高橋和希

MY TOP 10 MONSTER CARDS:

1. BLUE-EYES WHITE DRAGON. EVEN NOW, THERE'S NOTHING THAT CAN BEAT IT.

2. DARK MAGICIAN. AFTER ALL, IT'S THE MAIN CHARACTER'S CARD!

3. KURIBOH. WHAT'S THAT LOOK IN ITS EYES SUPPOSED TO MEAN?

4. RED-EYES BLACK DRAGON. I THINK IT'S A COOL MONSTER.

5. PANTHER WARRIOR. THE AMERICAN COMICS TOUCH IS A PLUS.

6. BUSTER BLADER. WHEN THIS CARD WAS ADVERTISED IN JAPAN, THE COMPUTER GRAPHICS USED IN THE COMMERCIAL WERE PRETTY COOL.

7. DARK MAGICIAN GIRL. BECAUSE THERE AREN'T THAT MANY FEMALE MONSTERS.

8. EXODIA THE FORBIDDEN ONE. THESE CARDS ARE ACTUALLY BASED ON MYTH.

9. TIME WIZARD. IT'S ACTUALLY MORE LIKE A SPELL CARD THAN A MONSTER CARD, BUT...

10. GAIA THE FIERCE KNIGHT. I LIKE IT, BUT IT'S A PAIN TO DRAW!

   –KAZUKI TAKAHASHI, 2000

Artist/author Kazuki Takahashi first tried to break into the manga business in 1982, but success eluded him until **Yu-Gi-Oh!** debuted in the Japanese **Weekly Shonen Jump** magazine in 1996. **Yu-Gi-Oh!**'s themes of friendship and fighting, together with Takahashi's weird and wonderful art, soon became enormously successful, spawning a real-world card game, video games, and two anime series. A lifelong gamer, Takahashi enjoys Shogi (Japanese chess), Mahjong, card games, and tabletop RPGs, among other games.

YU-GI-OH!: DUELIST VOL. 14
The SHONEN JUMP Manga Edition

STORY AND ART BY
KAZUKI TAKAHASHI

Translation & English Adaptation/Joe Yamazaki
Touch-up Art & Lettering/Eric Erbes
Design/Andrea Rice
Editor/Jason Thompson

Managing Editor/Elizabeth Kawasaki
Director of Production/Noboru Watanabe
Vice President of Publishing/Alvin Lu
Vice President & Editor in Chief/Yumi Hoashi
Sr. Director of Acquisitions/Rika Inouye
Vice President of Sales & Marketing/Liza Coppola
Publisher/ Hyoe Narita

In the original Japanese edition, YU-GI-OH!, YU-GI-OH!: DUELIST and YU-GI-OH!: MILLENNIUM WORLD are known collectively as YU-GI-OH!. The English YU-GI-OH!: DUELIST was originally volumes 8-31 of the Japanese YU-GI-OH!.

Printed in the U.S.A.

Published by VIZ Media, LLC
P.O. Box 77010
San Francisco, CA 94107

10 9 8 7 6 5 4 3 2
First printing, April 2006
Second printing, May 2010

PARENTAL ADVISORY
YU-GI-OH!: DUELIST is rated T for Teen and is recommended for ages 13 and up. Contains fantasy violence.
ratings.viz.com

THE WORLD'S
MOST POPULAR MANGA
SHONEN JUMP
www.shonenjump.com

www.viz.com

SHONEN JUMP MANGA

Vol. 14

DOUBLE DUEL

STORY AND ART BY

KAZUKI TAKAHASHI

THE STORY SO FAR...

YUGI MUTOU/
YU-GI-OH

When 10th grader Yugi solved the Millennium Puzzle, another spirit took up residence in his body…Yu-Gi-Oh, the King of Games, a dark avenger who challenges evildoers to "Shadow Games" of life and death!

YUGI FACES DEADLY ENEMIES!

Using his gaming skills, Yugi fights ruthless adversaries like Maximillion Pegasus, multimillionaire creator of the collectible card game "Duel Monsters," and Ryo Bakura, whose friendly personality turns evil when he is possessed by the spirit of the Millennium Ring. But Yugi's greatest rival is Seto Kaiba, the world's second-greatest gamer—and the ruthless teenage president of Kaiba Corporation. At first, Kaiba and Yugi are bitter enemies, but after fighting against a common adversary—Pegasus—they come to respect one another. But for all his powers, there is one thing Yu-Gi-Oh cannot do: remember who he is and where he came from.

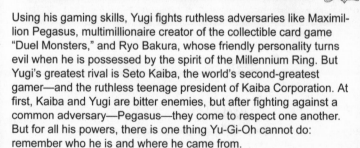

HIROTO HONDA

ANZU MAZAKI

KATSUYA JONOUCHI

MARIK

ISHIZU ISHTAR

SETO KAIBA

THE TABLET OF THE PHARAOH'S MEMORIES

Then one day, when an Egyptian museum exhibit comes to Japan, Yugi sees an ancient carving of himself as an Egyptian pharaoh! The curator of the exhibit, Ishizu Ishtar, explains that there are seven Millennium Items, which were made to fit into a stone tablet in a hidden shrine in Egypt. According to the legend, when the seven Items are brought together, the pharaoh will regain his memories of his past life.

THE EGYPTIAN GOD CARDS

But Ishizu has a message for Kaiba as well. Ishizu needs Kaiba's help to win back two of three Egyptian God Cards—the rarest cards on Earth—from the clutches of the "Rare Hunters," a criminal syndicate led by the evil Marik, Ishizu's brother. In order to draw out the thieves, Kaiba announces "Battle City," an enormous "Duel Monsters" tournament. As the tournament rages, Yugi, Kaiba and Marik struggle for possession of the three God Cards and the title of Duelist King. Meanwhile, Yugi's friend Jonouchi also fights his way through the tournament, unaware that he, too, is Marik's target! And now a new evil duelist has appeared on the scene…

Vol. 14

CONTENTS

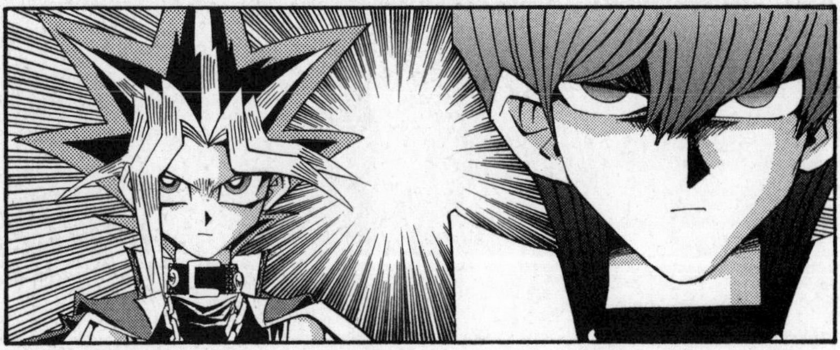

Duel 120: Full Strength!!

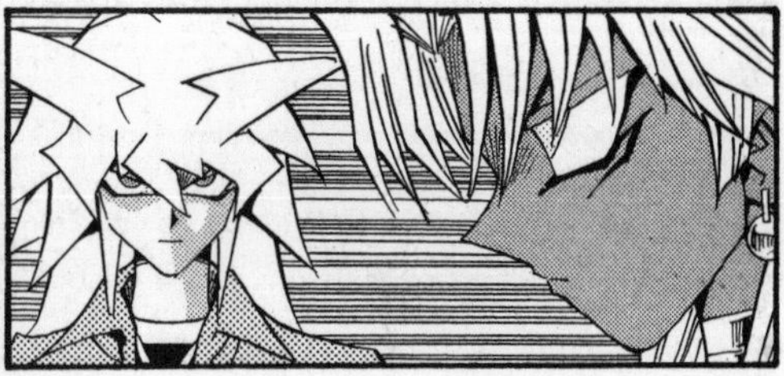

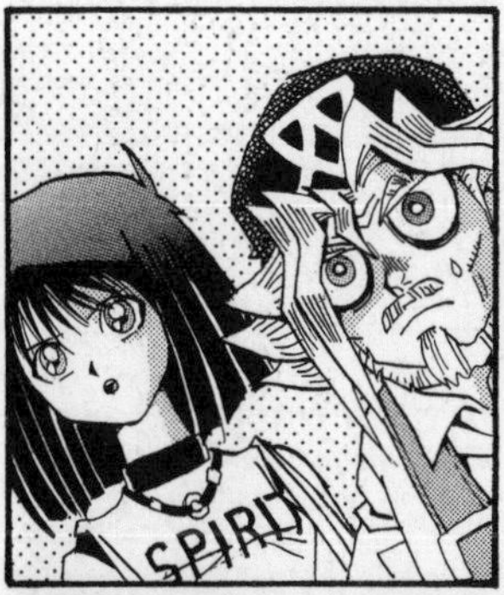

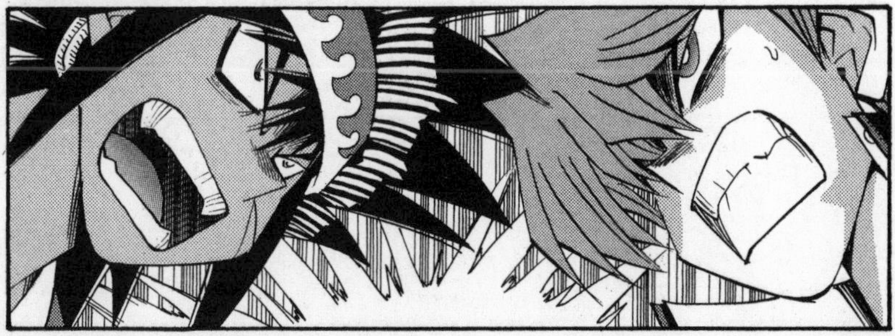

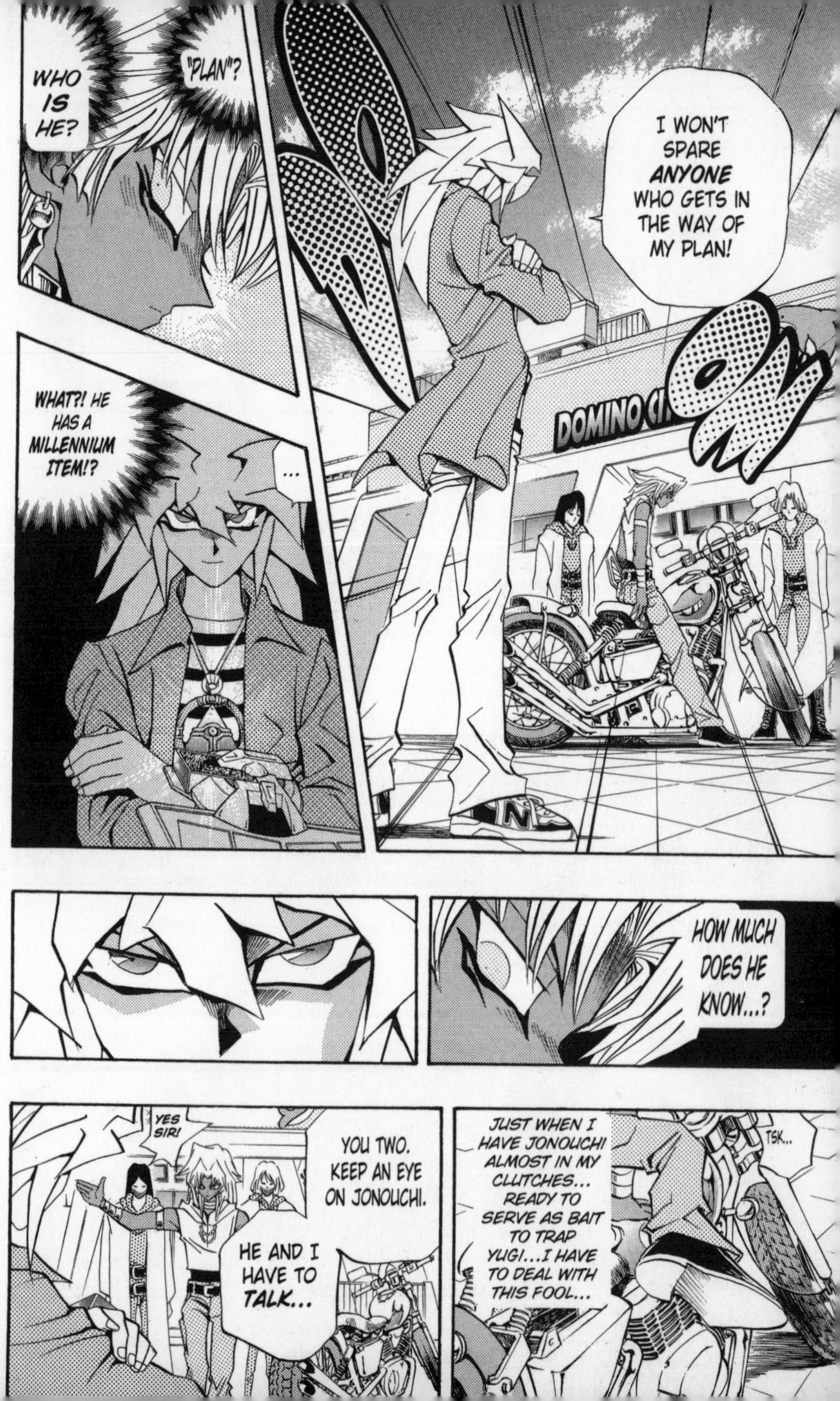
I WON'T SPARE ANYONE WHO GETS IN THE WAY OF MY PLAN!
DOMINO CI
"PLAN"?
WHO IS HE?
...
WHAT?! HE HAS A MILLENNIUM ITEM!?
HOW MUCH DOES HE KNOW...?
TSK...
JUST WHEN I HAVE JONOUCHI ALMOST IN MY CLUTCHES... READY TO SERVE AS BAIT TO TRAP YUGI...I HAVE TO DEAL WITH THIS FOOL...
YOU TWO. KEEP AN EYE ON JONOUCHI.
HE AND I HAVE TO TALK...
YES SIR!

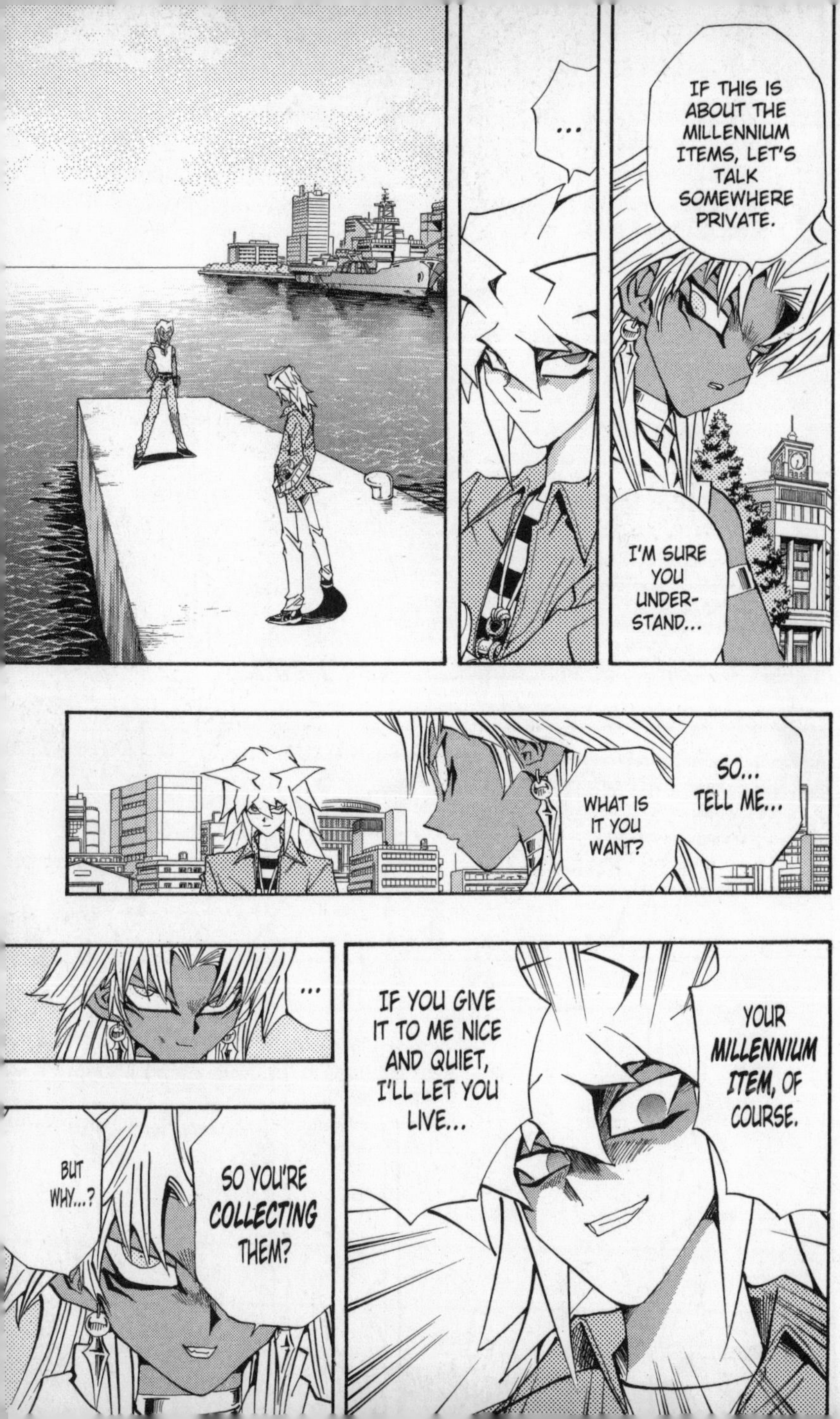
IF THIS IS ABOUT THE MILLENNIUM ITEMS, LET'S TALK SOMEWHERE PRIVATE.
I'M SURE YOU UNDER-STAND...
...
SO... TELL ME...
WHAT IS IT YOU WANT?
YOUR MILLENNIUM ITEM, OF COURSE.
IF YOU GIVE IT TO ME NICE AND QUIET, I'LL LET YOU LIVE...
...
SO YOU'RE COLLECTING THEM?
BUT WHY...?

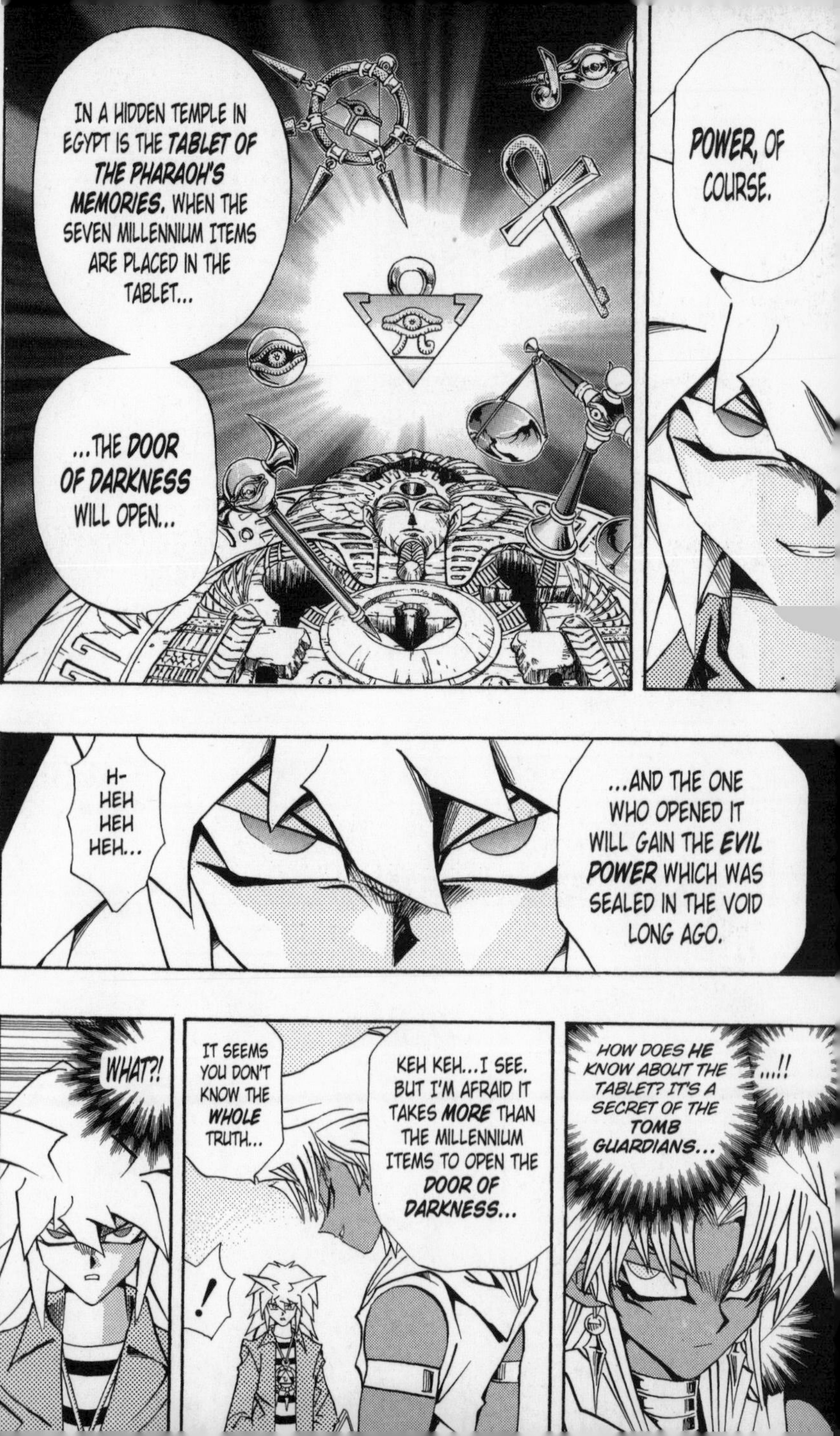
POWER, OF COURSE.
IN A HIDDEN TEMPLE IN EGYPT IS THE *TABLET OF THE PHARAOH'S MEMORIES.* WHEN THE SEVEN MILLENNIUM ITEMS ARE PLACED IN THE TABLET...
...THE *DOOR OF DARKNESS* WILL OPEN...
...AND THE ONE WHO OPENED IT WILL GAIN THE *EVIL POWER* WHICH WAS SEALED IN THE VOID LONG AGO.
H-HEH HEH HEH...
...!!
HOW DOES HE KNOW ABOUT THE TABLET? IT'S A SECRET OF THE TOMB GUARDIANS...
KEH KEH...I SEE. BUT I'M AFRAID IT TAKES *MORE* THAN THE MILLENNIUM ITEMS TO OPEN THE *DOOR OF DARKNESS...*
IT SEEMS YOU DON'T KNOW THE *WHOLE* TRUTH...
!
WHAT?!

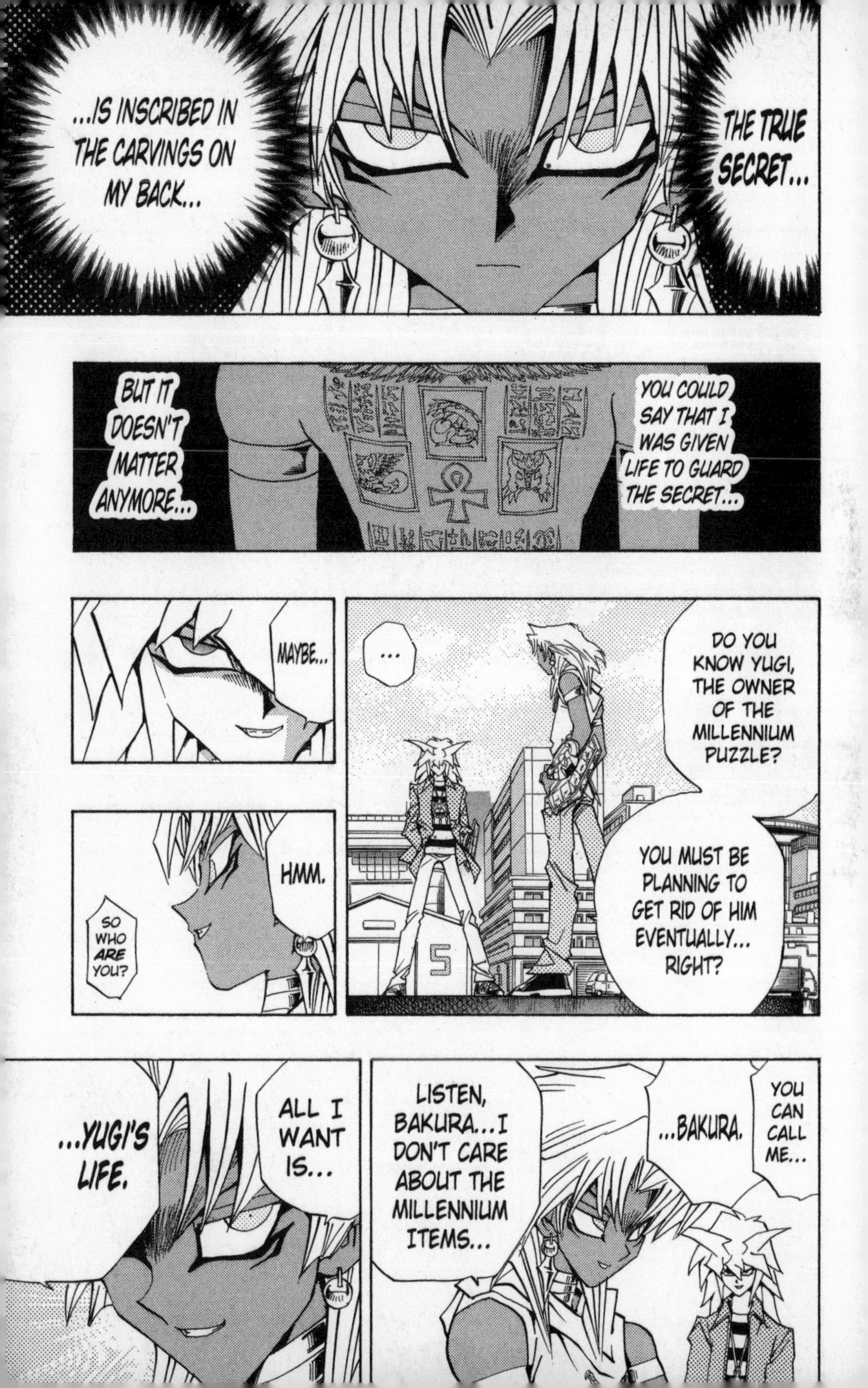
THE TRUE SECRET...
...IS INSCRIBED IN THE CARVINGS ON MY BACK...
YOU COULD SAY THAT I WAS GIVEN LIFE TO GUARD THE SECRET...
BUT IT DOESN'T MATTER ANYMORE...
DO YOU KNOW YUGI, THE OWNER OF THE MILLENNIUM PUZZLE?
...
YOU MUST BE PLANNING TO GET RID OF HIM EVENTUALLY... RIGHT?
MAYBE...
HMM.
SO WHO ARE YOU?
YOU CAN CALL ME...
...BAKURA.
LISTEN, BAKURA...I DON'T CARE ABOUT THE MILLENNIUM ITEMS...
ALL I WANT IS...
...YUGI'S LIFE.

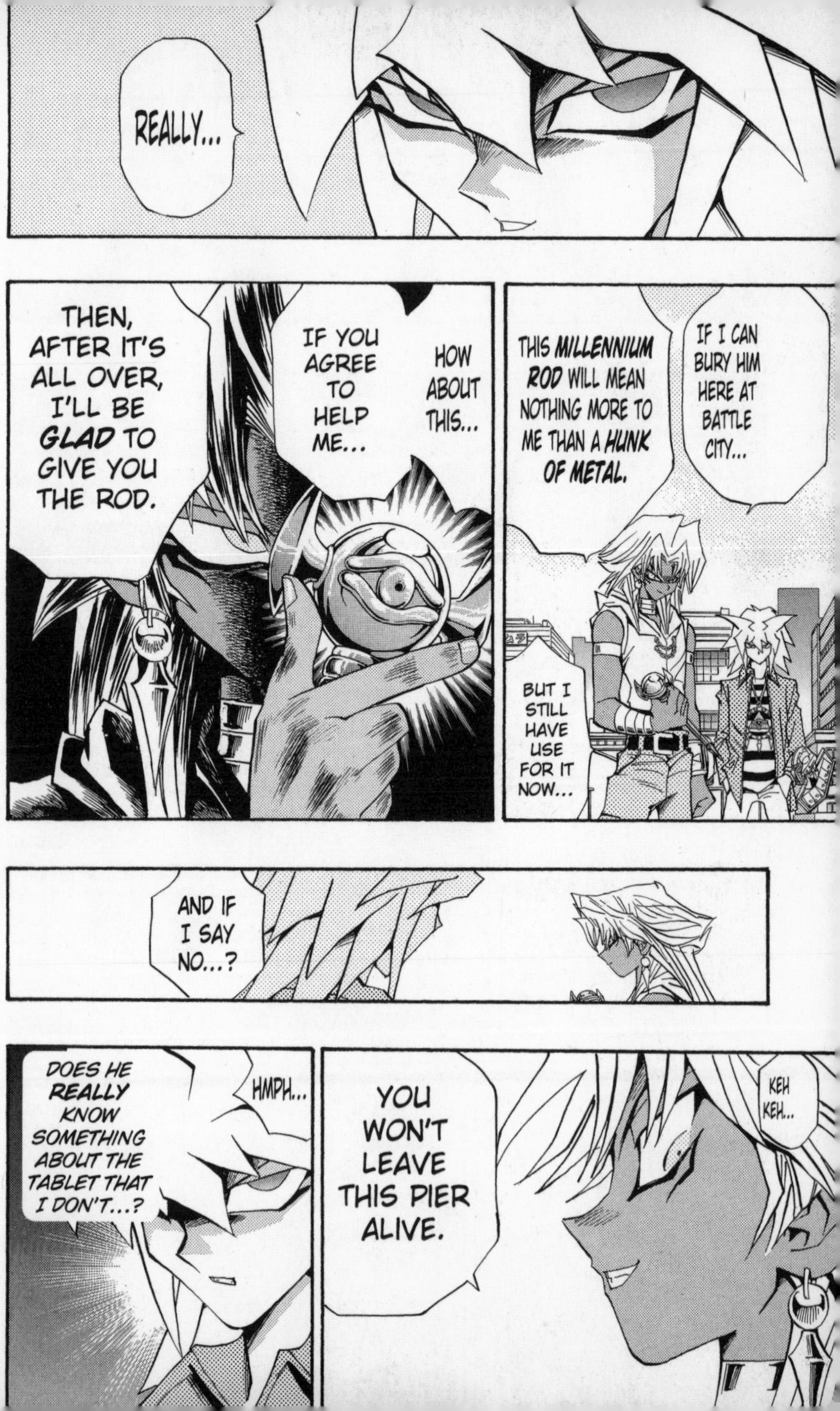
REALLY...
IF I CAN BURY HIM HERE AT BATTLE CITY...
THIS **MILLENNIUM ROD** WILL MEAN NOTHING MORE TO ME THAN A **HUNK OF METAL.**
BUT I STILL HAVE USE FOR IT NOW...
HOW ABOUT THIS...
IF YOU AGREE TO HELP ME...
THEN, AFTER IT'S ALL OVER, I'LL BE **GLAD** TO GIVE YOU THE ROD.
AND IF I SAY NO...?
KEH KEH...
YOU WON'T LEAVE THIS PIER ALIVE.
HMPH...
*DOES HE **REALLY** KNOW SOMETHING ABOUT THE TABLET THAT I DON'T...?*

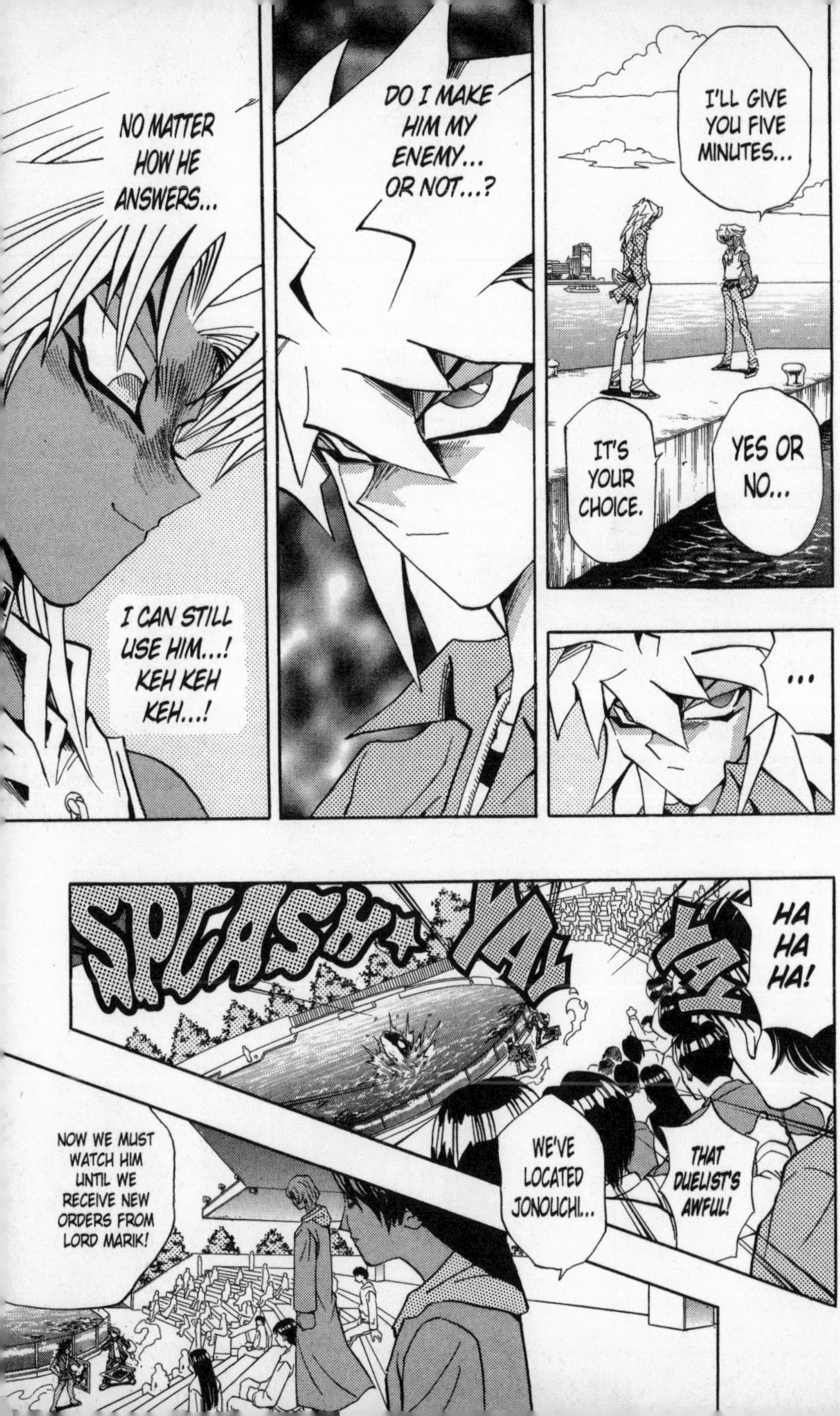
I'LL GIVE YOU FIVE MINUTES...
YES OR NO...
IT'S YOUR CHOICE.
...
DO I MAKE HIM MY ENEMY... OR NOT...?
NO MATTER HOW HE ANSWERS...
I CAN STILL USE HIM...! KEH KEH KEH...!
HA HA HA!
YA
YA
SPLASH
THAT DUELIST'S AWFUL!
WE'VE LOCATED JONOUCHI...
NOW WE MUST WATCH HIM UNTIL WE RECEIVE NEW ORDERS FROM LORD MARIK!

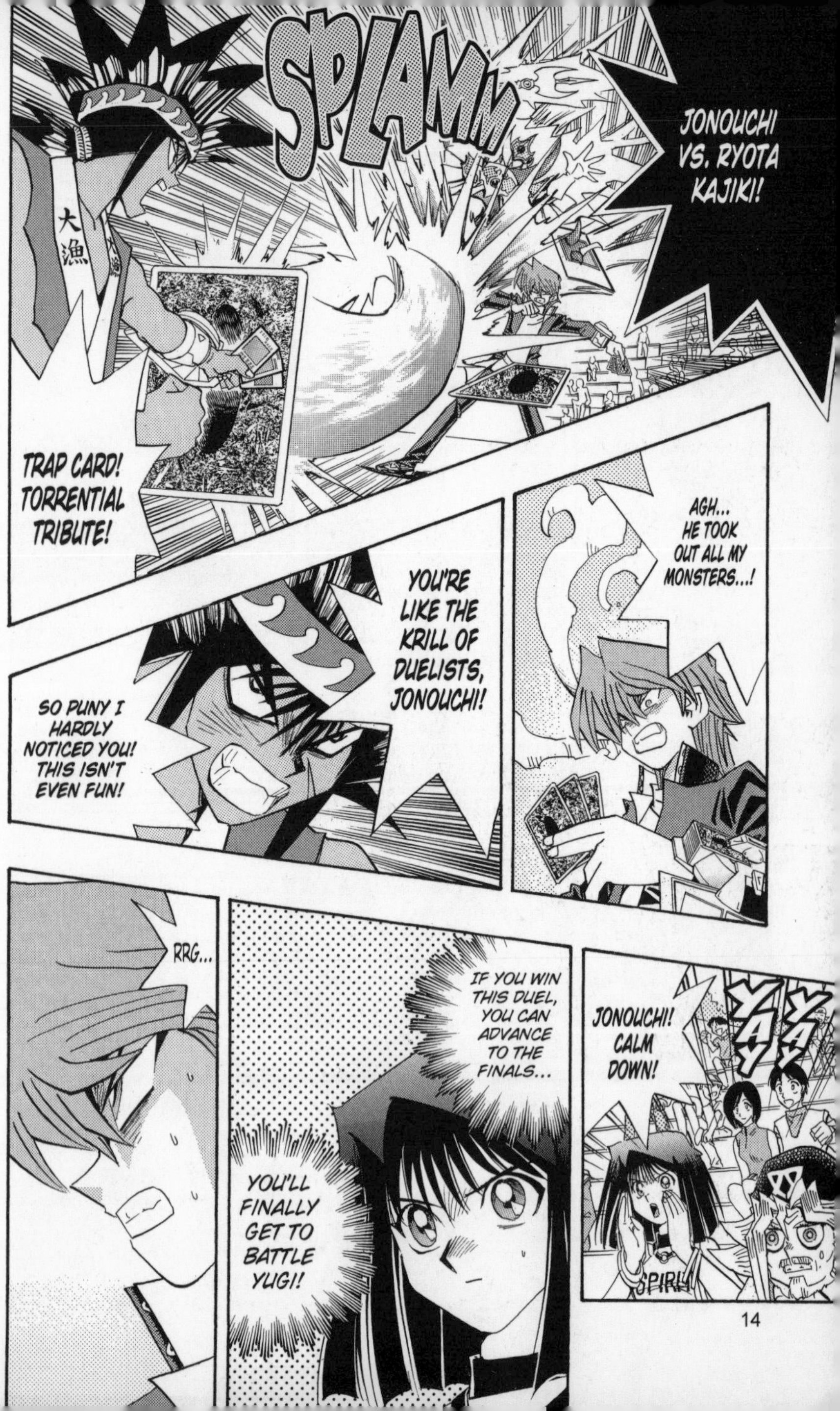
SPLAMM
JONOUCHI VS. RYOTA KAJIKI!
大漁
TRAP CARD! TORRENTIAL TRIBUTE!
AGH... HE TOOK OUT ALL MY MONSTERS...!
YOU'RE LIKE THE KRILL OF DUELISTS, JONOUCHI!
SO PUNY I HARDLY NOTICED YOU! THIS ISN'T EVEN FUN!
YAY YAY
JONOUCHI! CALM DOWN!
IF YOU WIN THIS DUEL, YOU CAN ADVANCE TO THE FINALS...
YOU'LL FINALLY GET TO BATTLE YUGI!
RRG...

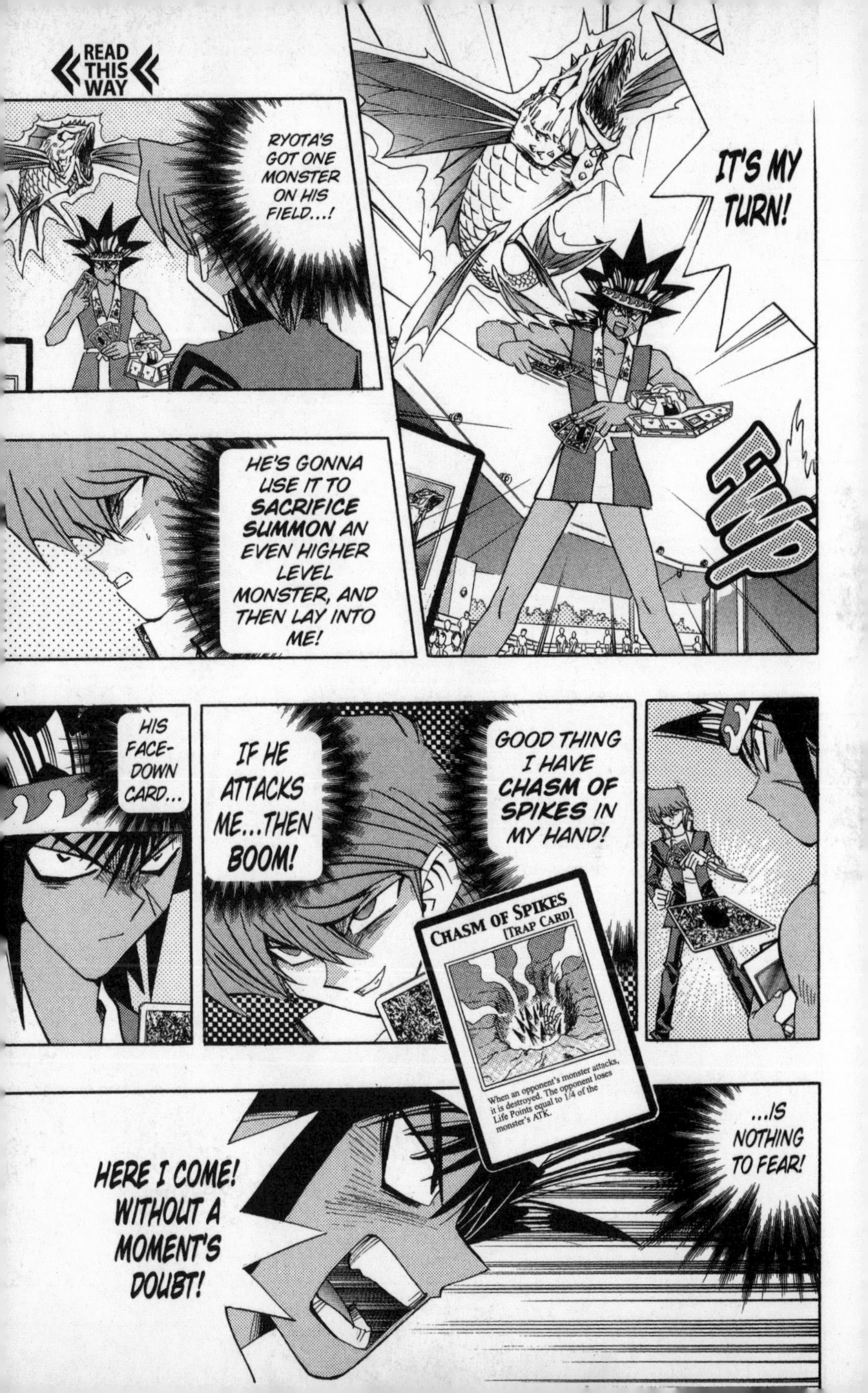
READ THIS WAY
IT'S MY TURN!
FWIP
RYOTA'S GOT ONE MONSTER ON HIS FIELD...!
HE'S GONNA USE IT TO SACRIFICE SUMMON AN EVEN HIGHER LEVEL MONSTER, AND THEN LAY INTO ME!
GOOD THING I HAVE CHASM OF SPIKES IN MY HAND!
IF HE ATTACKS ME...THEN BOOM!
CHASM OF SPIKES
[TRAP CARD]
When an opponent's monster attacks, it is destroyed. The opponent loses Life Points equal to 1/4 of the monster's ATK.
HIS FACE-DOWN CARD...
...IS NOTHING TO FEAR!
HERE I COME! WITHOUT A MOMENT'S DOUBT!

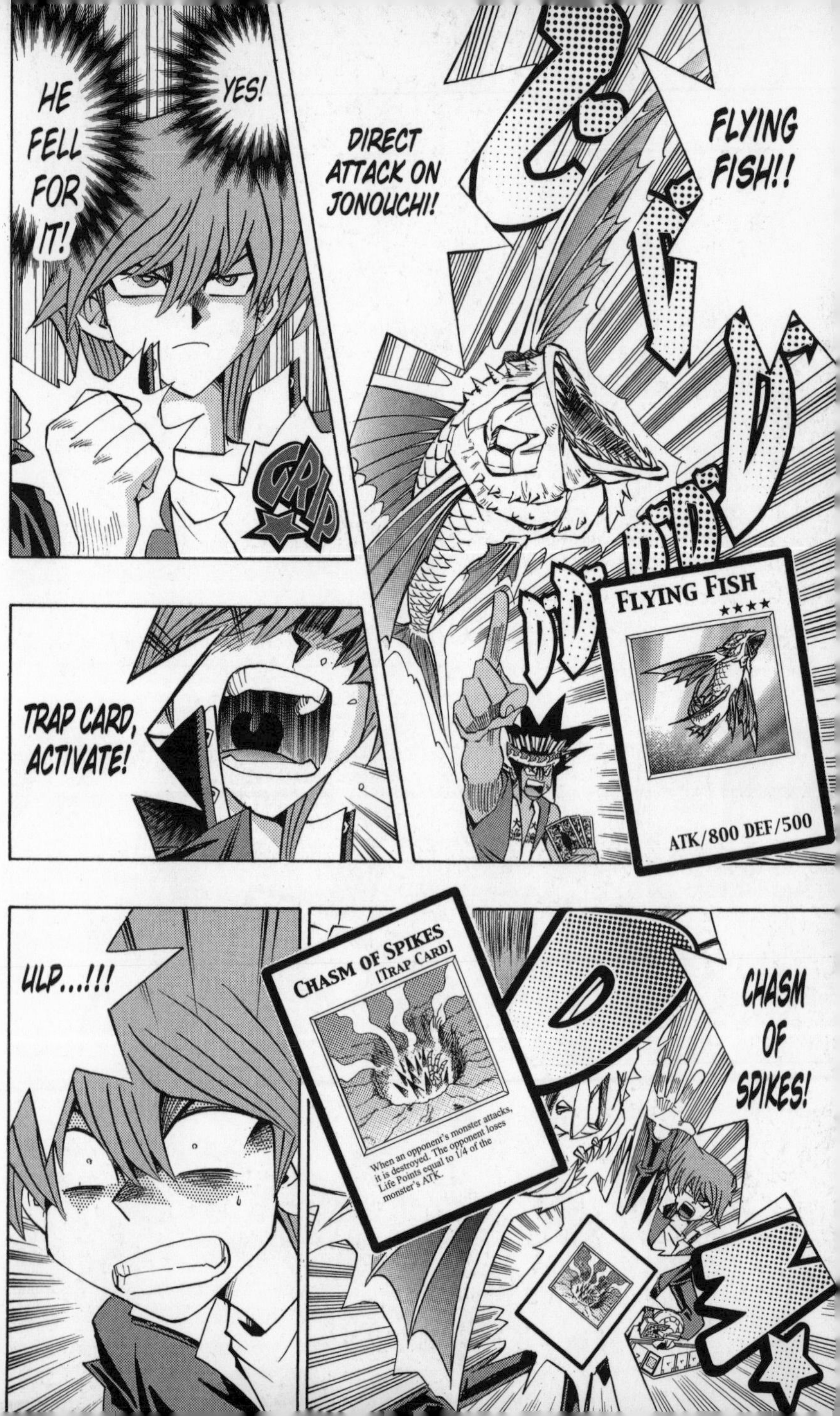
FLYING FISH!!
DIRECT ATTACK ON JONOUCHI!
FLYING FISH
★★★★
ATK/800 DEF/500
YES!
HE FELL FOR IT!
GRIP
TRAP CARD, ACTIVATE!
CHASM OF SPIKES!
CHASM OF SPIKES
[TRAP CARD]
When an opponent's monster attacks, it is destroyed. The opponent loses Life Points equal to 1/4 of the monster's ATK.
ULP...!!!

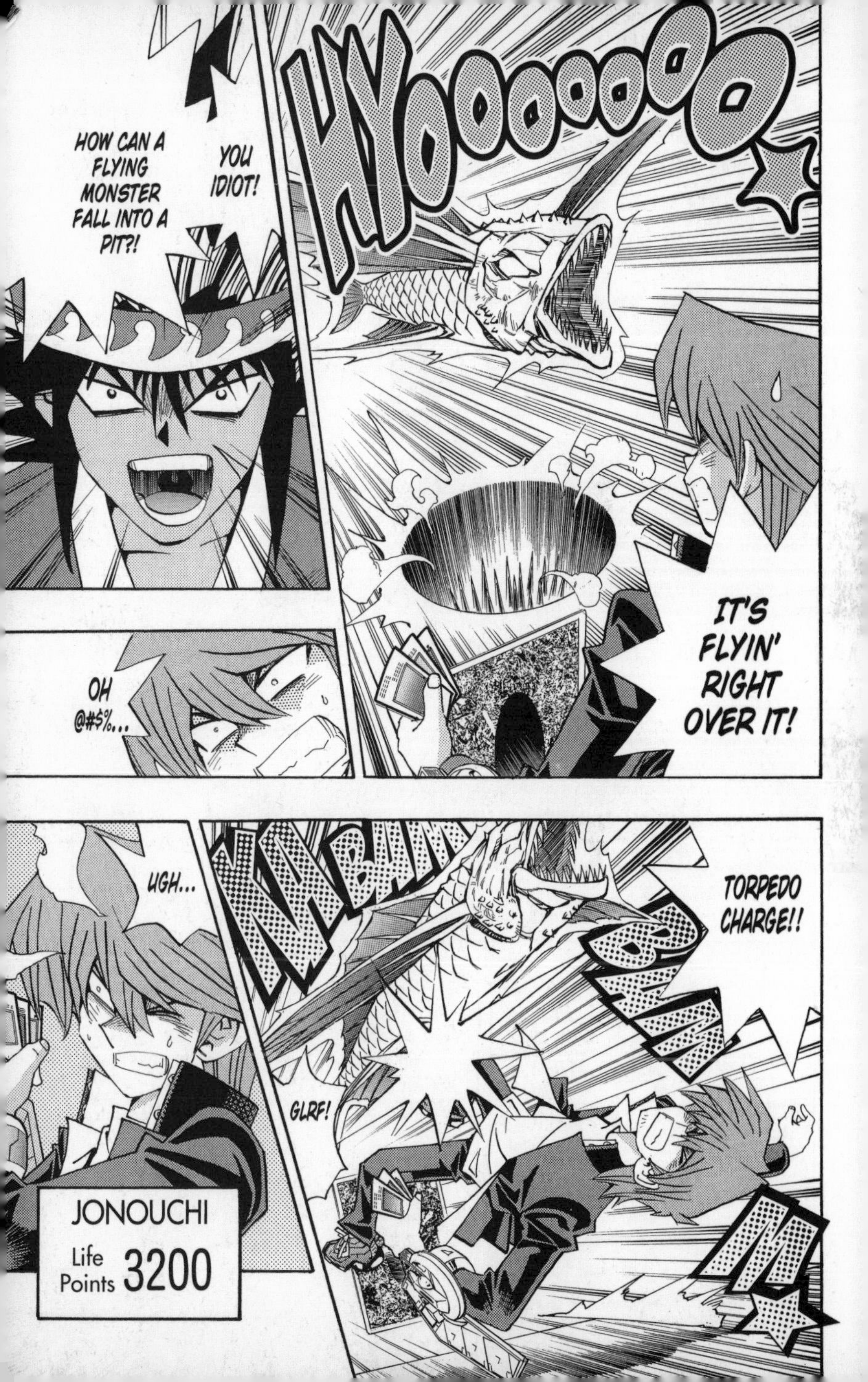
HYOOOOOO
IT'S FLYIN' RIGHT OVER IT!
YOU IDIOT!
HOW CAN A FLYING MONSTER FALL INTO A PIT?!
OH @#$%...
TORPEDO CHARGE!!
GLRF!
UGH...
JONOUCHI
Life Points 3200

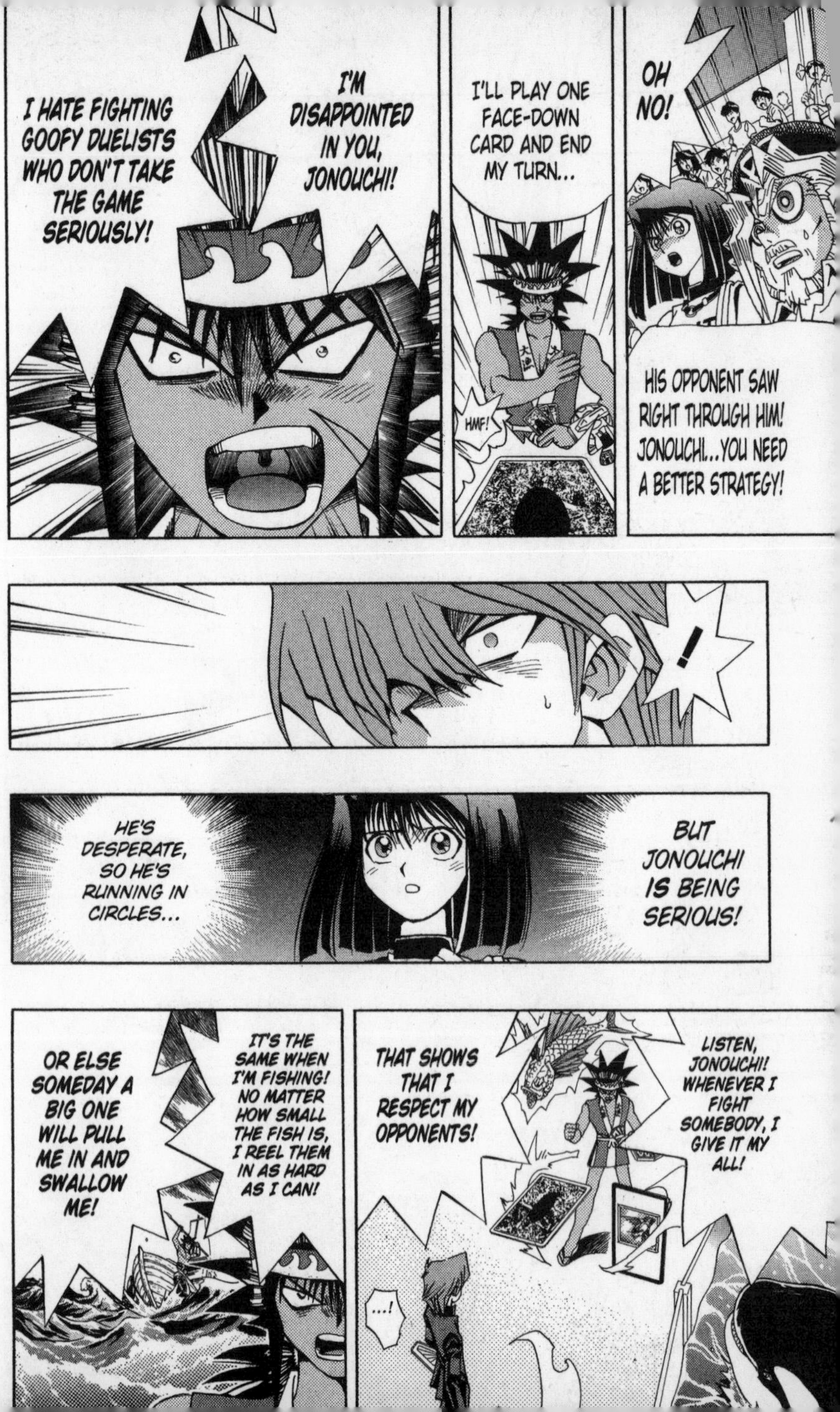
OH NO!
HIS OPPONENT SAW RIGHT THROUGH HIM! JONOUCHI...YOU NEED A BETTER STRATEGY!
I'LL PLAY ONE FACE-DOWN CARD AND END MY TURN...
HMF!
I'M DISAPPOINTED IN YOU, JONOUCHI!
I HATE FIGHTING GOOFY DUELISTS WHO DON'T TAKE THE GAME SERIOUSLY!
!
HE'S DESPERATE, SO HE'S RUNNING IN CIRCLES...
BUT JONOUCHI IS BEING SERIOUS!
LISTEN, JONOUCHI! WHENEVER I FIGHT SOMEBODY, I GIVE IT MY ALL!
THAT SHOWS THAT I RESPECT MY OPPONENTS!
...!
IT'S THE SAME WHEN I'M FISHING! NO MATTER HOW SMALL THE FISH IS, I REEL THEM IN AS HARD AS I CAN!
OR ELSE SOMEDAY A BIG ONE WILL PULL ME IN AND SWALLOW ME!

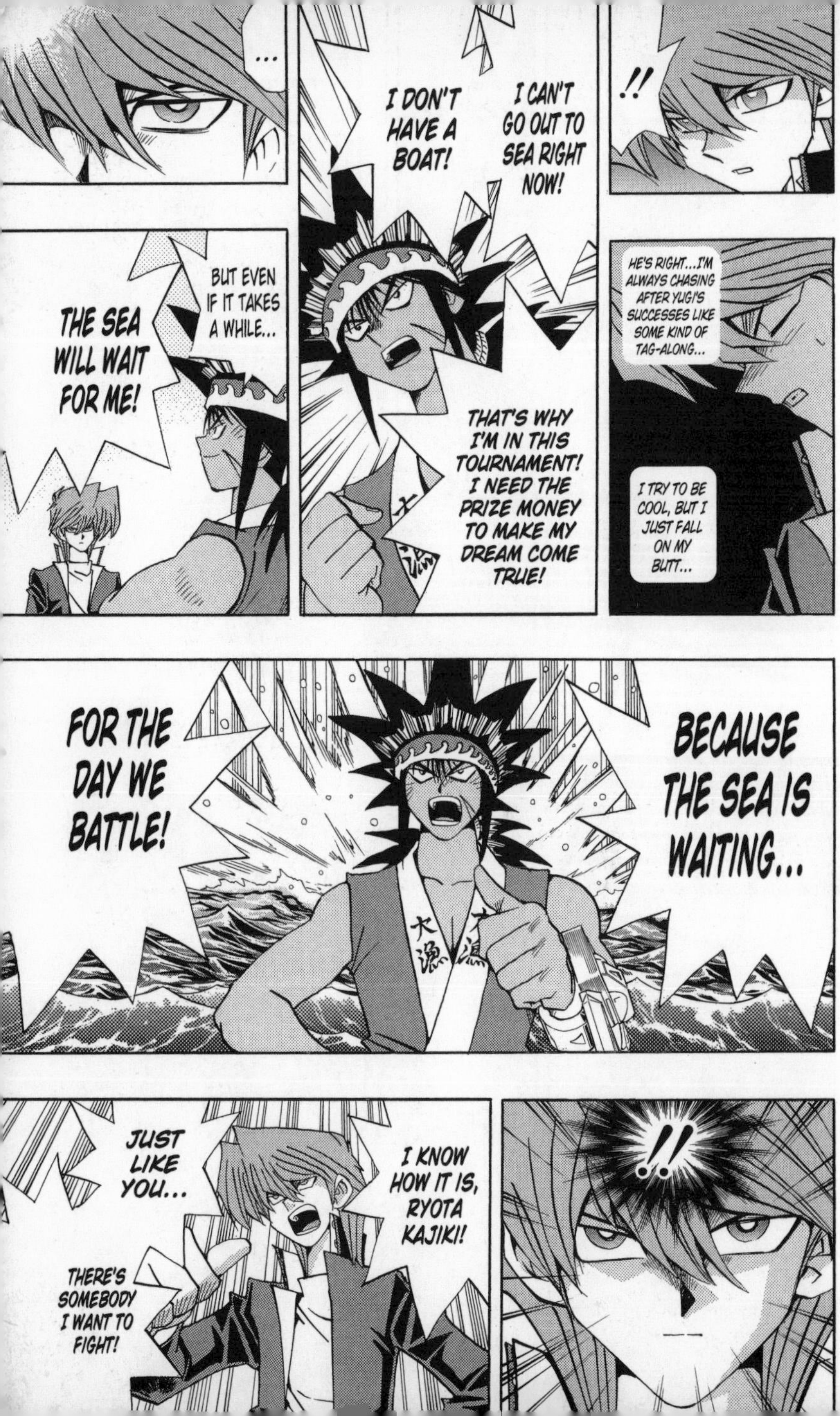
!!
HE'S RIGHT...I'M ALWAYS CHASING AFTER YUGI'S SUCCESSES LIKE SOME KIND OF TAG-ALONG...
I TRY TO BE COOL, BUT I JUST FALL ON MY BUTT...
I CAN'T GO OUT TO SEA RIGHT NOW!
I DON'T HAVE A BOAT!
THAT'S WHY I'M IN THIS TOURNAMENT! I NEED THE PRIZE MONEY TO MAKE MY DREAM COME TRUE!
...
BUT EVEN IF IT TAKES A WHILE...
THE SEA WILL WAIT FOR ME!
BECAUSE THE SEA IS WAITING...
FOR THE DAY WE BATTLE!
!!
——
I KNOW HOW IT IS, RYOTA KAJIKI!
JUST LIKE YOU...
THERE'S SOMEBODY I WANT TO FIGHT!

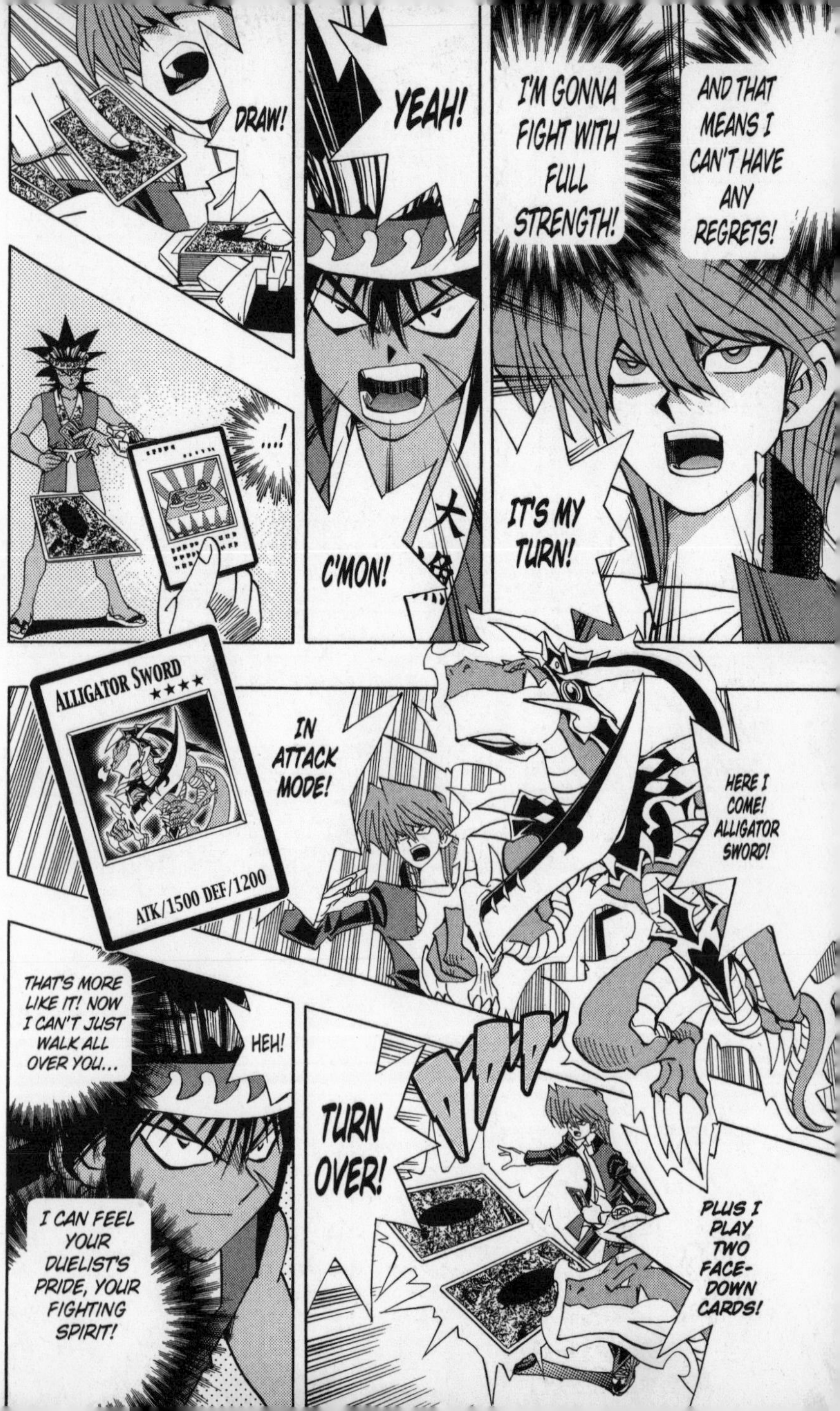
AND THAT MEANS I CAN'T HAVE ANY REGRETS!
I'M GONNA FIGHT WITH FULL STRENGTH!
IT'S MY TURN!
YEAH!
C'MON!
DRAW!
...!
ALLIGATOR SWORD ★★★★
ATK/1500 DEF/1200
HERE I COME! ALLIGATOR SWORD!
IN ATTACK MODE!
PLUS I PLAY TWO FACE-DOWN CARDS!
TURN OVER!
HEH!
THAT'S MORE LIKE IT! NOW I CAN'T JUST WALK ALL OVER YOU...
I CAN FEEL YOUR DUELIST'S PRIDE, YOUR FIGHTING SPIRIT!

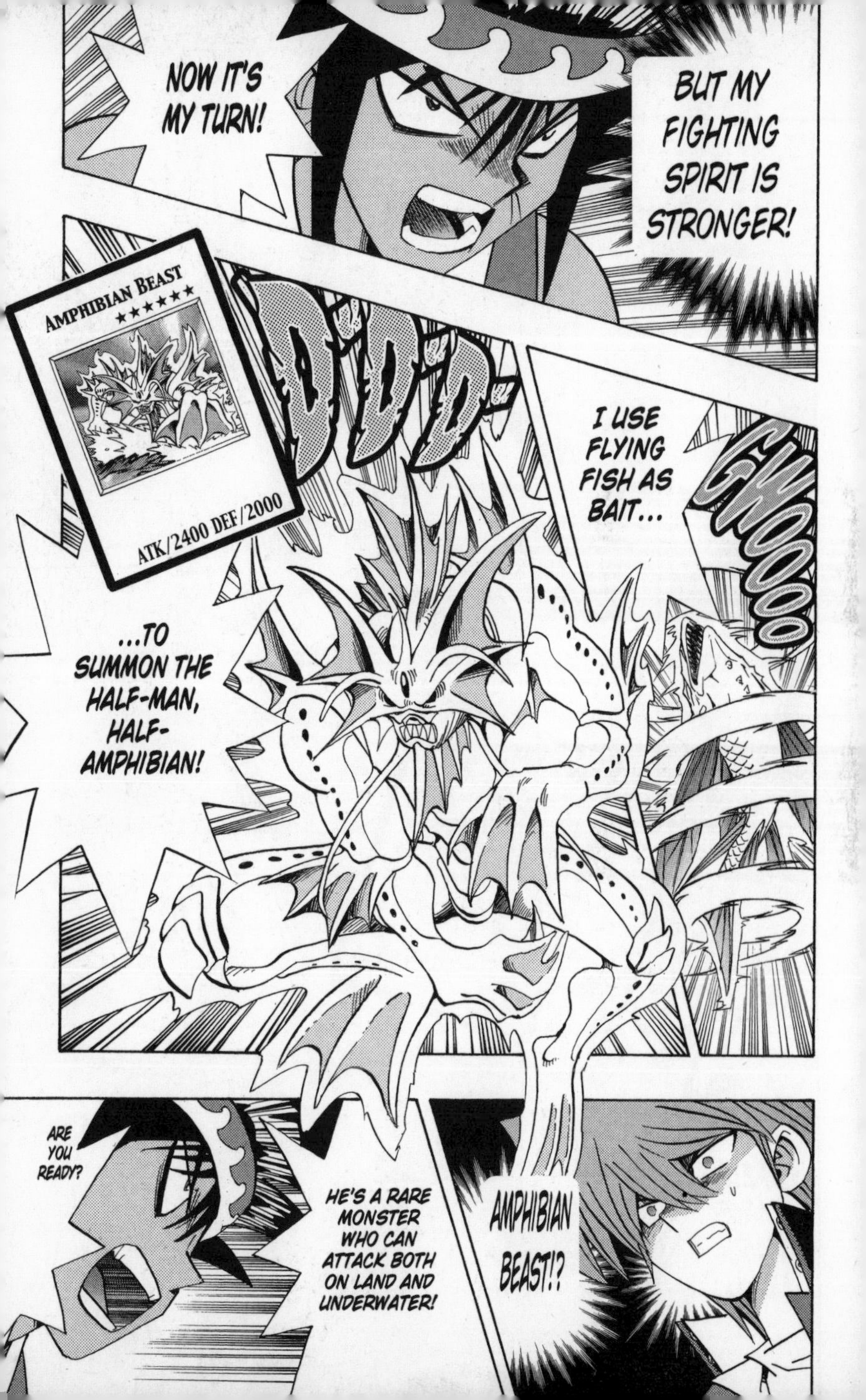
BUT MY FIGHTING SPIRIT IS STRONGER!
NOW IT'S MY TURN!
I USE FLYING FISH AS BAIT...
GHOOOOO
D'D'D-
AMPHIBIAN BEAST
★★★★★★
ATK/2400 DEF/2000
...TO SUMMON THE HALF-MAN, HALF-AMPHIBIAN!
AMPHIBIAN BEAST!?
HE'S A RARE MONSTER WHO CAN ATTACK BOTH ON LAND AND UNDERWATER!
ARE YOU READY?

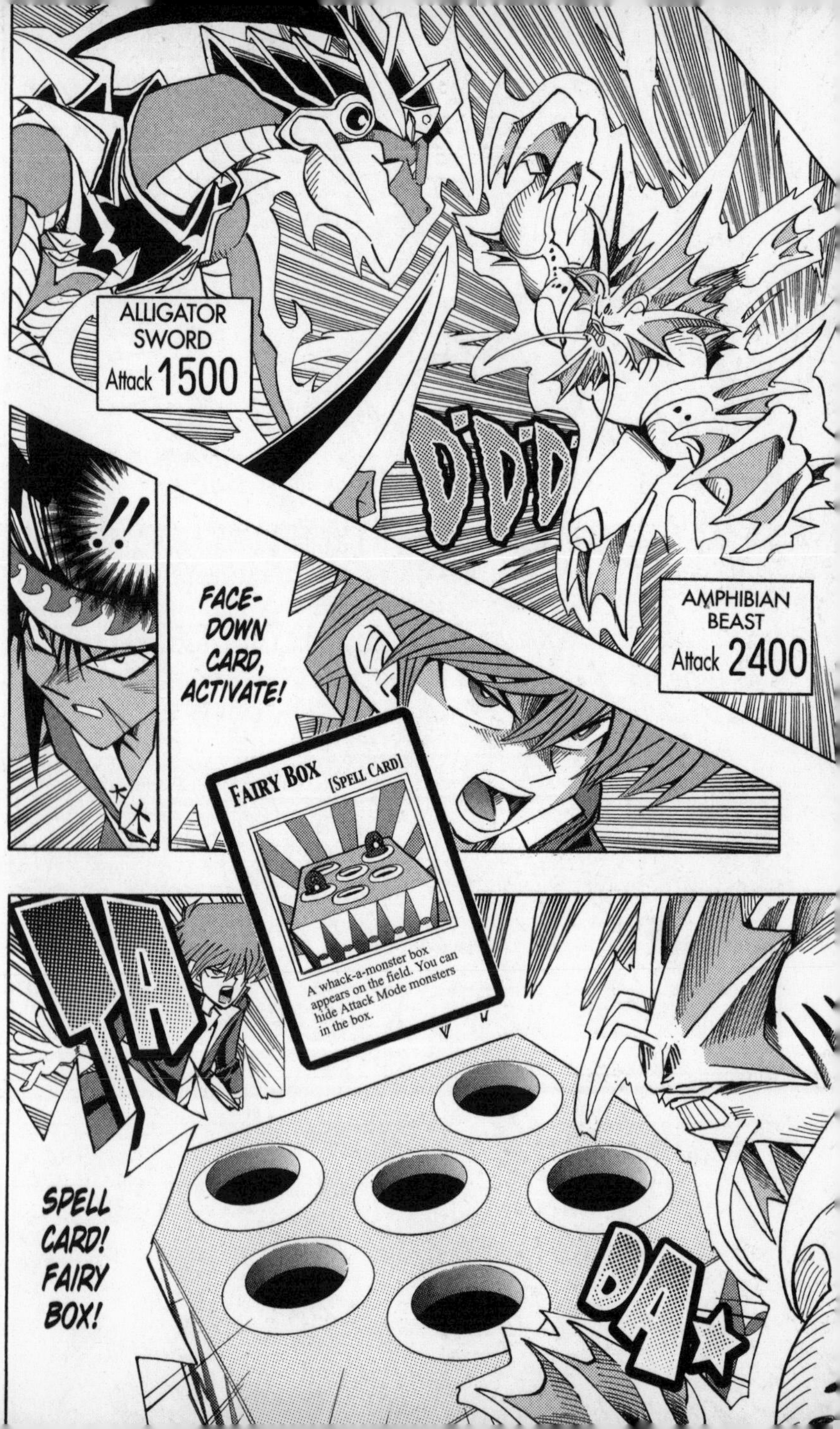

ALLIGATOR SWORD Attack 1500
DIDID
AMPHIBIAN BEAST Attack 2400
FACE-DOWN CARD, ACTIVATE!
!!
FAIRY BOX [SPELL CARD]
A whack-a-monster box appears on the field. You can hide Attack Mode monsters in the box.
DA☆
YA
SPELL CARD! FAIRY BOX!

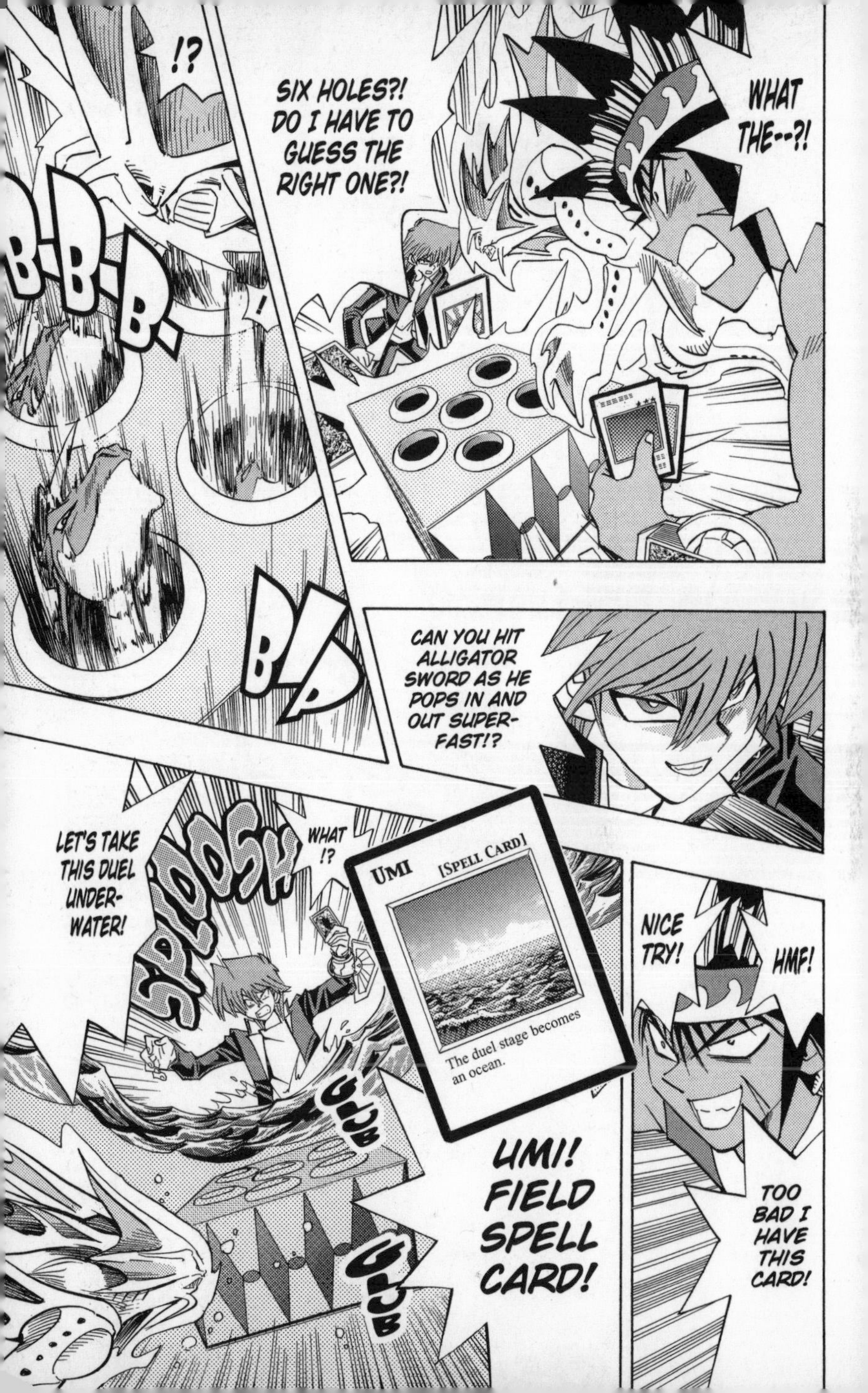
WHAT THE--?!
SIX HOLES?! DO I HAVE TO GUESS THE RIGHT ONE?!
CAN YOU HIT ALLIGATOR SWORD AS HE POPS IN AND OUT SUPER-FAST!?
!?
B-B-B-B.
!
B!P
NICE TRY!
HMF!
TOO BAD I HAVE THIS CARD!
UMI [SPELL CARD]
The duel stage becomes an ocean.
WHAT !?
SPLOOSH
LET'S TAKE THIS DUEL UNDER-WATER!
UMI! FIELD SPELL CARD!
GLUB
GLUB

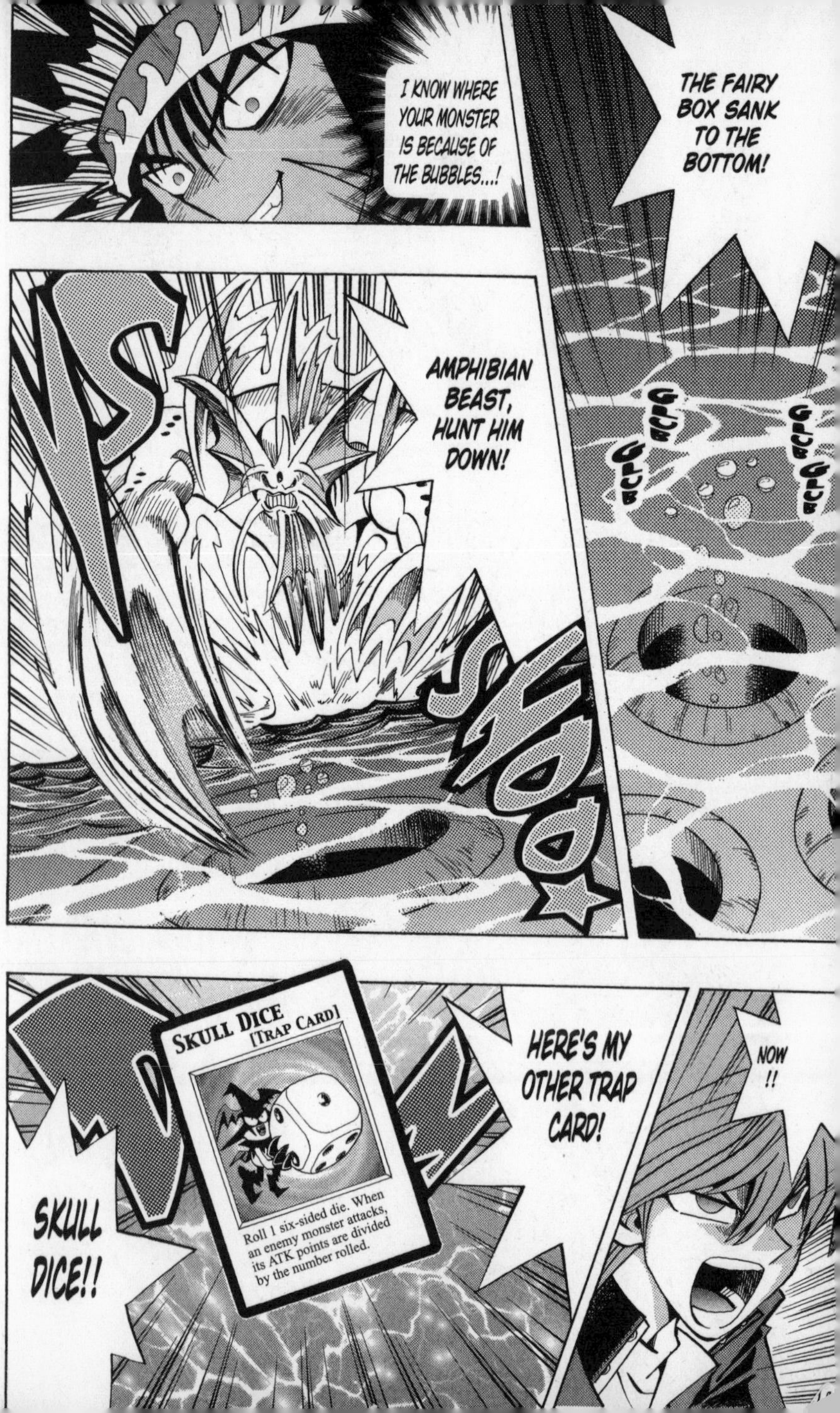
THE FAIRY BOX SANK TO THE BOTTOM!
GLUB GLUB
GLUB GLUB
I KNOW WHERE YOUR MONSTER IS BECAUSE OF THE BUBBLES...!
AMPHIBIAN BEAST, HUNT HIM DOWN!
SHOOP☆
NOW!!
HERE'S MY OTHER TRAP CARD!
SKULL DICE
[TRAP CARD]
Roll 1 six-sided die. When an enemy monster attacks, its ATK points are divided by the number rolled.
SKULL DICE!!

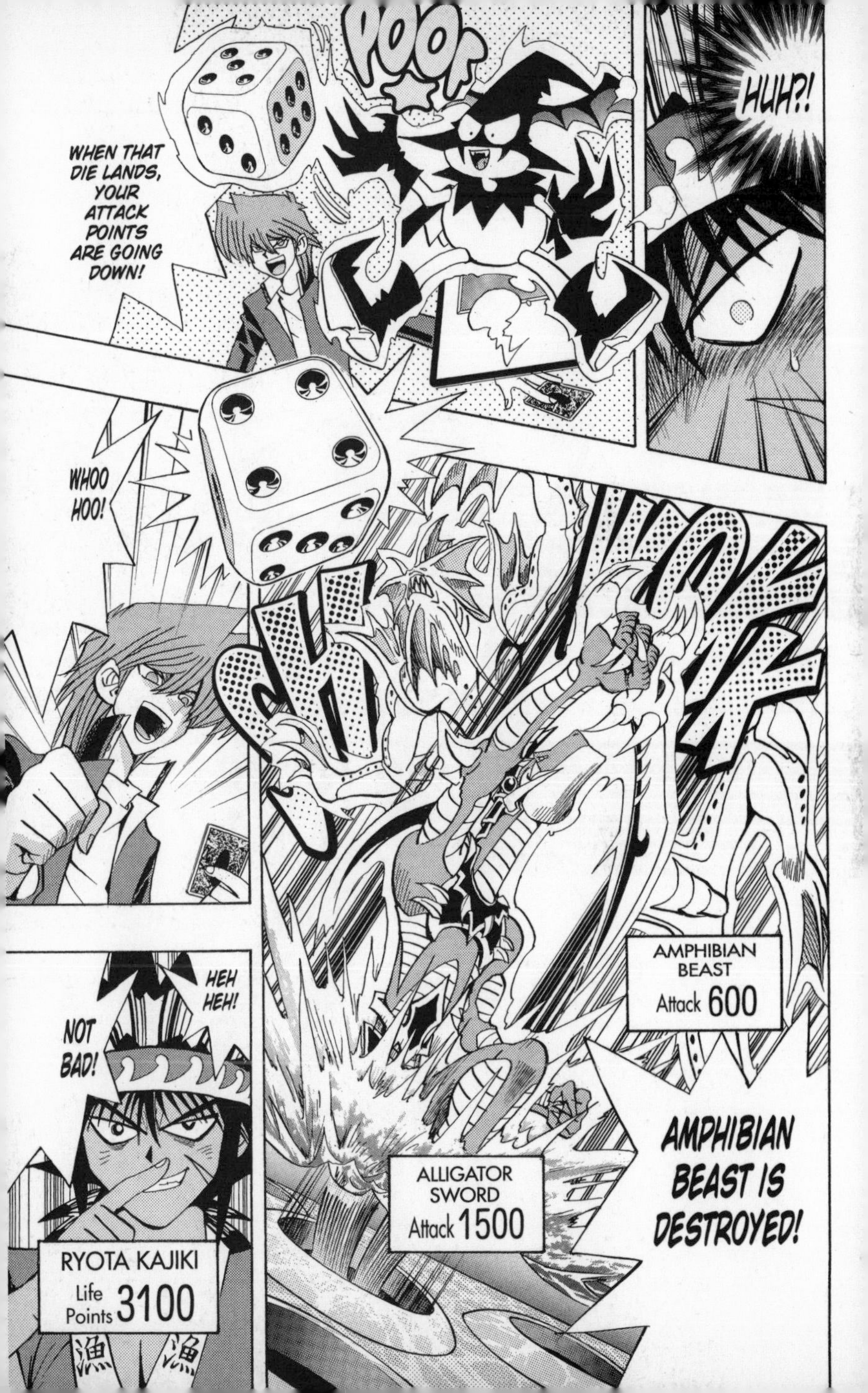
HUH?!
POOF
WHEN THAT DIE LANDS, YOUR ATTACK POINTS ARE GOING DOWN!
AMPHIBIAN BEAST Attack 600
AMPHIBIAN BEAST IS DESTROYED!
ALLIGATOR SWORD Attack 1500
WHOO HOO!
HEH HEH!
NOT BAD!
RYOTA KAJIKI Life Points 3100
漁
漁

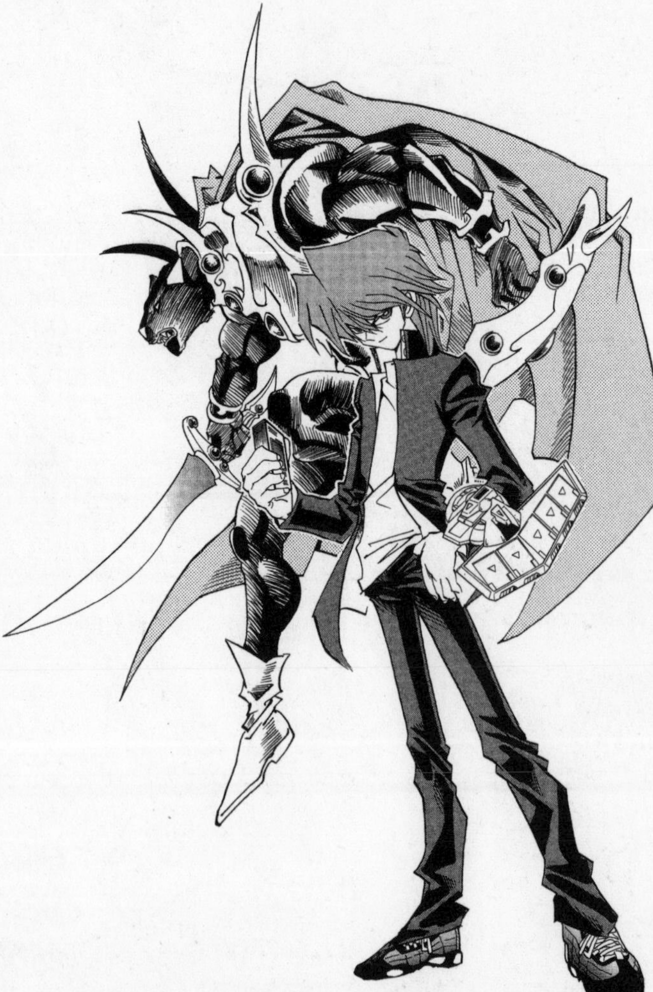

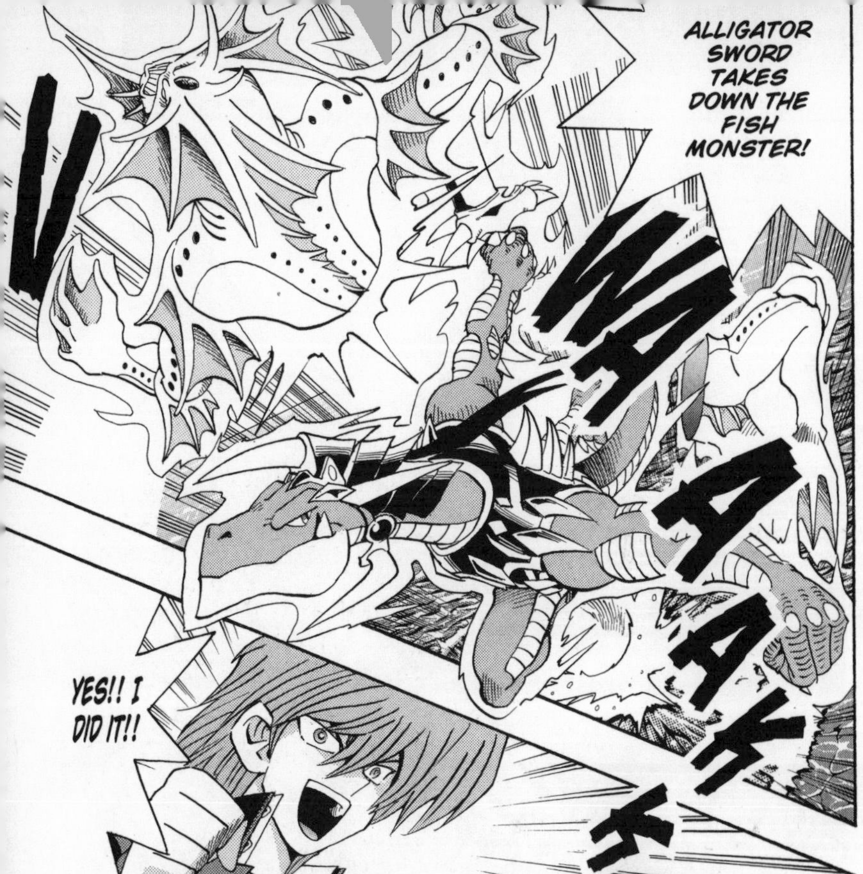
ALLIGATOR SWORD TAKES DOWN THE FISH MONSTER!
WHAAKK
YES!! I DID IT!!

DUEL 121: RETURN OF THE SEA SCOURGE

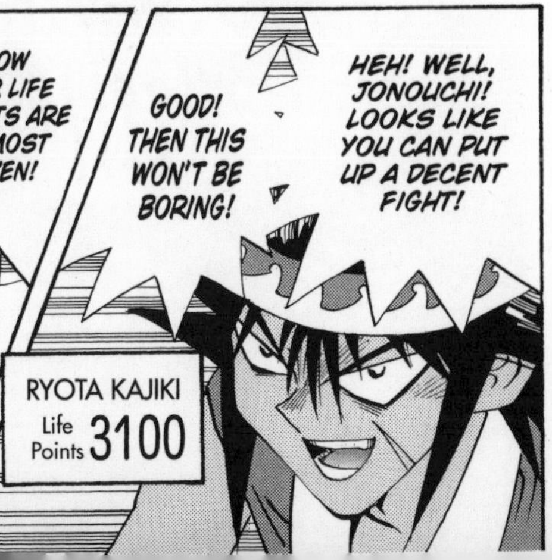
HEH! WELL, JONOUCHI! LOOKS LIKE YOU CAN PUT UP A DECENT FIGHT!
GOOD! THEN THIS WON'T BE BORING!
RYOTA KAJIKI Life Points 3100

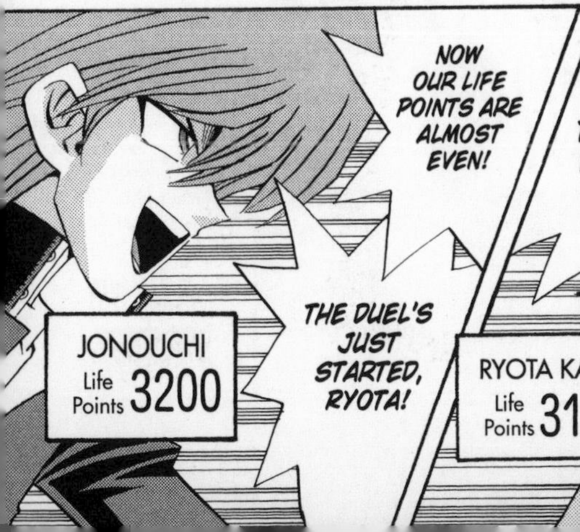
NOW OUR LIFE POINTS ARE ALMOST EVEN!
THE DUEL'S JUST STARTED, RYOTA!
JONOUCHI Life Points 3200

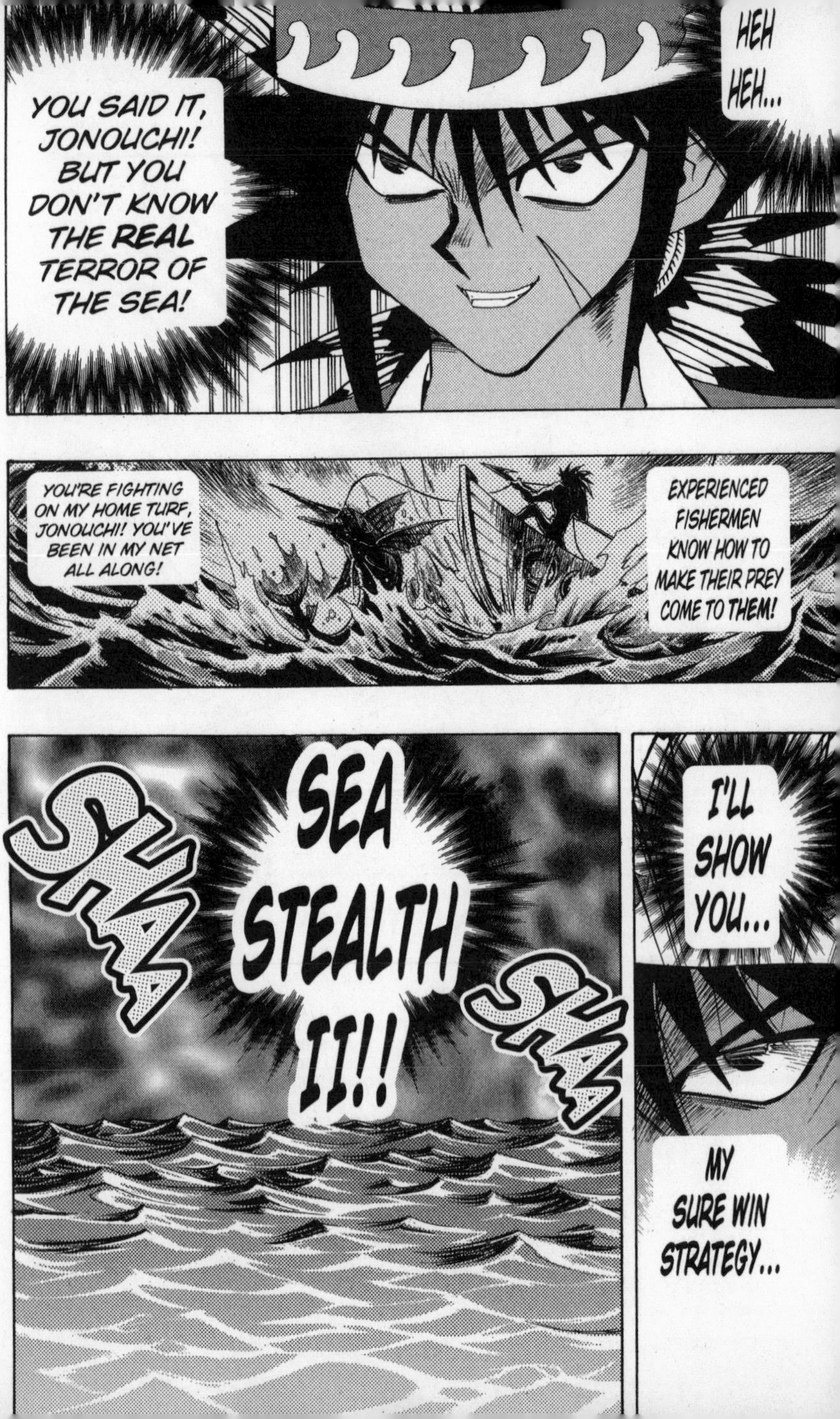
HEH HEH...
YOU SAID IT, JONOUCHI! BUT YOU DON'T KNOW THE REAL TERROR OF THE SEA!
EXPERIENCED FISHERMEN KNOW HOW TO MAKE THEIR PREY COME TO THEM!
YOU'RE FIGHTING ON MY HOME TURF, JONOUCHI! YOU'VE BEEN IN MY NET ALL ALONG!
I'LL SHOW YOU...
MY SURE WIN STRATEGY...
SEA STEALTH II!!
SHA
SHA

Duel 121: Return of the Sea Scourge

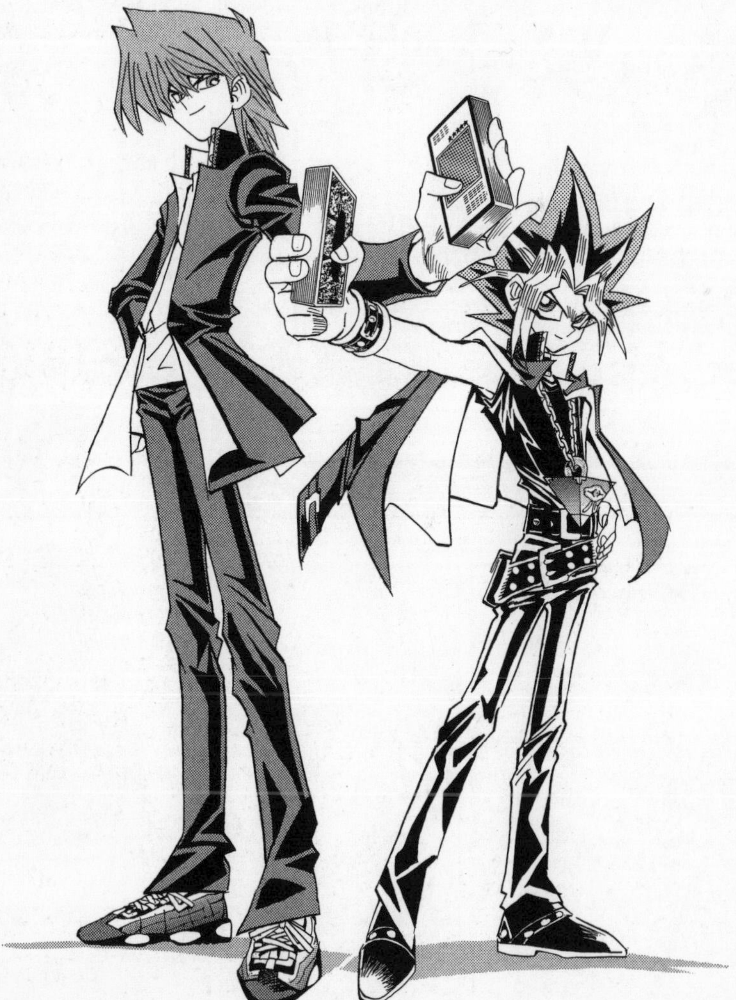

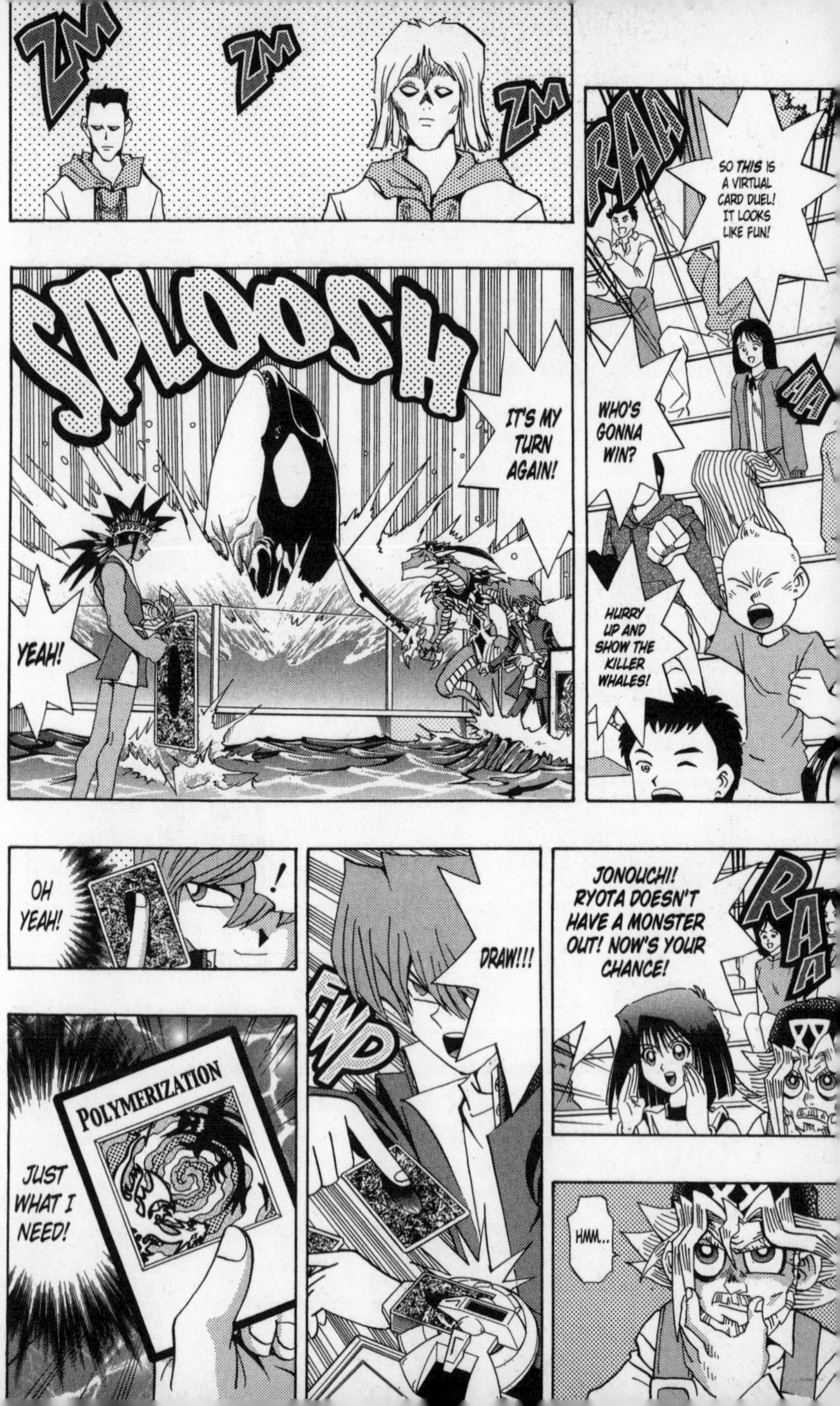
RAA
SO THIS IS A VIRTUAL CARD DUEL! IT LOOKS LIKE FUN!
WHO'S GONNA WIN?
HURRY UP AND SHOW THE KILLER WHALES!
ZM ZM ZM
SPLOOSH
IT'S MY TURN AGAIN!
YEAH!
JONOUCHI! RYOTA DOESN'T HAVE A MONSTER OUT! NOW'S YOUR CHANCE!
RAA
HMM...
DRAW!!!
!
OH YEAH!
POLYMERIZATION
JUST WHAT I NEED!

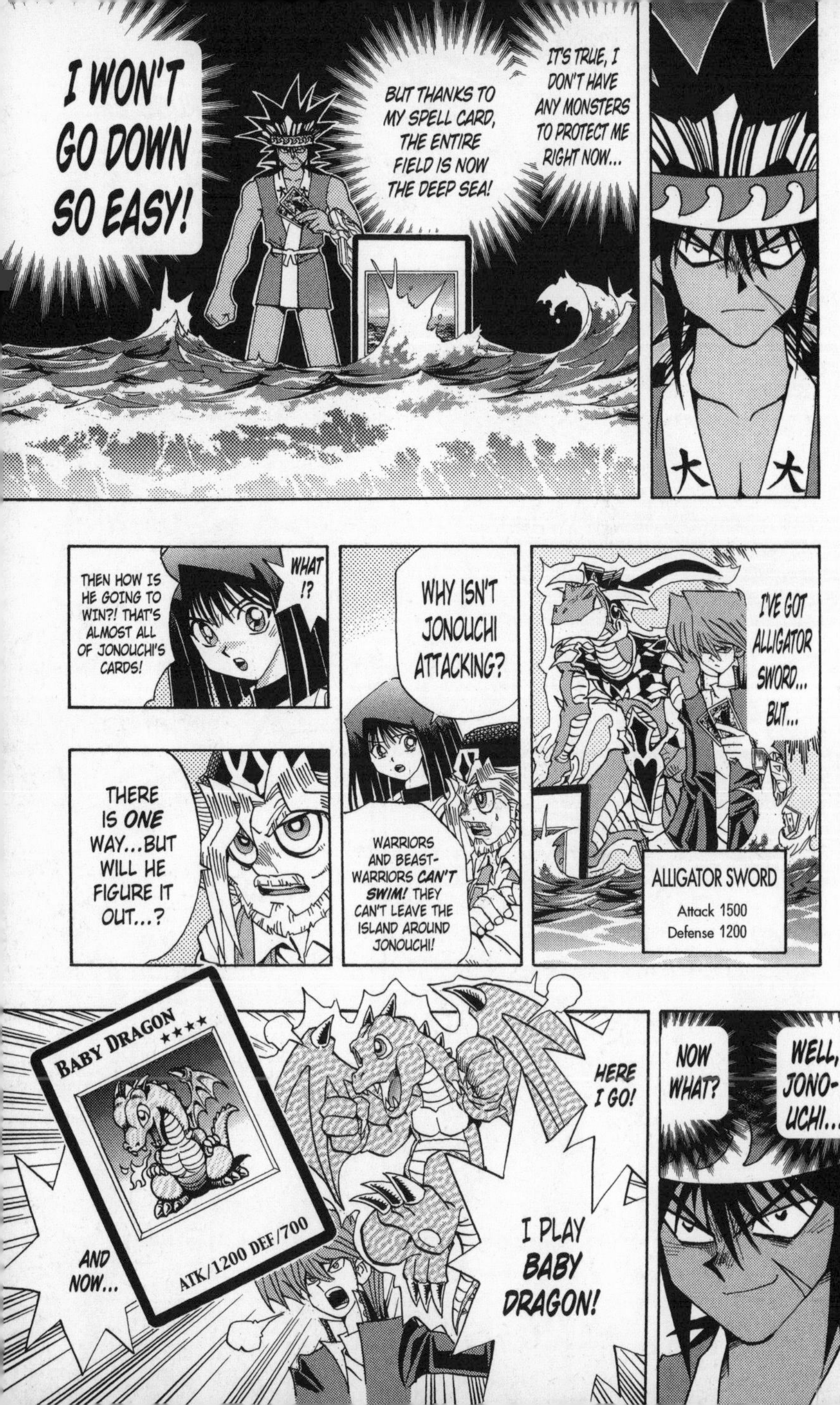
IT'S TRUE, I DON'T HAVE ANY MONSTERS TO PROTECT ME RIGHT NOW...
BUT THANKS TO MY SPELL CARD, THE ENTIRE FIELD IS NOW THE DEEP SEA!
I WON'T GO DOWN SO EASY!
I'VE GOT ALLIGATOR SWORD... BUT...
ALLIGATOR SWORD
Attack 1500
Defense 1200
WHY ISN'T JONOUCHI ATTACKING?
WARRIORS AND BEAST-WARRIORS CAN'T SWIM! THEY CAN'T LEAVE THE ISLAND AROUND JONOUCHI!
WHAT!?
THEN HOW IS HE GOING TO WIN?! THAT'S ALMOST ALL OF JONOUCHI'S CARDS!
THERE IS ONE WAY...BUT WILL HE FIGURE IT OUT...?
WELL, JONOUCHI...
NOW WHAT?
HERE I GO!
AND NOW...
I PLAY BABY DRAGON!
BABY DRAGON ★★★★
ATK/1200 DEF/700

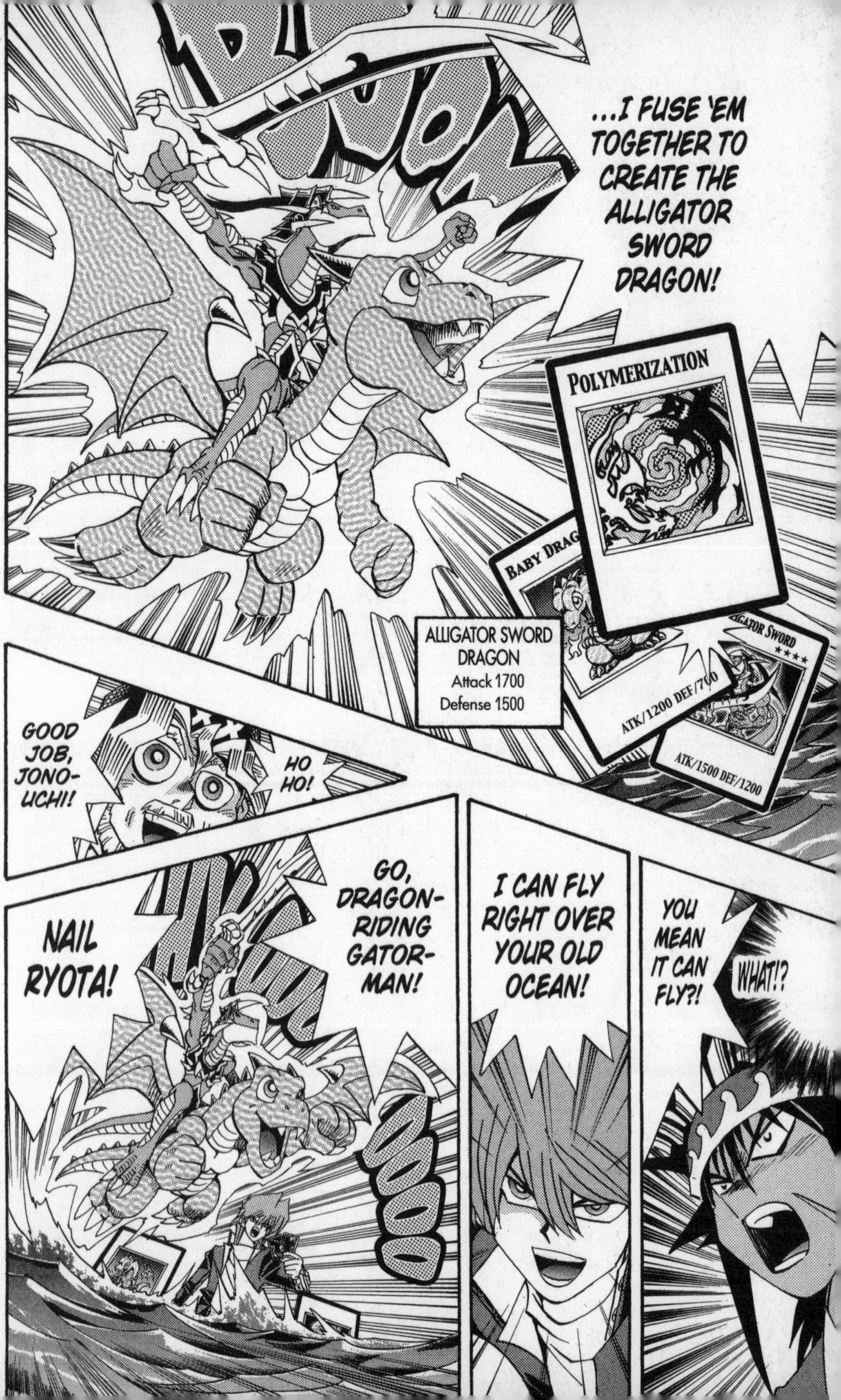
...I FUSE 'EM TOGETHER TO CREATE THE ALLIGATOR SWORD DRAGON!
POLYMERIZATION
BABY DRAG
ATK/1200 DEF/700
IGATOR SWORD
ATK/1500 DEF/1200
ALLIGATOR SWORD DRAGON
Attack 1700
Defense 1500
HO HO!
GOOD JOB, JONOUCHI!
WHAT!?
YOU MEAN IT CAN FLY?!
I CAN FLY RIGHT OVER YOUR OLD OCEAN!
GO, DRAGON-RIDING GATOR-MAN!
NAIL RYOTA!

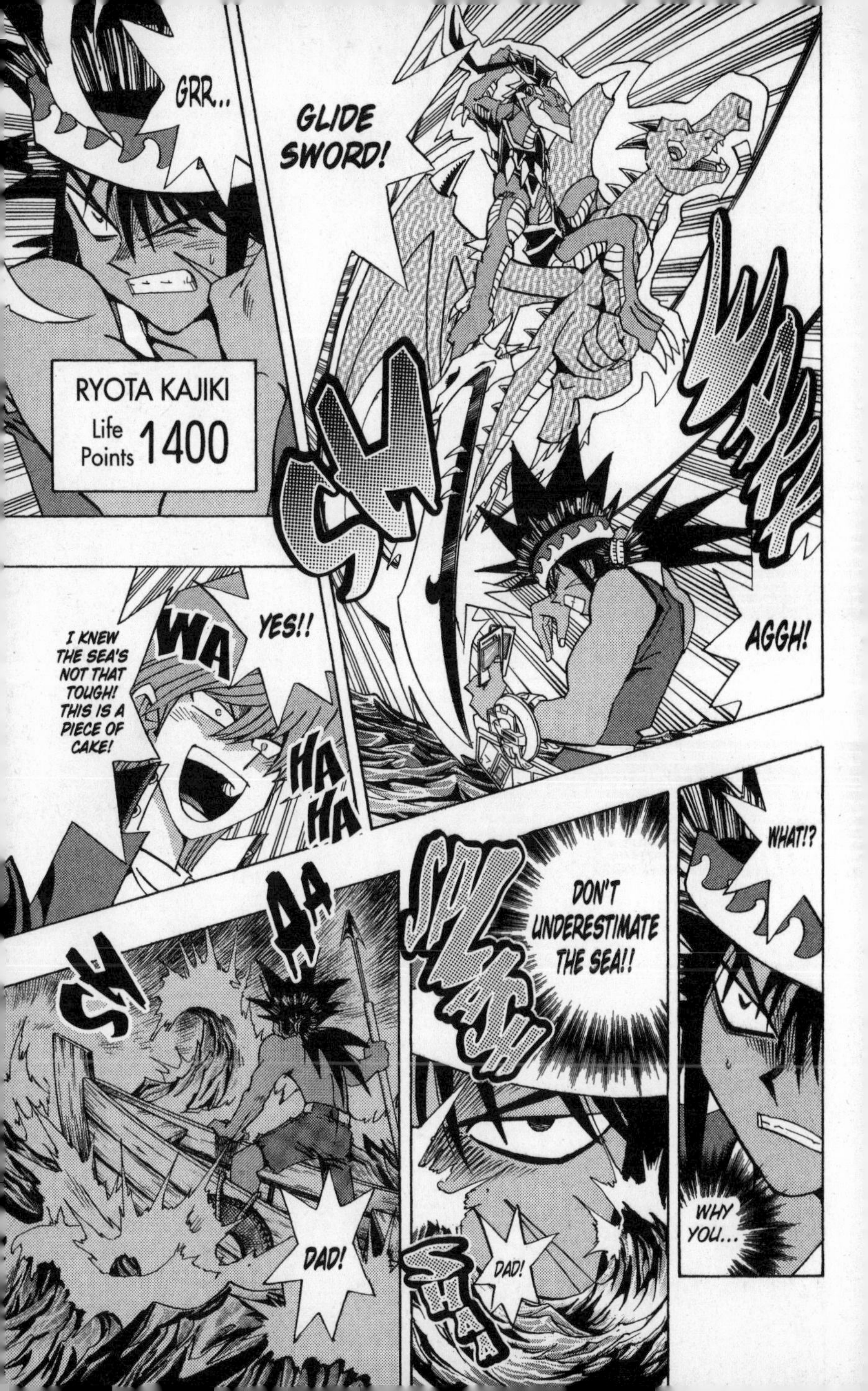
GLIDE SWORD!
AGGH!
GRR...
RYOTA KAJIKI
Life Points 1400
YES!!
WA
HA
HA
I KNEW THE SEA'S NOT THAT TOUGH! THIS IS A PIECE OF CAKE!
WHAT!?
WHY YOU...
DON'T UNDERESTIMATE THE SEA!!
DAD!
DAD!

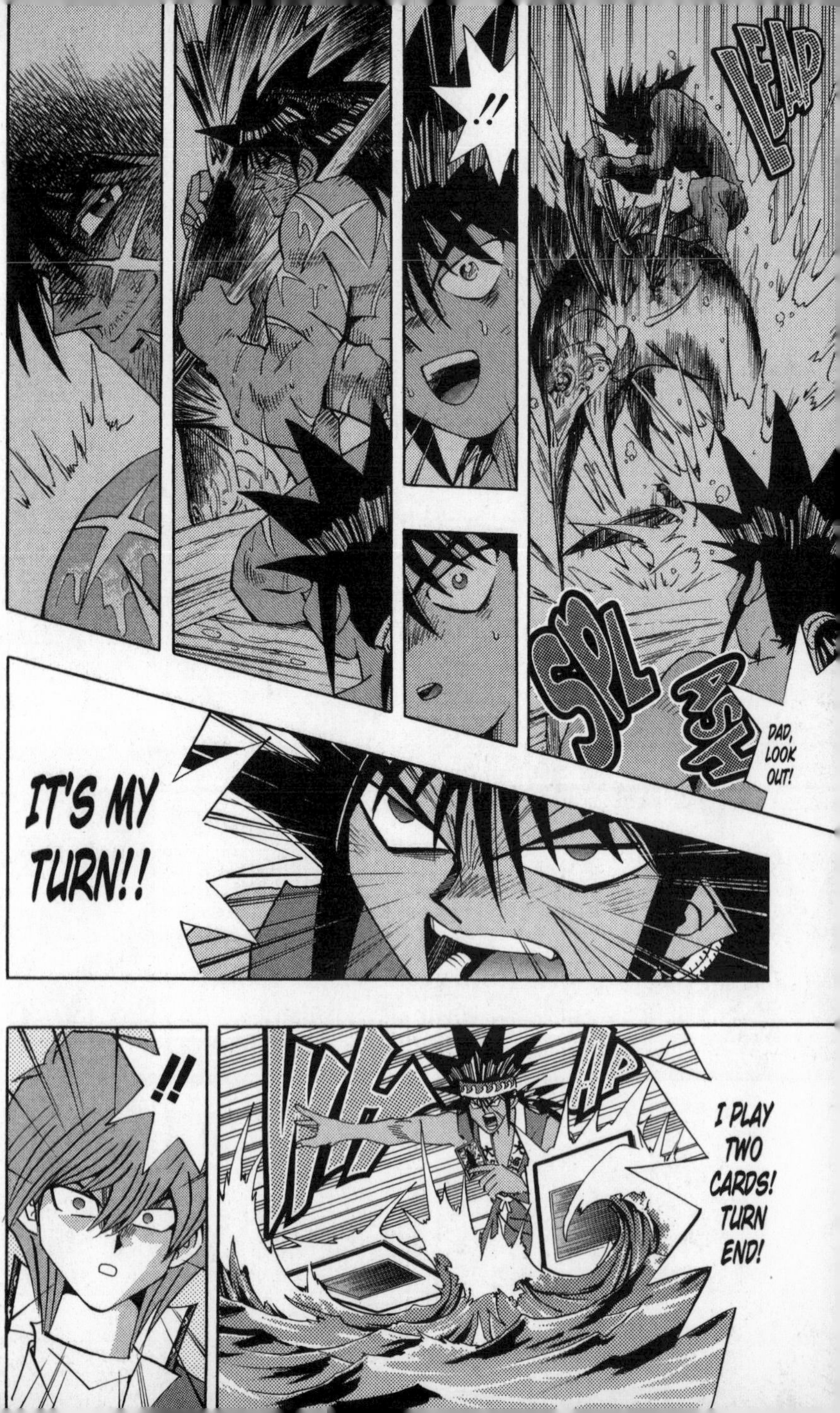

LEAP
SPLASH
DAD, LOOK OUT!
!!
IT'S MY TURN!!
WHAP
I PLAY TWO CARDS! TURN END!
!!

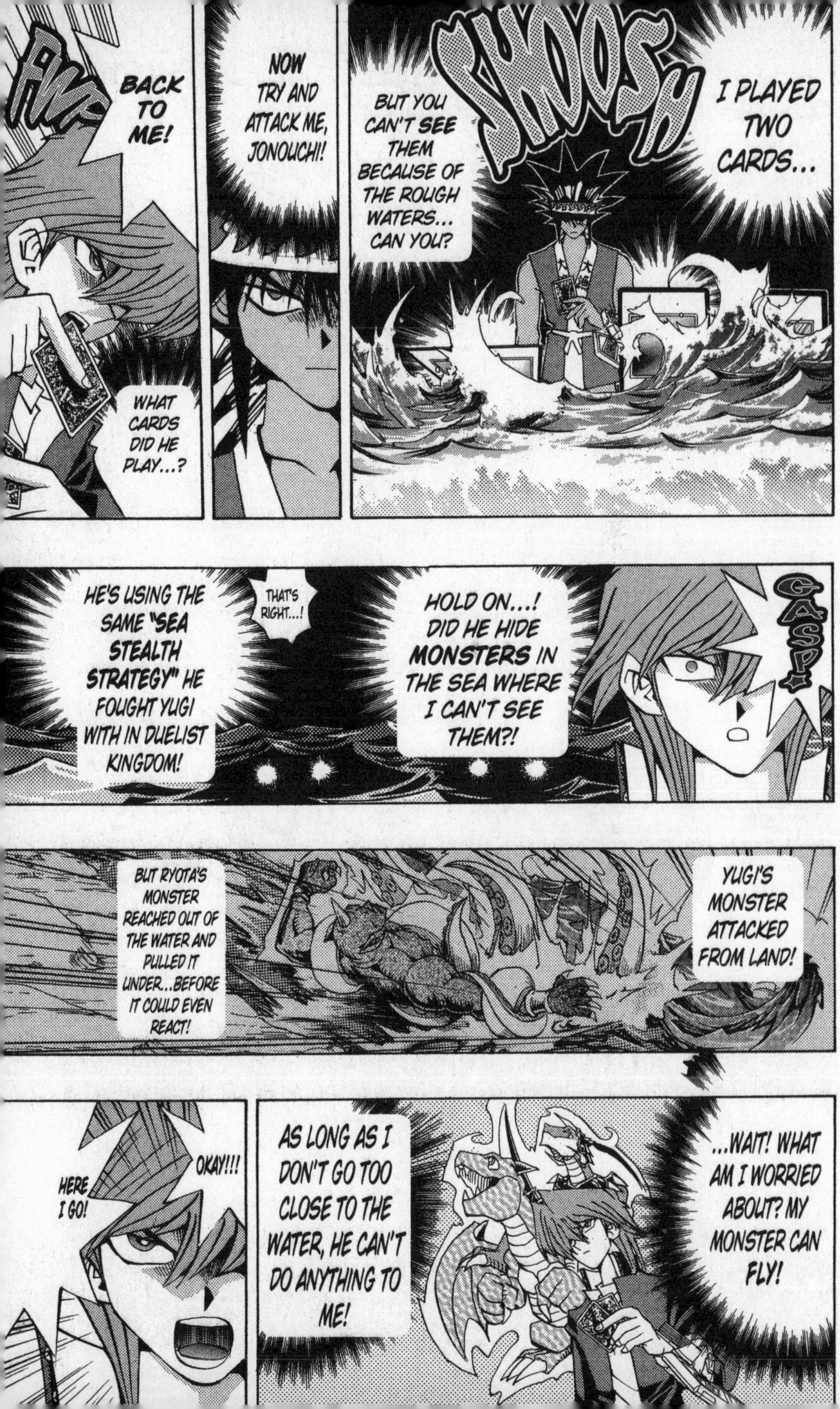
SHOOSH
I PLAYED TWO CARDS...
BUT YOU CAN'T SEE THEM BECAUSE OF THE ROUGH WATERS... CAN YOU?
NOW TRY AND ATTACK ME, JONOUCHI!
BACK TO ME!
WHAT CARDS DID HE PLAY...?
GASP!
HOLD ON...! DID HE HIDE MONSTERS IN THE SEA WHERE I CAN'T SEE THEM?!
THAT'S RIGHT...!
HE'S USING THE SAME "SEA STEALTH STRATEGY" HE FOUGHT YUGI WITH IN DUELIST KINGDOM!
YUGI'S MONSTER ATTACKED FROM LAND!
BUT RYOTA'S MONSTER REACHED OUT OF THE WATER AND PULLED IT UNDER...BEFORE IT COULD EVEN REACT!
...WAIT! WHAT AM I WORRIED ABOUT? MY MONSTER CAN FLY!
AS LONG AS I DON'T GO TOO CLOSE TO THE WATER, HE CAN'T DO ANYTHING TO ME!
OKAY!!!
HERE I GO!

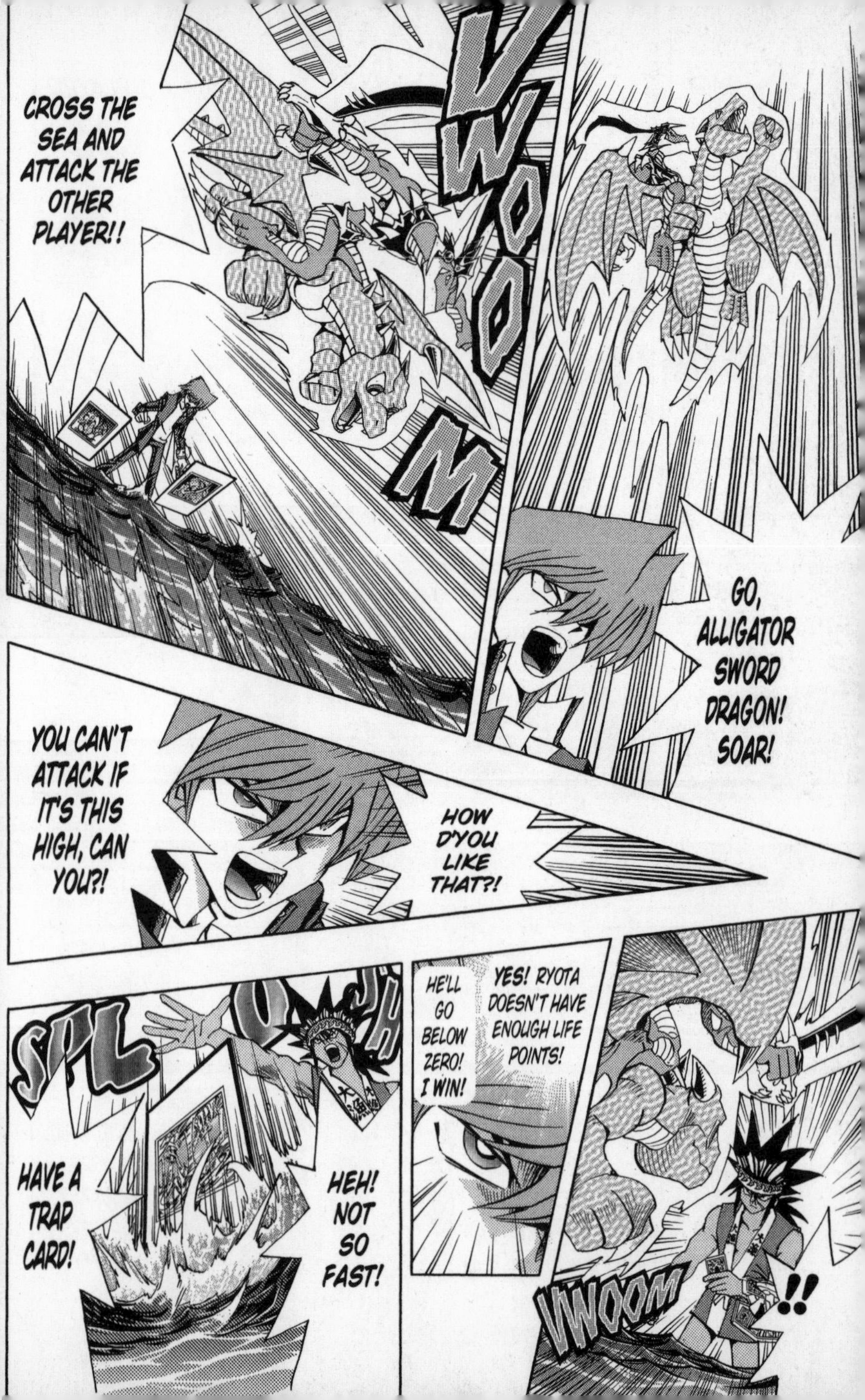
GO, ALLIGATOR SWORD DRAGON! SOAR!
VWOOOM
CROSS THE SEA AND ATTACK THE OTHER PLAYER!!
YOU CAN'T ATTACK IF IT'S THIS HIGH, CAN YOU?!
HOW D'YOU LIKE THAT?!
VWOOM
!!
YES! RYOTA DOESN'T HAVE ENOUGH LIFE POINTS!
HE'LL GO BELOW ZERO! I WIN!
SPL
HEH! NOT SO FAST!
HAVE A TRAP CARD!

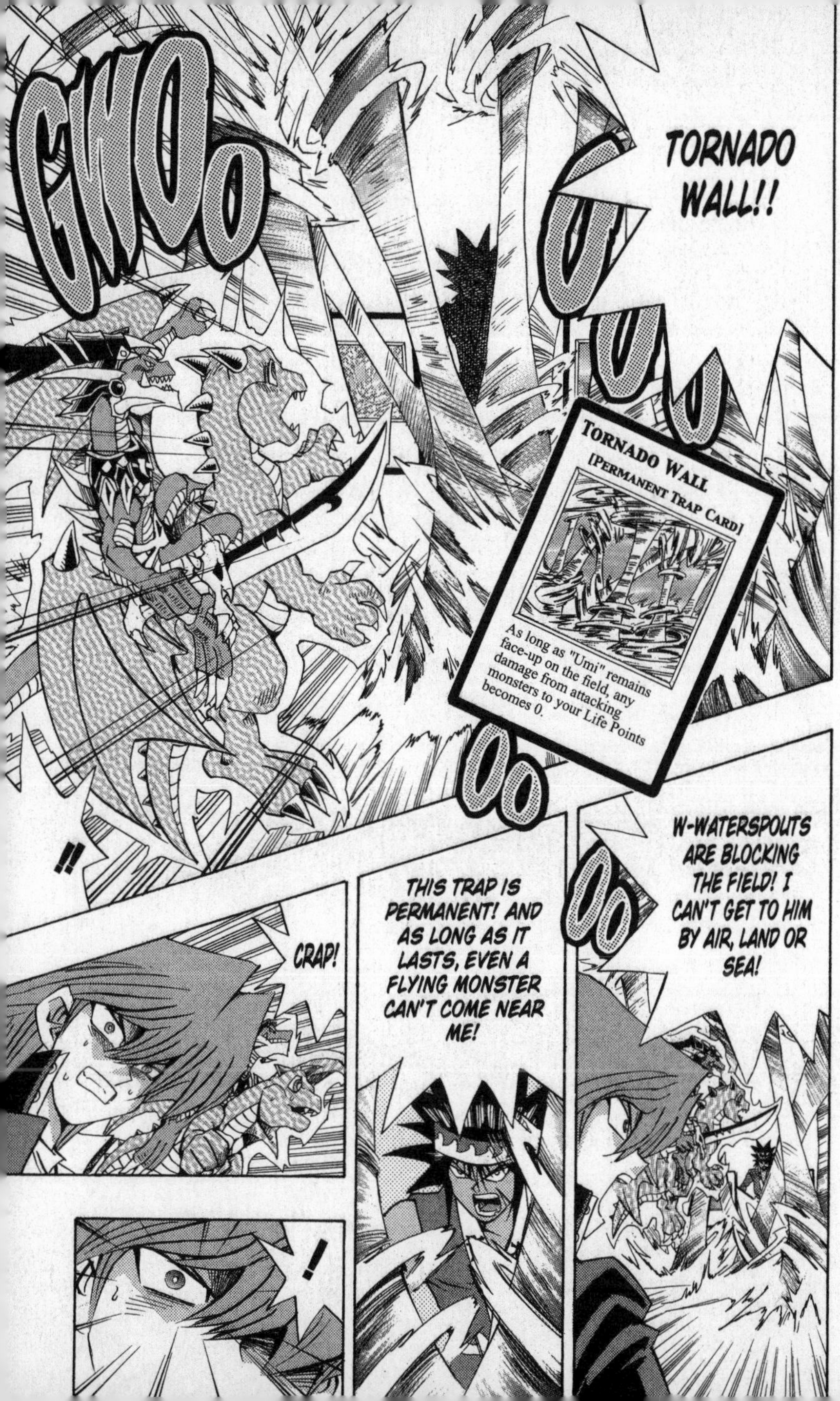
TORNADO WALL!!
GWOOOO
TORNADO WALL
[PERMANENT TRAP CARD]
As long as "Umi" remains face-up on the field, any damage from attacking monsters to your Life Points becomes 0.
!!
W-WATERSPOUTS ARE BLOCKING THE FIELD! I CAN'T GET TO HIM BY AIR, LAND OR SEA!
THIS TRAP IS PERMANENT! AND AS LONG AS IT LASTS, EVEN A FLYING MONSTER CAN'T COME NEAR ME!
CRAP!
!

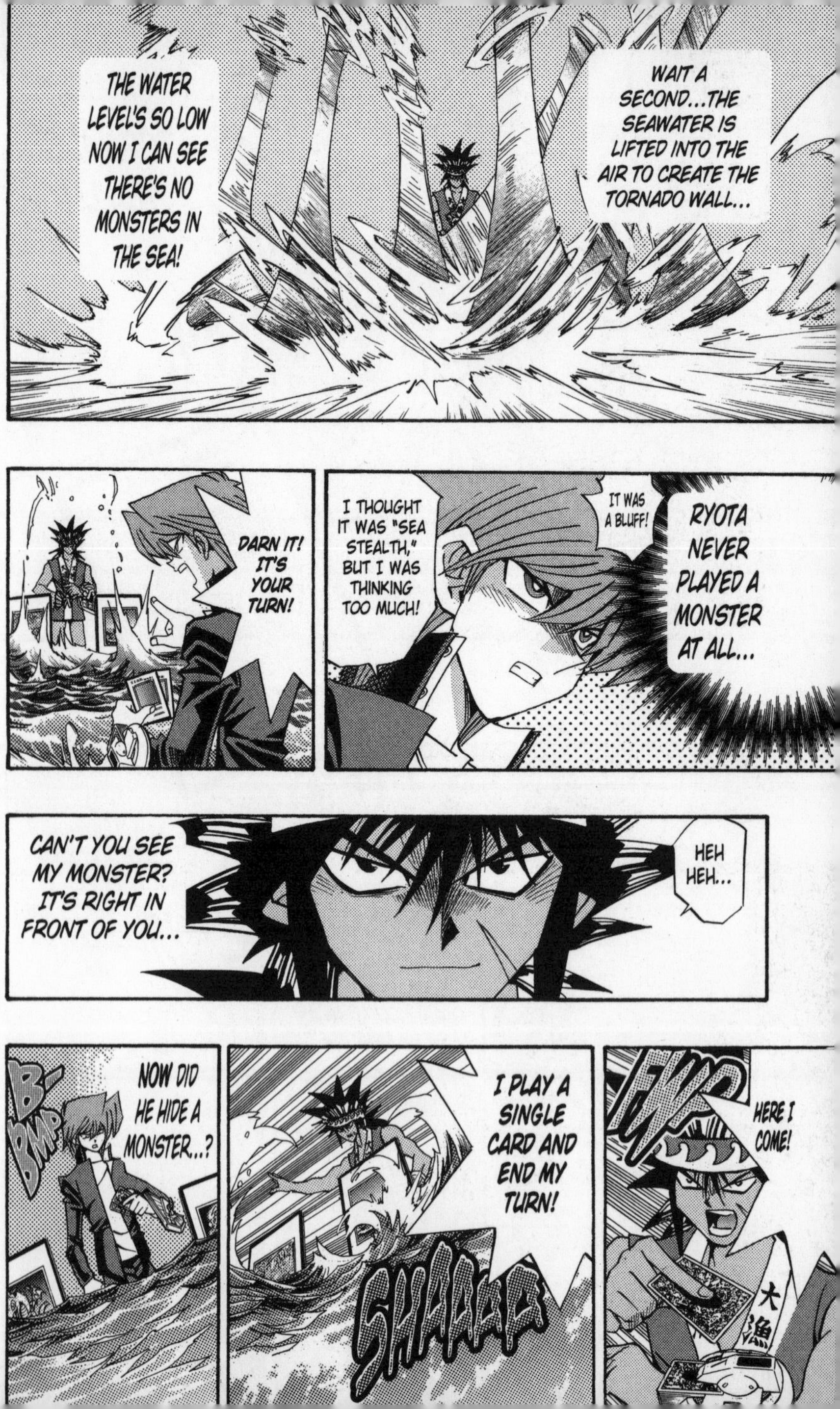
WAIT A SECOND...THE SEAWATER IS LIFTED INTO THE AIR TO CREATE THE TORNADO WALL...
THE WATER LEVEL'S SO LOW NOW I CAN SEE THERE'S NO MONSTERS IN THE SEA!
RYOTA NEVER PLAYED A MONSTER AT ALL...
IT WAS A BLUFF!
I THOUGHT IT WAS "SEA STEALTH," BUT I WAS THINKING TOO MUCH!
DARN IT! IT'S YOUR TURN!
HEH HEH...
CAN'T YOU SEE MY MONSTER? IT'S RIGHT IN FRONT OF YOU...
HERE I COME!
大漁
I PLAY A SINGLE CARD AND END MY TURN!
NOW DID HE HIDE A MONSTER...?

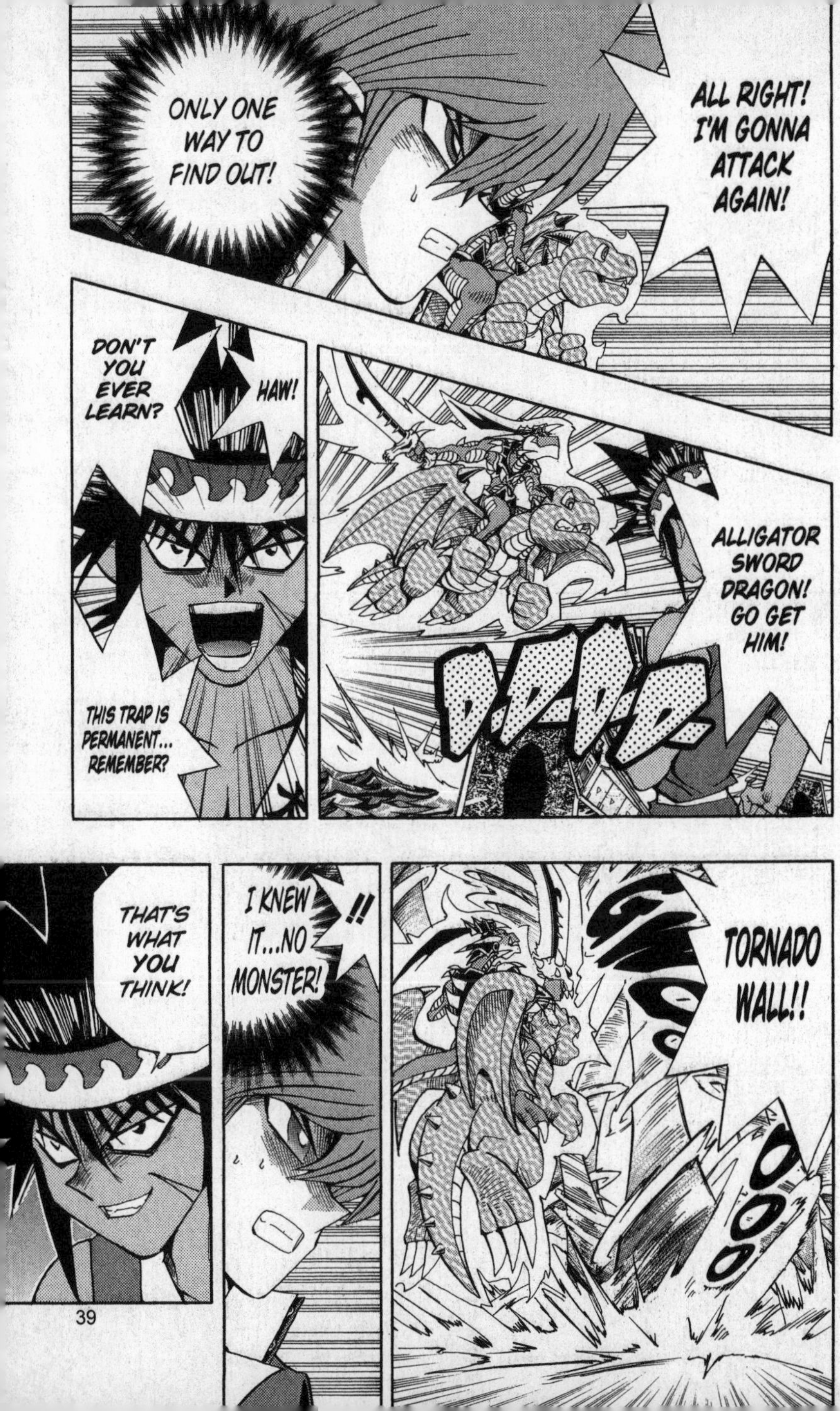
ALL RIGHT! I'M GONNA ATTACK AGAIN!
ONLY ONE WAY TO FIND OUT!
ALLIGATOR SWORD DRAGON! GO GET HIM!
HAW!
DON'T YOU EVER LEARN?
THIS TRAP IS PERMANENT... REMEMBER?
TORNADO WALL!!
!!
I KNEW IT...NO MONSTER!
THAT'S WHAT YOU THINK!

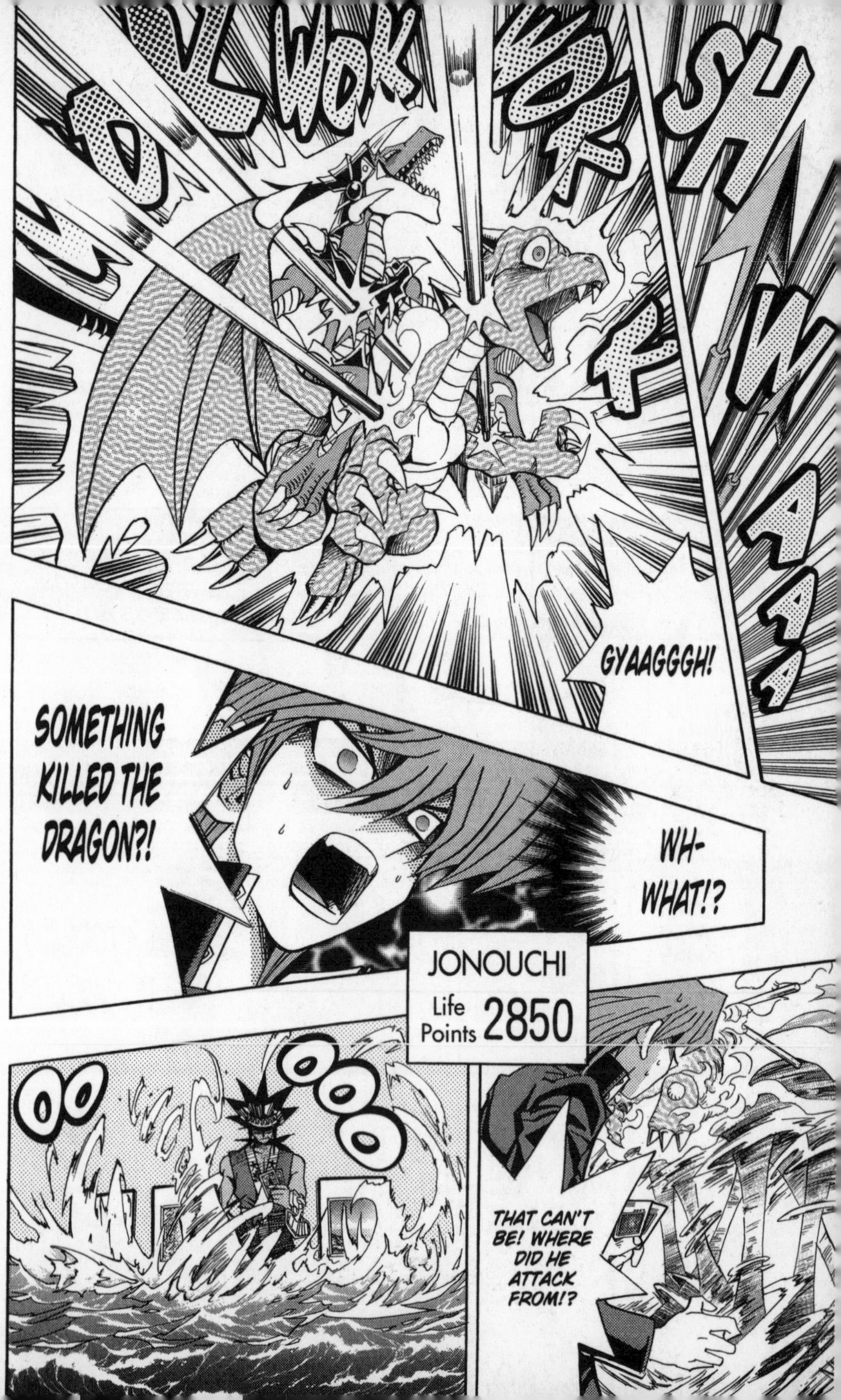
SHWAAA
GYAAGGGH!
WH-
WHAT!?
SOMETHING KILLED THE DRAGON?!
JONOUCHI
Life Points 2850
THAT CAN'T BE! WHERE DID HE ATTACK FROM!?

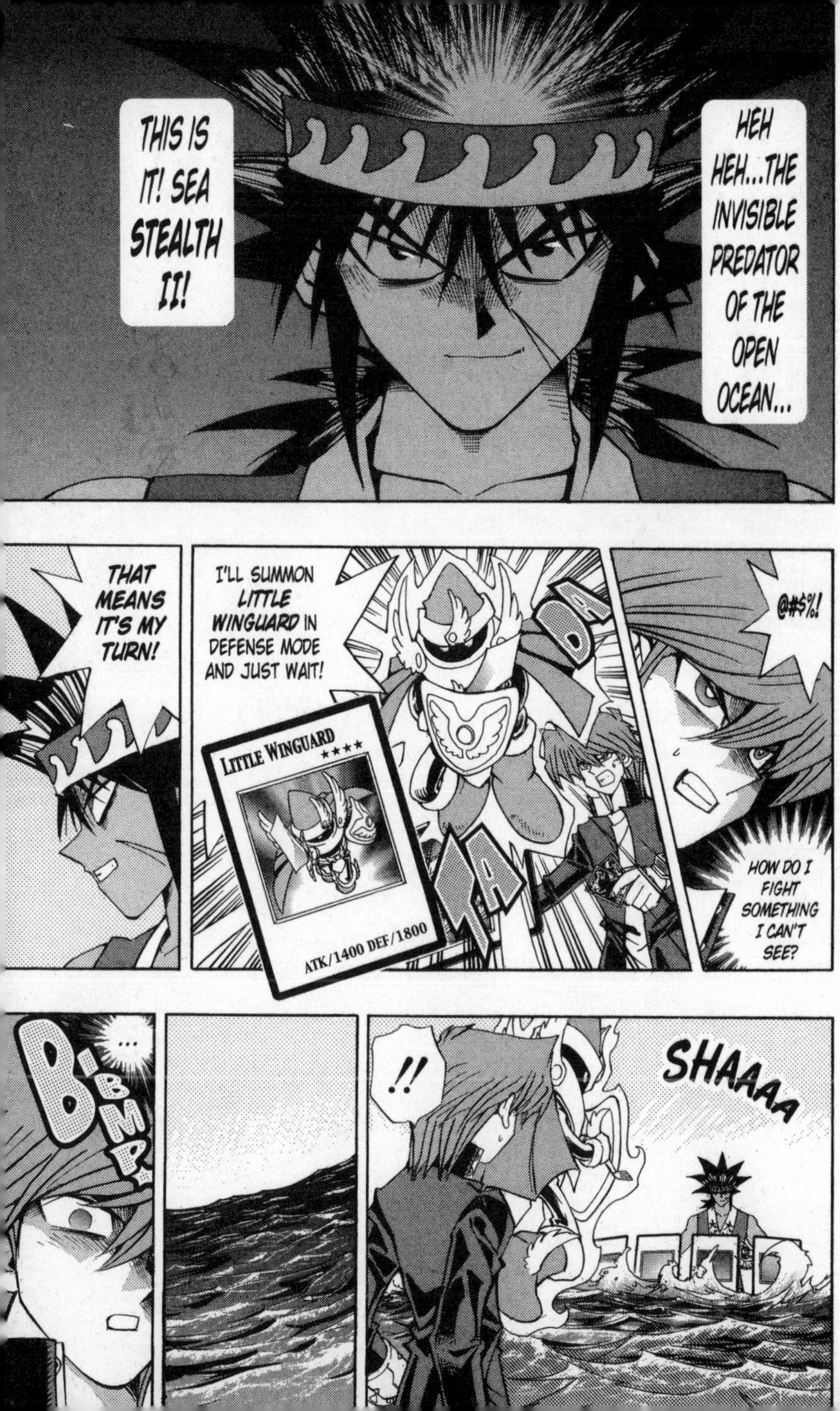
HEH HEH...THE INVISIBLE PREDATOR OF THE OPEN OCEAN...
THIS IS IT! SEA STEALTH II!
@#$%!
HOW DO I FIGHT SOMETHING I CAN'T SEE?
I'LL SUMMON LITTLE WINGUARD IN DEFENSE MODE AND JUST WAIT!
LITTLE WINGUARD
ATK/1400 DEF/1800
THAT MEANS IT'S MY TURN!
SHAAAA
!!
...

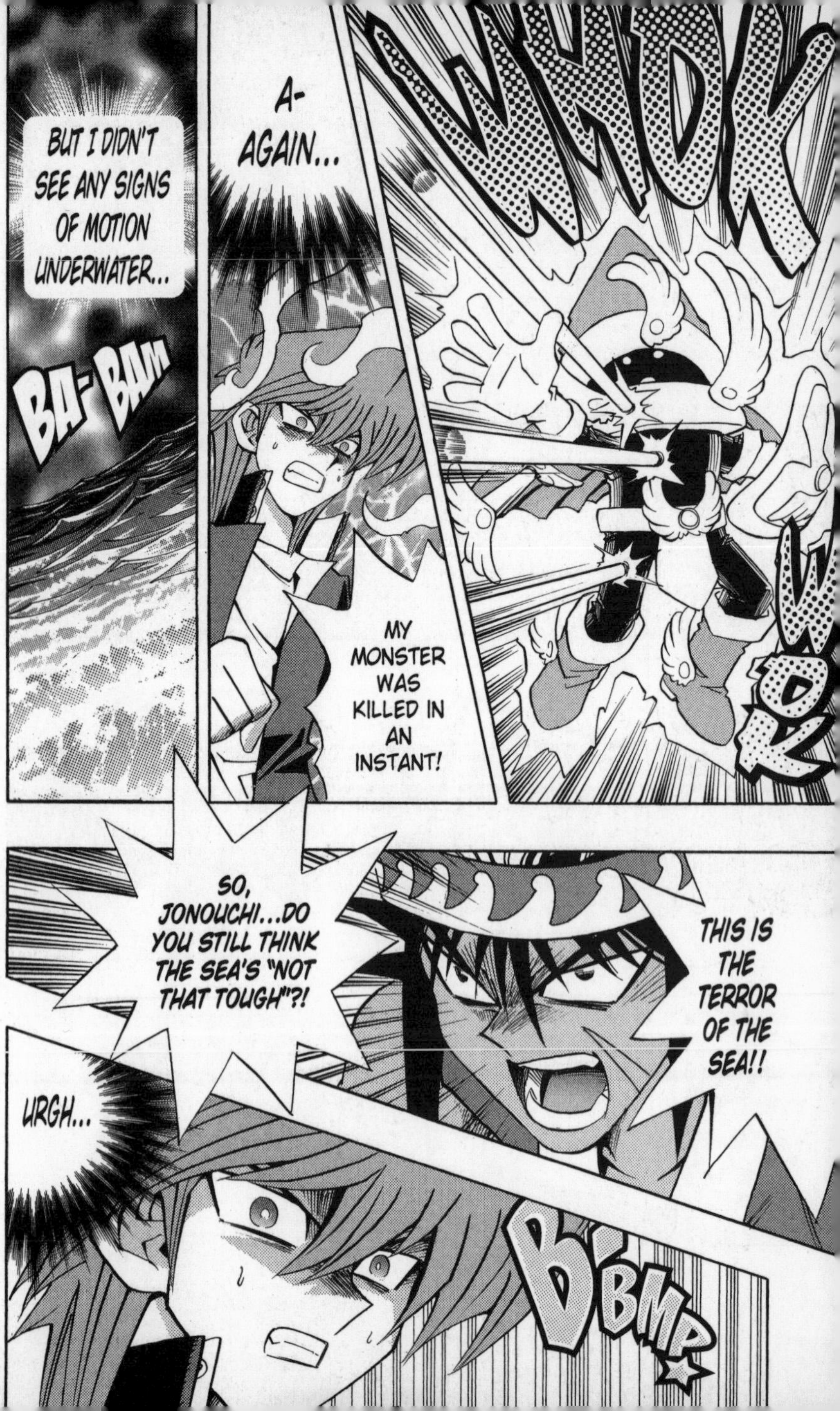
WHOK
WHOK
A- AGAIN...
MY MONSTER WAS KILLED IN AN INSTANT!
BUT I DIDN'T SEE ANY SIGNS OF MOTION UNDERWATER...
BA-BAM
SO, JONOUCHI...DO YOU STILL THINK THE SEA'S "NOT THAT TOUGH"?!
THIS IS THE TERROR OF THE SEA!!
URGH...
B'BMP

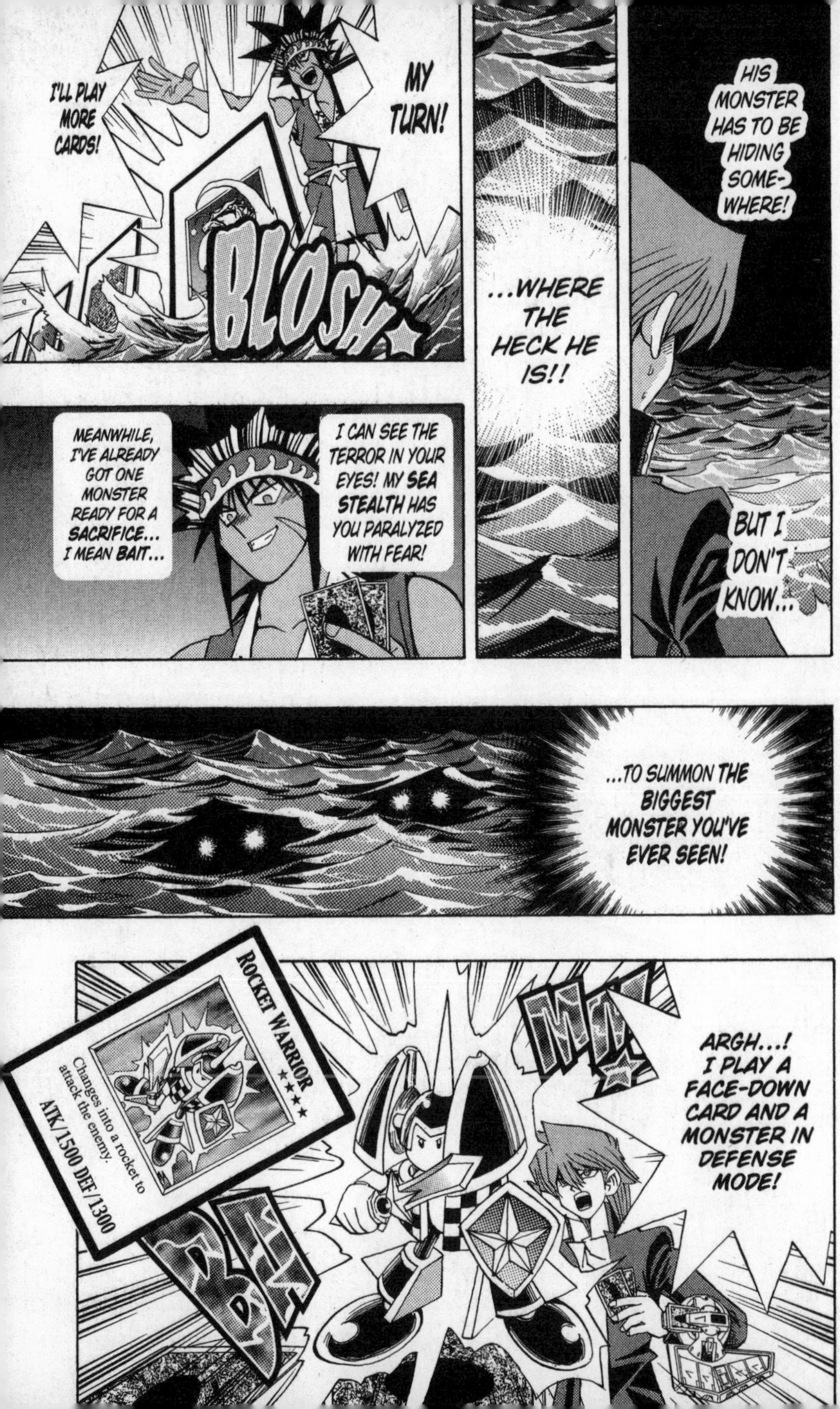
HIS MONSTER HAS TO BE HIDING SOME-WHERE!
BUT I DON'T KNOW...
...WHERE THE HECK HE IS!!
MY TURN!
I'LL PLAY MORE CARDS!
BLOSH
I CAN SEE THE TERROR IN YOUR EYES! MY SEA STEALTH HAS YOU PARALYZED WITH FEAR!
MEANWHILE, I'VE ALREADY GOT ONE MONSTER READY FOR A SACRIFICE... I MEAN BAIT...
...TO SUMMON THE BIGGEST MONSTER YOU'VE EVER SEEN!
ARGH...! I PLAY A FACE-DOWN CARD AND A MONSTER IN DEFENSE MODE!
ROCKET WARRIOR
Changes into a rocket to attack the enemy.
ATK/1500 DEF/1300

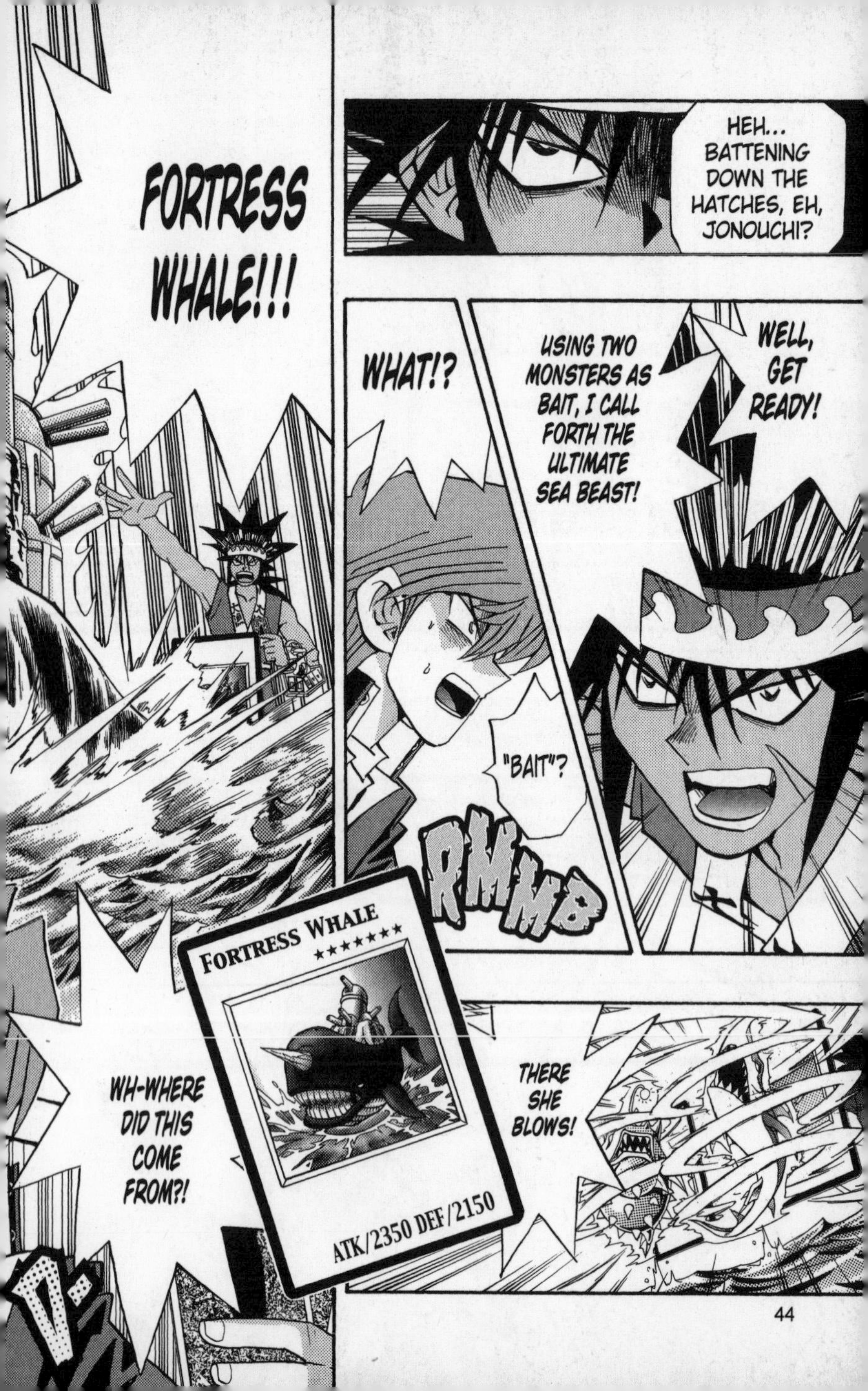
HEH... BATTENING DOWN THE HATCHES, EH, JONOUCHI?
WELL, GET READY!
USING TWO MONSTERS AS BAIT, I CALL FORTH THE ULTIMATE SEA BEAST!
RMMB
WHAT!?
"BAIT"?
THERE SHE BLOWS!
FORTRESS WHALE!!!
FORTRESS WHALE
ATK/2350 DEF/2150
WH-WHERE DID THIS COME FROM?!

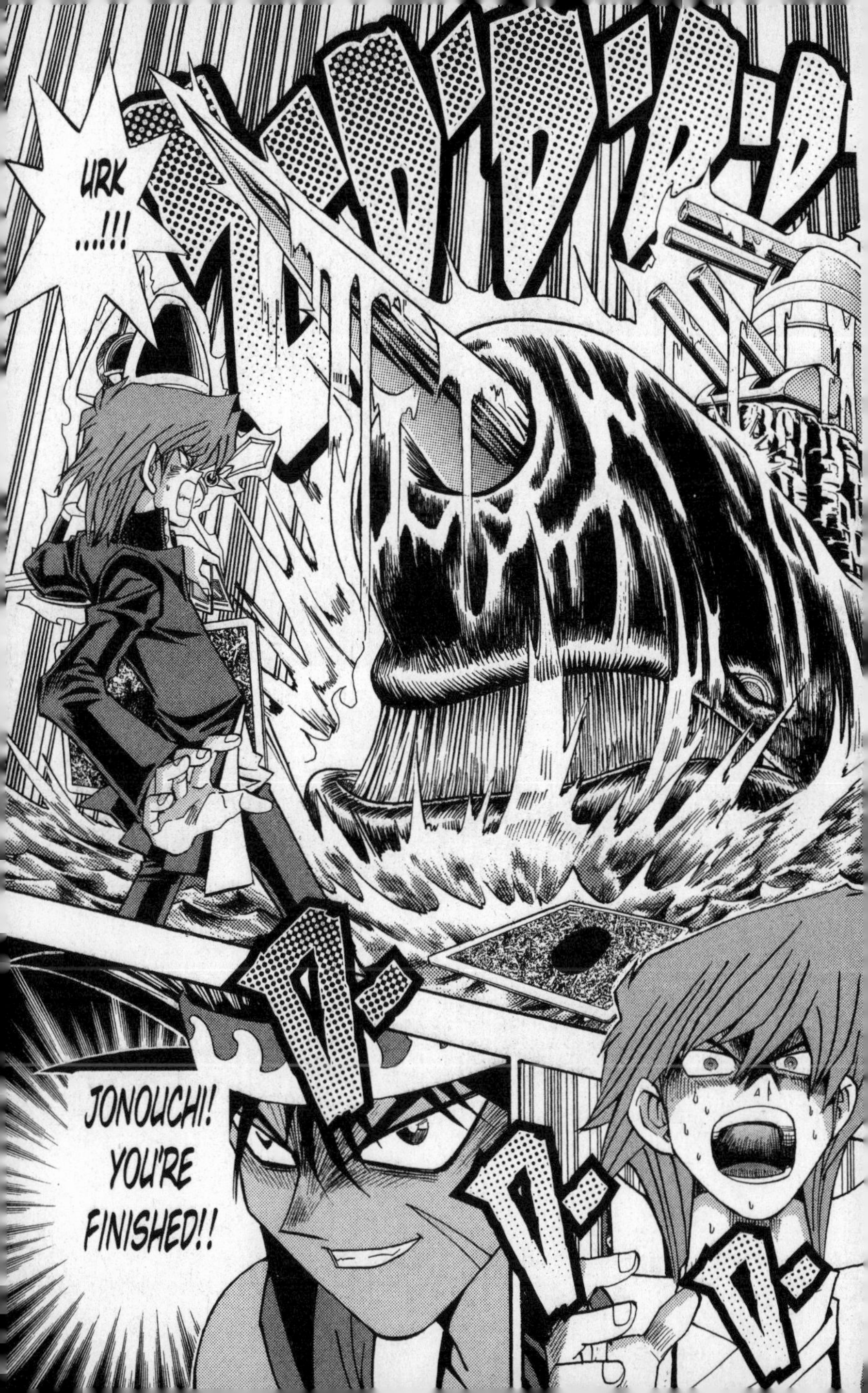
URK ...!!!
JONOUCHI! YOU'RE FINISHED!!

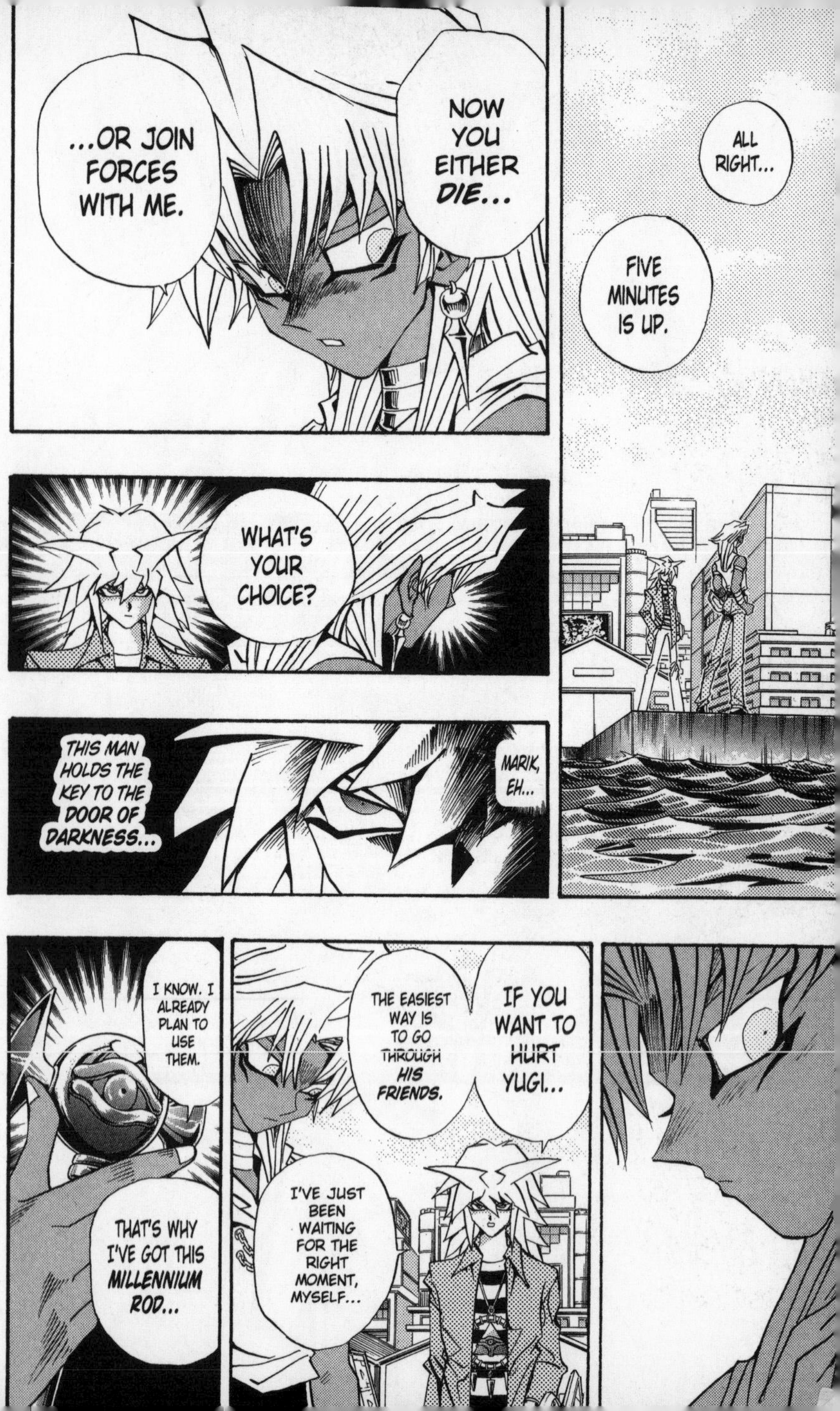
ALL RIGHT...
FIVE MINUTES IS UP.
NOW YOU EITHER *DIE*...
...OR JOIN FORCES WITH ME.
WHAT'S YOUR CHOICE?
MARIK, EH...
THIS MAN HOLDS THE KEY TO THE DOOR OF DARKNESS...
IF YOU WANT TO HURT YUGI...
THE EASIEST WAY IS TO GO THROUGH *HIS FRIENDS.*
I'VE JUST BEEN WAITING FOR THE RIGHT MOMENT, MYSELF...
I KNOW. I ALREADY PLAN TO USE THEM.
THAT'S WHY I'VE GOT THIS *MILLENNIUM ROD*...

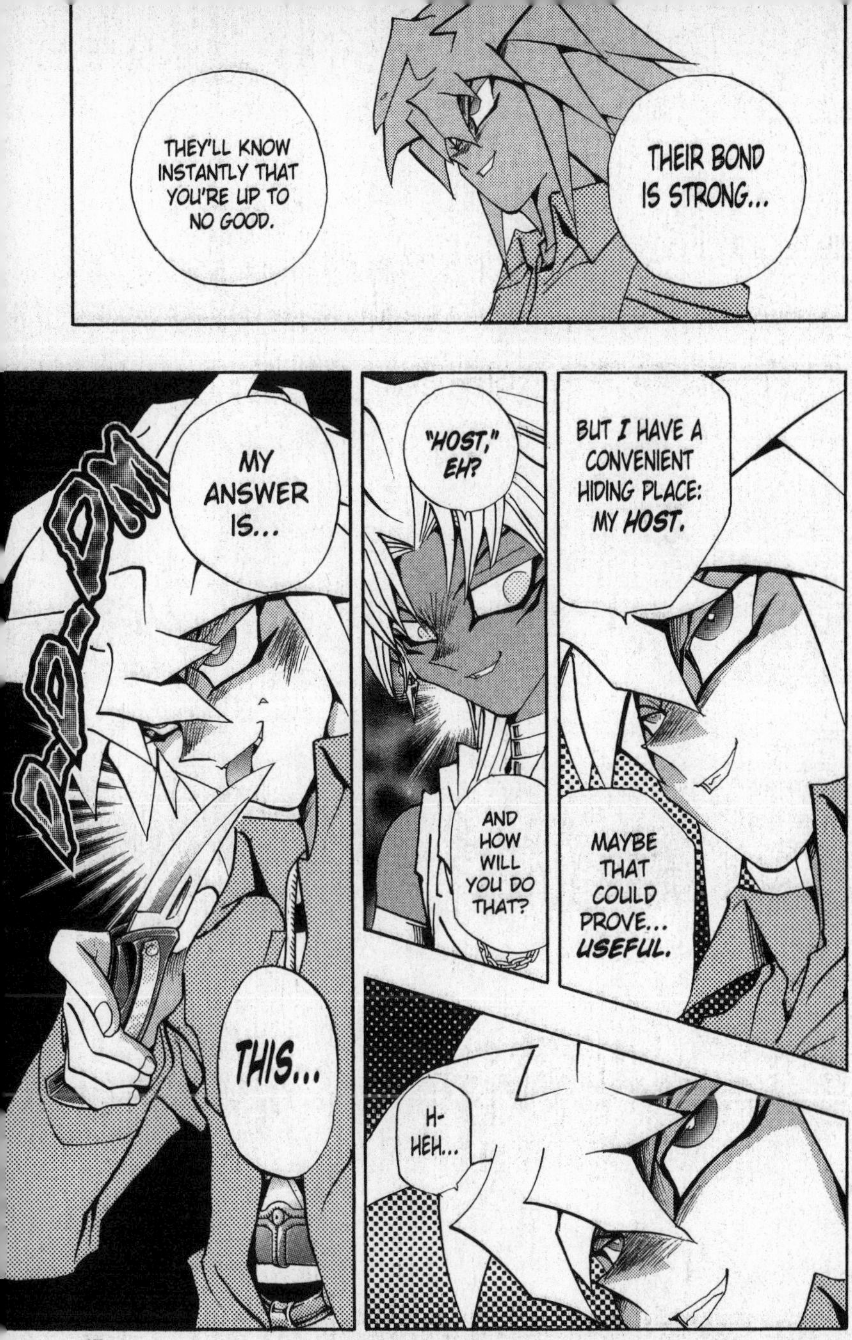
THEIR BOND IS STRONG...
THEY'LL KNOW INSTANTLY THAT YOU'RE UP TO NO GOOD.
BUT I HAVE A CONVENIENT HIDING PLACE: MY *HOST.*
MAYBE THAT COULD PROVE... *USEFUL.*
"HOST," EH?
AND HOW WILL YOU DO THAT?
H-HEH...
MY ANSWER IS...
D-D-DOM
THIS...

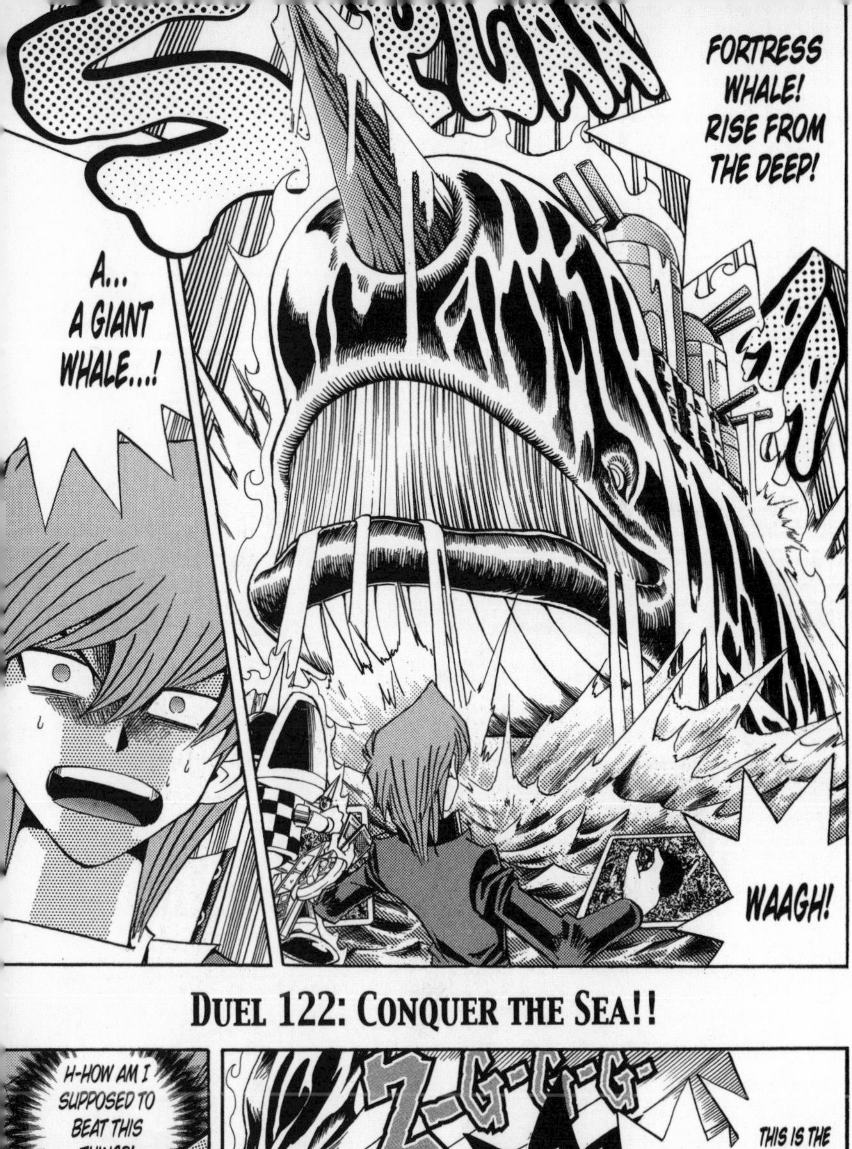
FORTRESS WHALE! RISE FROM THE DEEP!
WAAGH!
A... A GIANT WHALE...!

Duel 122: Conquer the Sea!!

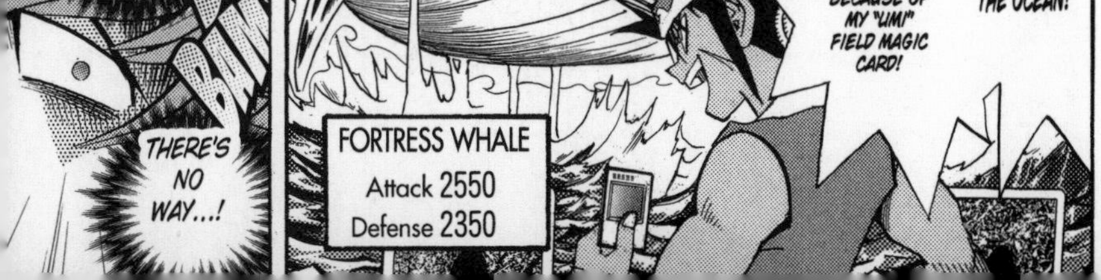
THIS IS THE BIGGEST BEAST IN THE OCEAN!
AND IT'S POWERED UP BECAUSE OF MY "UMI" FIELD MAGIC CARD!
Z-G-G-G-
FORTRESS WHALE
Attack 2550
Defense 2350
H-HOW AM I SUPPOSED TO BEAT THIS THING?!
THERE'S NO WAY...!

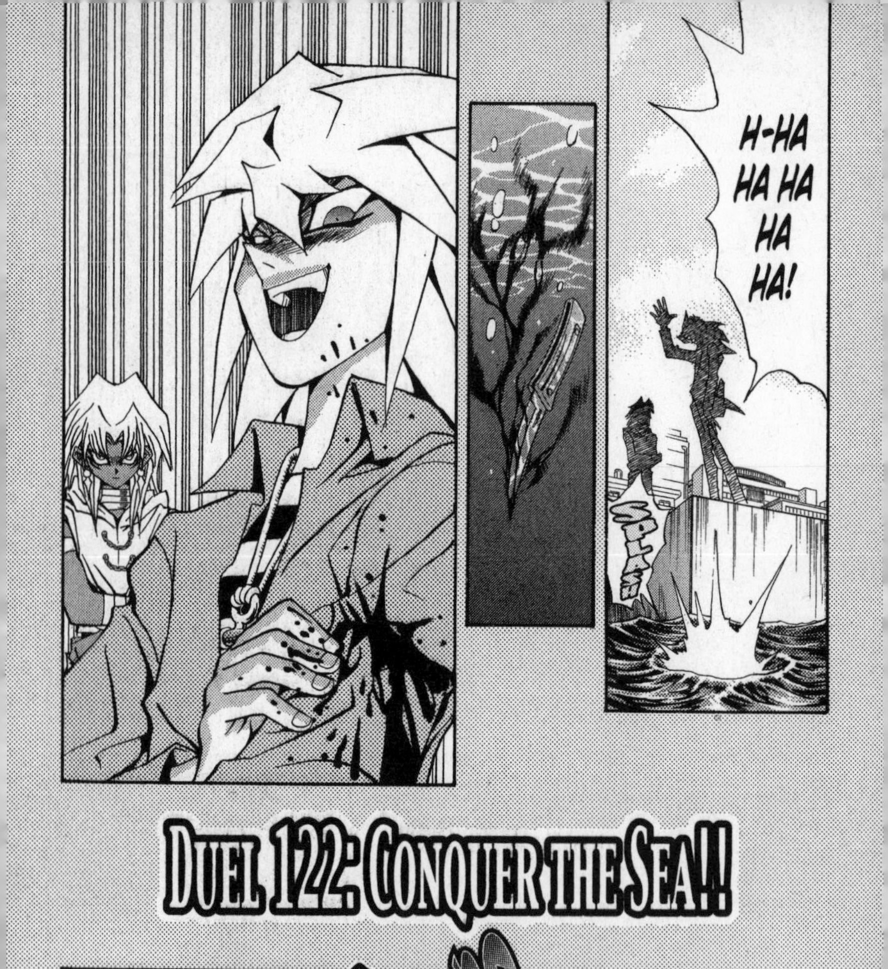
H-HA HA HA HA HA!
SPLASH

DUEL 122: CONQUER THE SEA!!

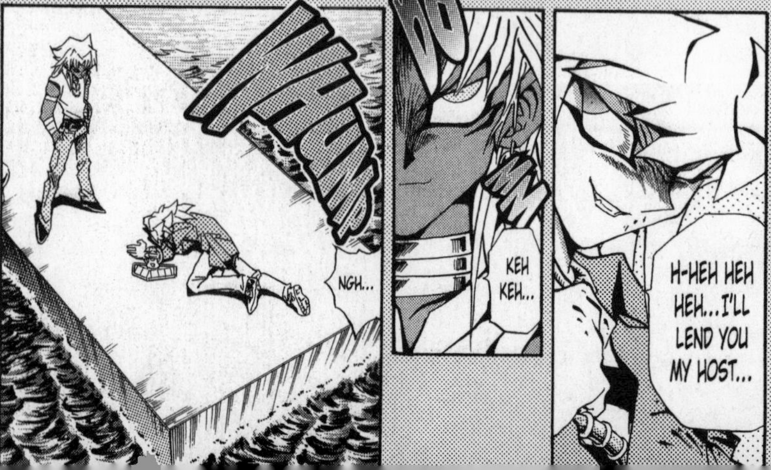
H-HEH HEH HEH...I'LL LEND YOU MY HOST...
DO
KEH KEH...
WHUMP
NGH...

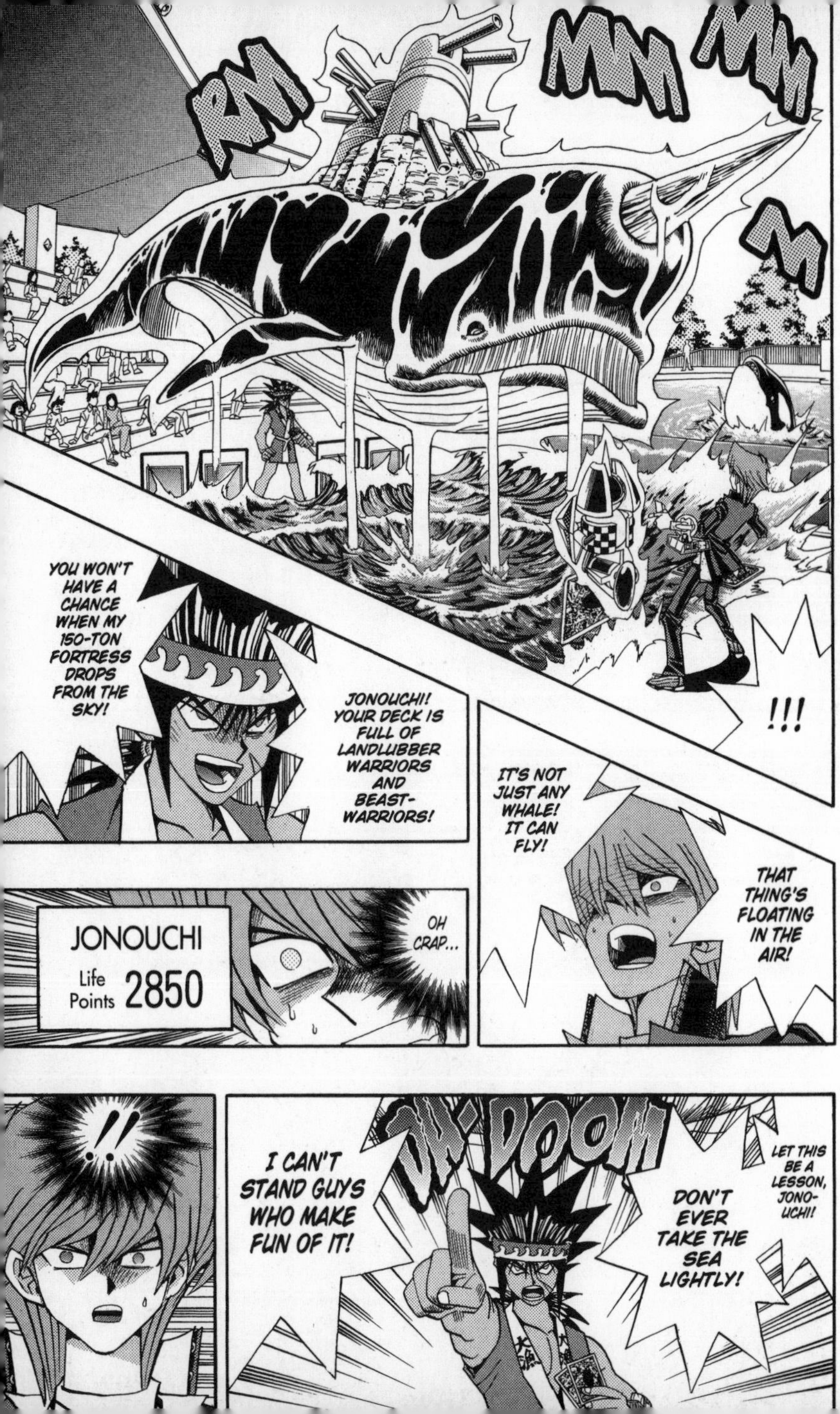
RMMMMMMM
!!!
IT'S NOT JUST ANY WHALE! IT CAN FLY!
THAT THING'S FLOATING IN THE AIR!
JONOUCHI! YOUR DECK IS FULL OF LANDLUBBER WARRIORS AND BEAST-WARRIORS!
YOU WON'T HAVE A CHANCE WHEN MY 150-TON FORTRESS DROPS FROM THE SKY!
OH CRAP...
JONOUCHI
Life Points 2850
LET THIS BE A LESSON, JONO-UCHI!
JA-DOOM
DON'T EVER TAKE THE SEA LIGHTLY!
I CAN'T STAND GUYS WHO MAKE FUN OF IT!
!!

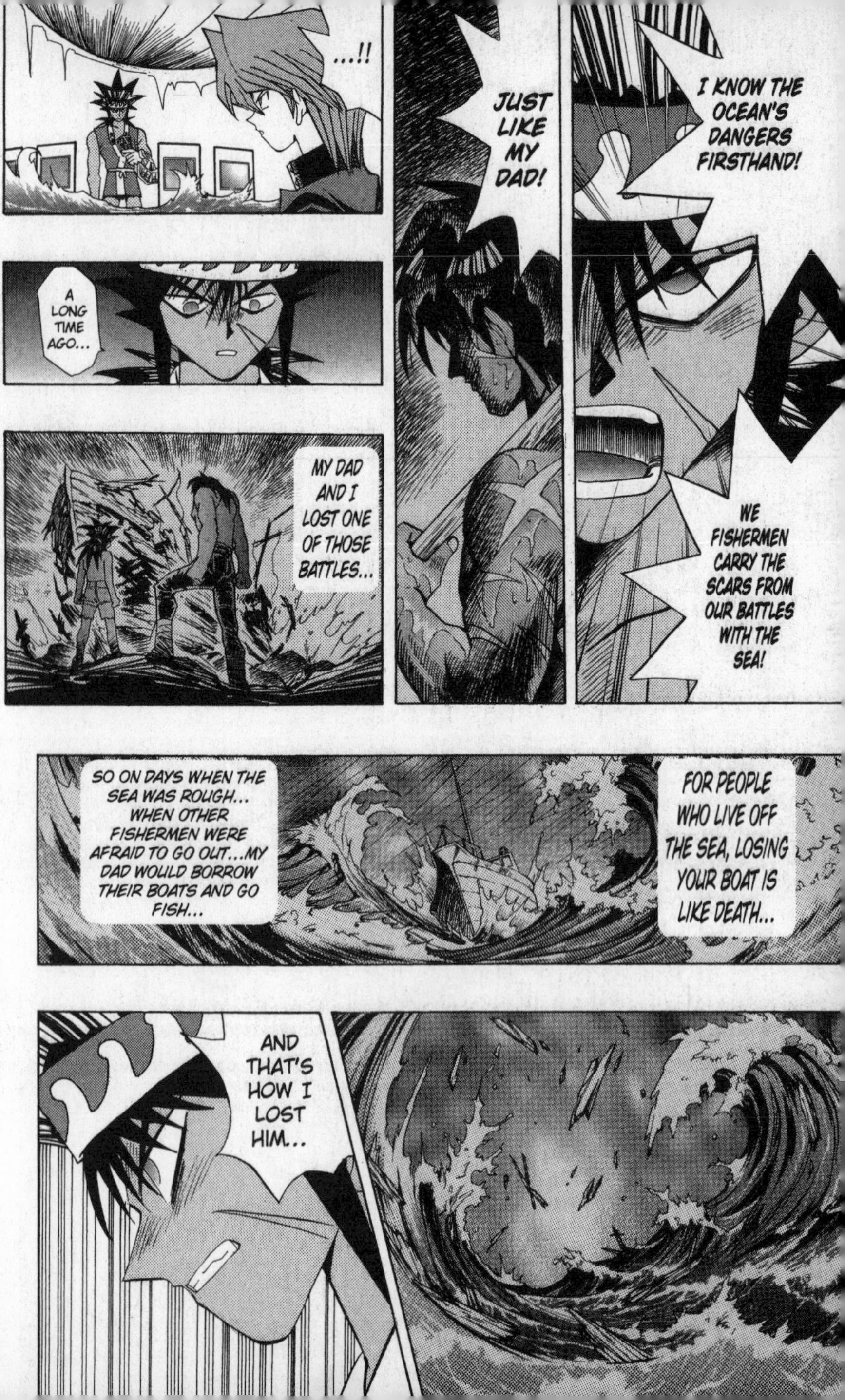
I KNOW THE OCEAN'S DANGERS FIRSTHAND!
WE FISHERMEN CARRY THE SCARS FROM OUR BATTLES WITH THE SEA!
JUST LIKE MY DAD!
...!!
A LONG TIME AGO...
MY DAD AND I LOST ONE OF THOSE BATTLES...
FOR PEOPLE WHO LIVE OFF THE SEA, LOSING YOUR BOAT IS LIKE DEATH...
SO ON DAYS WHEN THE SEA WAS ROUGH... WHEN OTHER FISHERMEN WERE AFRAID TO GO OUT...MY DAD WOULD BORROW THEIR BOATS AND GO FISH...
AND THAT'S HOW I LOST HIM...

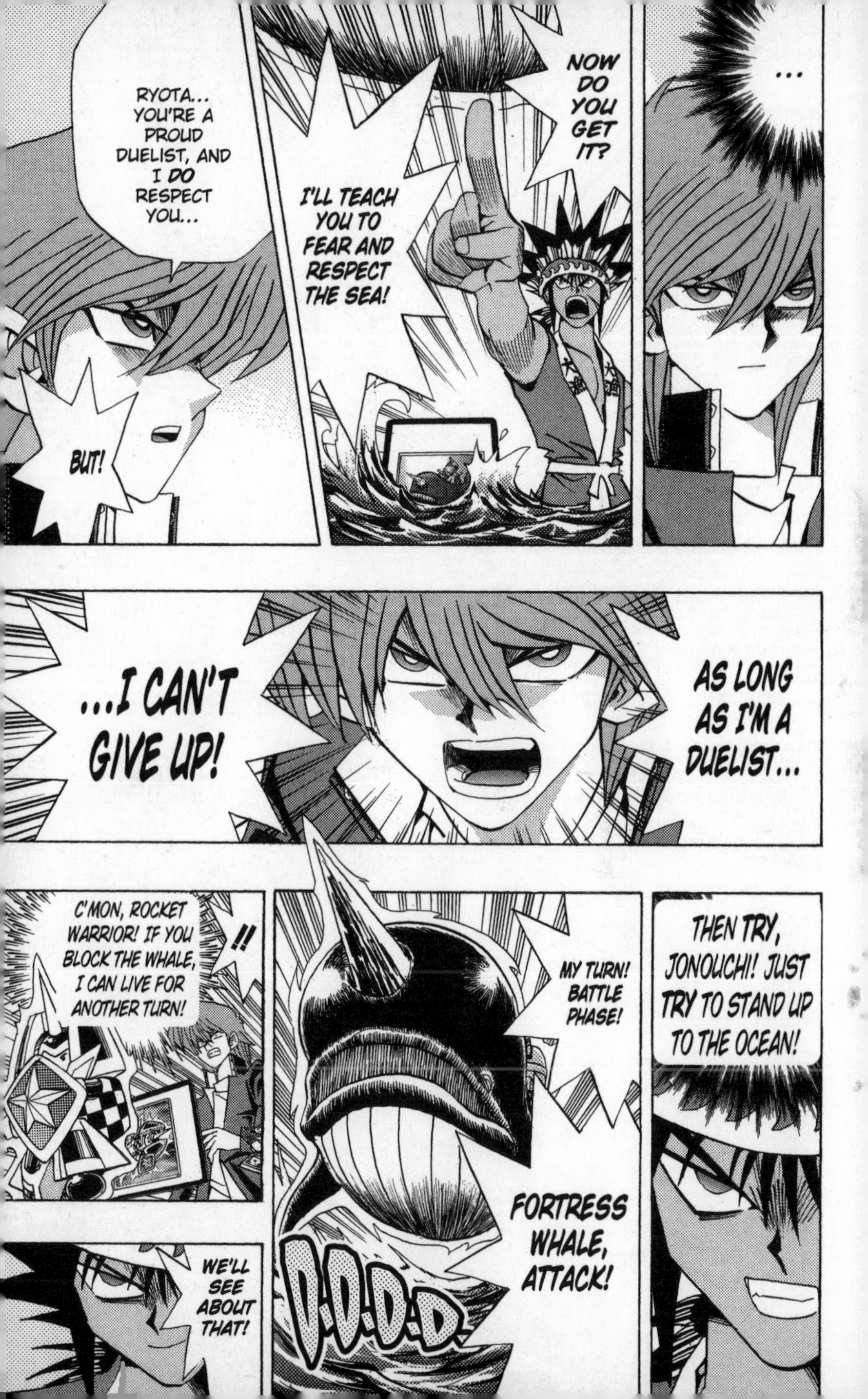
...
NOW DO YOU GET IT?
I'LL TEACH YOU TO FEAR AND RESPECT THE SEA!
RYOTA... YOU'RE A PROUD DUELIST, AND I *DO* RESPECT YOU...
BUT!
AS LONG AS I'M A DUELIST...
...I CAN'T GIVE UP!
THEN TRY, JONOUCHI! JUST TRY TO STAND UP TO THE OCEAN!
MY TURN! BATTLE PHASE!
FORTRESS WHALE, ATTACK!
D-D-D-D
!!
C'MON, ROCKET WARRIOR! IF YOU BLOCK THE WHALE, I CAN LIVE FOR ANOTHER TURN!
WE'LL SEE ABOUT THAT!

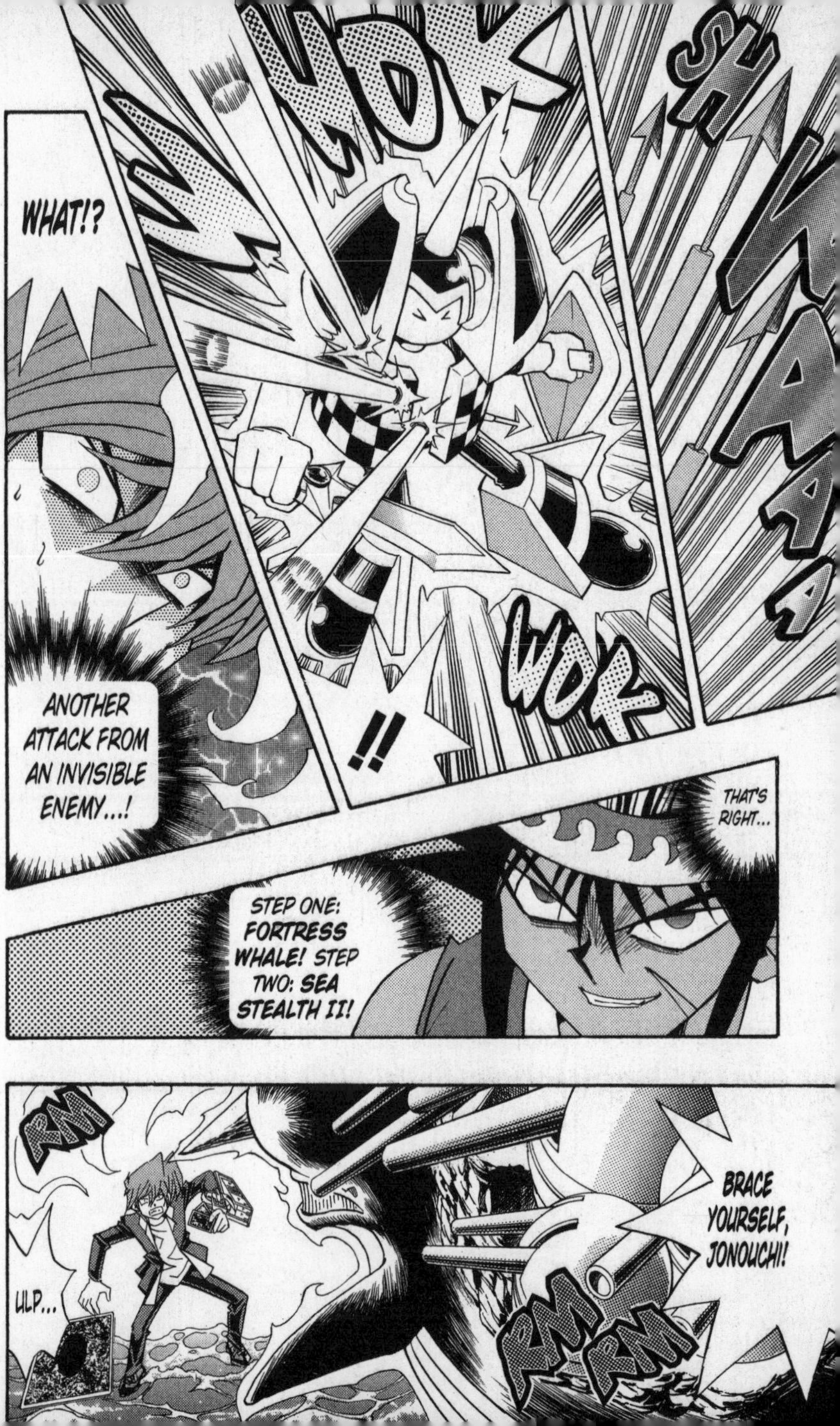

WOK
WOK
!!
WHAT!?
ANOTHER ATTACK FROM AN INVISIBLE ENEMY...!
THAT'S RIGHT...
STEP ONE: FORTRESS WHALE! STEP TWO: SEA STEALTH II!
BRACE YOURSELF, JONOUCHI!
RM
RM RM
ULP...

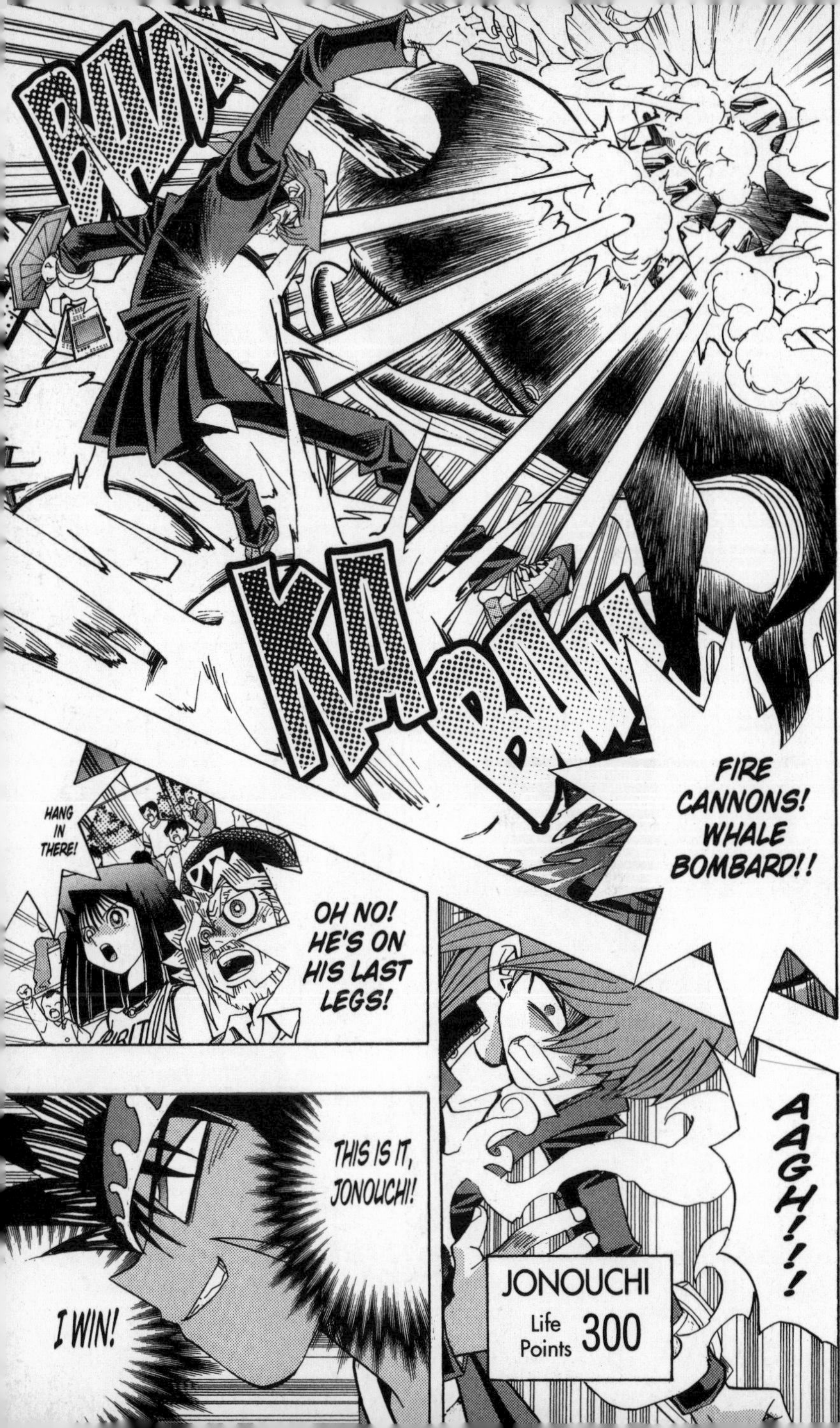
BAM
KABAM
FIRE CANNONS! WHALE BOMBARD!!
AAGH!!!
JONOUCHI
Life Points 300
OH NO! HE'S ON HIS LAST LEGS!
HANG IN THERE!
THIS IS IT, JONOUCHI!
I WIN!

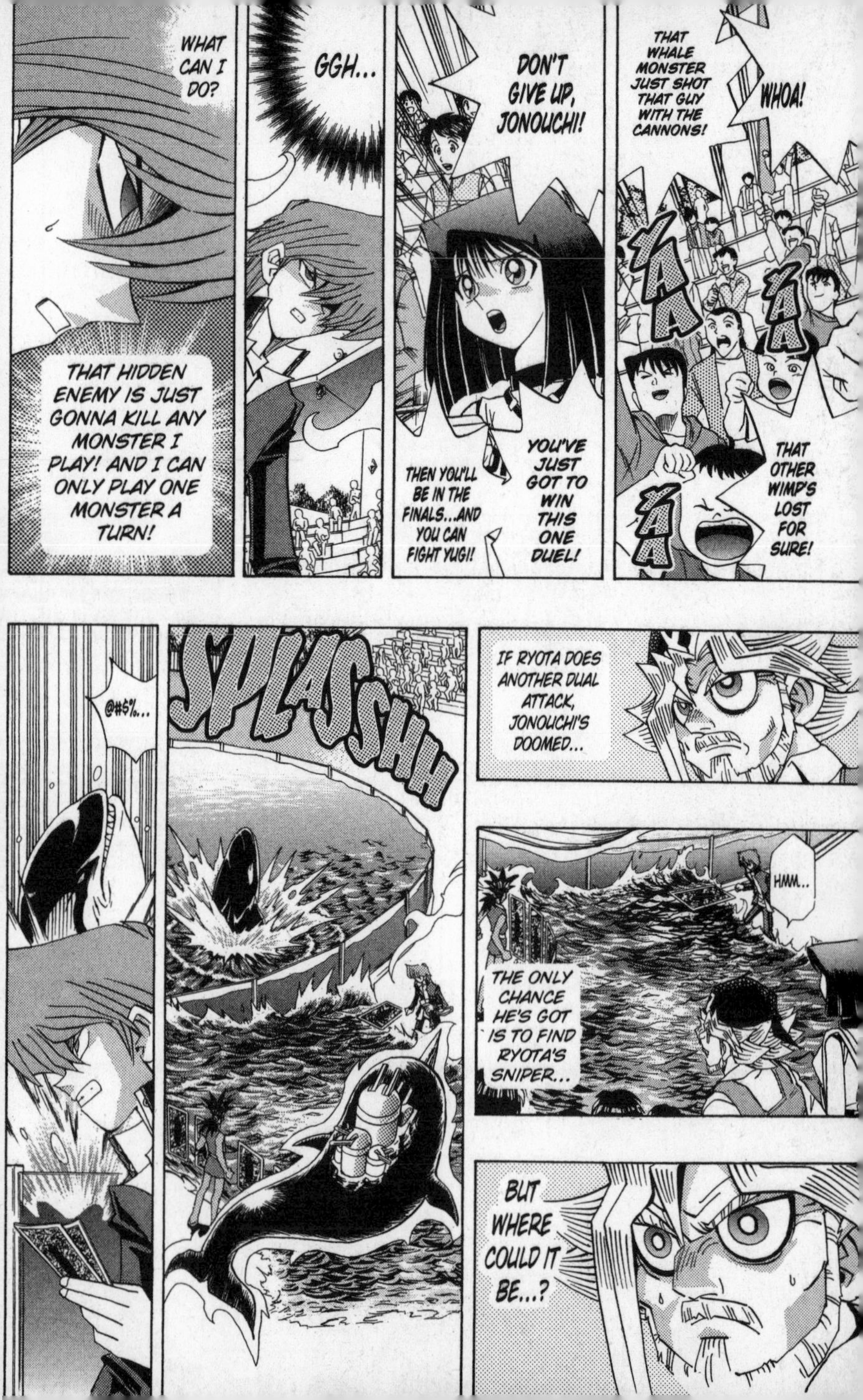
WHOA!
THAT WHALE MONSTER JUST SHOT THAT GUY WITH THE CANNONS!
YAA
YAA
YAA
THAT OTHER WIMP'S LOST FOR SURE!
DON'T GIVE UP, JONOUCHI!
YOU'VE JUST GOT TO WIN THIS ONE DUEL!
THEN YOU'LL BE IN THE FINALS...AND YOU CAN FIGHT YUGI!
GGH...
WHAT CAN I DO?
THAT HIDDEN ENEMY IS JUST GONNA KILL ANY MONSTER I PLAY! AND I CAN ONLY PLAY ONE MONSTER A TURN!
IF RYOTA DOES ANOTHER DUAL ATTACK, JONOUCHI'S DOOMED...
HMM...
THE ONLY CHANCE HE'S GOT IS TO FIND RYOTA'S SNIPER...
BUT WHERE COULD IT BE...?
SPLASSHH
@#$%...

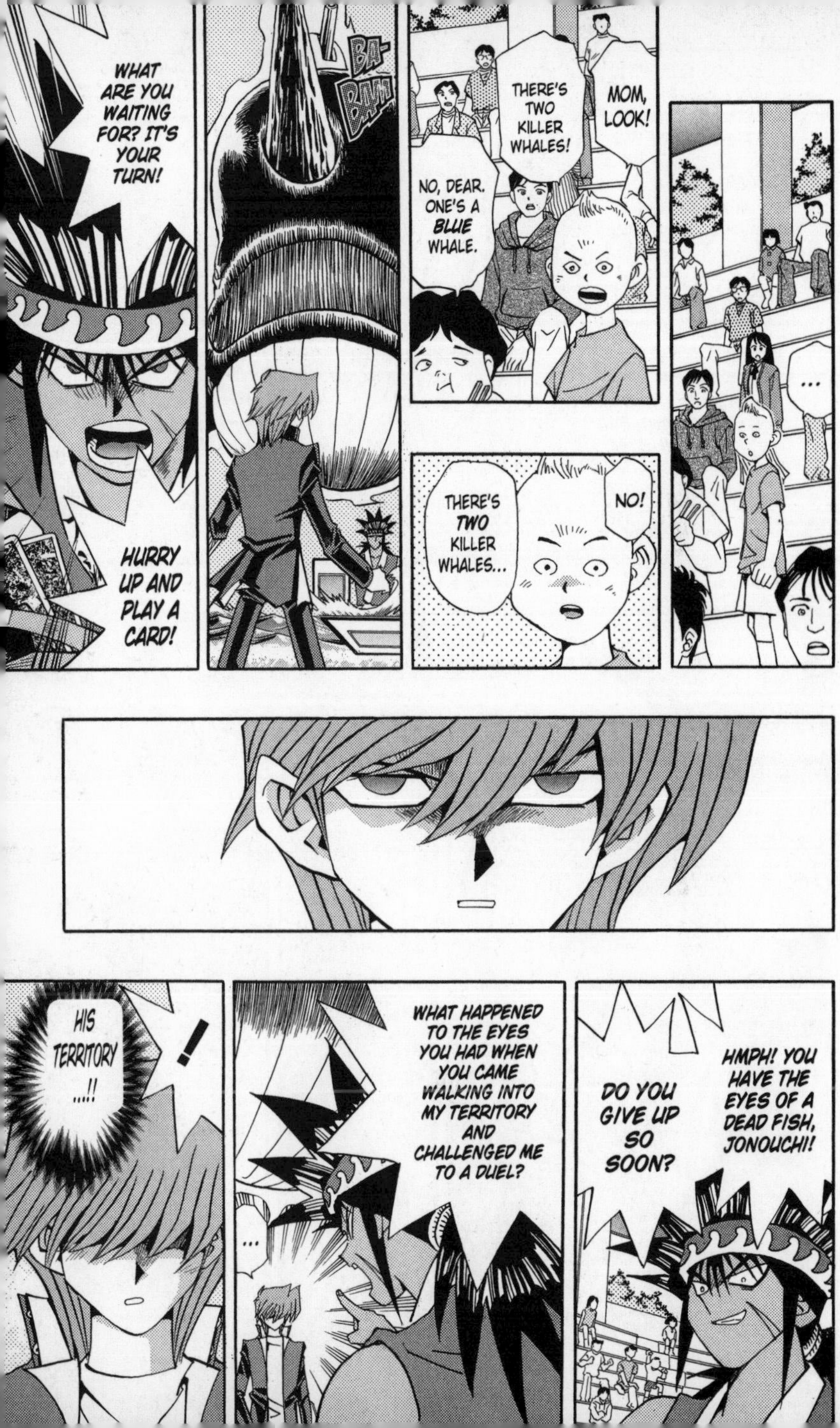
MOM, LOOK!
THERE'S TWO KILLER WHALES!
NO, DEAR. ONE'S A BLUE WHALE.
NO!
THERE'S TWO KILLER WHALES...
...
BA-BAM
WHAT ARE YOU WAITING FOR? IT'S YOUR TURN!
HURRY UP AND PLAY A CARD!
HMPH! YOU HAVE THE EYES OF A DEAD FISH, JONOUCHI!
DO YOU GIVE UP SO SOON?
WHAT HAPPENED TO THE EYES YOU HAD WHEN YOU CAME WALKING INTO MY TERRITORY AND CHALLENGED ME TO A DUEL?
...
!
HIS TERRITORY ...!!

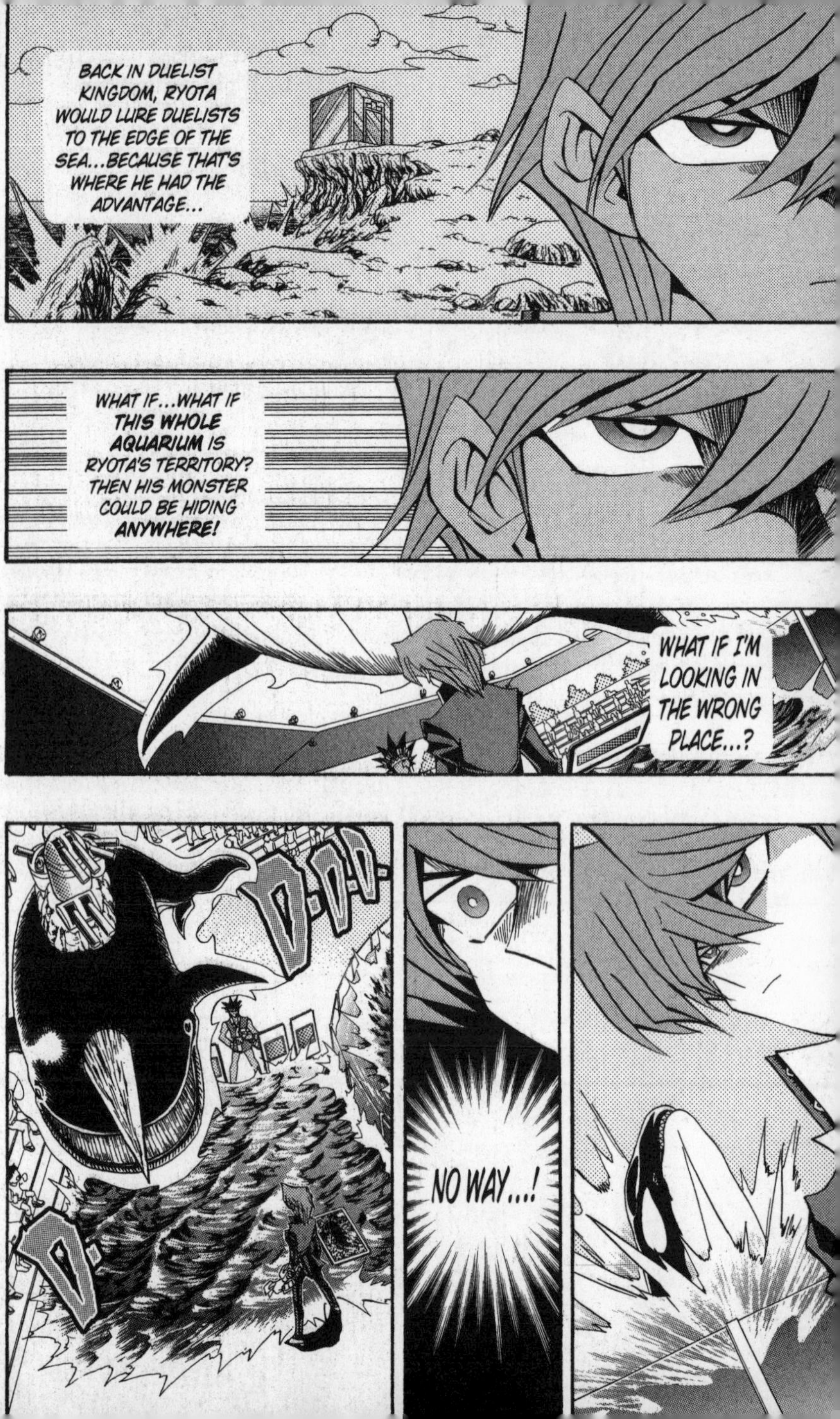
BACK IN DUELIST KINGDOM, RYOTA WOULD LURE DUELISTS TO THE EDGE OF THE SEA...BECAUSE THAT'S WHERE HE HAD THE ADVANTAGE...
WHAT IF...WHAT IF **THIS WHOLE AQUARIUM** IS RYOTA'S TERRITORY? THEN HIS MONSTER COULD BE HIDING **ANYWHERE!**
WHAT IF I'M LOOKING IN THE WRONG PLACE...?
NO WAY...!

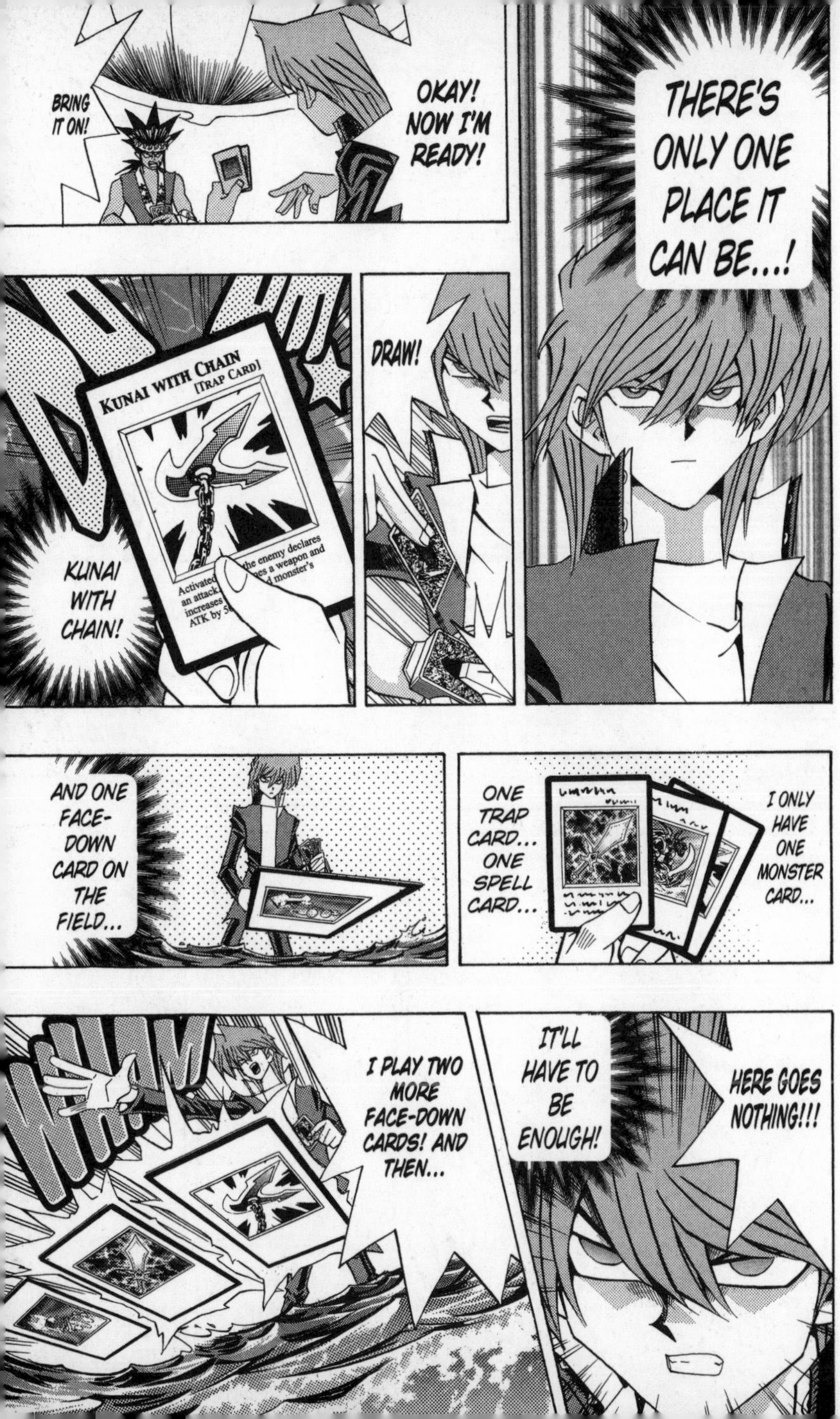
THERE'S ONLY ONE PLACE IT CAN BE...!
OKAY! NOW I'M READY!
BRING IT ON!
DRAW!
KUNAI WITH CHAIN [TRAP CARD]
Activated ... the enemy declares an attack ... es a weapon and increases ... d monster's ATK by 50
KUNAI WITH CHAIN!
I ONLY HAVE ONE MONSTER CARD...
ONE TRAP CARD... ONE SPELL CARD...
AND ONE FACE-DOWN CARD ON THE FIELD...
HERE GOES NOTHING!!!
IT'LL HAVE TO BE ENOUGH!
I PLAY TWO MORE FACE-DOWN CARDS! AND THEN...

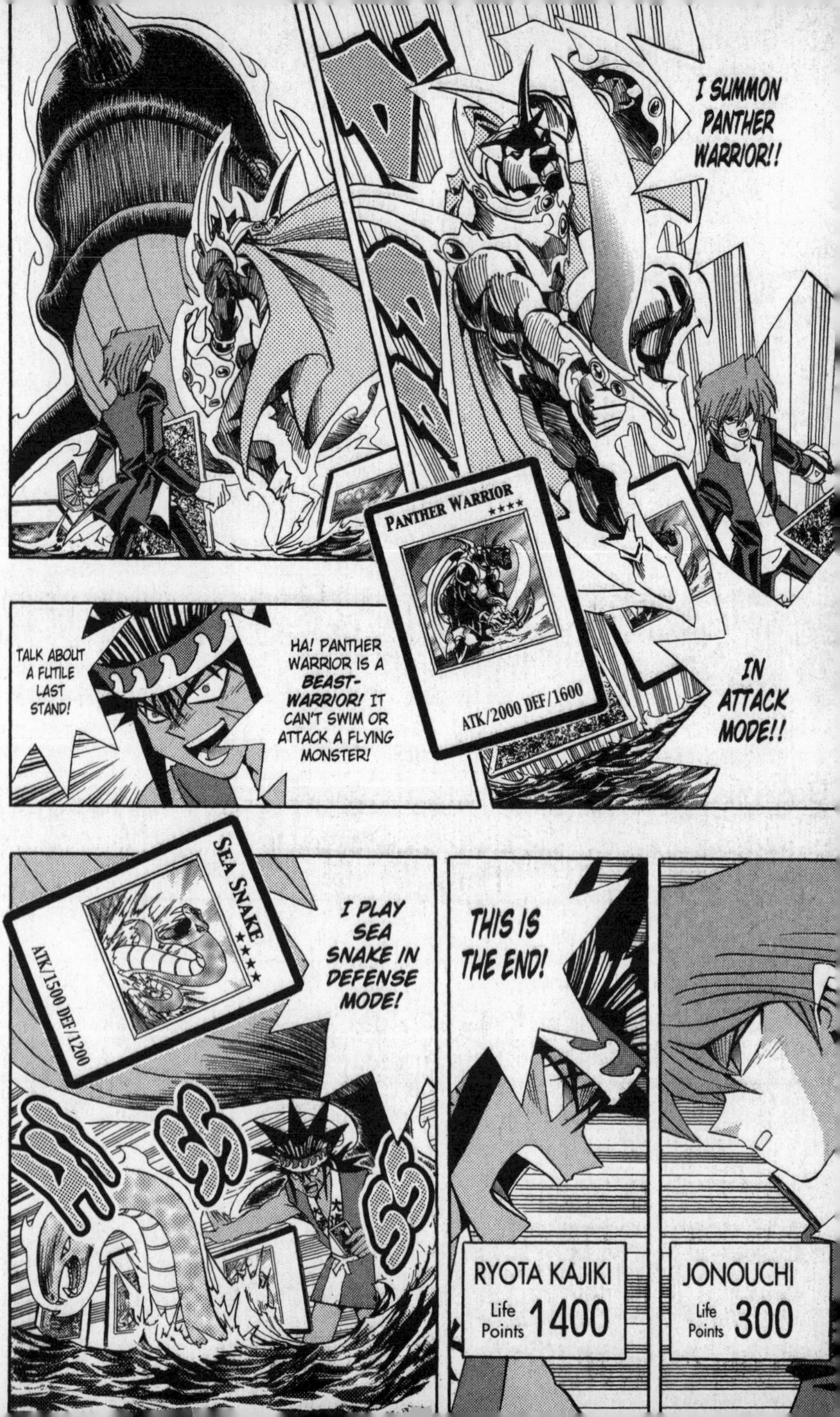

I SUMMON PANTHER WARRIOR!!
PANTHER WARRIOR ★★★★
ATK/2000 DEF/1600
IN ATTACK MODE!!
HA! PANTHER WARRIOR IS A BEAST-WARRIOR! IT CAN'T SWIM OR ATTACK A FLYING MONSTER!
TALK ABOUT A FUTILE LAST STAND!
JONOUCHI
Life Points 300
THIS IS THE END!
RYOTA KAJIKI
Life Points 1400
I PLAY SEA SNAKE IN DEFENSE MODE!
SEA SNAKE ★★★★
ATK/1500 DEF/1200

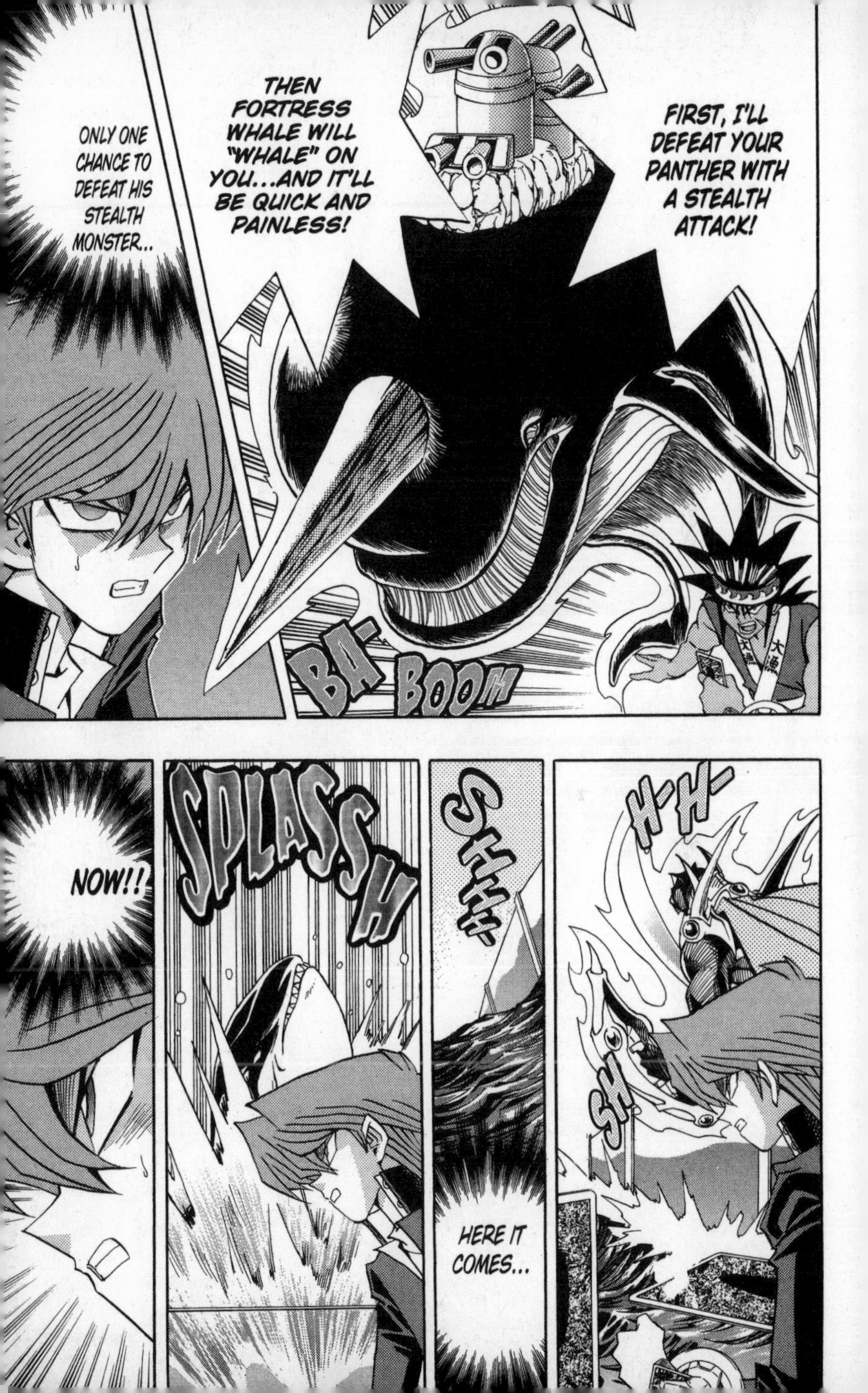
FIRST, I'LL DEFEAT YOUR PANTHER WITH A STEALTH ATTACK!
THEN FORTRESS WHALE WILL "WHALE" ON YOU...AND IT'LL BE QUICK AND PAINLESS!
BA-BOOM
ONLY ONE CHANCE TO DEFEAT HIS STEALTH MONSTER...
H-H-
SH
SHHH
HERE IT COMES...
SPLASSH
NOW!!

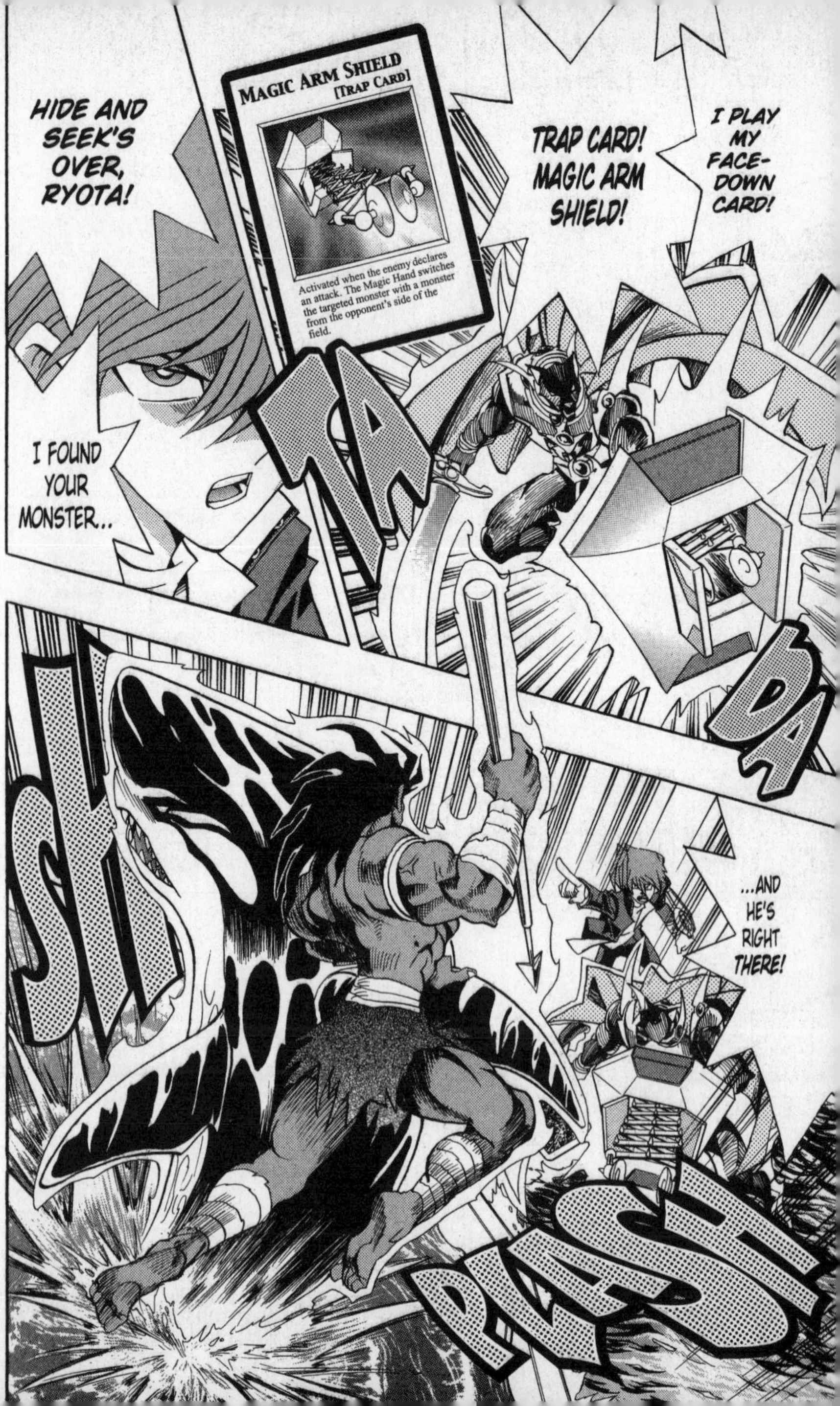
I PLAY MY FACE-DOWN CARD!
TRAP CARD! MAGIC ARM SHIELD!
MAGIC ARM SHIELD
[TRAP CARD]
Activated when the enemy declares an attack. The Magic Hand switches the targeted monster with a monster from the opponent's side of the field.
HIDE AND SEEK'S OVER, RYOTA!
I FOUND YOUR MONSTER...
TA
DA
...AND HE'S RIGHT THERE!
SH
PLASH

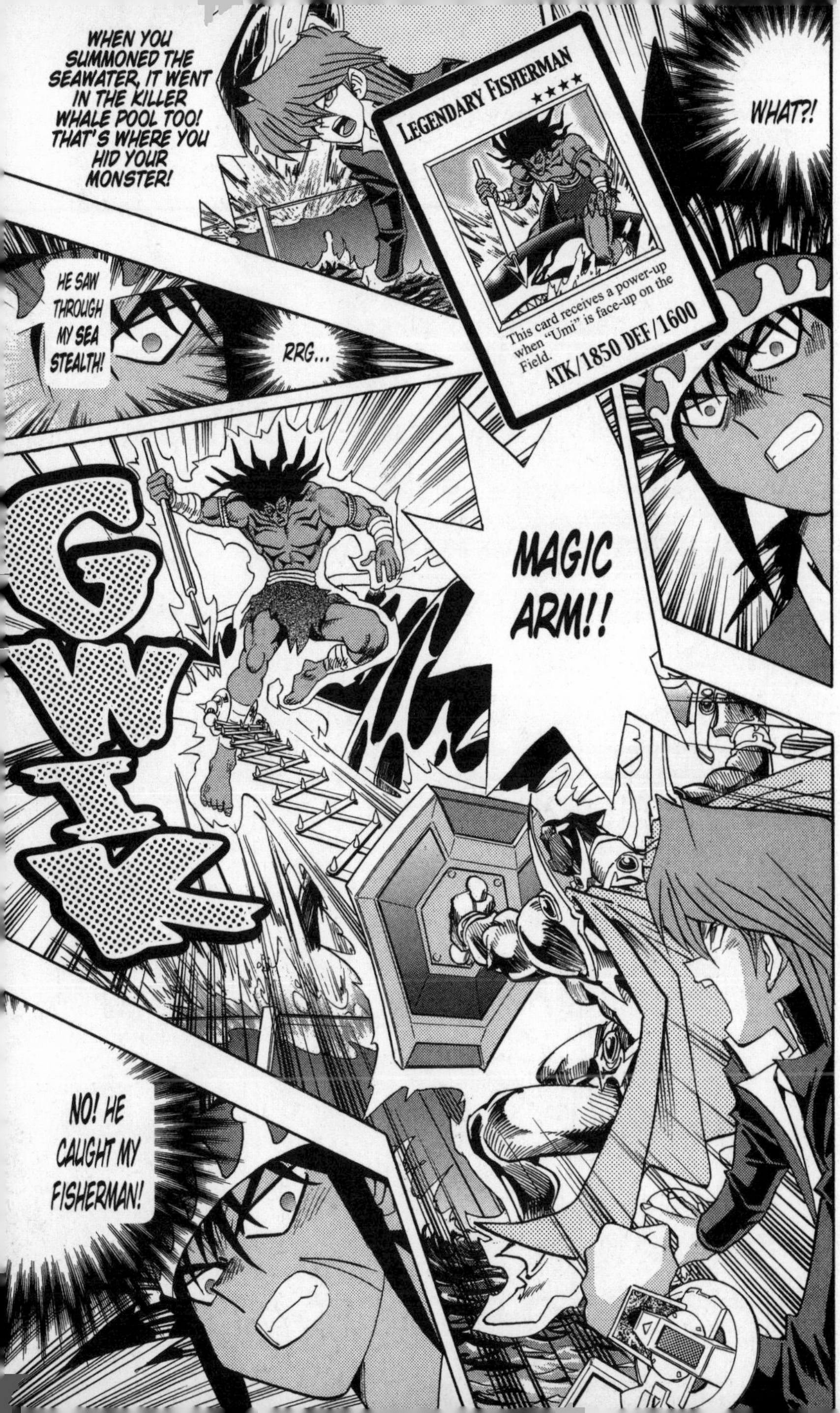
WHAT?!
LEGENDARY FISHERMAN
★★★★
This card receives a power-up when "Umi" is face-up on the Field.
ATK/1850 DEF/1600
WHEN YOU SUMMONED THE SEAWATER, IT WENT IN THE KILLER WHALE POOL TOO! THAT'S WHERE YOU HID YOUR MONSTER!
HE SAW THROUGH MY SEA STEALTH!
RRG...
MAGIC ARM!!
GWIK
NO! HE CAUGHT MY FISHERMAN!

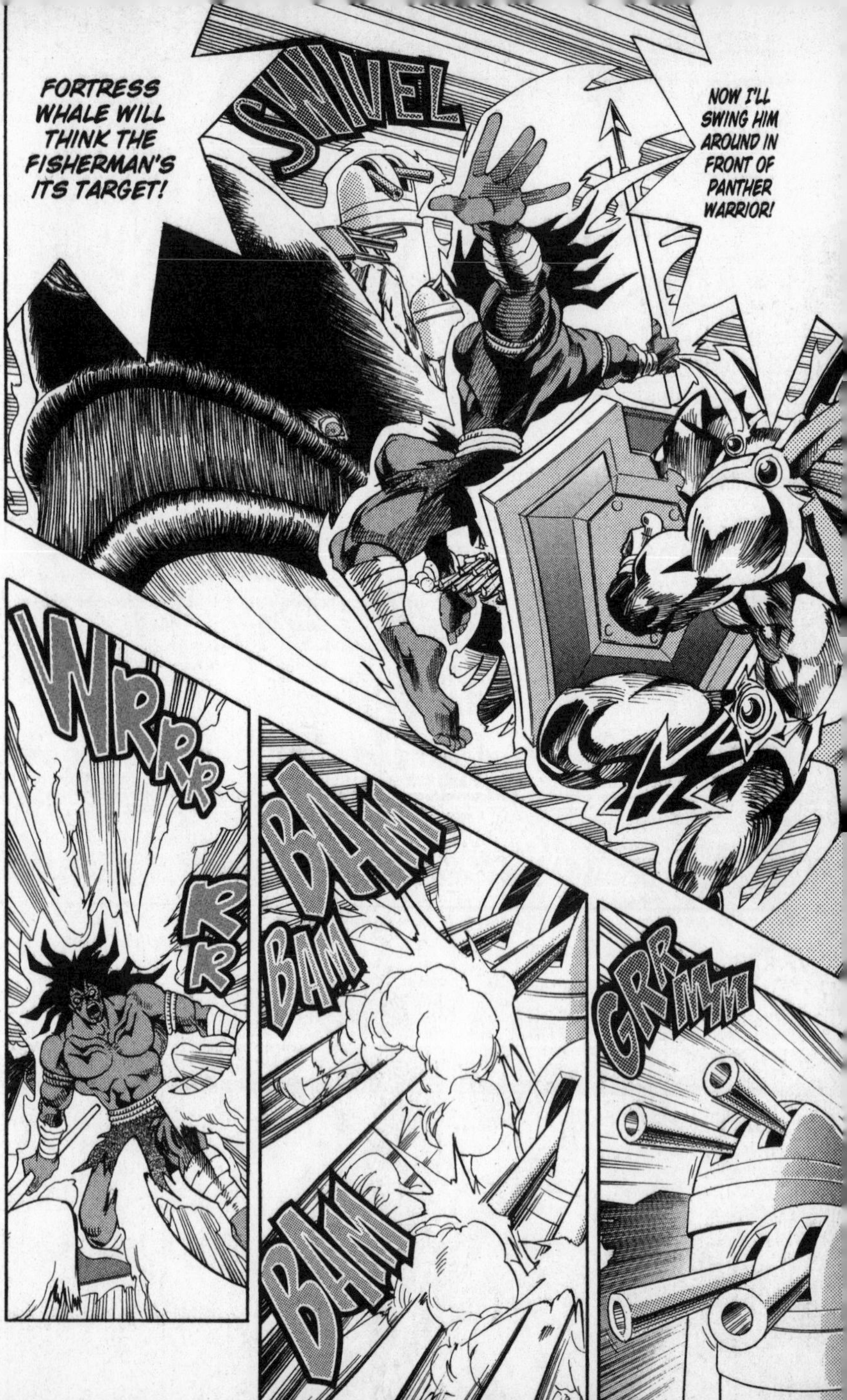
NOW I'LL SWING HIM AROUND IN FRONT OF PANTHER WARRIOR!
SWIVEL
FORTRESS WHALE WILL THINK THE FISHERMAN'S ITS TARGET!
GRRMMM
BAM BAM
BAM
BAM
WRRRR
RRR

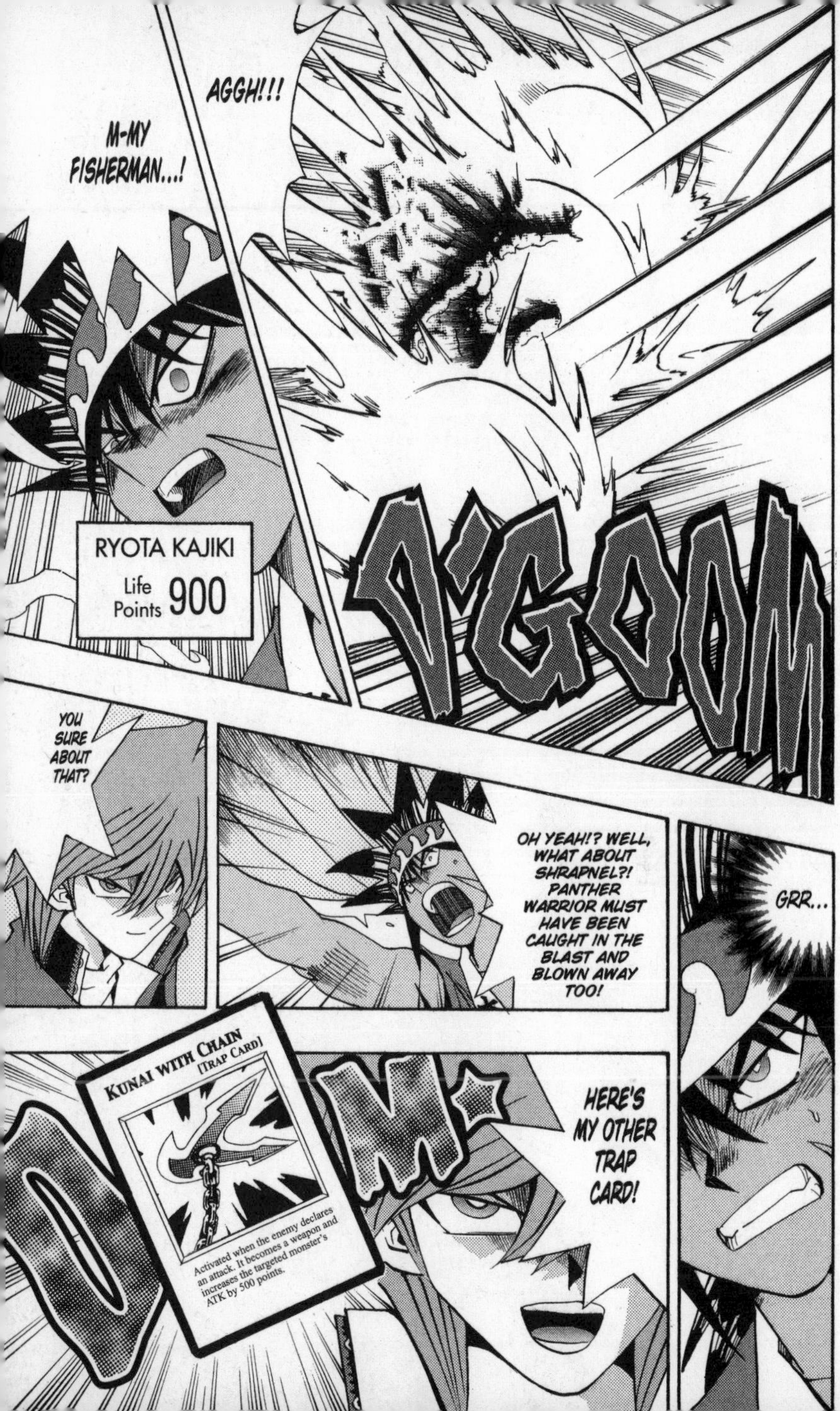
AGGH!!!
M-MY FISHERMAN...!
D'GOOM
RYOTA KAJIKI
Life Points 900
GRR...
OH YEAH!? WELL, WHAT ABOUT SHRAPNEL?! PANTHER WARRIOR MUST HAVE BEEN CAUGHT IN THE BLAST AND BLOWN AWAY TOO!
YOU SURE ABOUT THAT?
HERE'S MY OTHER TRAP CARD!
KUNAI WITH CHAIN
[TRAP CARD]
Activated when the enemy declares an attack. It becomes a weapon and increases the targeted monster's ATK by 500 points.

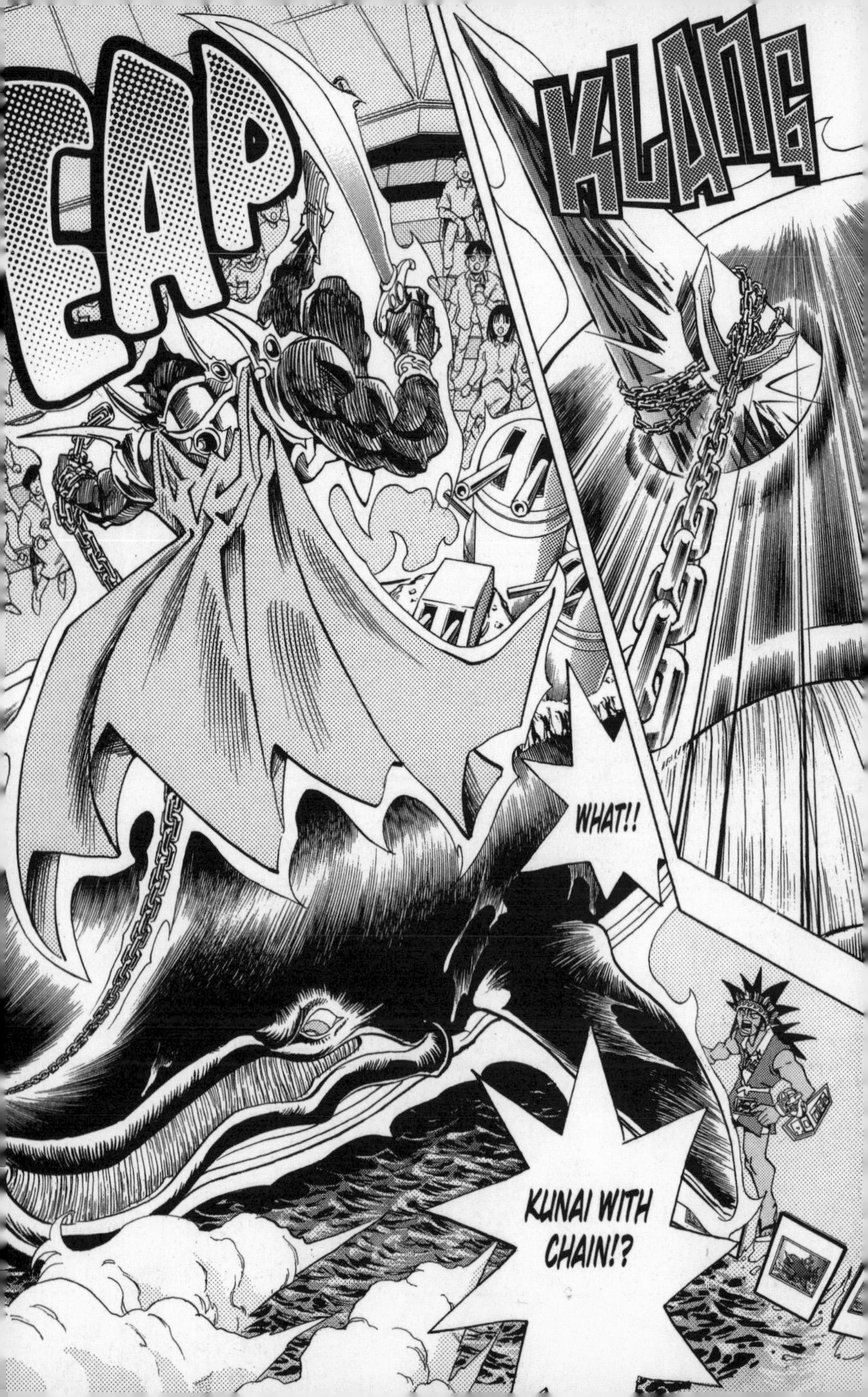
KLANG
FLAP
WHAT!!
KUNAI WITH CHAIN!?

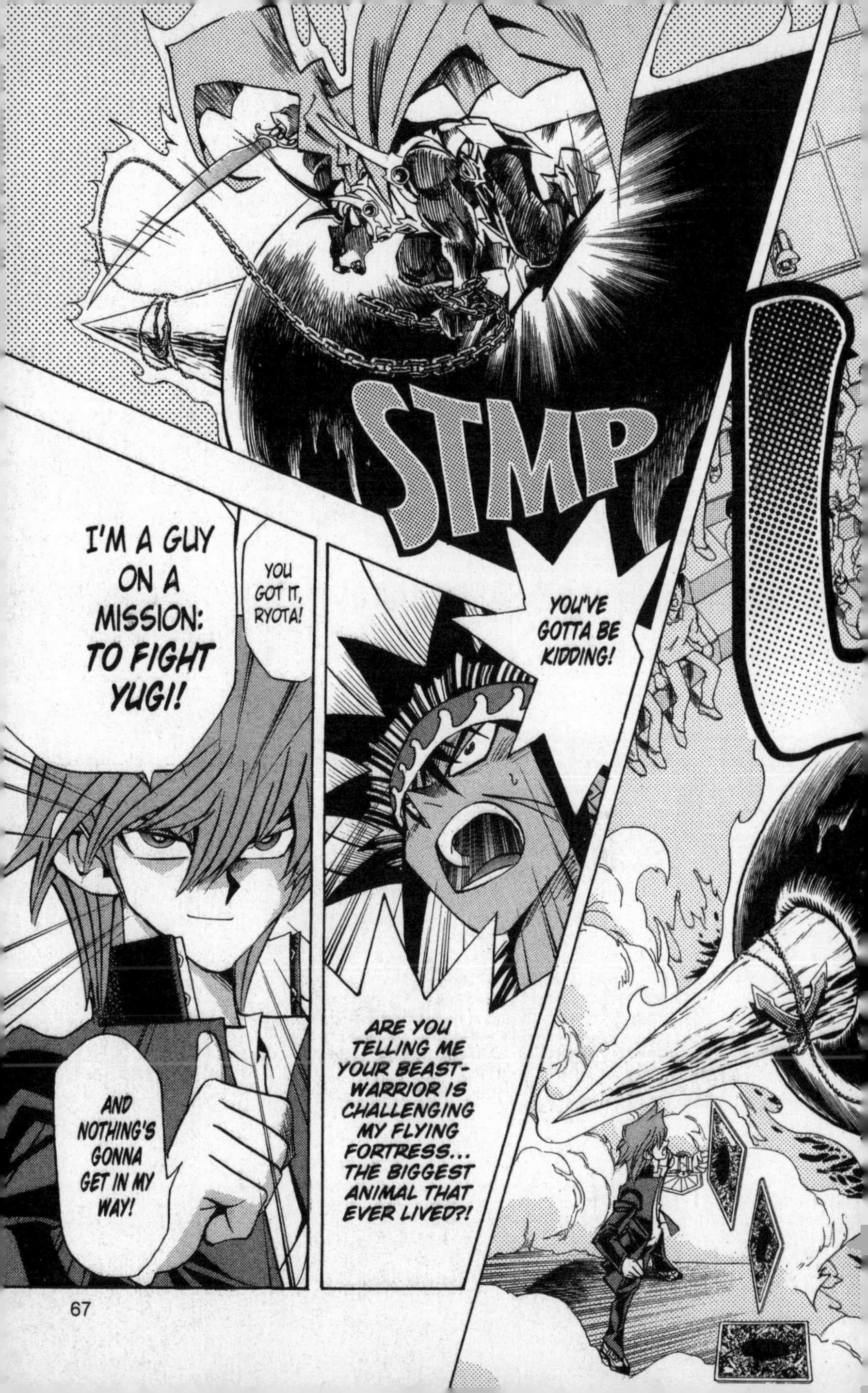
STMP
YOU'VE GOTTA BE KIDDING!
ARE YOU TELLING ME YOUR BEAST-WARRIOR IS CHALLENGING MY FLYING FORTRESS... THE BIGGEST ANIMAL THAT EVER LIVED?!
YOU GOT IT, RYOTA!
I'M A GUY ON A MISSION: TO FIGHT YUGI!
AND NOTHING'S GONNA GET IN MY WAY!

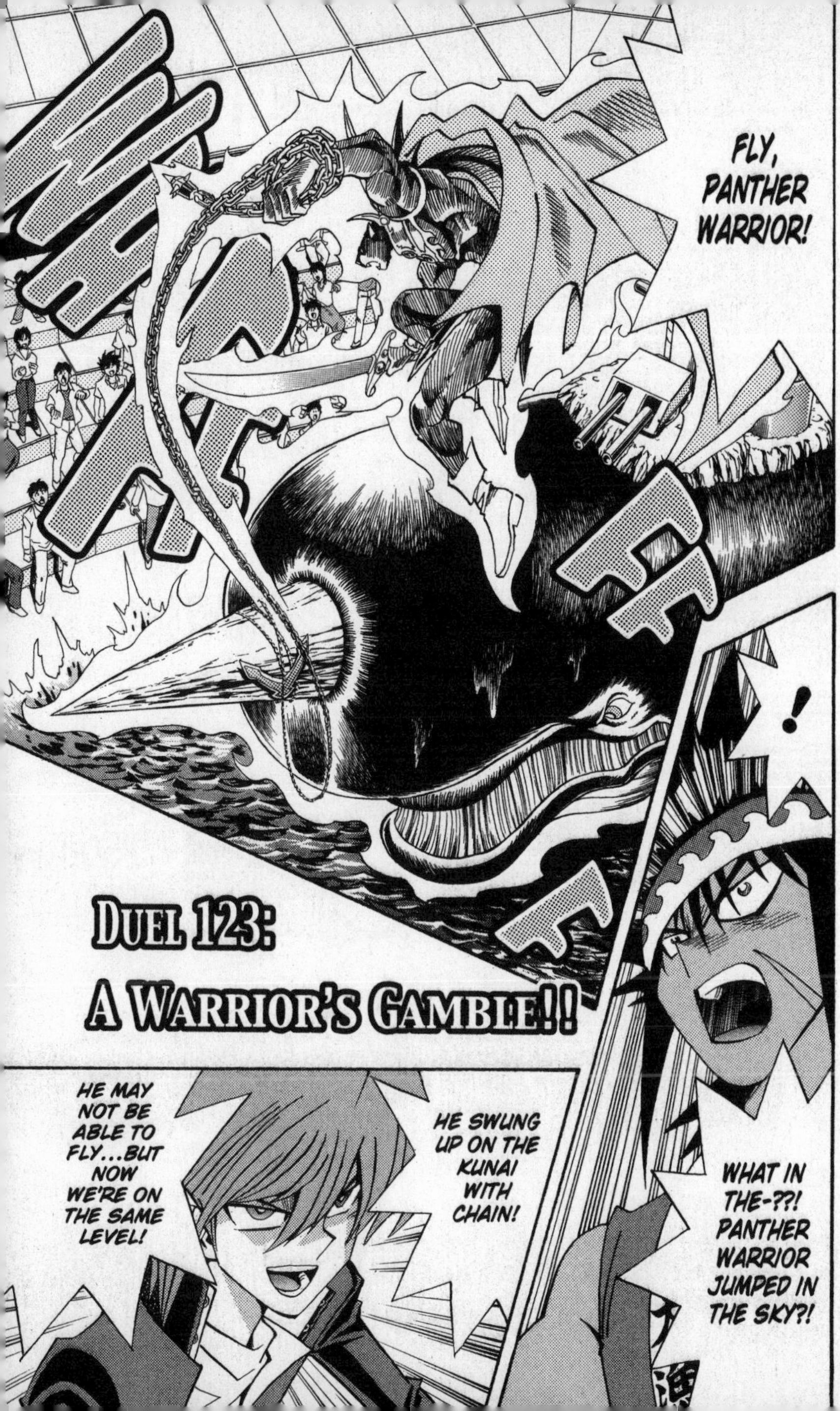
FLY, PANTHER WARRIOR!
DUEL 123:
A WARRIOR'S GAMBLE!!
!
WHAT IN THE-??! PANTHER WARRIOR JUMPED IN THE SKY?!
HE SWUNG UP ON THE KUNAI WITH CHAIN!
HE MAY NOT BE ABLE TO FLY...BUT NOW WE'RE ON THE SAME LEVEL!

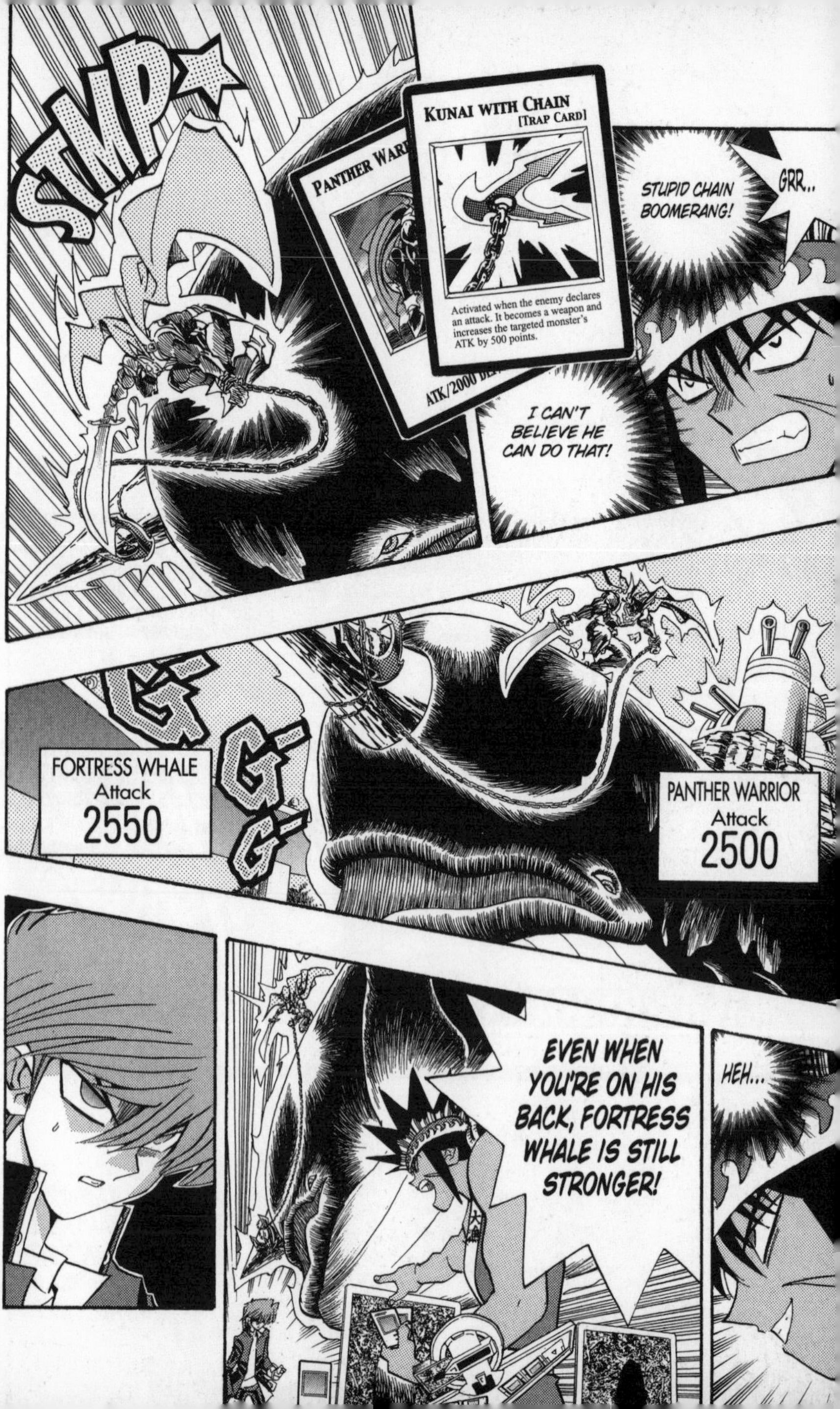
GRR..
STUPID CHAIN BOOMERANG!
I CAN'T BELIEVE HE CAN DO THAT!
STMP
KUNAI WITH CHAIN
[TRAP CARD]
Activated when the enemy declares an attack. It becomes a weapon and increases the targeted monster's ATK by 500 points.
PANTHER WARRIOR Attack 2500
G-G-G-
FORTRESS WHALE Attack 2550
HEH...
EVEN WHEN YOU'RE ON HIS BACK, FORTRESS WHALE IS STILL STRONGER!

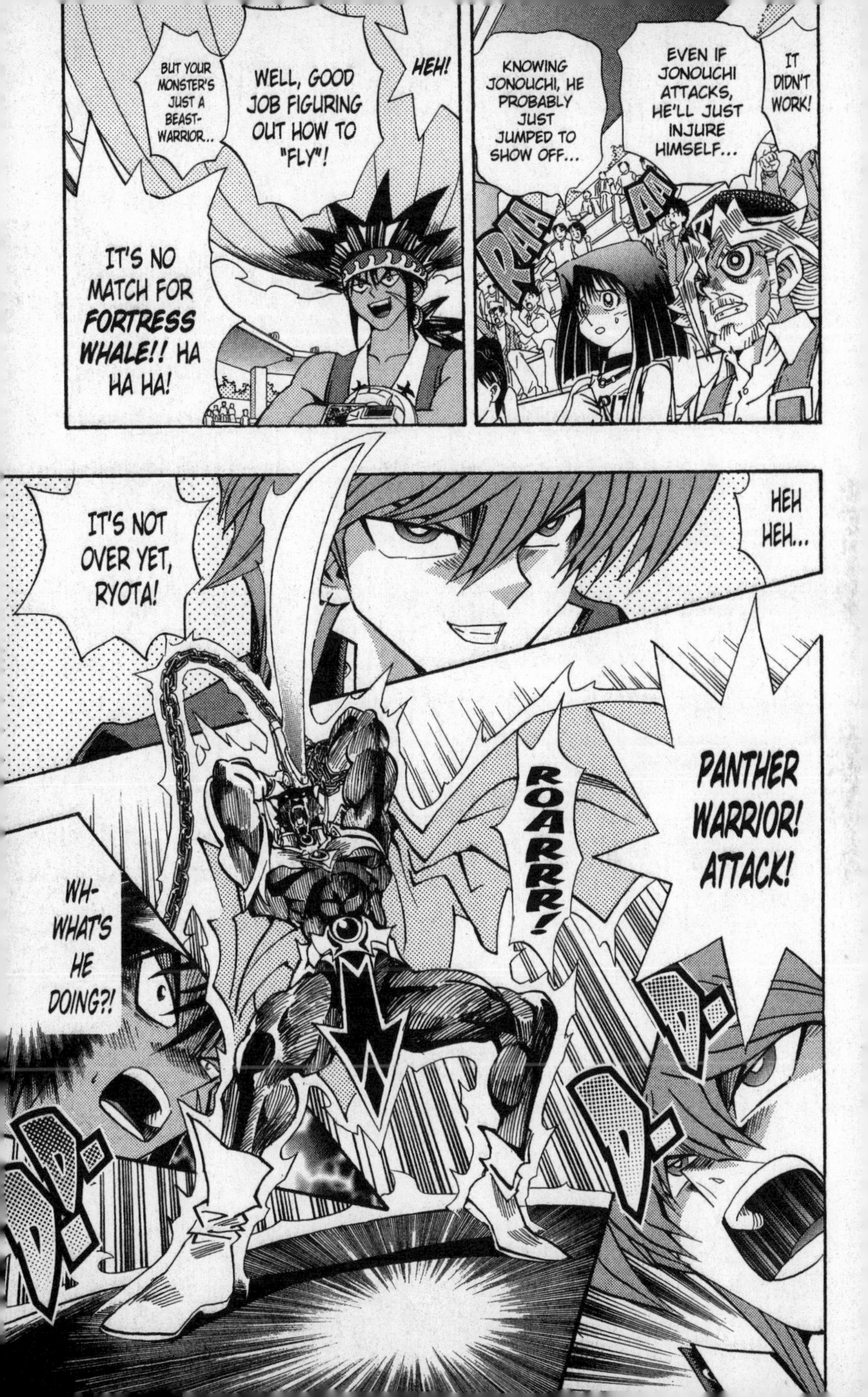
IT DIDN'T WORK!
EVEN IF JONOUCHI ATTACKS, HE'LL JUST INJURE HIMSELF...
KNOWING JONOUCHI, HE PROBABLY JUST JUMPED TO SHOW OFF...
RAA
AA
HEH!
WELL, GOOD JOB FIGURING OUT HOW TO "FLY"!
BUT YOUR MONSTER'S JUST A BEAST-WARRIOR...
IT'S NO MATCH FOR FORTRESS WHALE!! HA HA HA!
HEH HEH...
IT'S NOT OVER YET, RYOTA!
PANTHER WARRIOR! ATTACK!
ROARRR!
WH-WHAT'S HE DOING?!

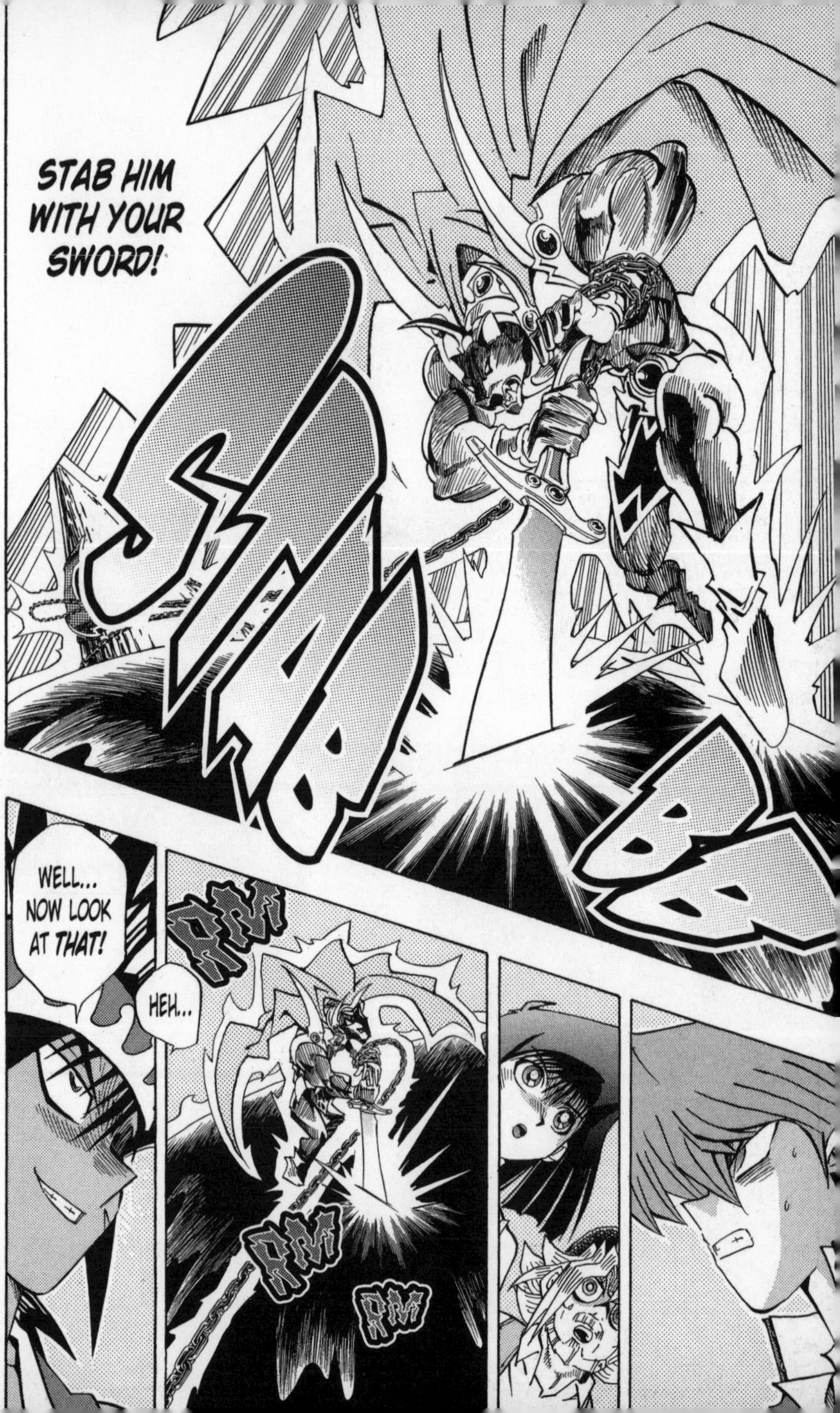
STAB HIM WITH YOUR SWORD!
RM
RM
RM
HEH...
WELL... NOW LOOK AT THAT!

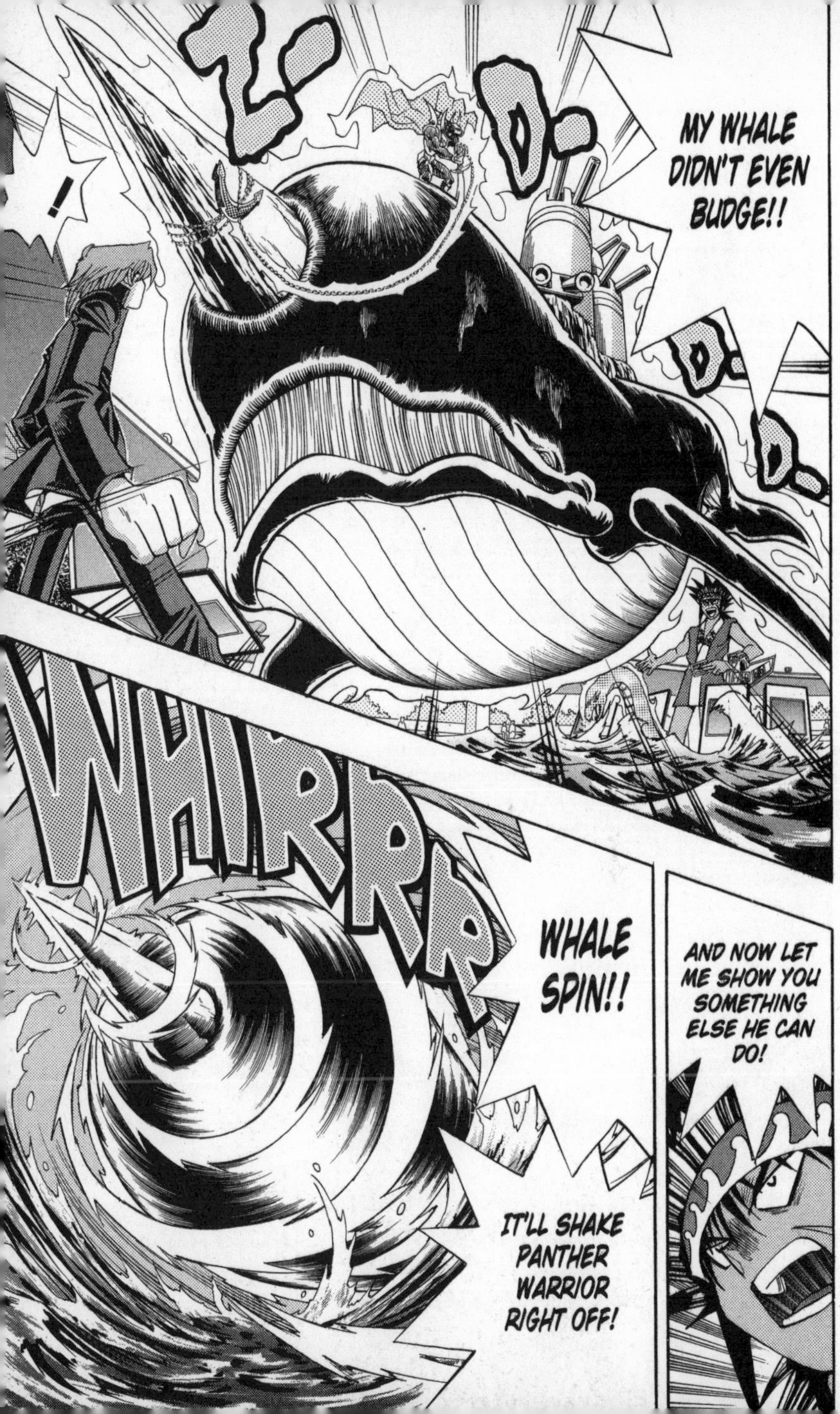
MY WHALE DIDN'T EVEN BUDGE!!
Z.. D..
D.. D..
!
AND NOW LET ME SHOW YOU SOMETHING ELSE HE CAN DO!
WHALE SPIN!!
IT'LL SHAKE PANTHER WARRIOR RIGHT OFF!
WHIRRR

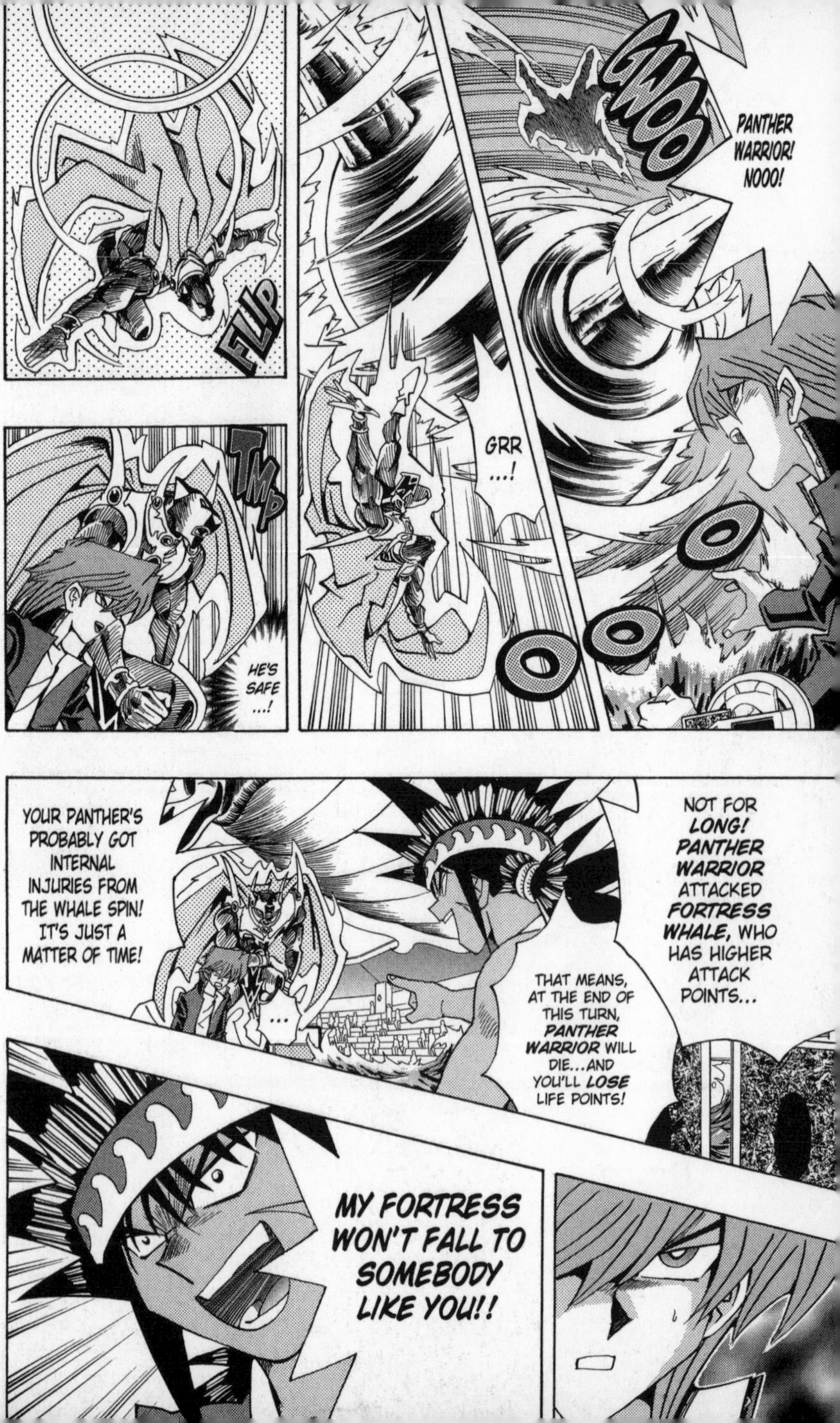
GWOO
PANTHER WARRIOR! NOOO!
OOO
GRR ...!
FLIP
TMP
HE'S SAFE ...!
NOT FOR LONG! PANTHER WARRIOR ATTACKED FORTRESS WHALE, WHO HAS HIGHER ATTACK POINTS...
THAT MEANS, AT THE END OF THIS TURN, PANTHER WARRIOR WILL DIE...AND YOU'LL LOSE LIFE POINTS!
YOUR PANTHER'S PROBABLY GOT INTERNAL INJURIES FROM THE WHALE SPIN! IT'S JUST A MATTER OF TIME!
...
MY FORTRESS WON'T FALL TO SOMEBODY LIKE YOU!!

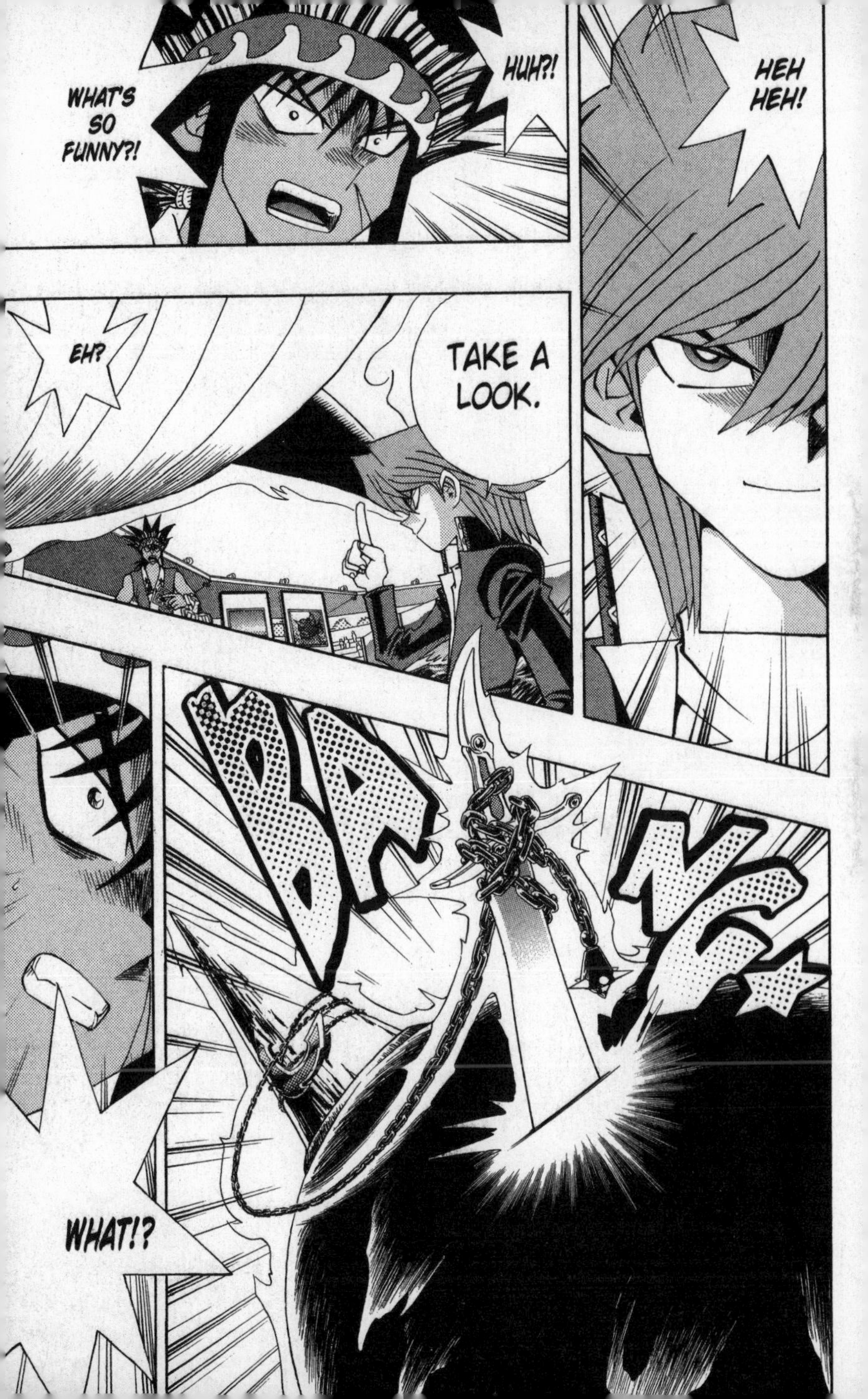
HEH HEH!
HUH?!
WHAT'S SO FUNNY?!
TAKE A LOOK.
EH?
BANG
WHAT!?

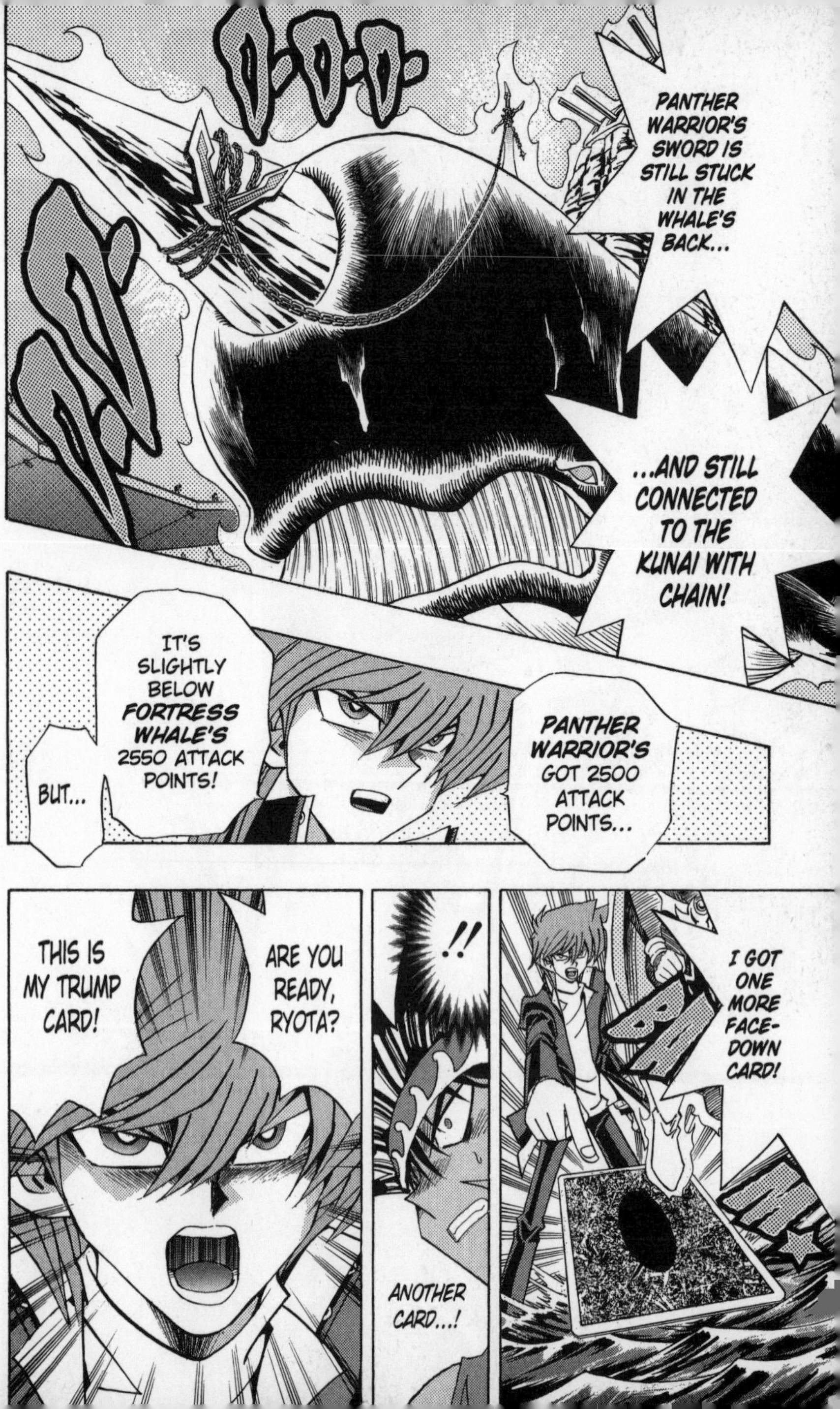
PANTHER WARRIOR'S SWORD IS STILL STUCK IN THE WHALE'S BACK...
...AND STILL CONNECTED TO THE KUNAI WITH CHAIN!
PANTHER WARRIOR'S GOT 2500 ATTACK POINTS...
IT'S SLIGHTLY BELOW FORTRESS WHALE'S 2550 ATTACK POINTS!
BUT...
I GOT ONE MORE FACE-DOWN CARD!
!!
ANOTHER CARD...!
ARE YOU READY, RYOTA?
THIS IS MY TRUMP CARD!

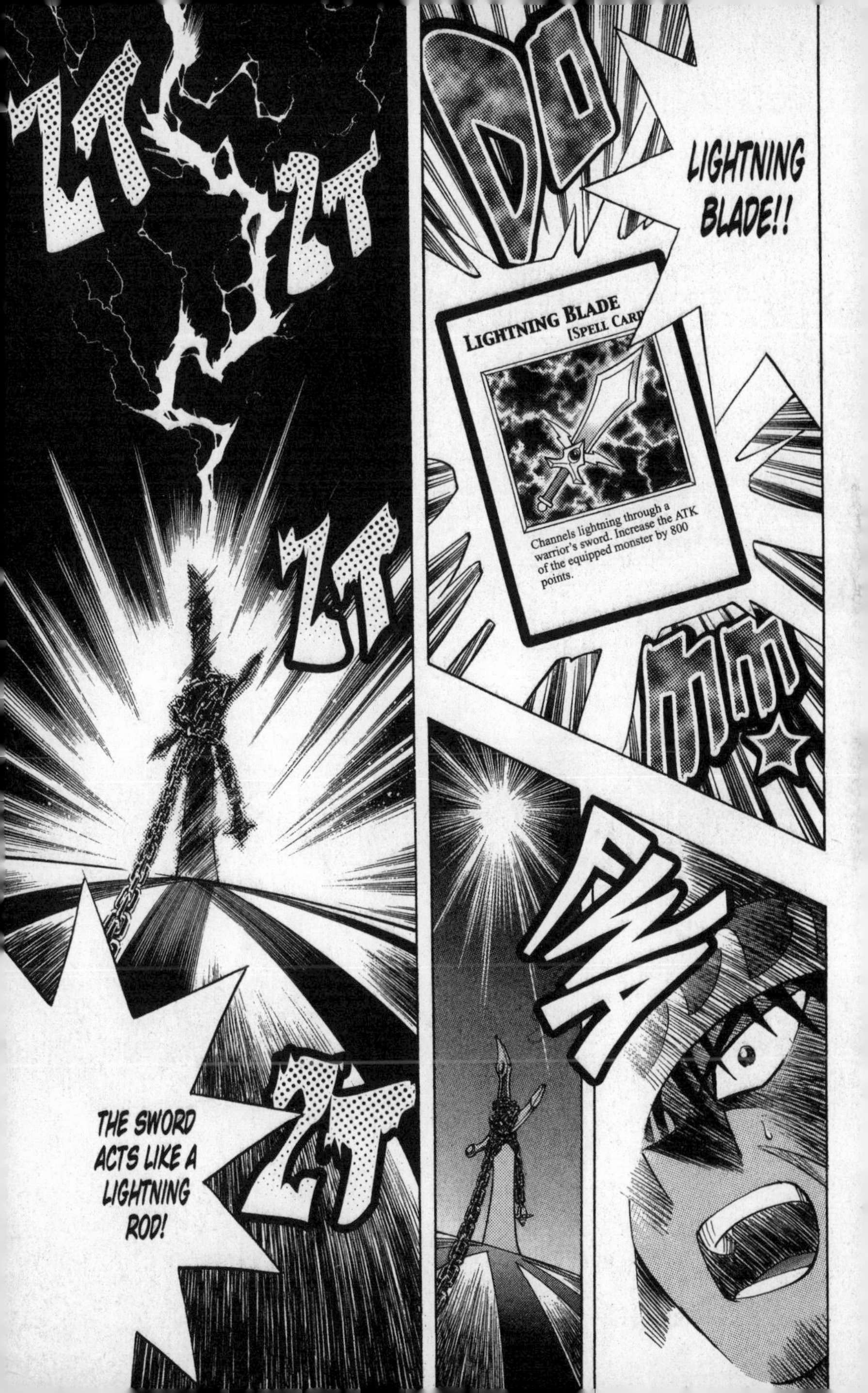
LIGHTNING BLADE!!
LIGHTNING BLADE
[SPELL CARD
Channels lightning through a warrior's sword. Increase the ATK of the equipped monster by 800 points.
FWA
THE SWORD ACTS LIKE A LIGHTNING ROD!

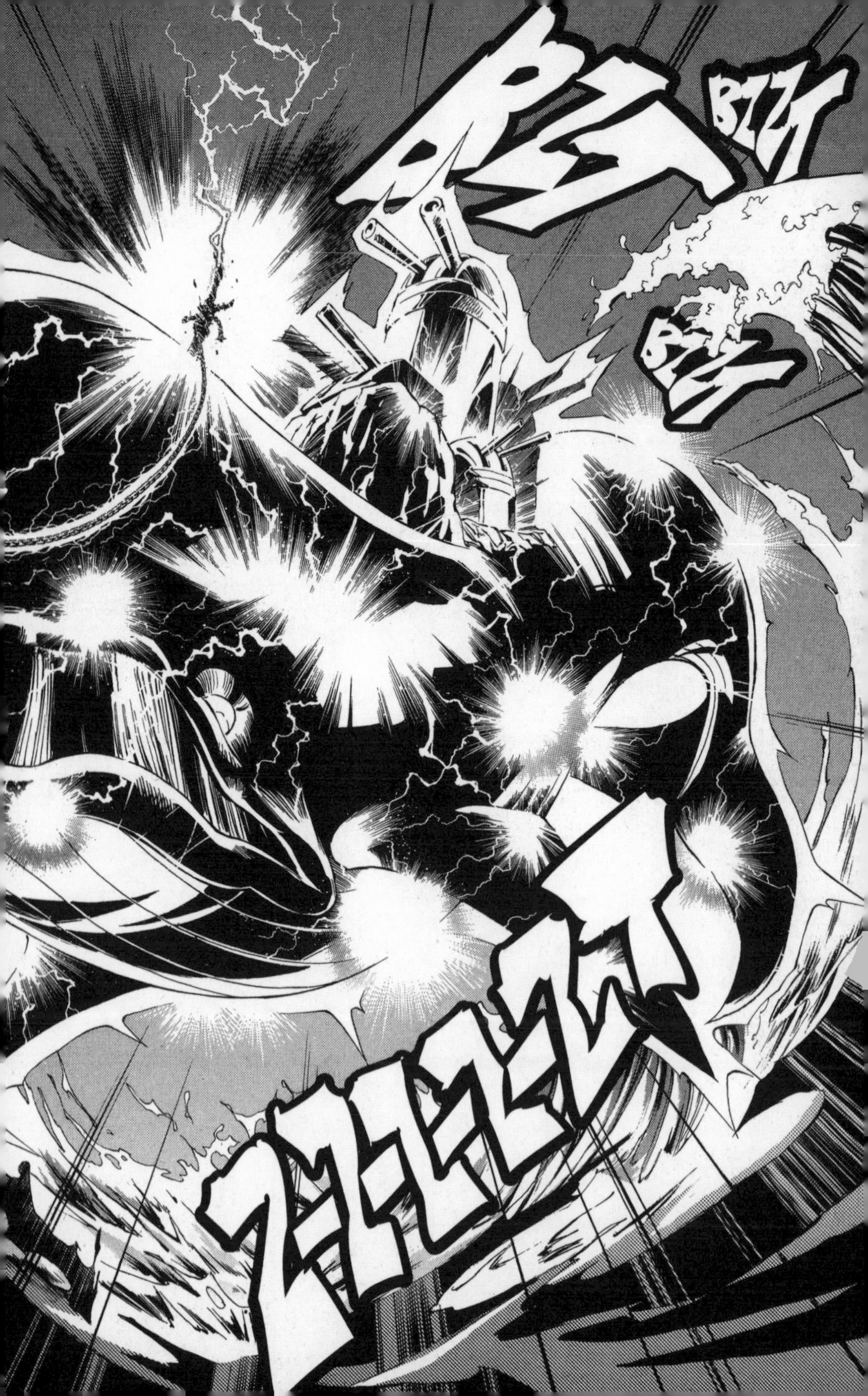
BZZT
BZT
BZZ
ZZZZZT

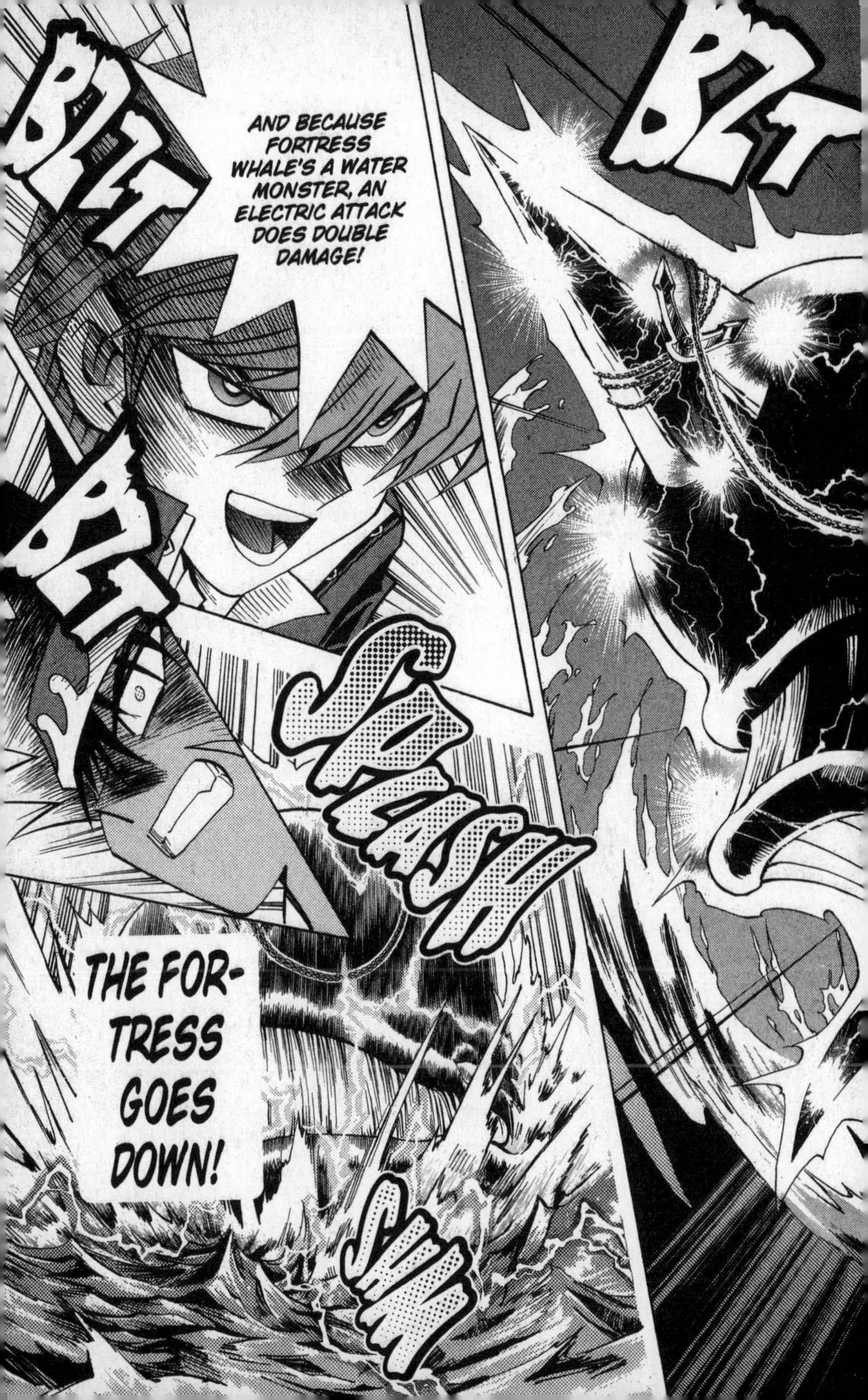
BZT
AND BECAUSE FORTRESS WHALE'S A WATER MONSTER, AN ELECTRIC ATTACK DOES DOUBLE DAMAGE!
BZT
BZT
SPLASH
THE FOR-TRESS GOES DOWN!
SPLASH

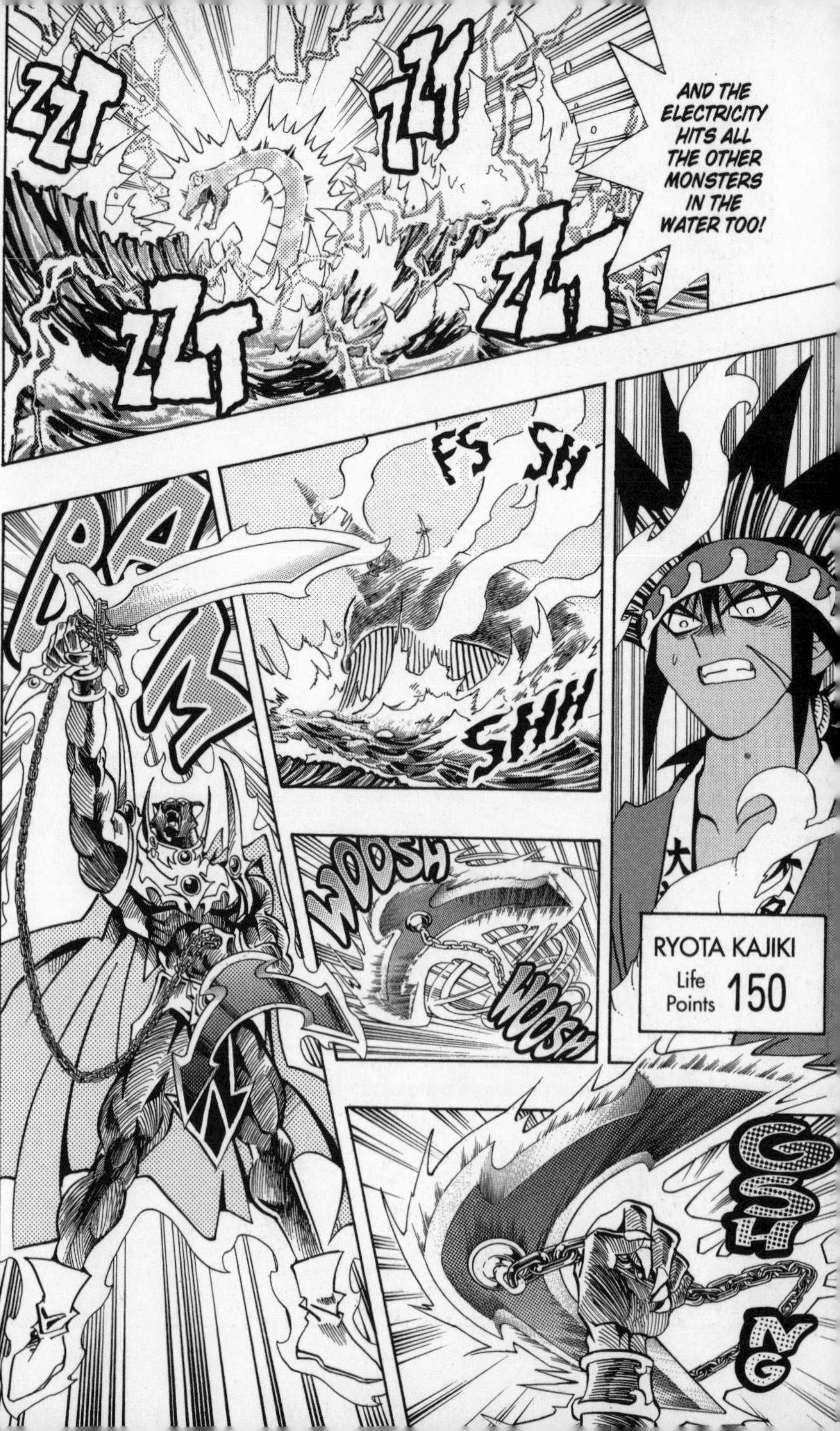
ZZT
ZZT
AND THE ELECTRICITY HITS ALL THE OTHER MONSTERS IN THE WATER TOO!
ZZT
ZZT
RYOTA KAJIKI
Life Points 150
FS SH
SHH
WOOSH
WOOSH
BAM
GSH
NG

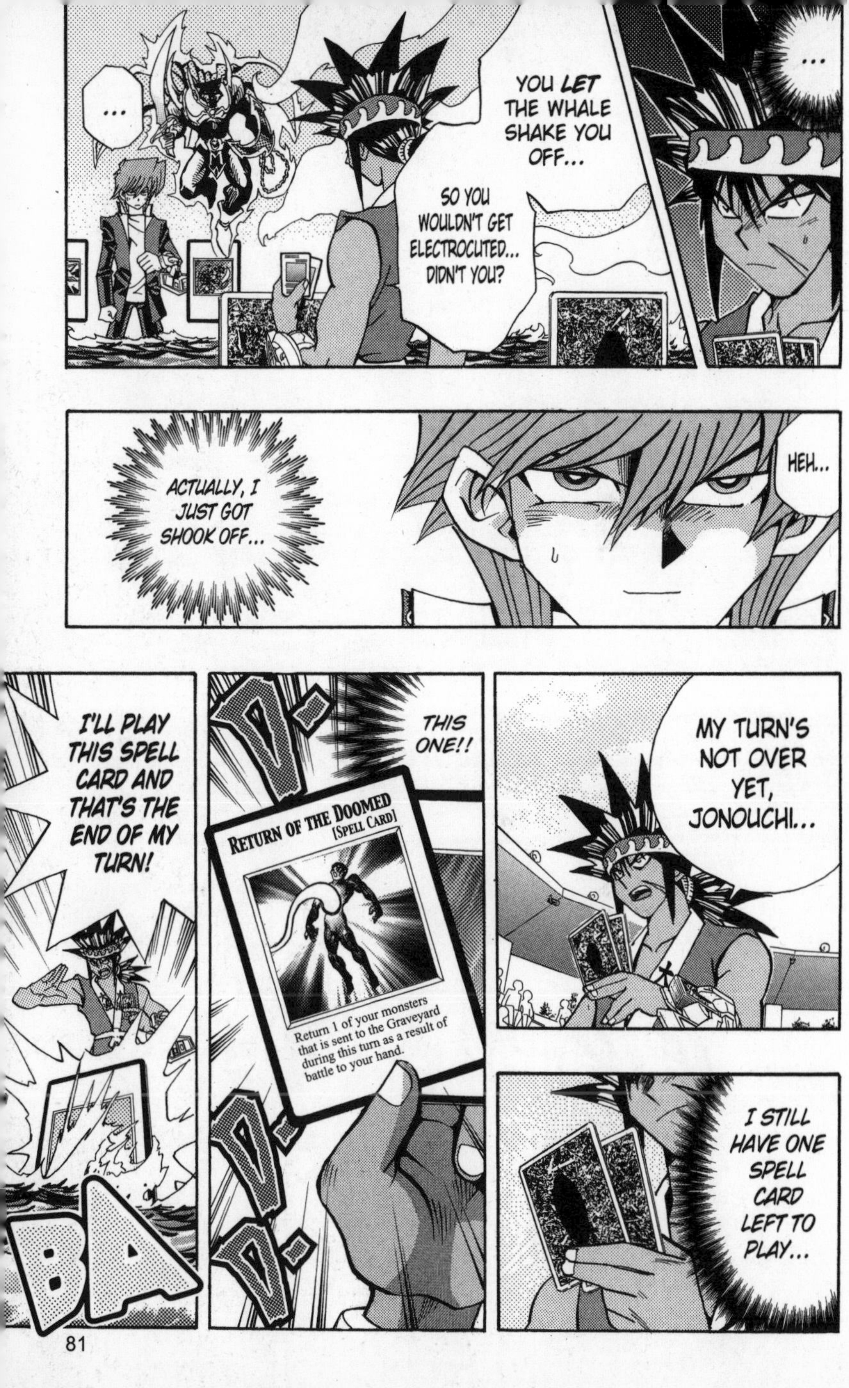
...
YOU LET THE WHALE SHAKE YOU OFF...
SO YOU WOULDN'T GET ELECTROCUTED... DIDN'T YOU?
...
HEH...
ACTUALLY, I JUST GOT SHOOK OFF...
MY TURN'S NOT OVER YET, JONOUCHI...
I STILL HAVE ONE SPELL CARD LEFT TO PLAY...
THIS ONE!!
RETURN OF THE DOOMED
[SPELL CARD]
Return 1 of your monsters that is sent to the Graveyard during this turn as a result of battle to your hand.
I'LL PLAY THIS SPELL CARD AND THAT'S THE END OF MY TURN!
BA

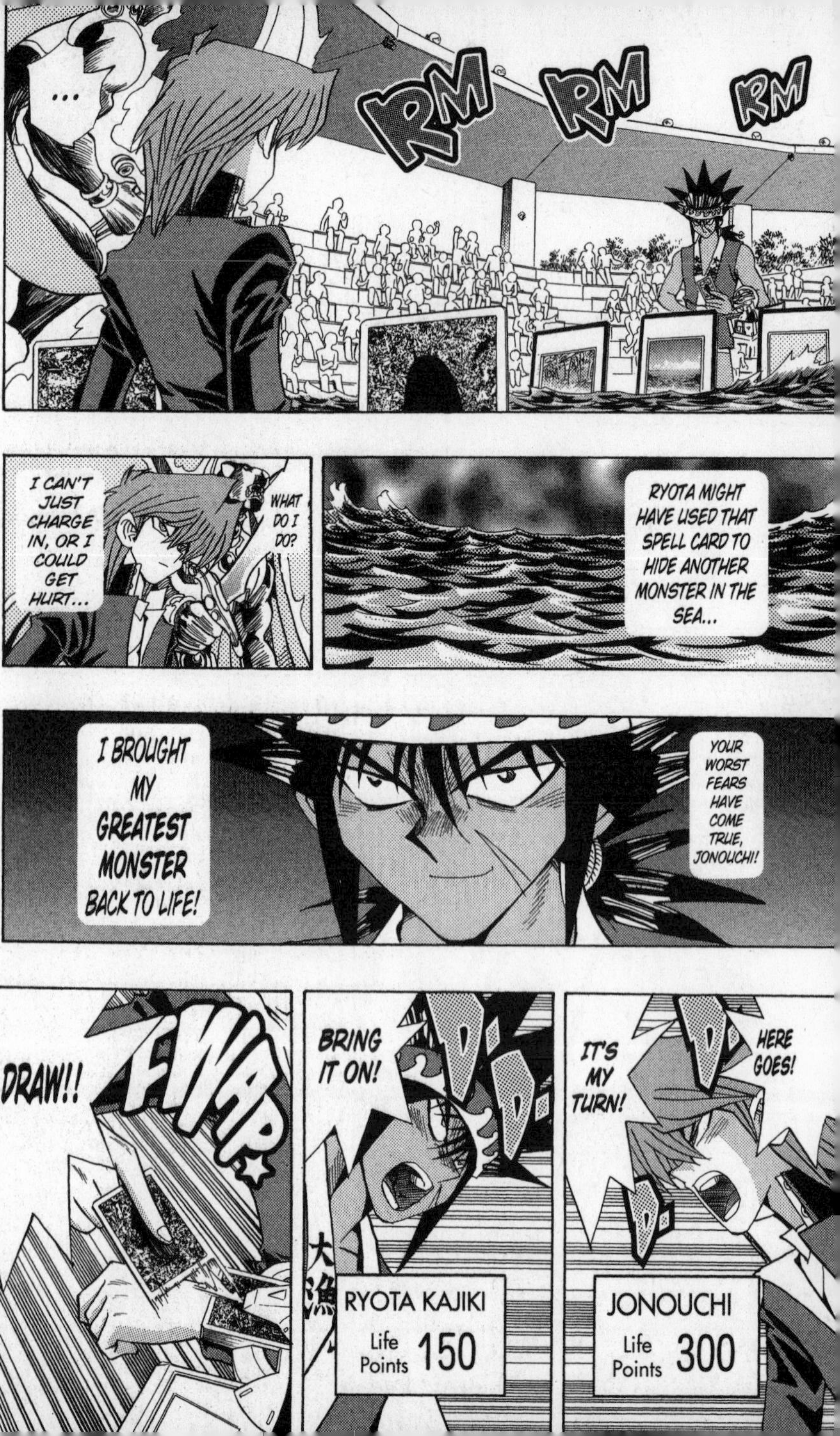
RM
RM
RM
...
RYOTA MIGHT HAVE USED THAT SPELL CARD TO HIDE ANOTHER MONSTER IN THE SEA...
WHAT DO I DO?
I CAN'T JUST CHARGE IN, OR I COULD GET HURT...
YOUR WORST FEARS HAVE COME TRUE, JONOUCHI!
I BROUGHT MY GREATEST MONSTER BACK TO LIFE!
HERE GOES!
IT'S MY TURN!
JONOUCHI
Life Points 300
BRING IT ON!
大漁
RYOTA KAJIKI
Life Points 150
FWAP
DRAW!!

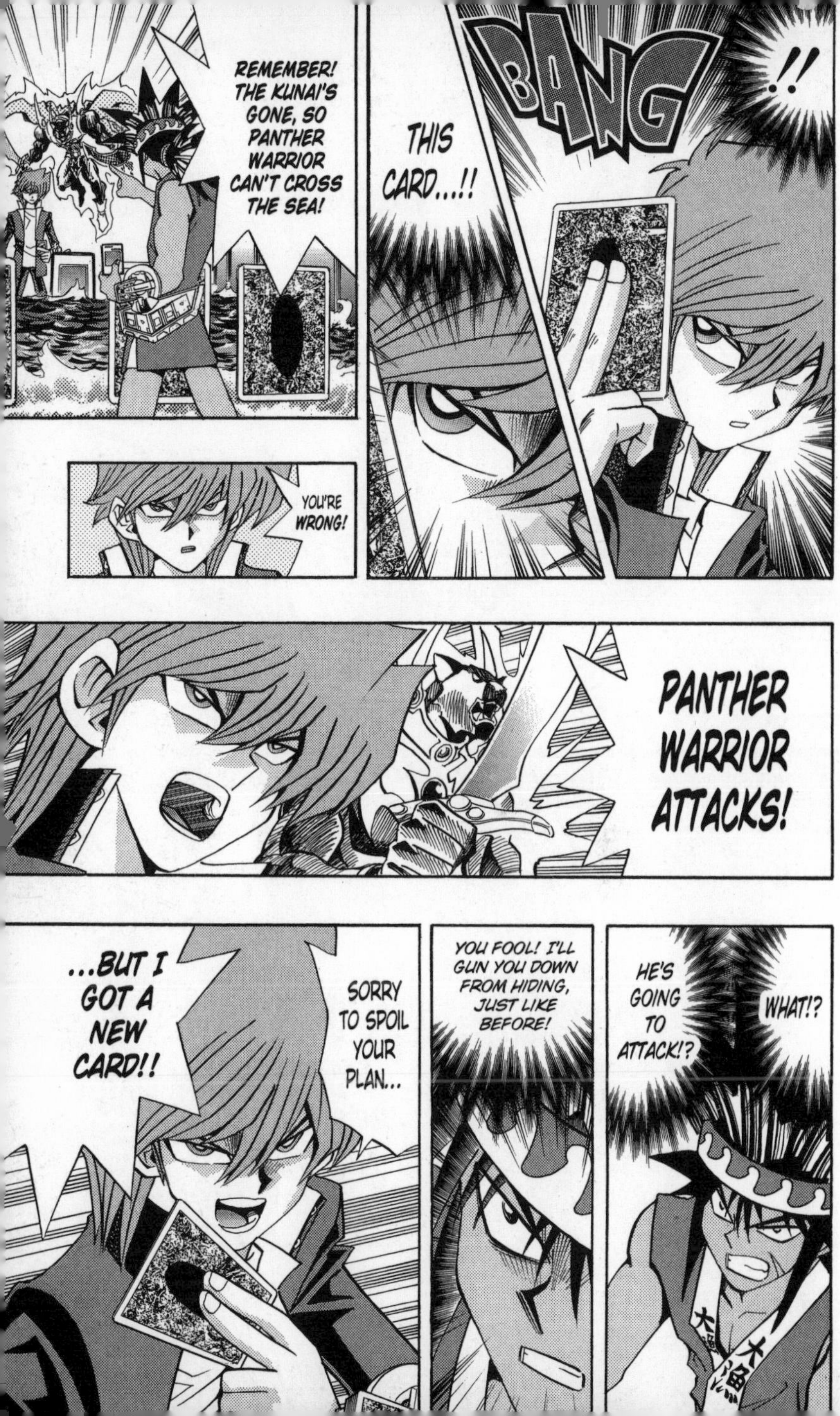
BANG
!!
THIS CARD...!!
REMEMBER! THE KUNAI'S GONE, SO PANTHER WARRIOR CAN'T CROSS THE SEA!
YOU'RE WRONG!
PANTHER WARRIOR ATTACKS!
WHAT!?
HE'S GOING TO ATTACK!?
YOU FOOL! I'LL GUN YOU DOWN FROM HIDING, JUST LIKE BEFORE!
SORRY TO SPOIL YOUR PLAN...
...BUT I GOT A NEW CARD!!

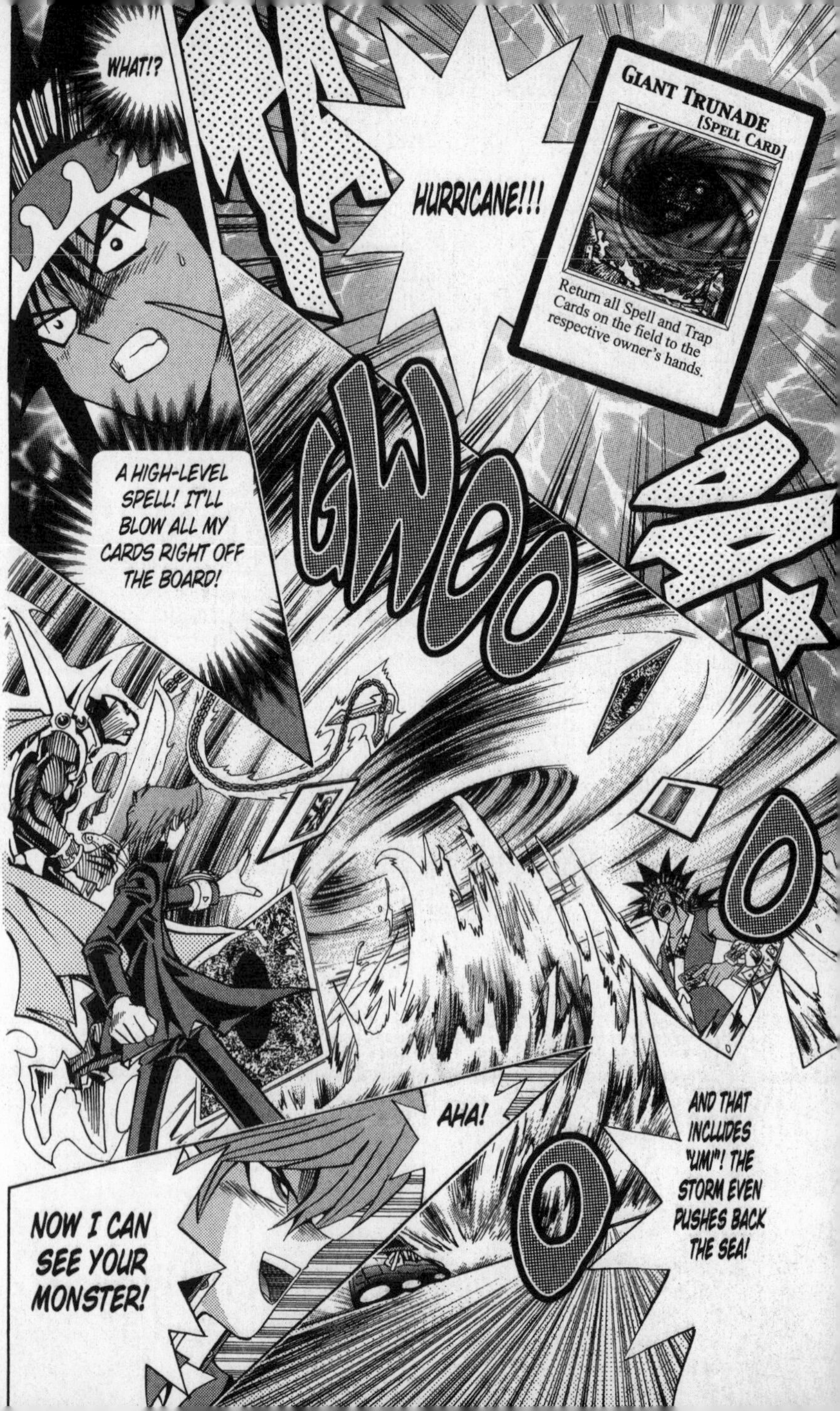

GIANT TRUNADE
[SPELL CARD]
Return all Spell and Trap Cards on the field to the respective owner's hands.
HURRICANE!!!
WHAT!?
A HIGH-LEVEL SPELL! IT'LL BLOW ALL MY CARDS RIGHT OFF THE BOARD!
GWOOO
AND THAT INCLUDES "UMI"! THE STORM EVEN PUSHES BACK THE SEA!
AHA!
NOW I CAN SEE YOUR MONSTER!

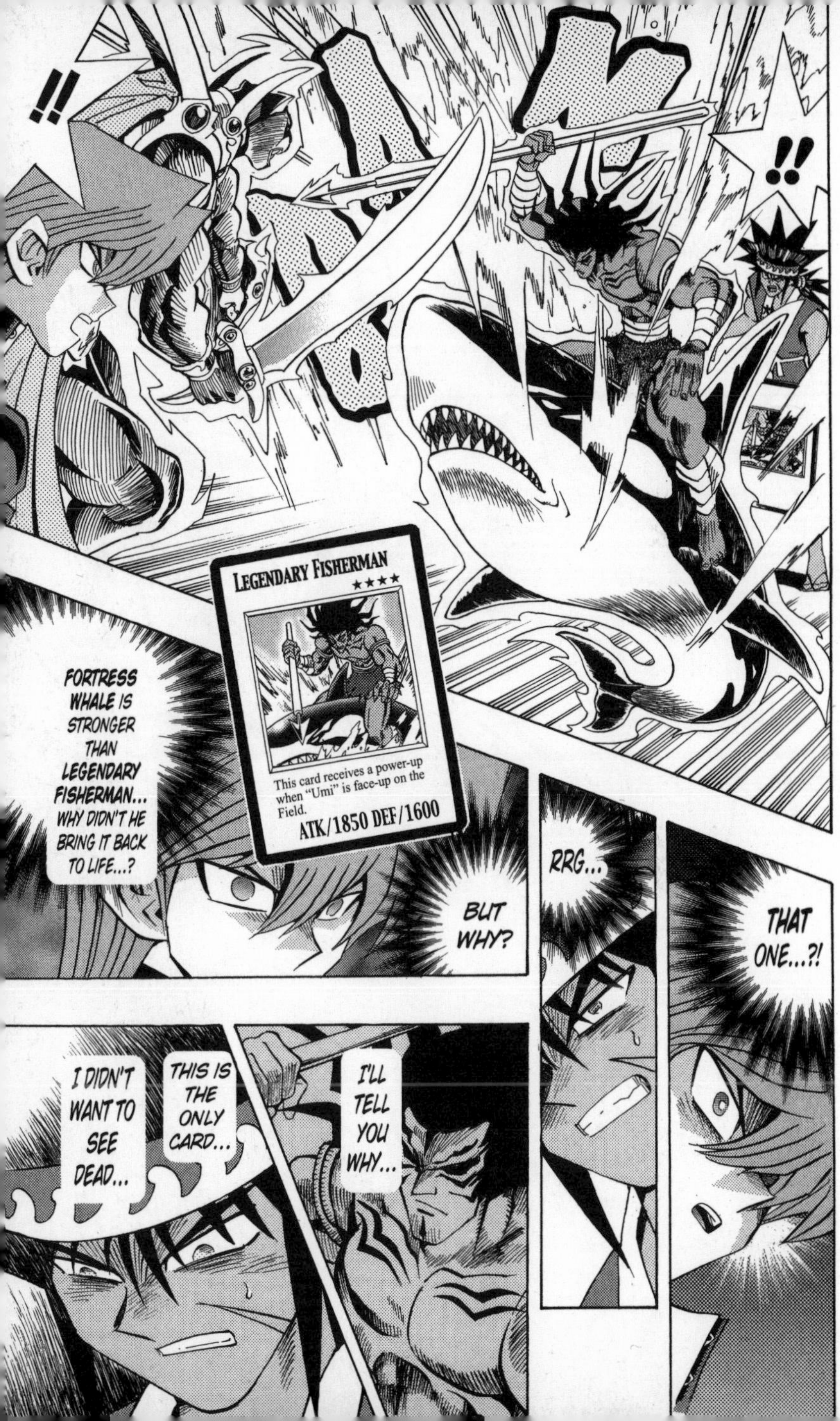
!!
!!
LEGENDARY FISHERMAN
★★★★
This card receives a power-up when "Umi" is face-up on the Field.
ATK/1850 DEF/1600
FORTRESS WHALE IS STRONGER THAN LEGENDARY FISHERMAN... WHY DIDN'T HE BRING IT BACK TO LIFE...?
BUT WHY?
THAT ONE...?!
RRG...
I'LL TELL YOU WHY...
THIS IS THE ONLY CARD...
I DIDN'T WANT TO SEE DEAD...

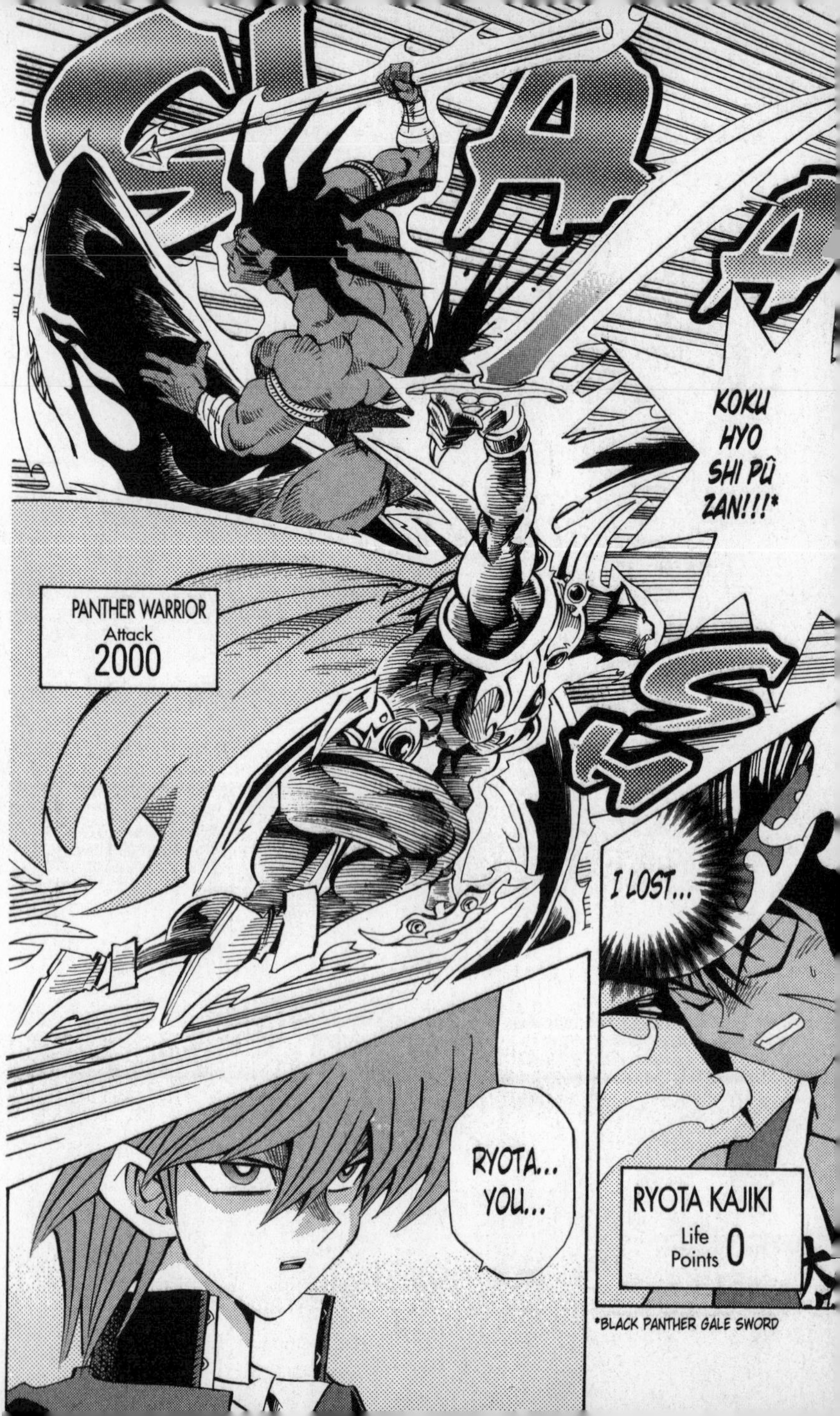
KOKU HYO SHI PÛ ZAN!!!*
PANTHER WARRIOR Attack 2000
I LOST...
RYOTA KAJIKI Life Points 0
RYOTA... YOU...

*BLACK PANTHER GALE SWORD

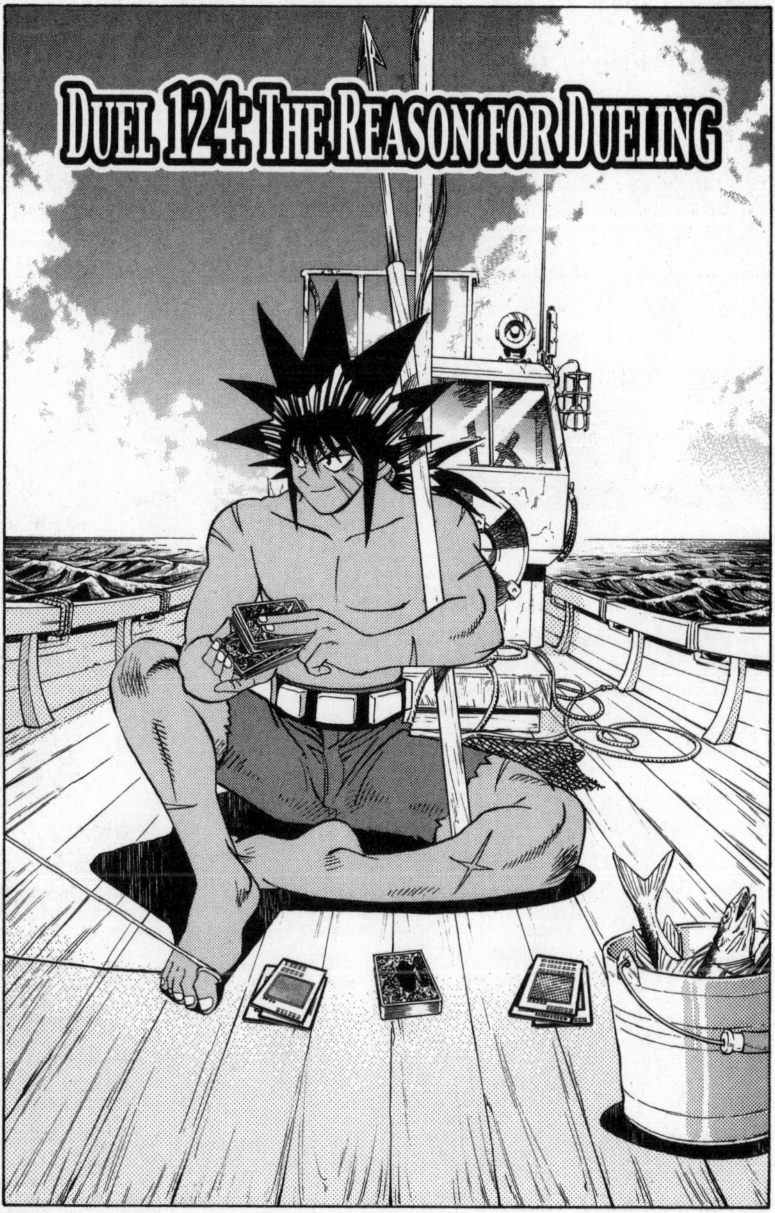
DUEL 124: THE REASON FOR DUELING

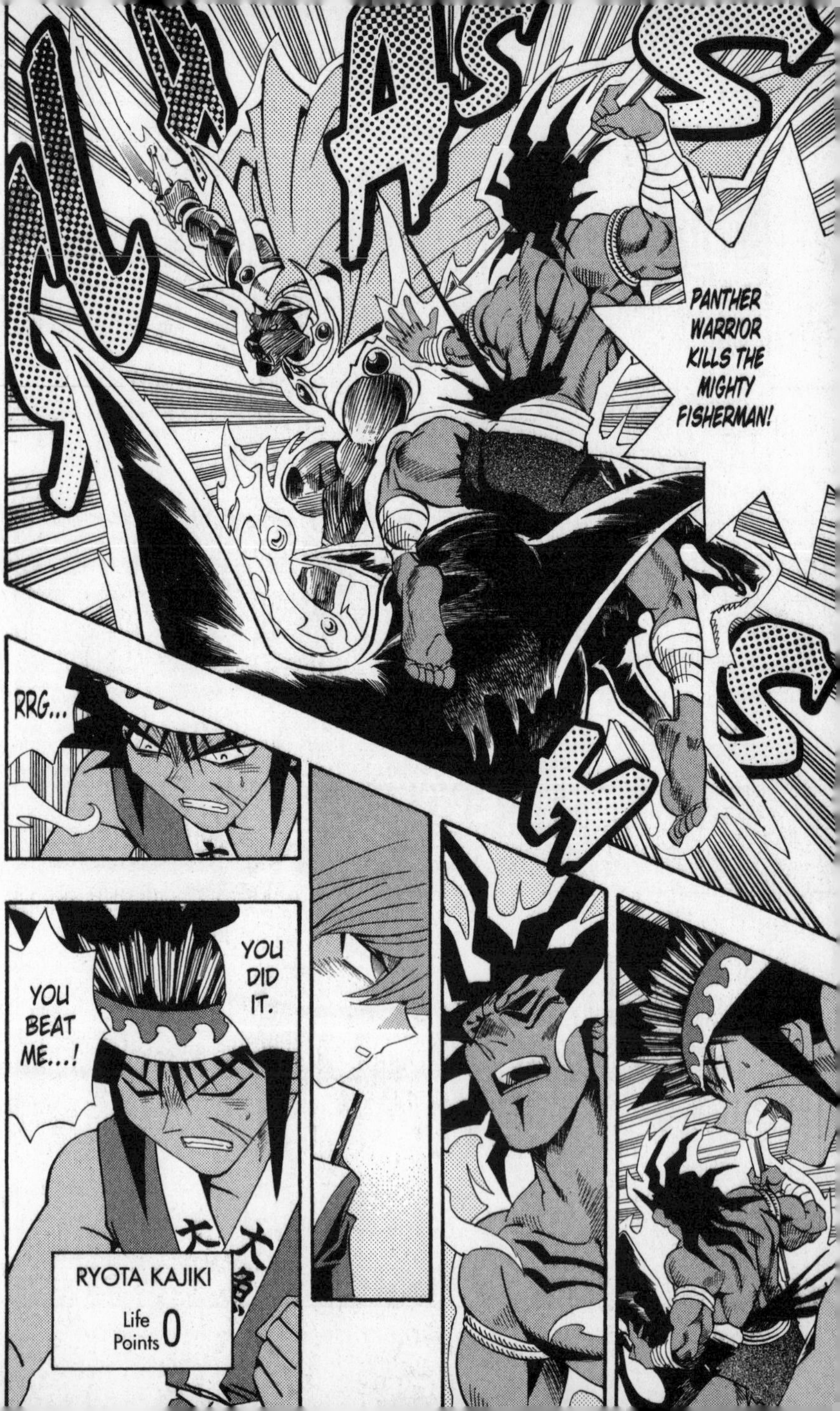
PANTHER WARRIOR KILLS THE MIGHTY FISHERMAN!
RRG...
YOU DID IT.
YOU BEAT ME...!
RYOTA KAJIKI
Life Points 0

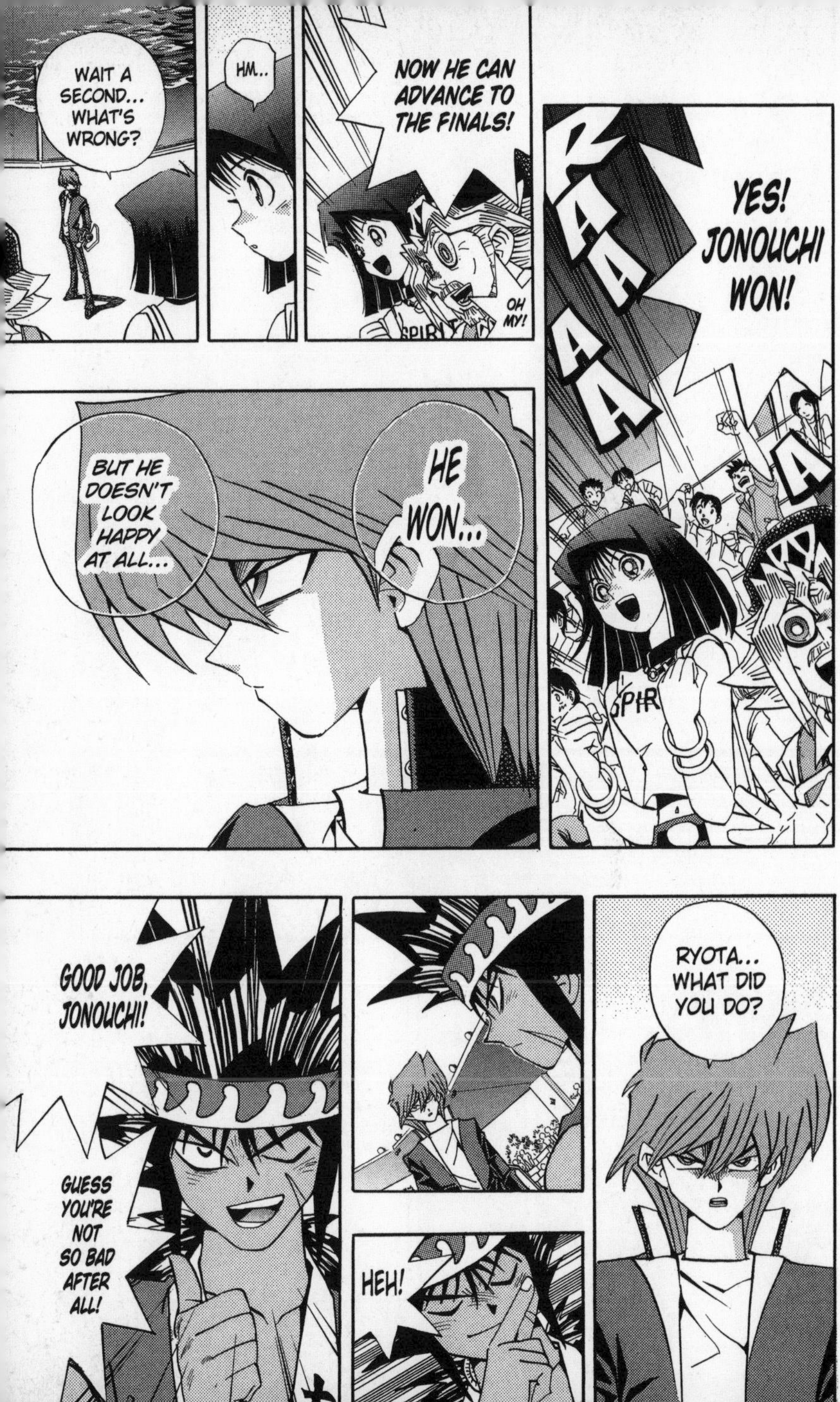
RAAAAA
YES! JONOUCHI WON!
NOW HE CAN ADVANCE TO THE FINALS!
OH MY!
HM...
WAIT A SECOND... WHAT'S WRONG?
HE WON...
BUT HE DOESN'T LOOK HAPPY AT ALL...
RYOTA... WHAT DID YOU DO?
HEH!
GOOD JOB, JONOUCHI!
GUESS YOU'RE NOT SO BAD AFTER ALL!

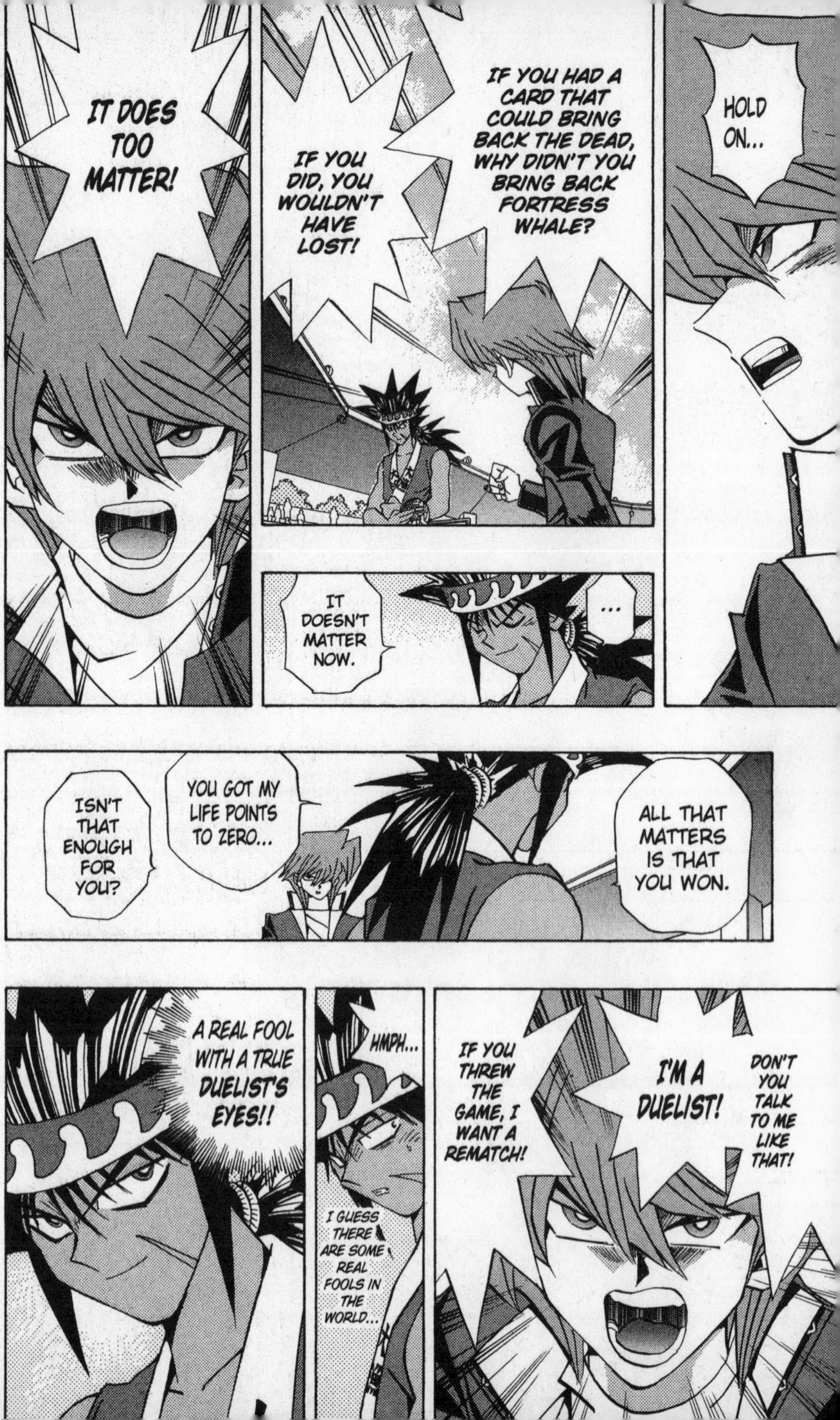
HOLD ON...
IF YOU HAD A CARD THAT COULD BRING BACK THE DEAD, WHY DIDN'T YOU BRING BACK FORTRESS WHALE?
IF YOU DID, YOU WOULDN'T HAVE LOST!
...
IT DOESN'T MATTER NOW.
IT DOES TOO MATTER!
ALL THAT MATTERS IS THAT YOU WON.
YOU GOT MY LIFE POINTS TO ZERO...
ISN'T THAT ENOUGH FOR YOU?
DON'T YOU TALK TO ME LIKE THAT!
I'M A DUELIST!
IF YOU THREW THE GAME, I WANT A REMATCH!
HMPH...
I GUESS THERE ARE SOME REAL FOOLS IN THE WORLD...
A REAL FOOL WITH A TRUE DUELIST'S EYES!!

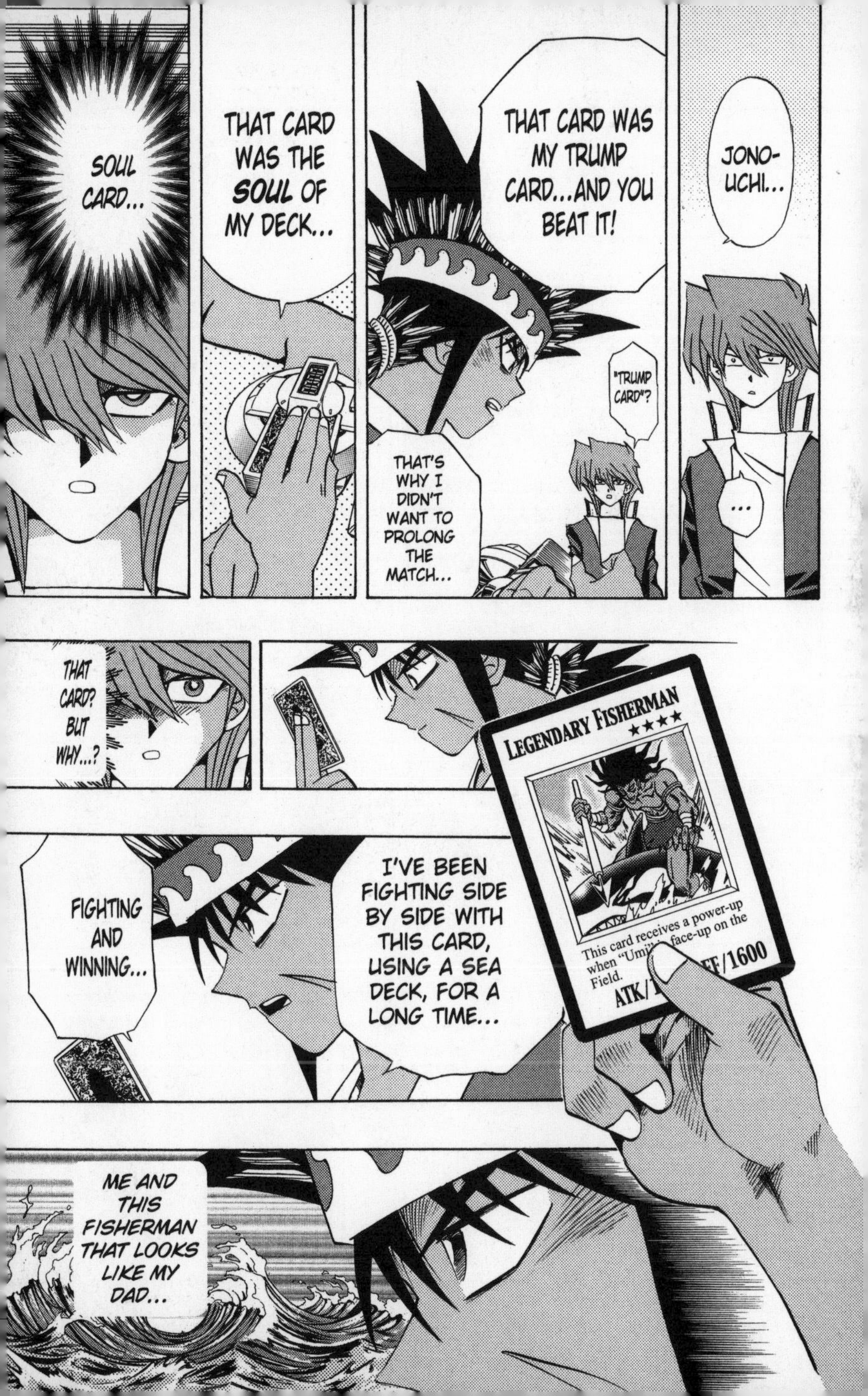
JONO-UCHI...
...
THAT CARD WAS MY TRUMP CARD...AND YOU BEAT IT!
"TRUMP CARD"?
THAT'S WHY I DIDN'T WANT TO PROLONG THE MATCH...
THAT CARD WAS THE SOUL OF MY DECK...
SOUL CARD...
LEGENDARY FISHERMAN
This card receives a power-up
when "Umi face-up on the
Field.
ATK/1
EF/1600
THAT CARD? BUT WHY...?
I'VE BEEN FIGHTING SIDE BY SIDE WITH THIS CARD, USING A SEA DECK, FOR A LONG TIME...
FIGHTING AND WINNING...
ME AND THIS FISHERMAN THAT LOOKS LIKE MY DAD...

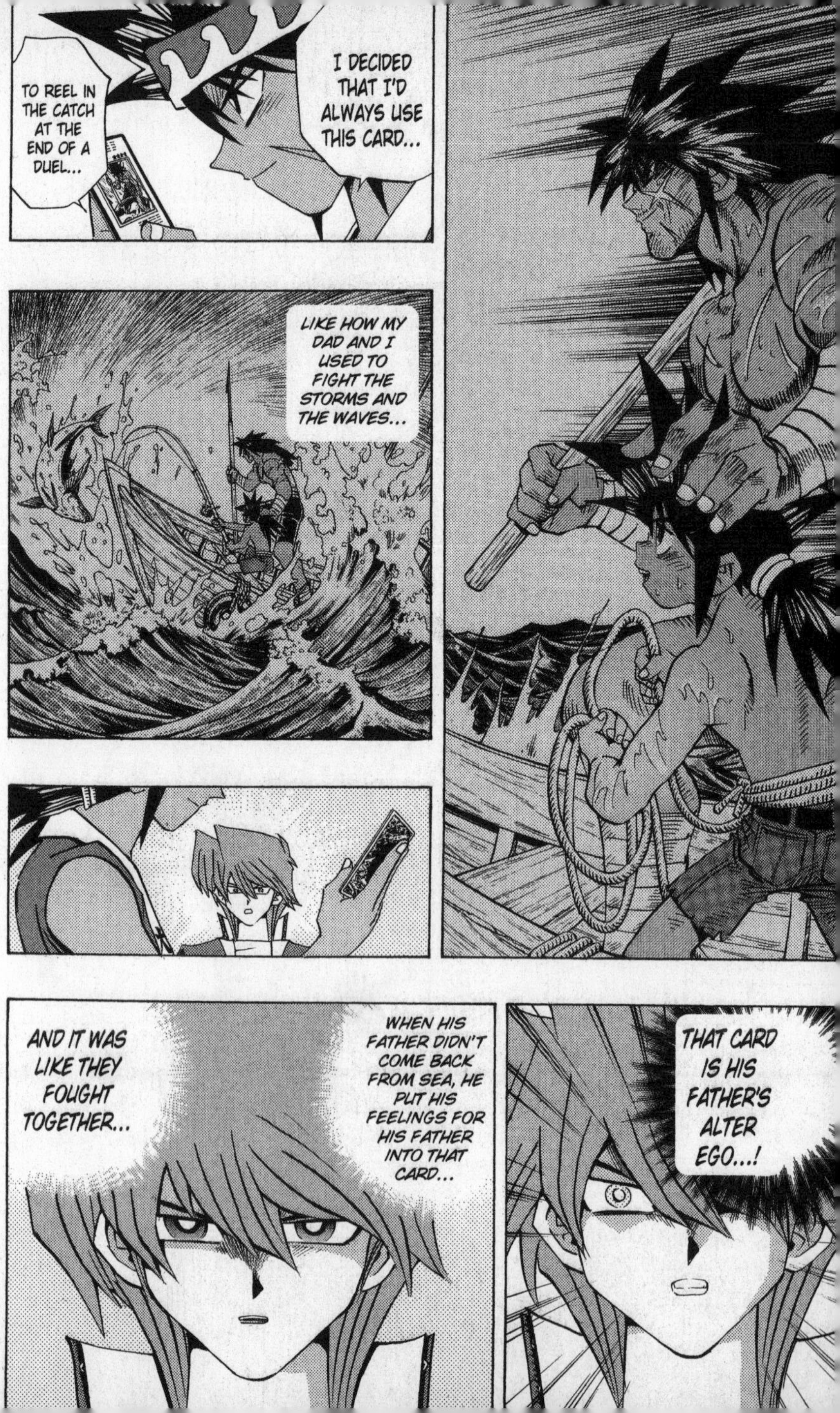
I DECIDED THAT I'D ALWAYS USE THIS CARD...
TO REEL IN THE CATCH AT THE END OF A DUEL...
LIKE HOW MY DAD AND I USED TO FIGHT THE STORMS AND THE WAVES...
THAT CARD IS HIS FATHER'S ALTER EGO...!
WHEN HIS FATHER DIDN'T COME BACK FROM SEA, HE PUT HIS FEELINGS FOR HIS FATHER INTO THAT CARD...
AND IT WAS LIKE THEY FOUGHT TOGETHER...

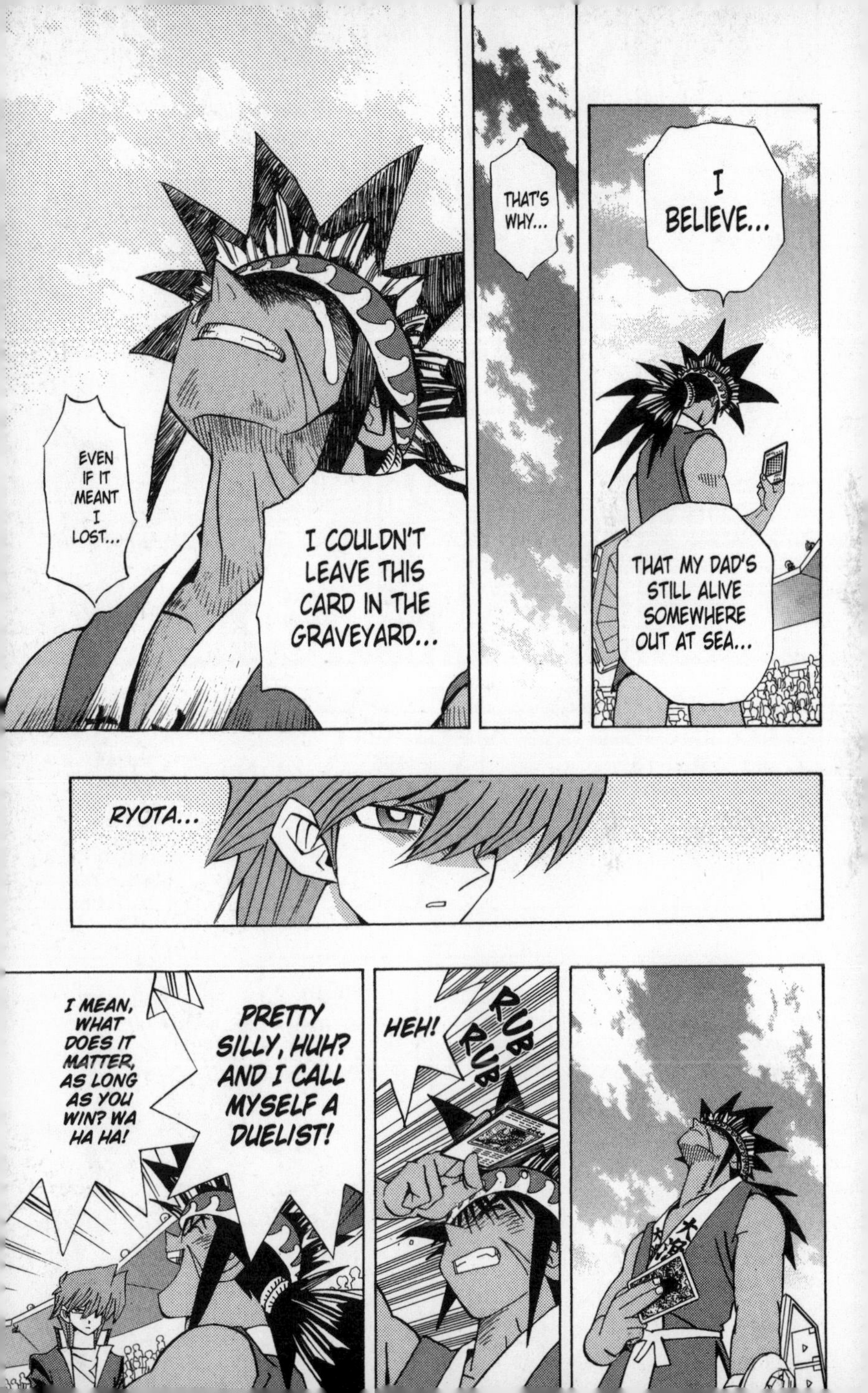
I BELIEVE...
THAT MY DAD'S STILL ALIVE SOMEWHERE OUT AT SEA...
THAT'S WHY...
I COULDN'T LEAVE THIS CARD IN THE GRAVEYARD...
EVEN IF IT MEANT I LOST...
RYOTA...
RUB RUB
HEH!
PRETTY SILLY, HUH? AND I CALL MYSELF A DUELIST!
I MEAN, WHAT DOES IT MATTER, AS LONG AS YOU WIN? WA HA HA!

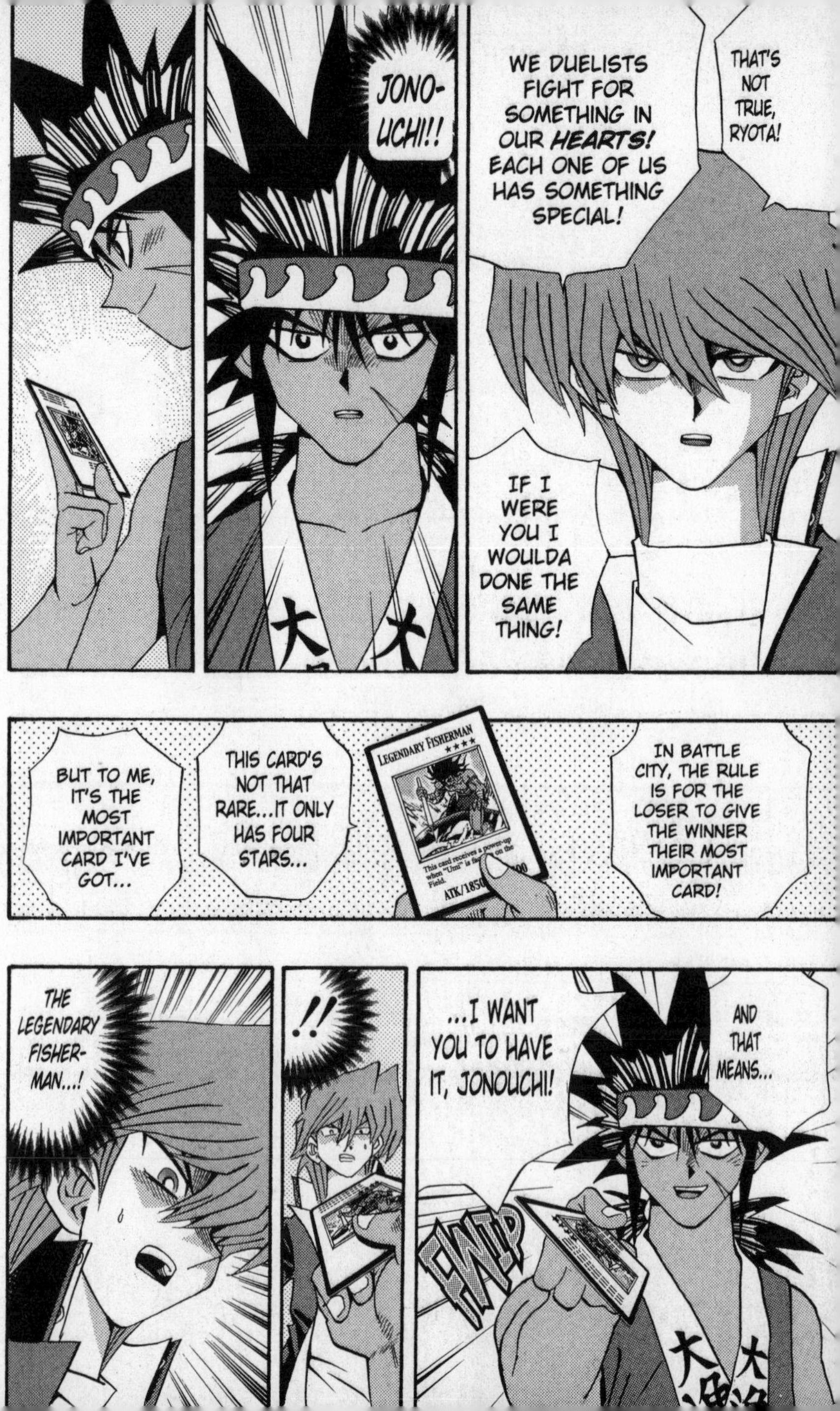
THAT'S NOT TRUE, RYOTA!
WE DUELISTS FIGHT FOR SOMETHING IN OUR **HEARTS!** EACH ONE OF US HAS SOMETHING SPECIAL!
IF I WERE YOU I WOULDA DONE THE SAME THING!
JONO-UCHI!!
IN BATTLE CITY, THE RULE IS FOR THE LOSER TO GIVE THE WINNER THEIR MOST IMPORTANT CARD!
LEGENDARY FISHERMAN
THIS CARD'S NOT THAT RARE...IT ONLY HAS FOUR STARS...
BUT TO ME, IT'S THE MOST IMPORTANT CARD I'VE GOT...
AND THAT MEANS...
...I WANT YOU TO HAVE IT, JONOUCHI!
FWIP
!!
THE LEGENDARY FISHER-MAN...!

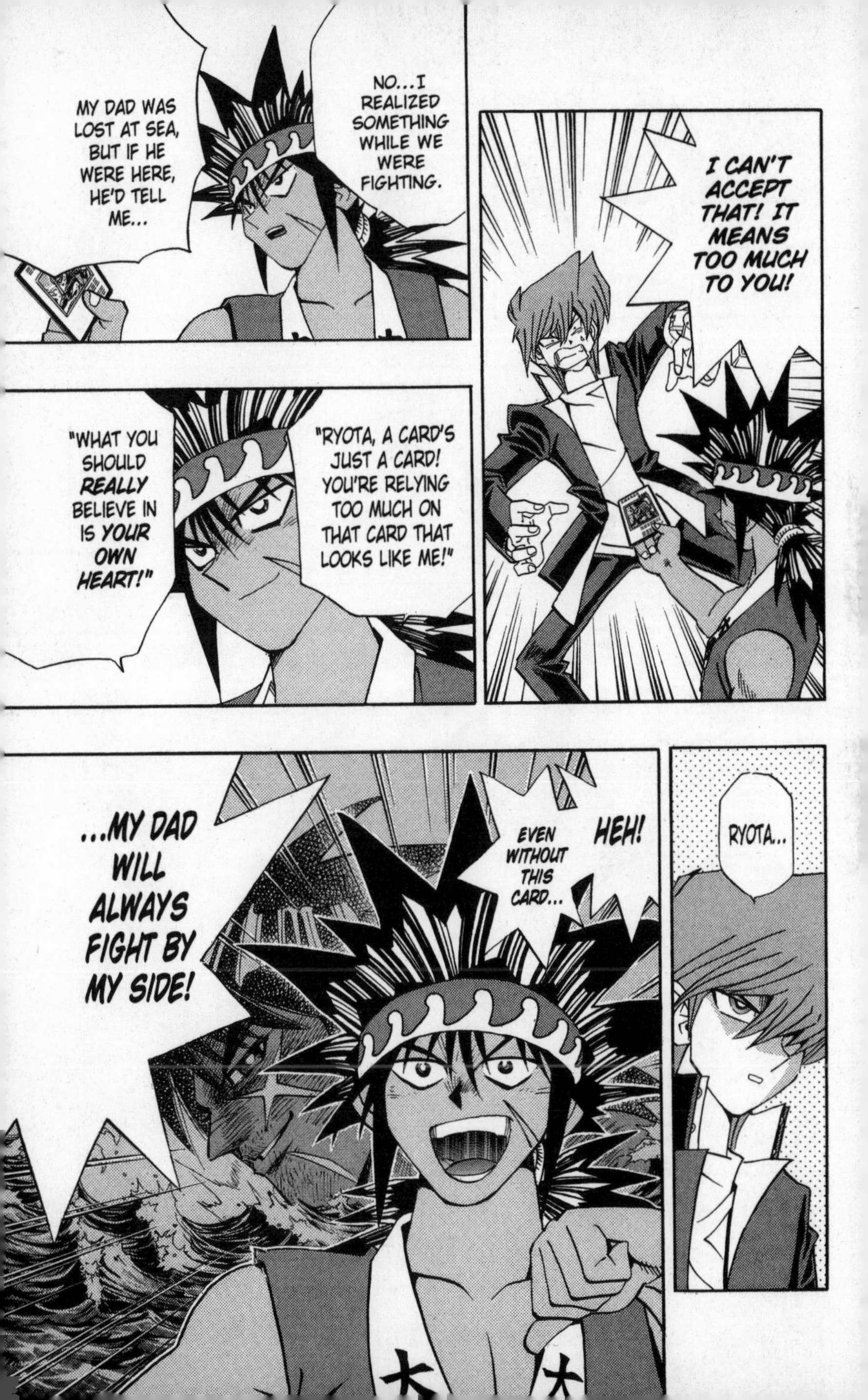
NO...I REALIZED SOMETHING WHILE WE WERE FIGHTING.
MY DAD WAS LOST AT SEA, BUT IF HE WERE HERE, HE'D TELL ME...
"RYOTA, A CARD'S JUST A CARD! YOU'RE RELYING TOO MUCH ON THAT CARD THAT LOOKS LIKE ME!"
"WHAT YOU SHOULD REALLY BELIEVE IN IS YOUR OWN HEART!"
I CAN'T ACCEPT THAT! IT MEANS TOO MUCH TO YOU!
RYOTA...
HEH!
EVEN WITHOUT THIS CARD...
...MY DAD WILL ALWAYS FIGHT BY MY SIDE!

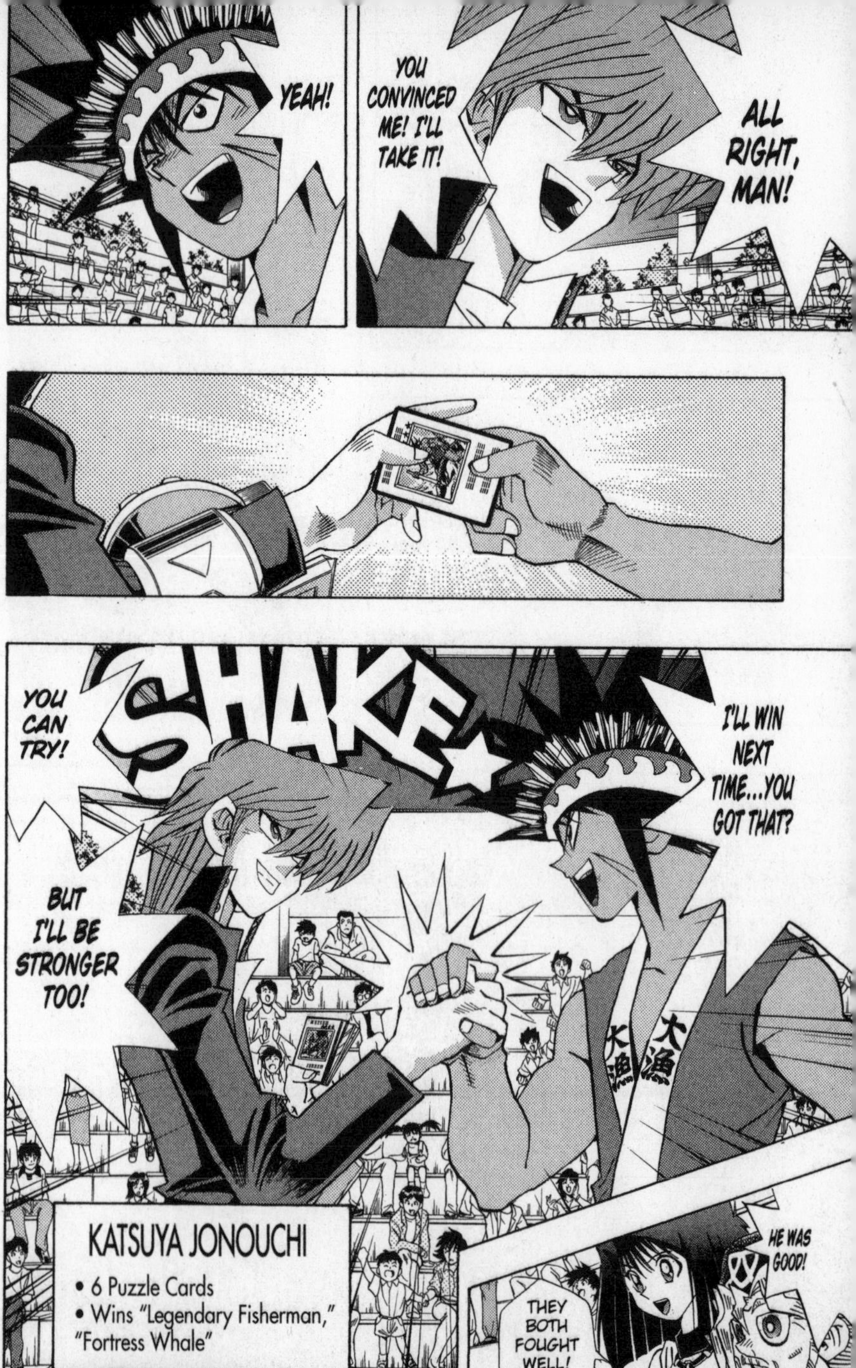
ALL RIGHT, MAN!
YOU CONVINCED ME! I'LL TAKE IT!
YEAH!
I'LL WIN NEXT TIME...YOU GOT THAT?
SHAKE
YOU CAN TRY!
BUT I'LL BE STRONGER TOO!
大漁
大漁
HE WAS GOOD!
THEY BOTH FOUGHT WELL!
KATSUYA JONOUCHI
• 6 Puzzle Cards
• Wins "Legendary Fisherman," "Fortress Whale"

READ THIS WAY

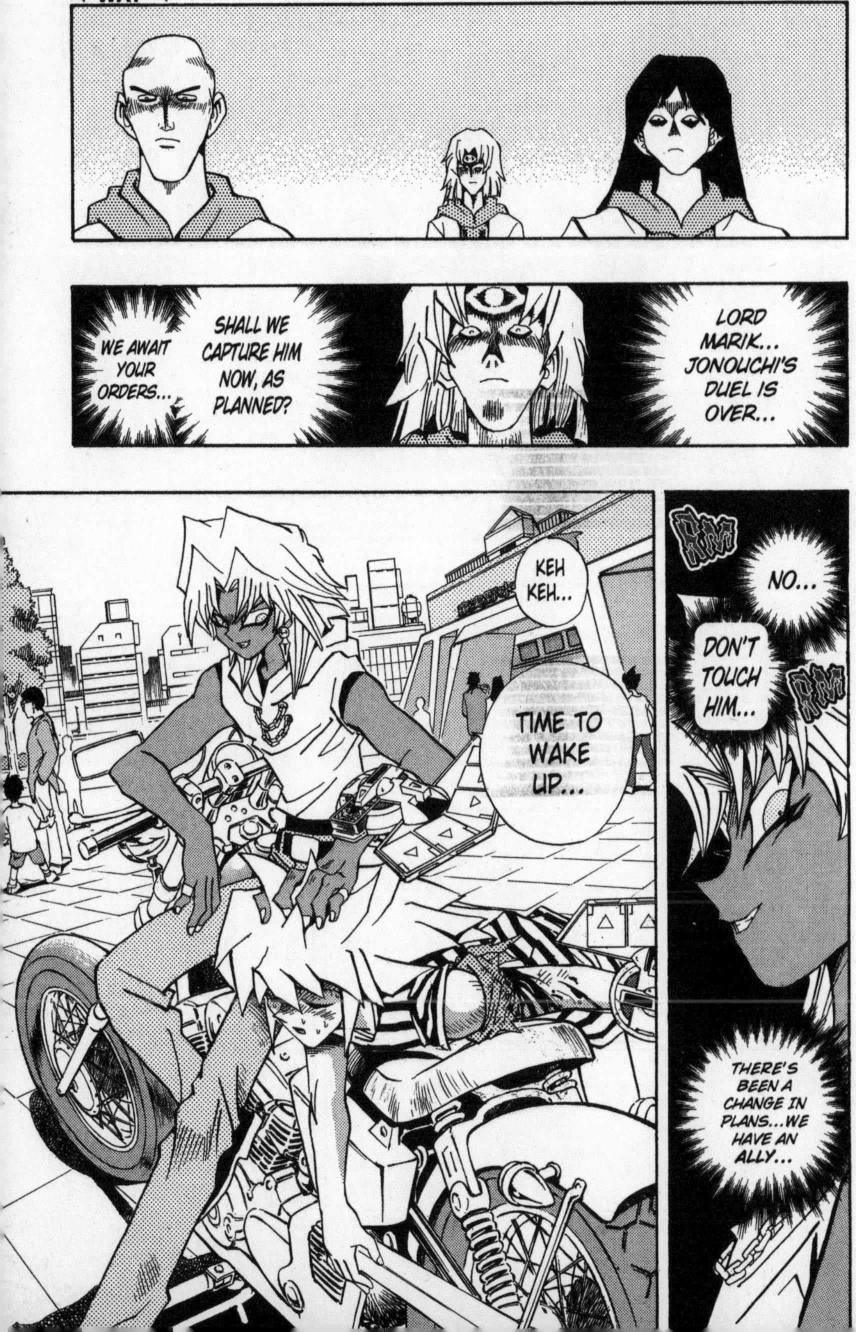
LORD MARIK... JONOUCHI'S DUEL IS OVER...
SHALL WE CAPTURE HIM NOW, AS PLANNED?
WE AWAIT YOUR ORDERS...
NO...
DON'T TOUCH HIM...
THERE'S BEEN A CHANGE IN PLANS...WE HAVE AN ALLY...
KEH KEH...
TIME TO WAKE UP...

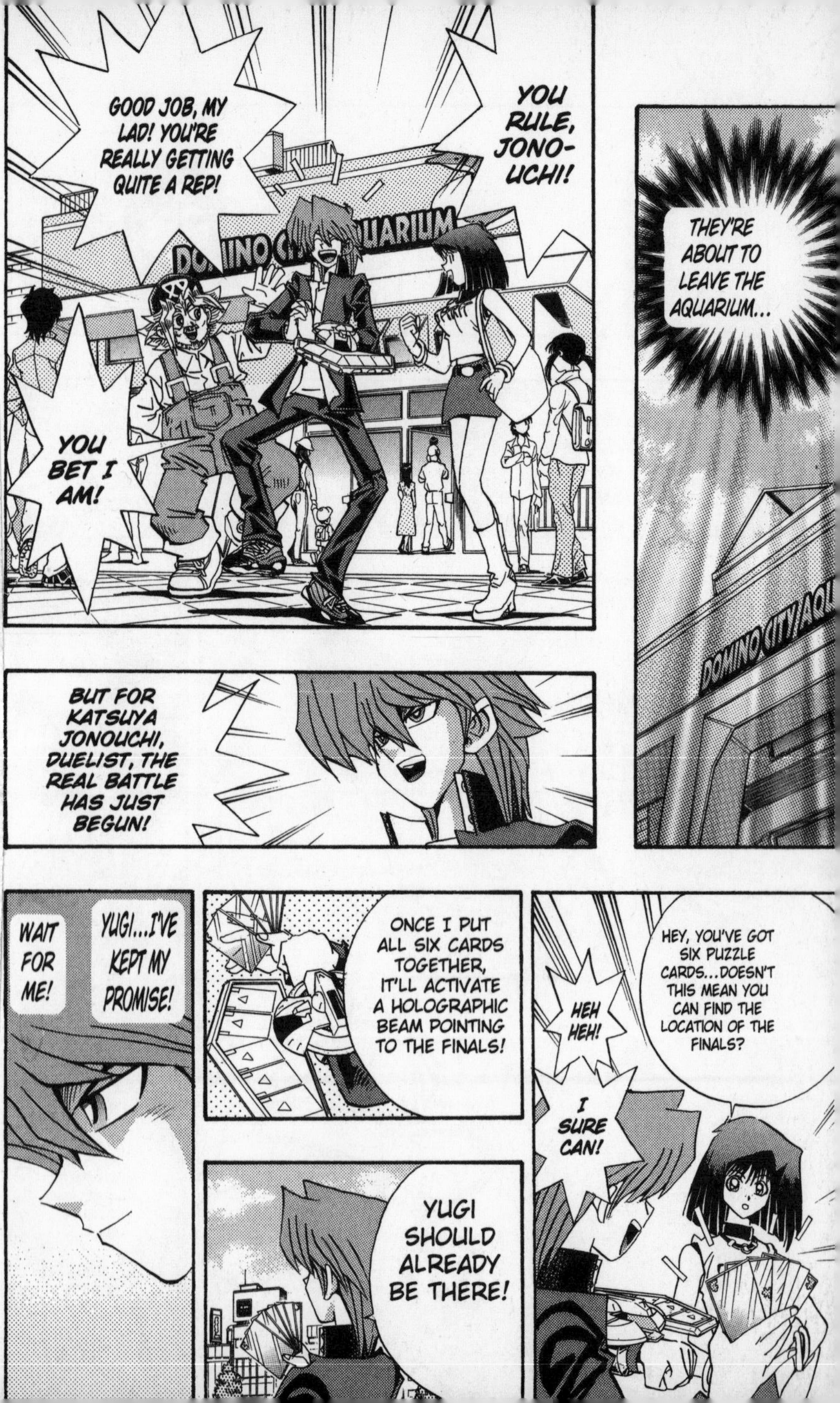
THEY'RE ABOUT TO LEAVE THE AQUARIUM...
YOU RULE, JONOUCHI!
GOOD JOB, MY LAD! YOU'RE REALLY GETTING QUITE A REP!
YOU BET I AM!
BUT FOR KATSUYA JONOUCHI, DUELIST, THE REAL BATTLE HAS JUST BEGUN!
HEY, YOU'VE GOT SIX PUZZLE CARDS...DOESN'T THIS MEAN YOU CAN FIND THE LOCATION OF THE FINALS?
HEH HEH!
I SURE CAN!
ONCE I PUT ALL SIX CARDS TOGETHER, IT'LL ACTIVATE A HOLOGRAPHIC BEAM POINTING TO THE FINALS!
YUGI SHOULD ALREADY BE THERE!
YUGI...I'VE KEPT MY PROMISE!
WAIT FOR ME!

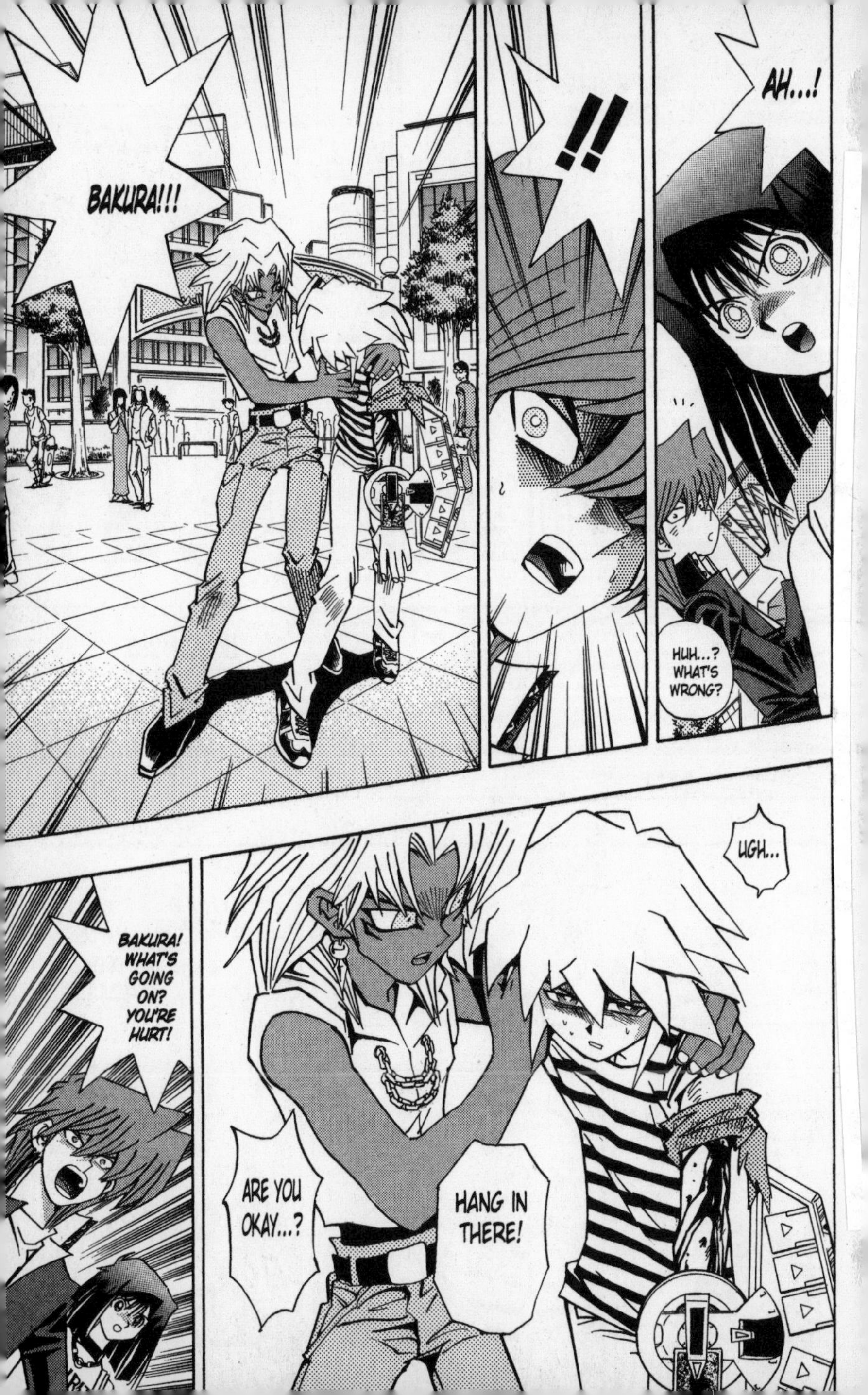
AH...!
HUH...? WHAT'S WRONG?
!!
BAKURA!!!
UGH...
HANG IN THERE!
ARE YOU OKAY...?
BAKURA! WHAT'S GOING ON? YOU'RE HURT!

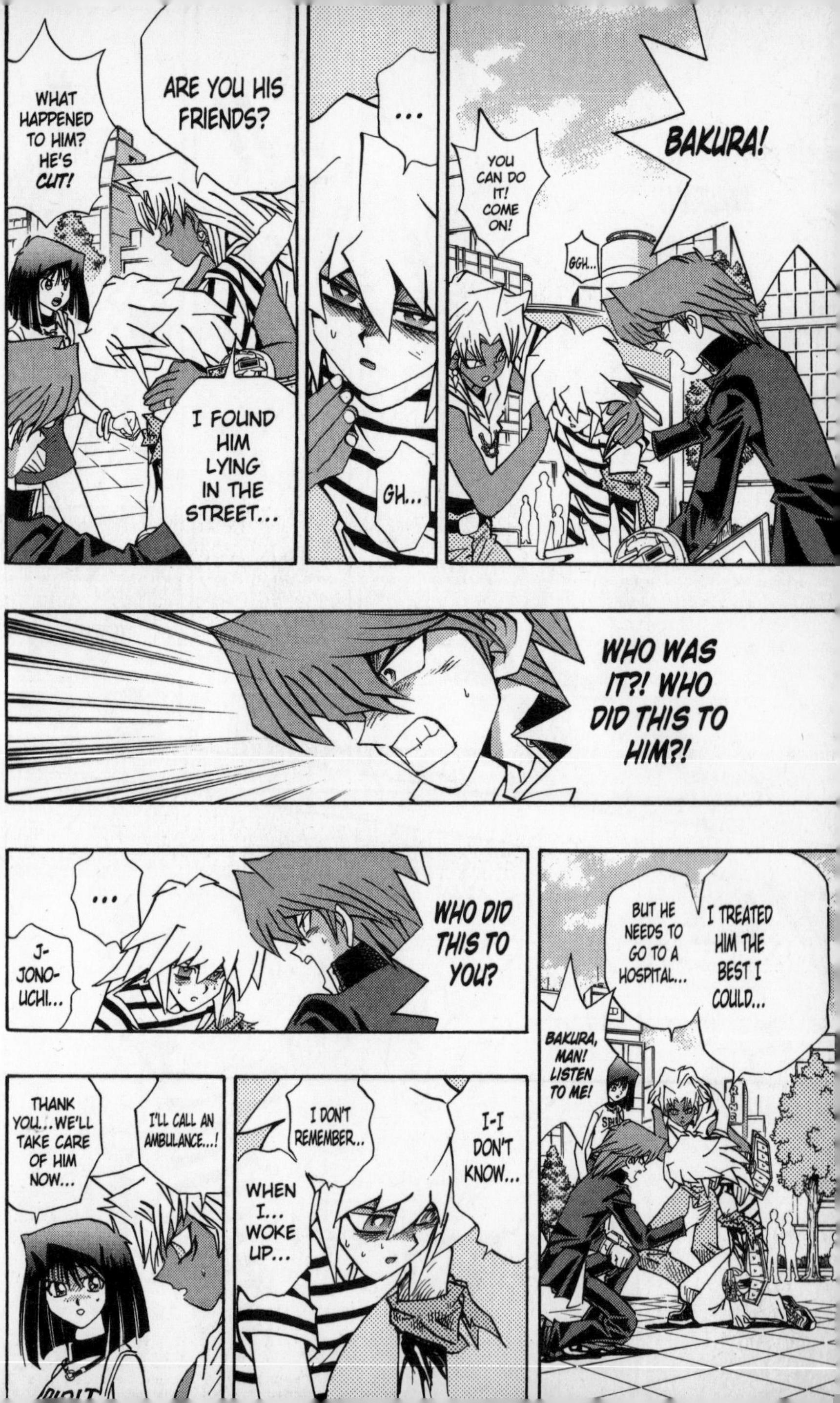
BAKURA!
YOU CAN DO IT! COME ON!
GGH...
...
GH...
ARE YOU HIS FRIENDS?
WHAT HAPPENED TO HIM? HE'S CUT!
I FOUND HIM LYING IN THE STREET...
WHO WAS IT?! WHO DID THIS TO HIM?!
I TREATED HIM THE BEST I COULD...
BUT HE NEEDS TO GO TO A HOSPITAL...
BAKURA, MAN! LISTEN TO ME!
WHO DID THIS TO YOU?
...
J-JONOUCHI...
I-I DON'T KNOW...
I DON'T REMEMBER..
WHEN I... WOKE UP...
I'LL CALL AN AMBULANCE...!
THANK YOU...WE'LL TAKE CARE OF HIM NOW...

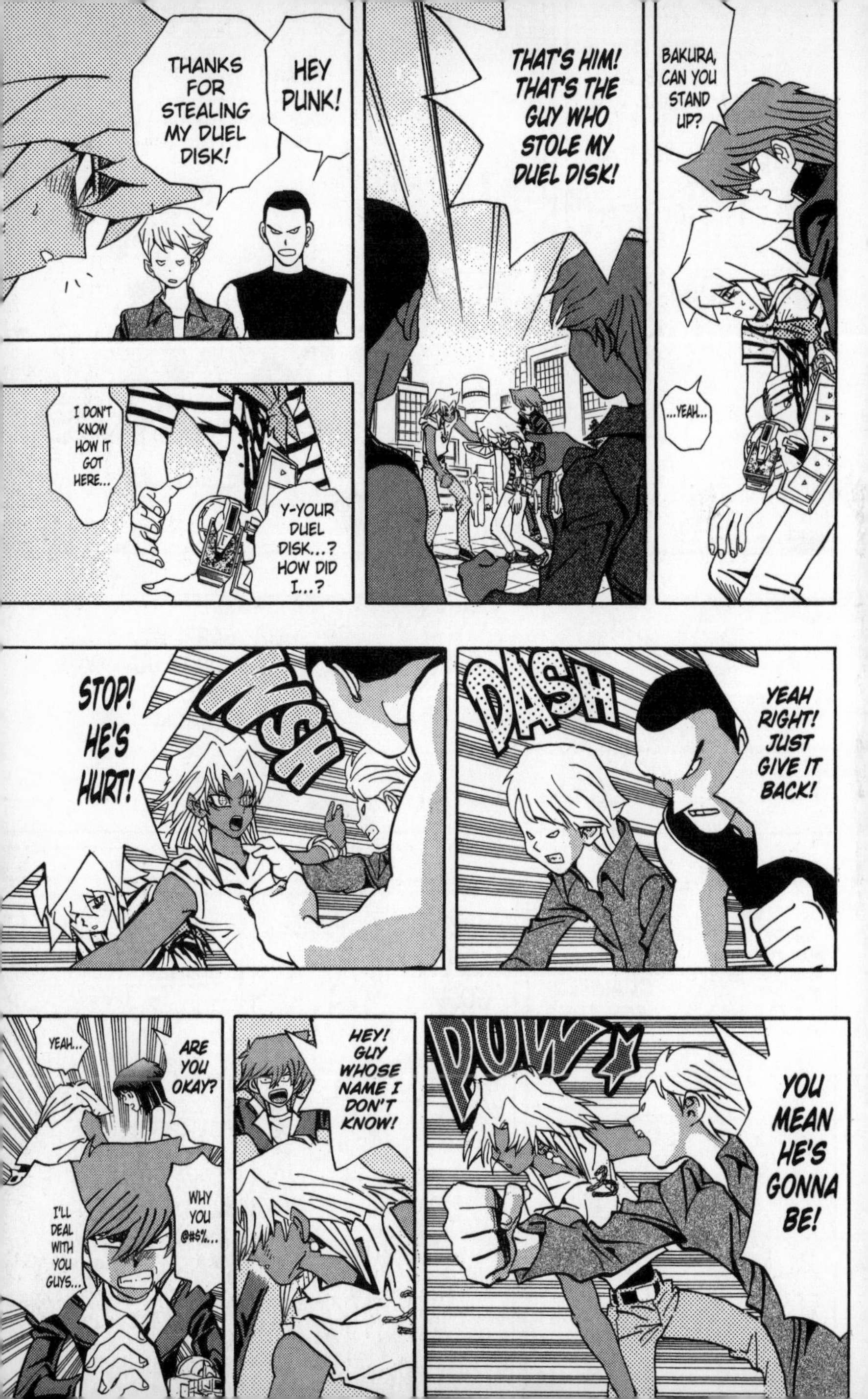
BAKURA, CAN YOU STAND UP?
...YEAH...
THAT'S HIM! THAT'S THE GUY WHO STOLE MY DUEL DISK!
HEY PUNK!
THANKS FOR STEALING MY DUEL DISK!
Y-YOUR DUEL DISK...? HOW DID I...?
I DON'T KNOW HOW IT GOT HERE...
DASH
YEAH RIGHT! JUST GIVE IT BACK!
STOP! HE'S HURT!
POW
YOU MEAN HE'S GONNA BE!
HEY! GUY WHOSE NAME I DON'T KNOW!
WHY YOU @#$%...
ARE YOU OKAY?
YEAH...
I'LL DEAL WITH YOU GUYS...

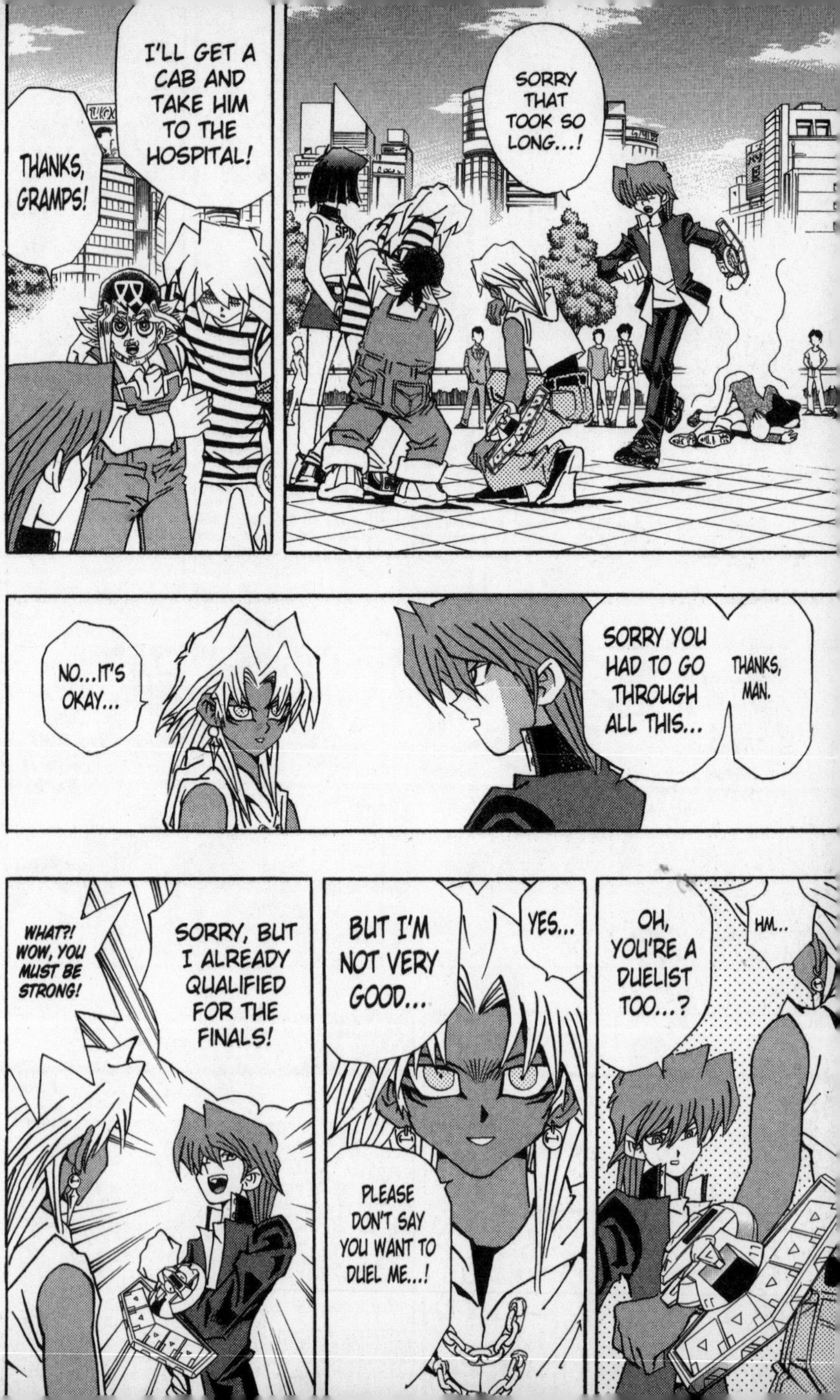
SORRY THAT TOOK SO LONG...!
I'LL GET A CAB AND TAKE HIM TO THE HOSPITAL!
THANKS, GRAMPS!
THANKS, MAN.
SORRY YOU HAD TO GO THROUGH ALL THIS...
NO...IT'S OKAY...
HM...
OH, YOU'RE A DUELIST TOO...?
YES...
BUT I'M NOT VERY GOOD...
PLEASE DON'T SAY YOU WANT TO DUEL ME...!
SORRY, BUT I ALREADY QUALIFIED FOR THE FINALS!
WHAT?! WOW, YOU MUST BE STRONG!

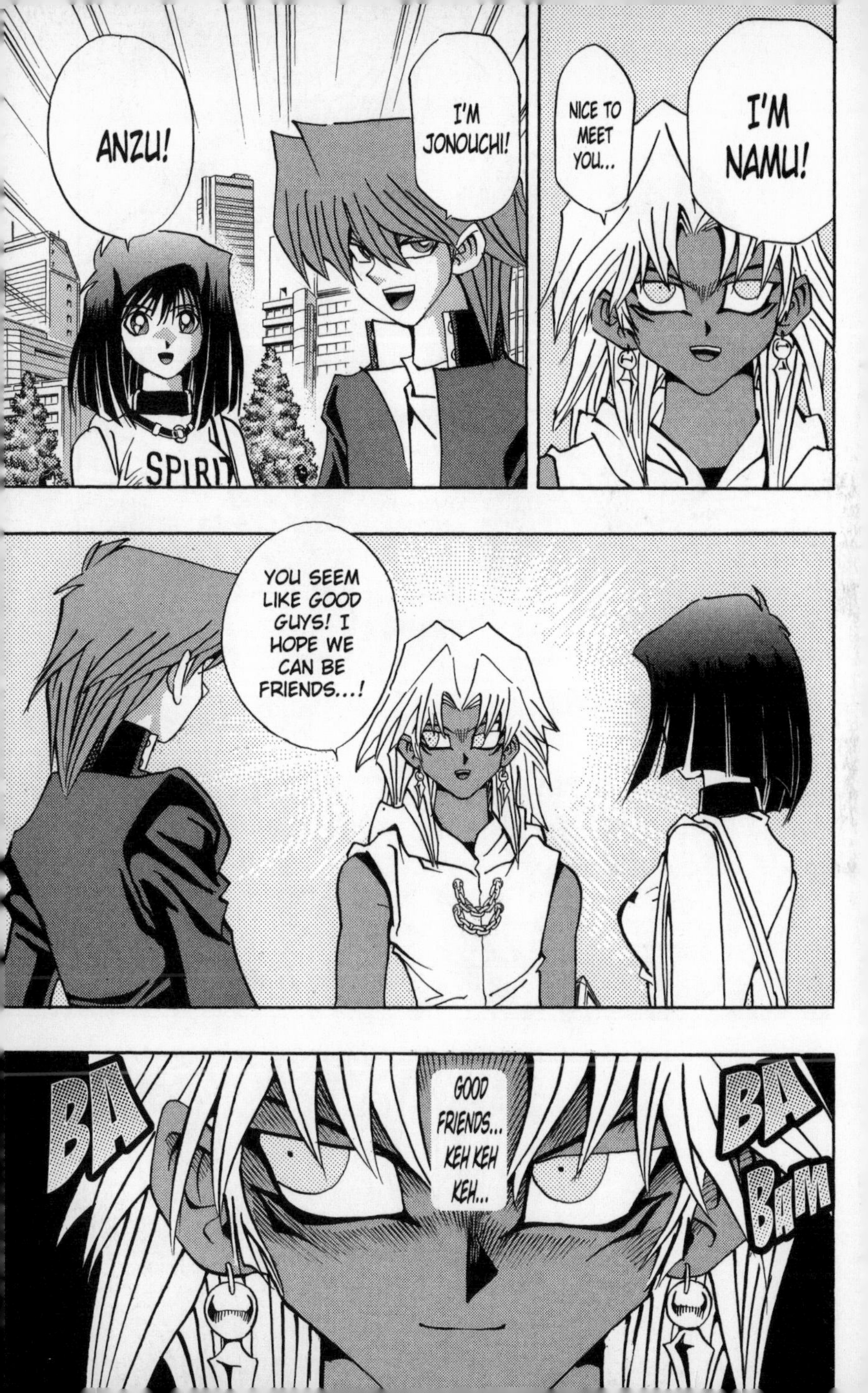
I'M NAMU!
NICE TO MEET YOU...
I'M JONOUCHI!
ANZU!
YOU SEEM LIKE GOOD GUYS! I HOPE WE CAN BE FRIENDS...!
BA BAM
GOOD FRIENDS... KEH KEH KEH...
BA

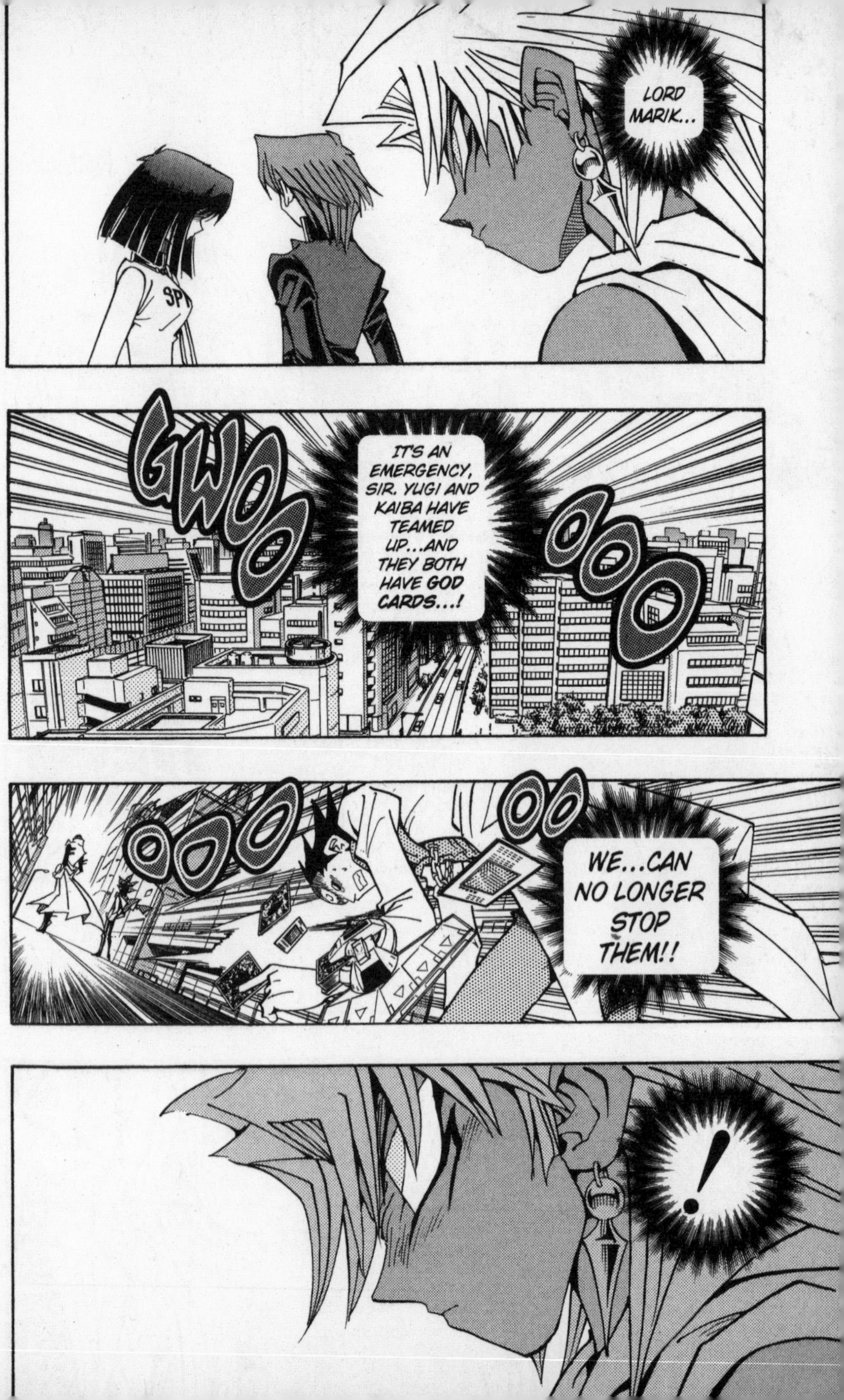
LORD MARIK...
GWOOOOOOOOOOO
IT'S AN EMERGENCY, SIR. YUGI AND KAIBA HAVE TEAMED UP...AND THEY BOTH HAVE GOD CARDS...!
WE...CAN NO LONGER STOP THEM!!
!

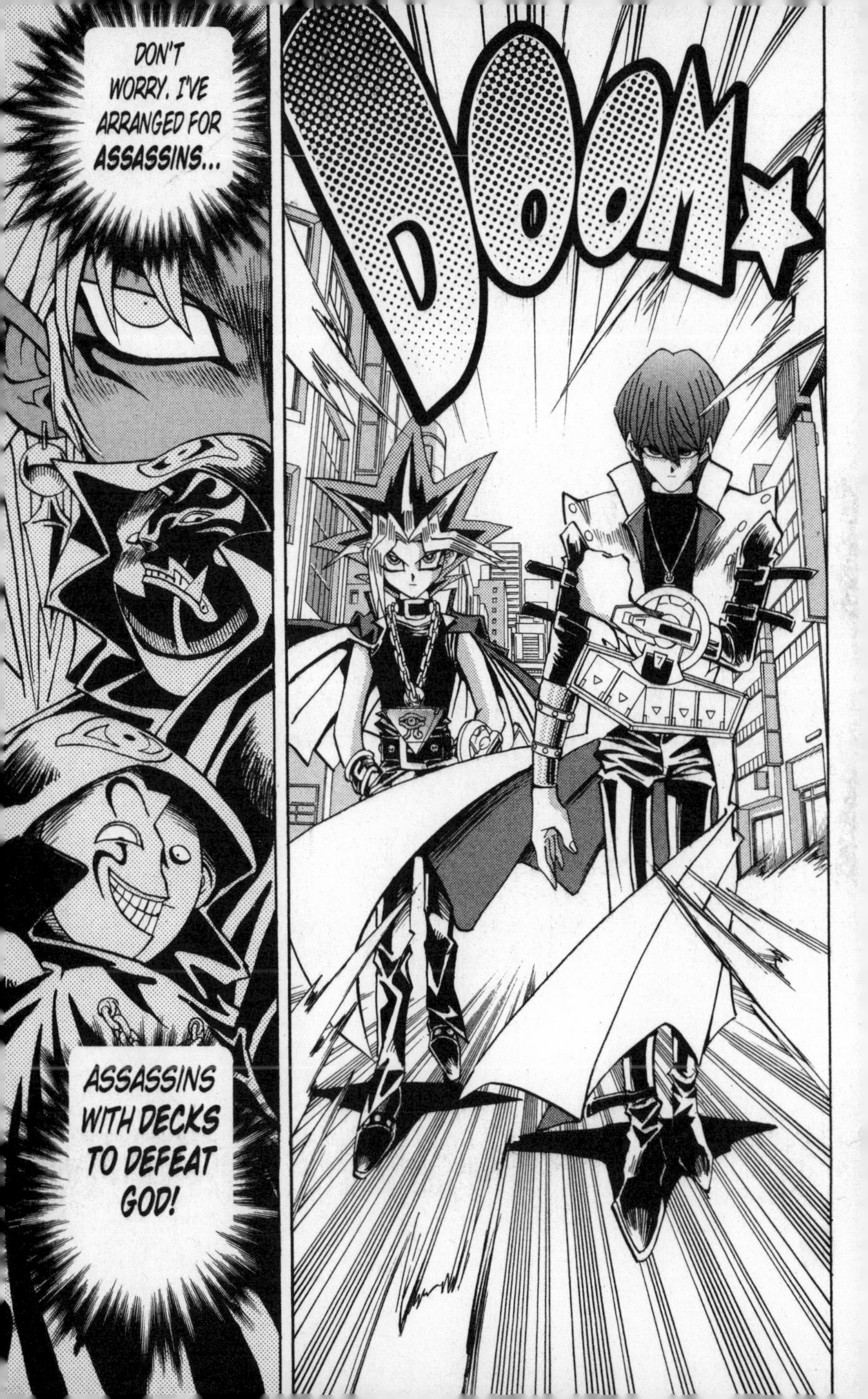
DOOM☆
DON'T WORRY. I'VE ARRANGED FOR ASSASSINS...
ASSASSINS WITH DECKS TO DEFEAT GOD!

DUEL 125: ARENA OF DEATH!!

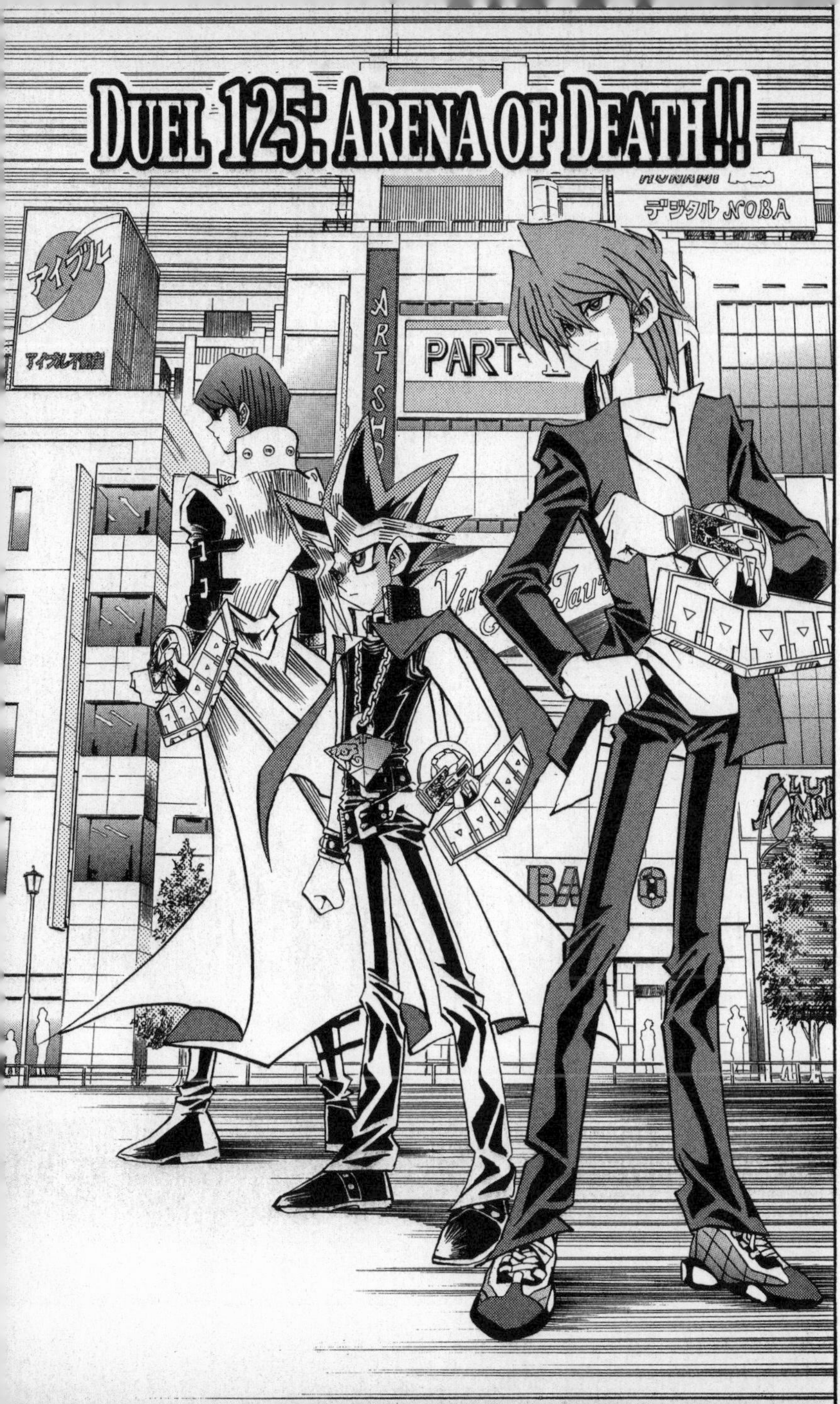
デジタル NOBA
PART

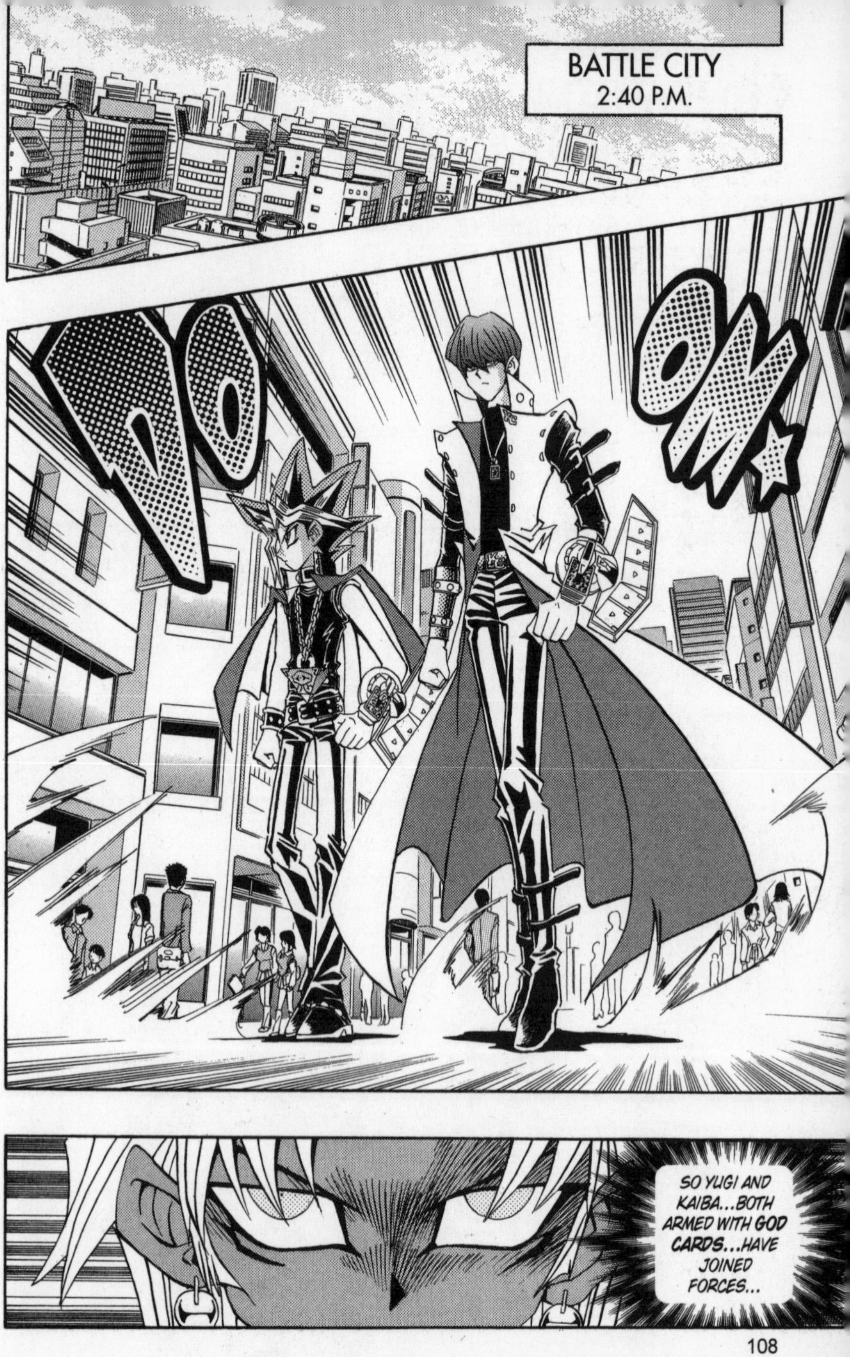
BATTLE CITY
2:40 P.M.
DOOM
SO YUGI AND KAIBA...BOTH ARMED WITH GOD CARDS...HAVE JOINED FORCES...

ANTI-GOD ATTACK FORCE!

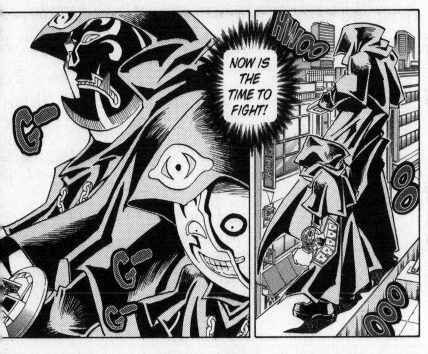

NOW IS THE TIME TO FIGHT!

HWOO

IN THE MEANTIME, I'LL MAKE YUGI'S FRIENDS INTO MY PAWNS!

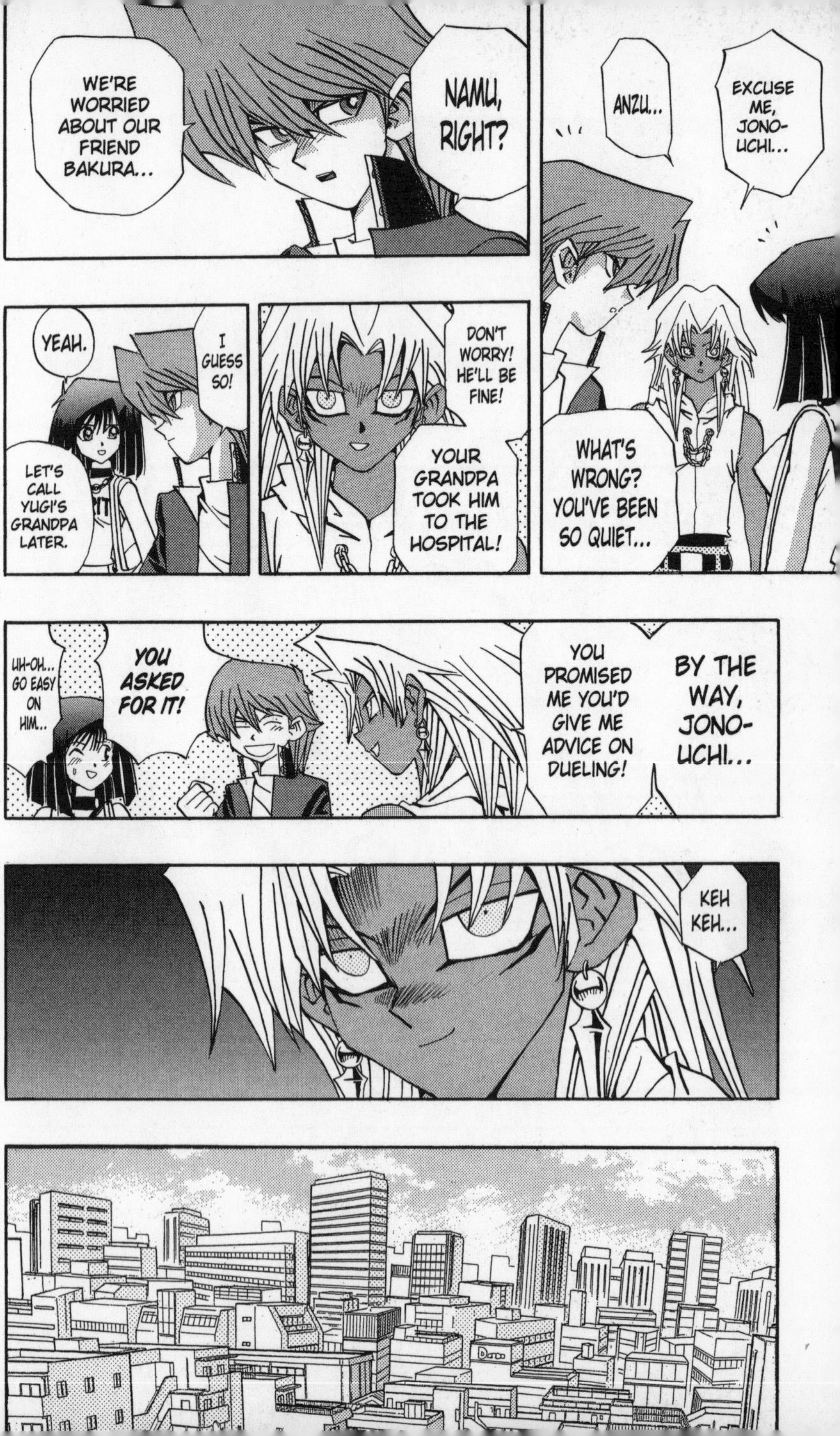
EXCUSE ME, JONO-UCHI...
ANZU...
WHAT'S WRONG? YOU'VE BEEN SO QUIET...
NAMU, RIGHT?
WE'RE WORRIED ABOUT OUR FRIEND BAKURA...
DON'T WORRY! HE'LL BE FINE!
YOUR GRANDPA TOOK HIM TO THE HOSPITAL!
I GUESS SO!
YEAH.
LET'S CALL YUGI'S GRANDPA LATER.
BY THE WAY, JONO-UCHI...
YOU PROMISED ME YOU'D GIVE ME ADVICE ON DUELING!
YOU ASKED FOR IT!
UH-OH... GO EASY ON HIM...
KEH KEH...

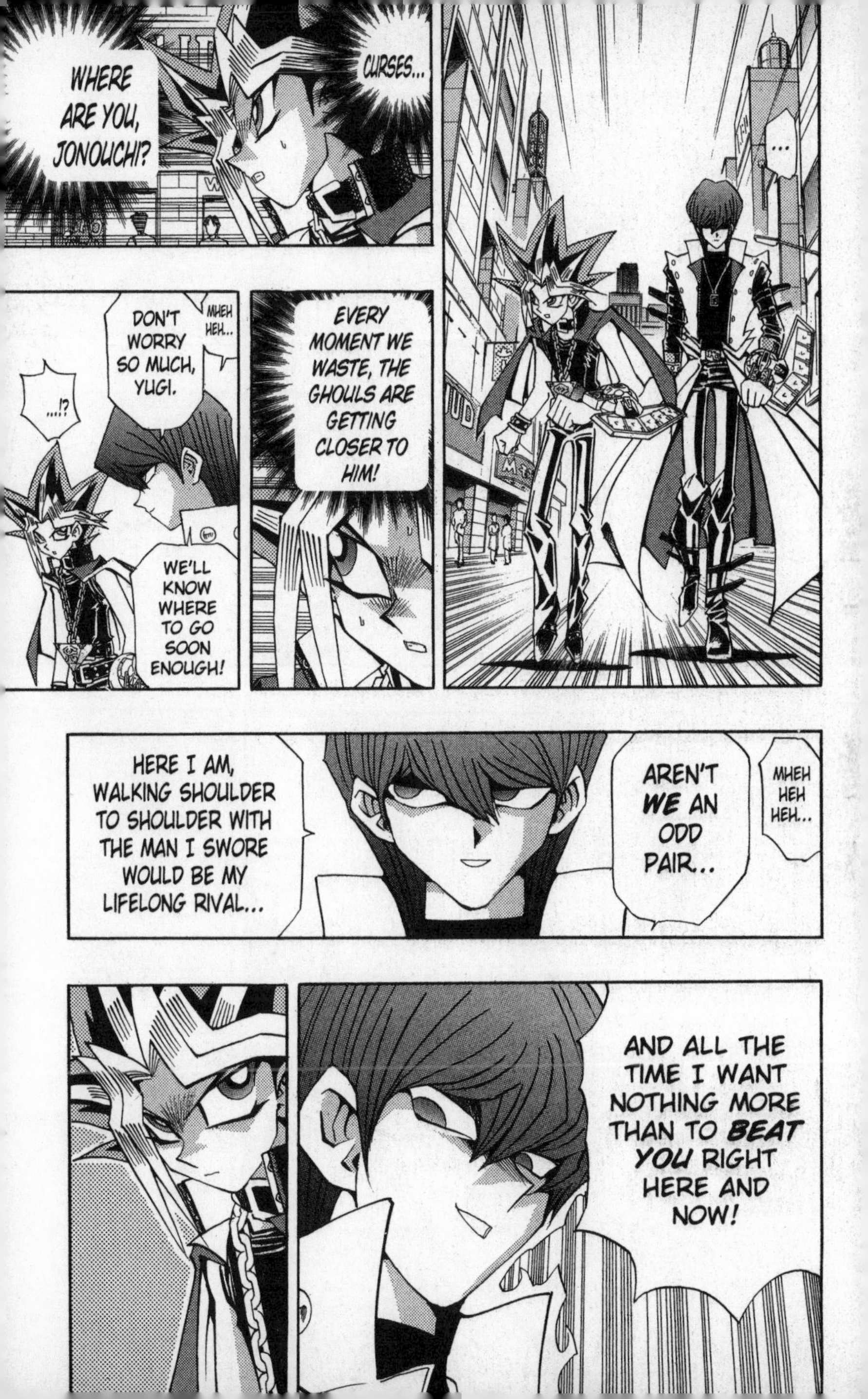
...
CURSES...
WHERE ARE YOU, JONOUCHI?
EVERY MOMENT WE WASTE, THE GHOULS ARE GETTING CLOSER TO HIM!
MHEH HEH...
DON'T WORRY SO MUCH, YUGI.
...!?
WE'LL KNOW WHERE TO GO SOON ENOUGH!
MHEH HEH HEH...
AREN'T WE AN ODD PAIR...
HERE I AM, WALKING SHOULDER TO SHOULDER WITH THE MAN I SWORE WOULD BE MY LIFELONG RIVAL...
AND ALL THE TIME I WANT NOTHING MORE THAN TO BEAT YOU RIGHT HERE AND NOW!

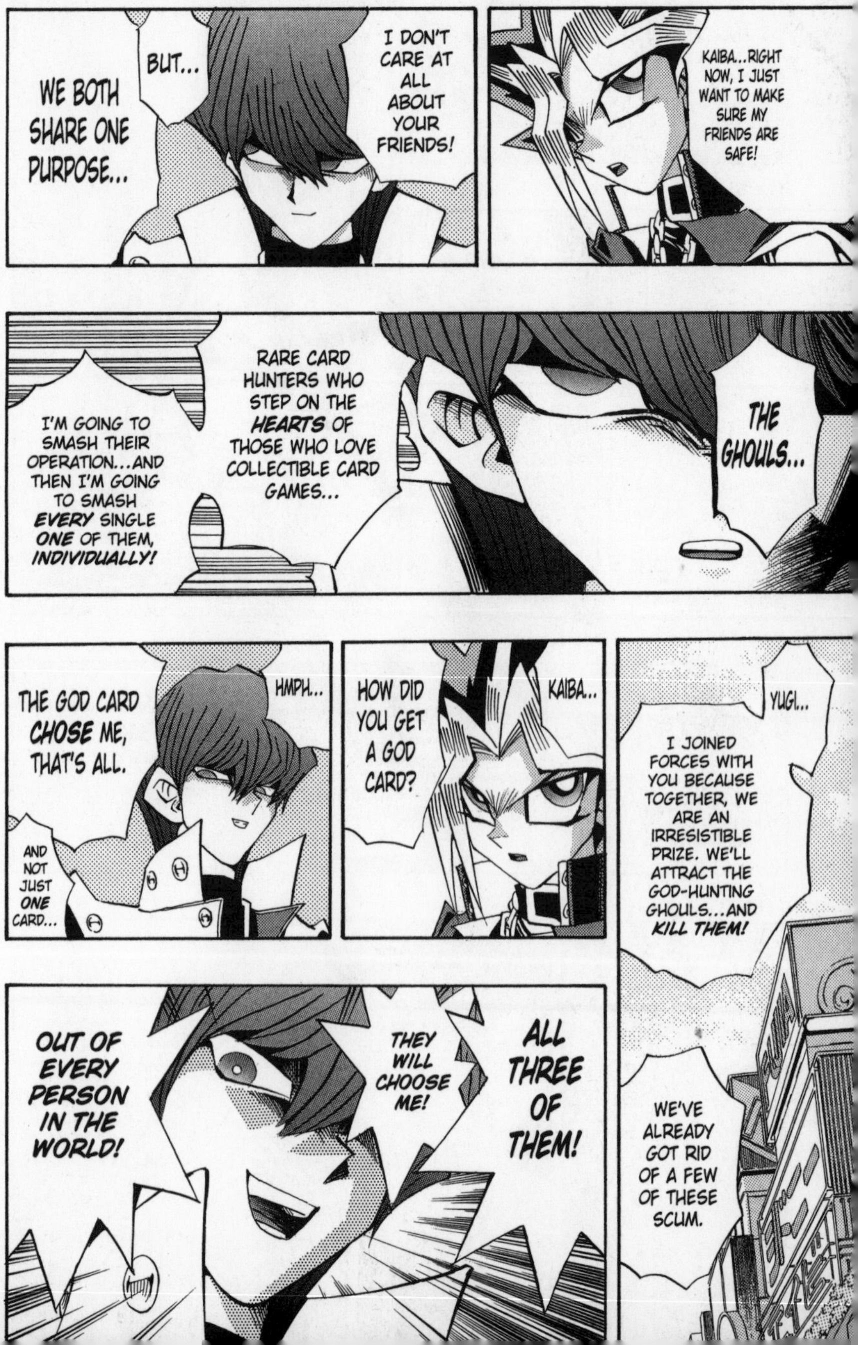
KAIBA...RIGHT NOW, I JUST WANT TO MAKE SURE MY FRIENDS ARE SAFE!
I DON'T CARE AT ALL ABOUT YOUR FRIENDS!
BUT...
WE BOTH SHARE ONE PURPOSE...
THE GHOULS...
RARE CARD HUNTERS WHO STEP ON THE *HEARTS* OF THOSE WHO LOVE COLLECTIBLE CARD GAMES...
I'M GOING TO SMASH THEIR OPERATION...AND THEN I'M GOING TO SMASH *EVERY* SINGLE *ONE* OF THEM, *INDIVIDUALLY!*
YUGI...
I JOINED FORCES WITH YOU BECAUSE TOGETHER, WE ARE AN IRRESISTIBLE PRIZE. WE'LL ATTRACT THE GOD-HUNTING GHOULS...AND *KILL THEM!*
WE'VE ALREADY GOT RID OF A FEW OF THESE SCUM.
KAIBA...
HOW DID YOU GET A GOD CARD?
HMPH...
THE GOD CARD *CHOSE* ME, THAT'S ALL.
AND NOT JUST *ONE* CARD...
ALL THREE OF THEM!
THEY WILL CHOOSE ME!
OUT OF EVERY PERSON IN THE WORLD!

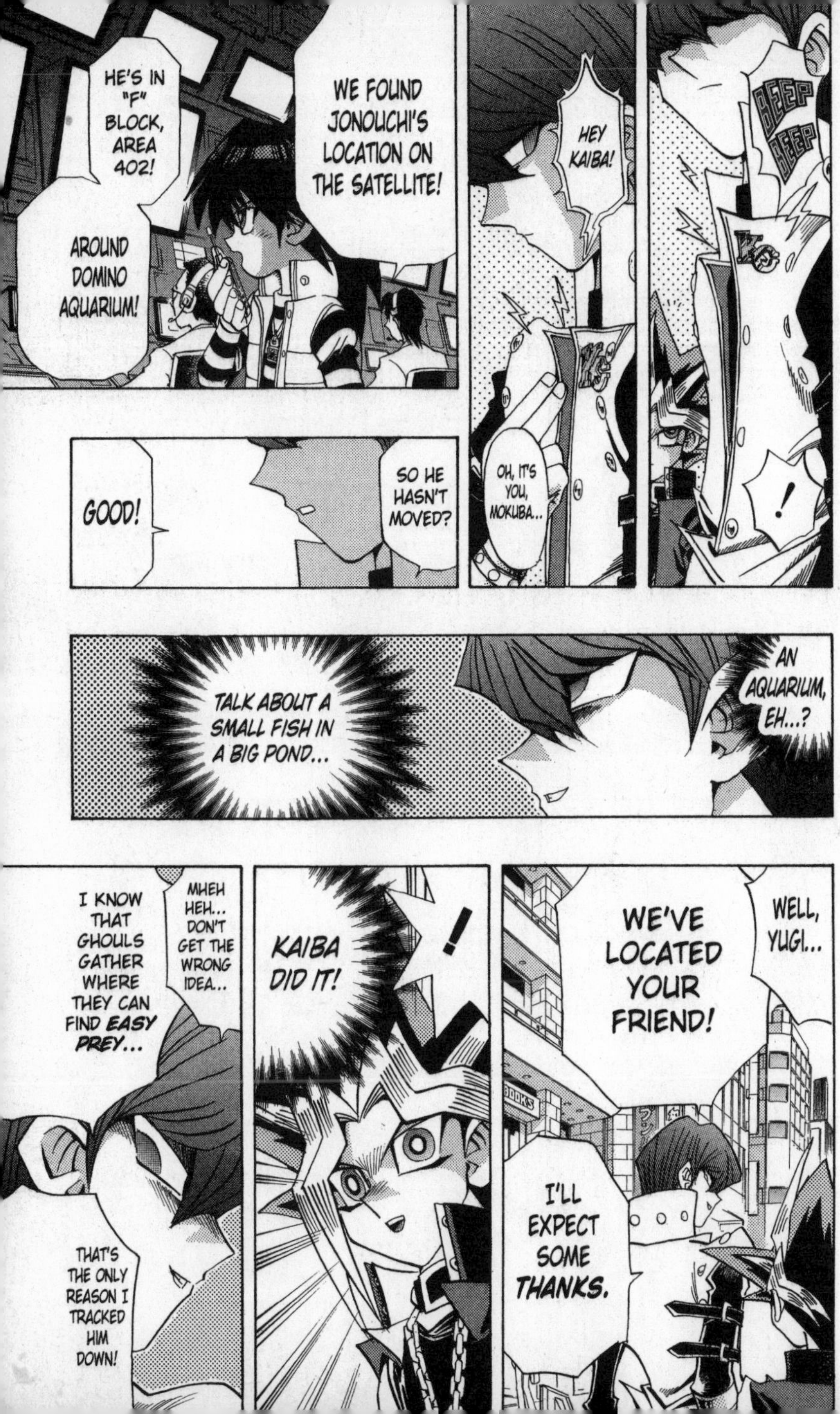
BEEP
BEEP
!
HEY KAIBA!
OH, IT'S YOU, MOKUBA...
WE FOUND JONOUCHI'S LOCATION ON THE SATELLITE!
HE'S IN "F" BLOCK, AREA 402!
AROUND DOMINO AQUARIUM!
SO HE HASN'T MOVED?
GOOD!
AN AQUARIUM, EH...?
TALK ABOUT A SMALL FISH IN A BIG POND...
WELL, YUGI...
WE'VE LOCATED YOUR FRIEND!
I'LL EXPECT SOME *THANKS.*
!
KAIBA DID IT!
MHEH HEH... DON'T GET THE WRONG IDEA...
I KNOW THAT GHOULS GATHER WHERE THEY CAN FIND ***EASY PREY...***
THAT'S THE ONLY REASON I TRACKED HIM DOWN!

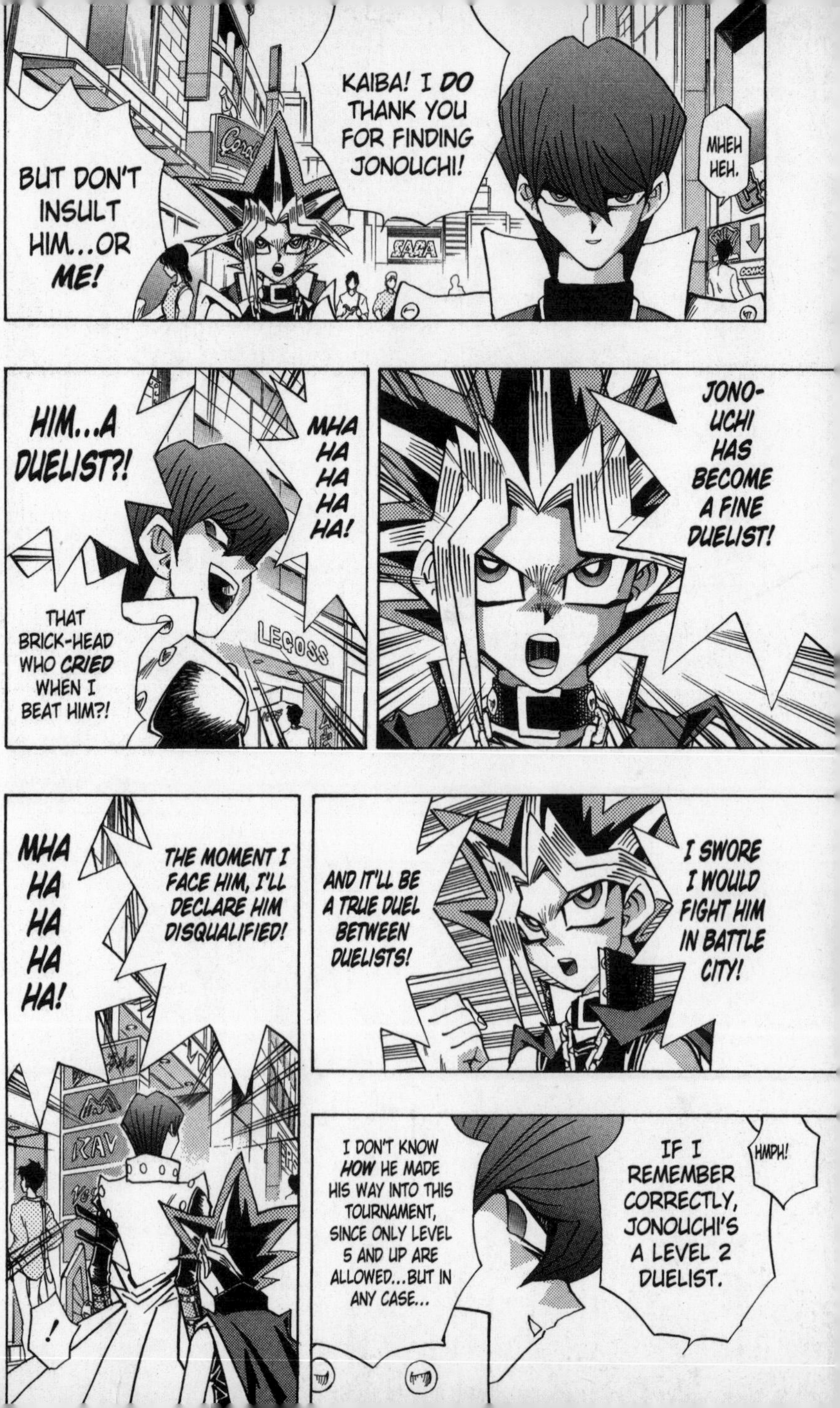
MHEH HEH.
KAIBA! I *DO* THANK YOU FOR FINDING JONOUCHI!
BUT DON'T INSULT HIM...OR *ME!*
JONOUCHI HAS BECOME A FINE DUELIST!
MHA HA HA HA HA!
HIM...A DUELIST?!
THAT BRICK-HEAD WHO *CRIED* WHEN I BEAT HIM?!
I SWORE I WOULD FIGHT HIM IN BATTLE CITY!
AND IT'LL BE A TRUE DUEL BETWEEN DUELISTS!
HMPH!
IF I REMEMBER CORRECTLY, JONOUCHI'S A LEVEL 2 DUELIST.
I DON'T KNOW *HOW* HE MADE HIS WAY INTO THIS TOURNAMENT, SINCE ONLY LEVEL 5 AND UP ARE ALLOWED...BUT IN ANY CASE...
THE MOMENT I FACE HIM, I'LL DECLARE HIM DISQUALIFIED!
MHA HA HA HA HA!
!

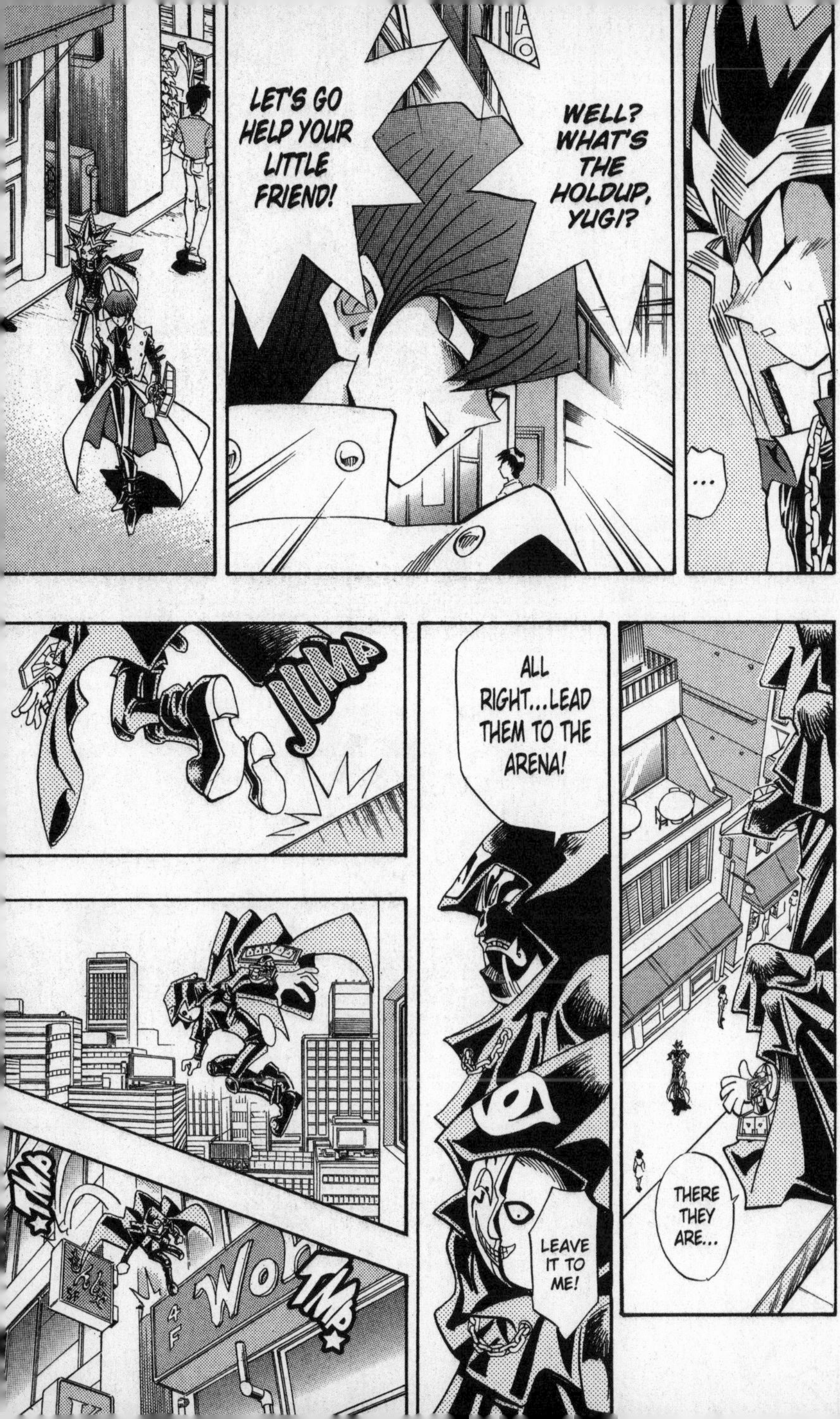
...
WELL? WHAT'S THE HOLDUP, YUGI?
LET'S GO HELP YOUR LITTLE FRIEND!
THERE THEY ARE...
ALL RIGHT...LEAD THEM TO THE ARENA!
LEAVE IT TO ME!
JUMP
TMP
TMP

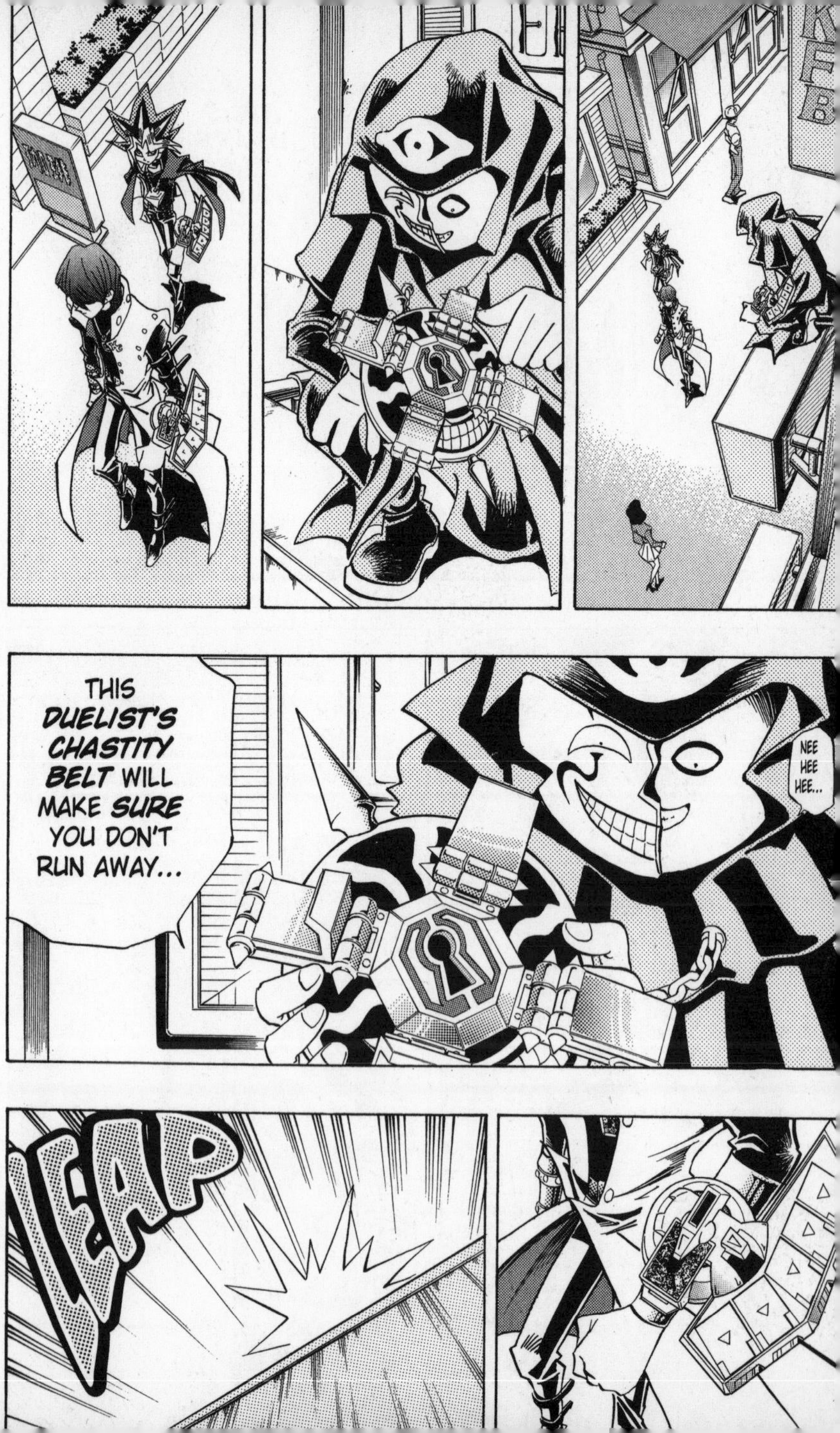
NEE HEE HEE...
THIS DUELIST'S CHASTITY BELT WILL MAKE SURE YOU DON'T RUN AWAY...
LEAP

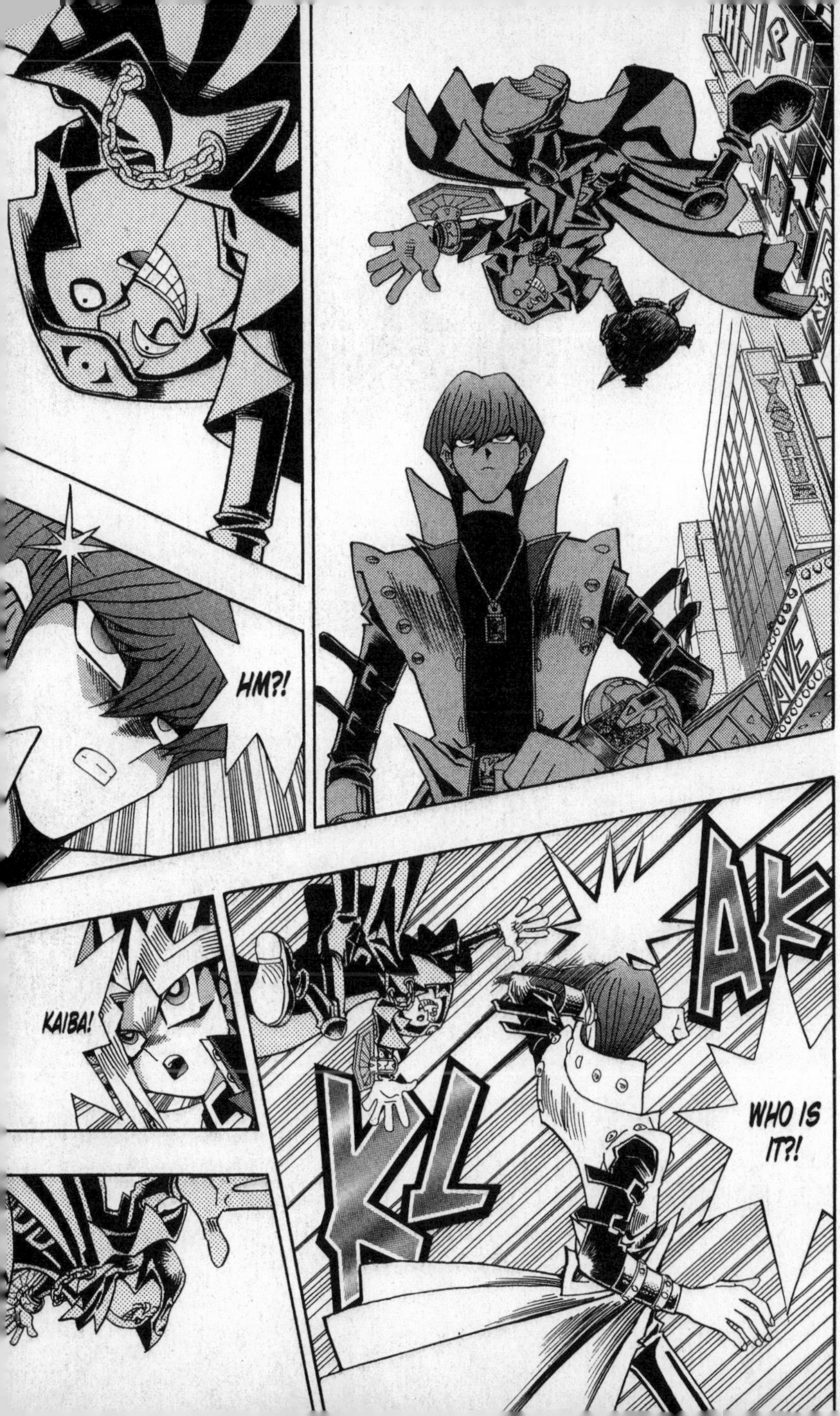
HM?!
WHO IS IT?!
KAIBA!

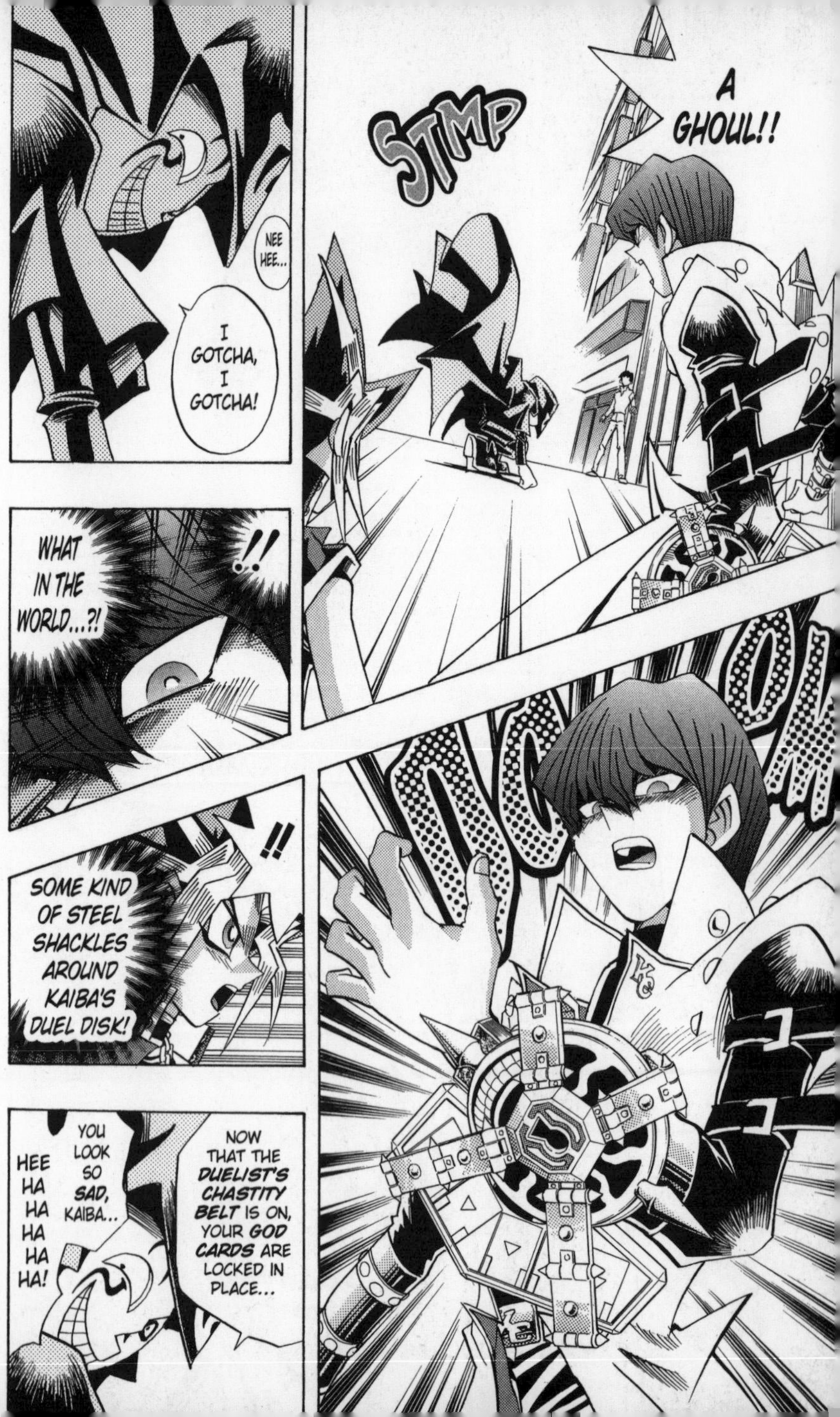

A GHOUL!!
STMP
NEE HEE...
I GOTCHA, I GOTCHA!
!!
WHAT IN THE WORLD...?!
!!
SOME KIND OF STEEL SHACKLES AROUND KAIBA'S DUEL DISK!
NOW THAT THE DUELIST'S CHASTITY BELT IS ON, YOUR GOD CARDS ARE LOCKED IN PLACE...
YOU LOOK SO SAD, KAIBA...
HEE HA HA HA HA HA!

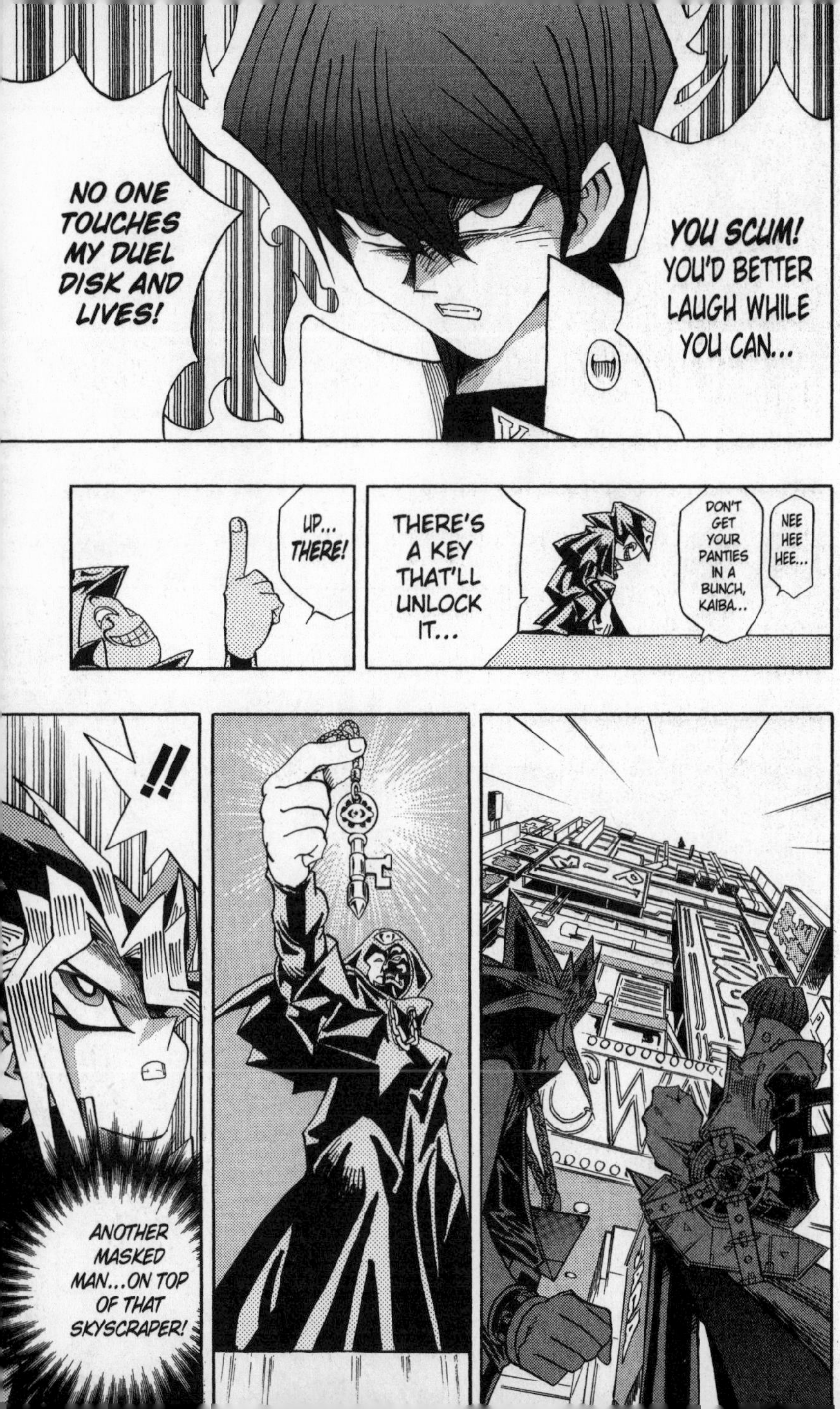
YOU SCUM! YOU'D BETTER LAUGH WHILE YOU CAN...
NO ONE TOUCHES MY DUEL DISK AND LIVES!
NEE HEE HEE...
DON'T GET YOUR PANTIES IN A BUNCH, KAIBA...
THERE'S A KEY THAT'LL UNLOCK IT...
UP... THERE!
!!
ANOTHER MASKED MAN...ON TOP OF THAT SKYSCRAPER!

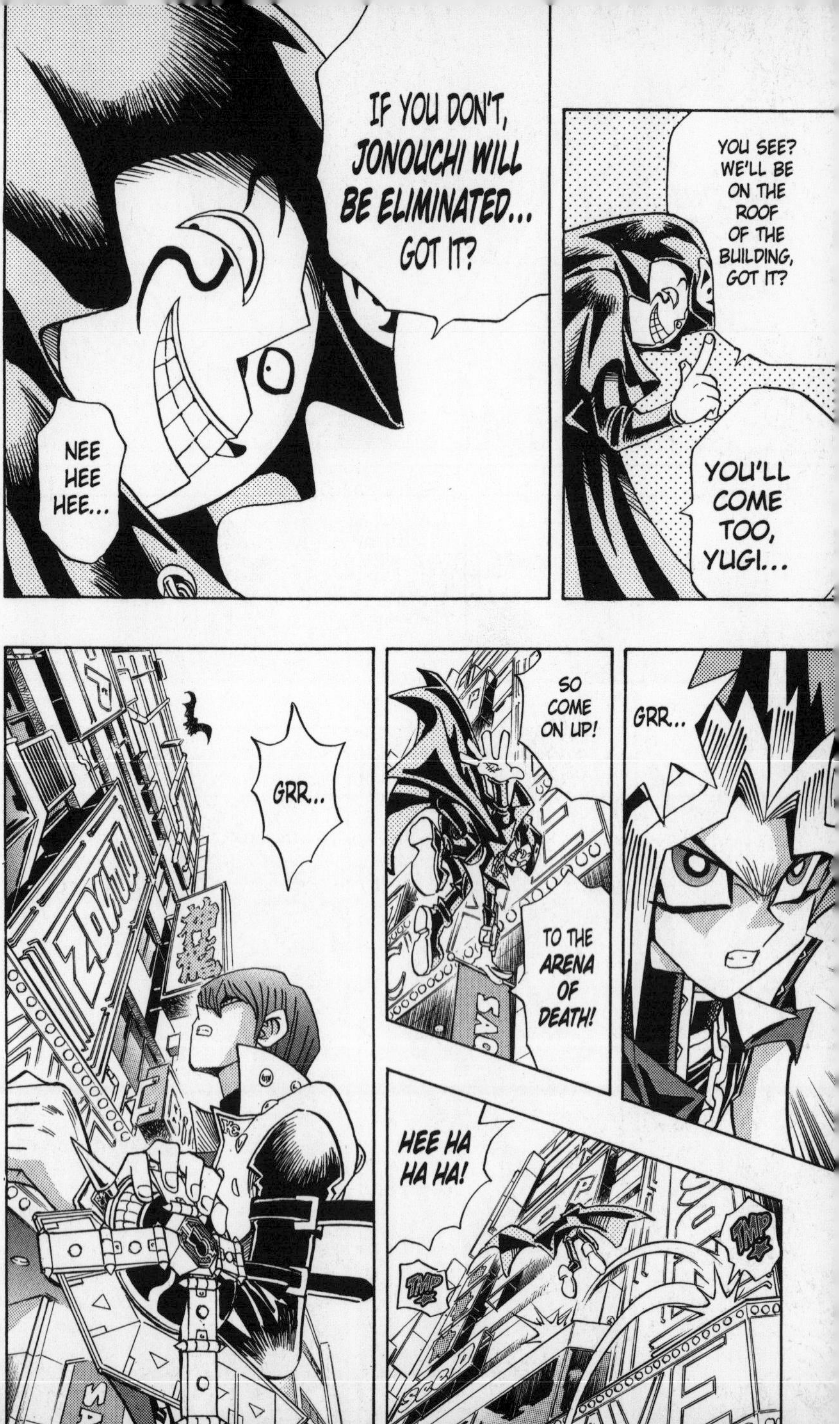
YOU SEE? WE'LL BE ON THE ROOF OF THE BUILDING, GOT IT?
YOU'LL COME TOO, YUGI...
IF YOU DON'T, JONOUCHI WILL BE ELIMINATED... GOT IT?
NEE HEE HEE...
GRR...
SO COME ON UP!
TO THE ARENA OF DEATH!
HEE HA HA HA!
TMP
TMP
GRR...

YES!

YUGI! WE HAVE NO CHOICE!

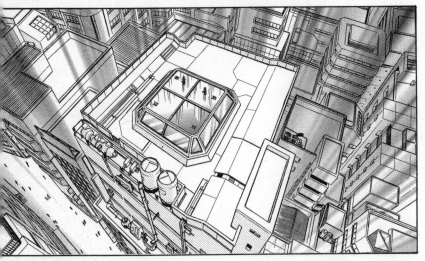

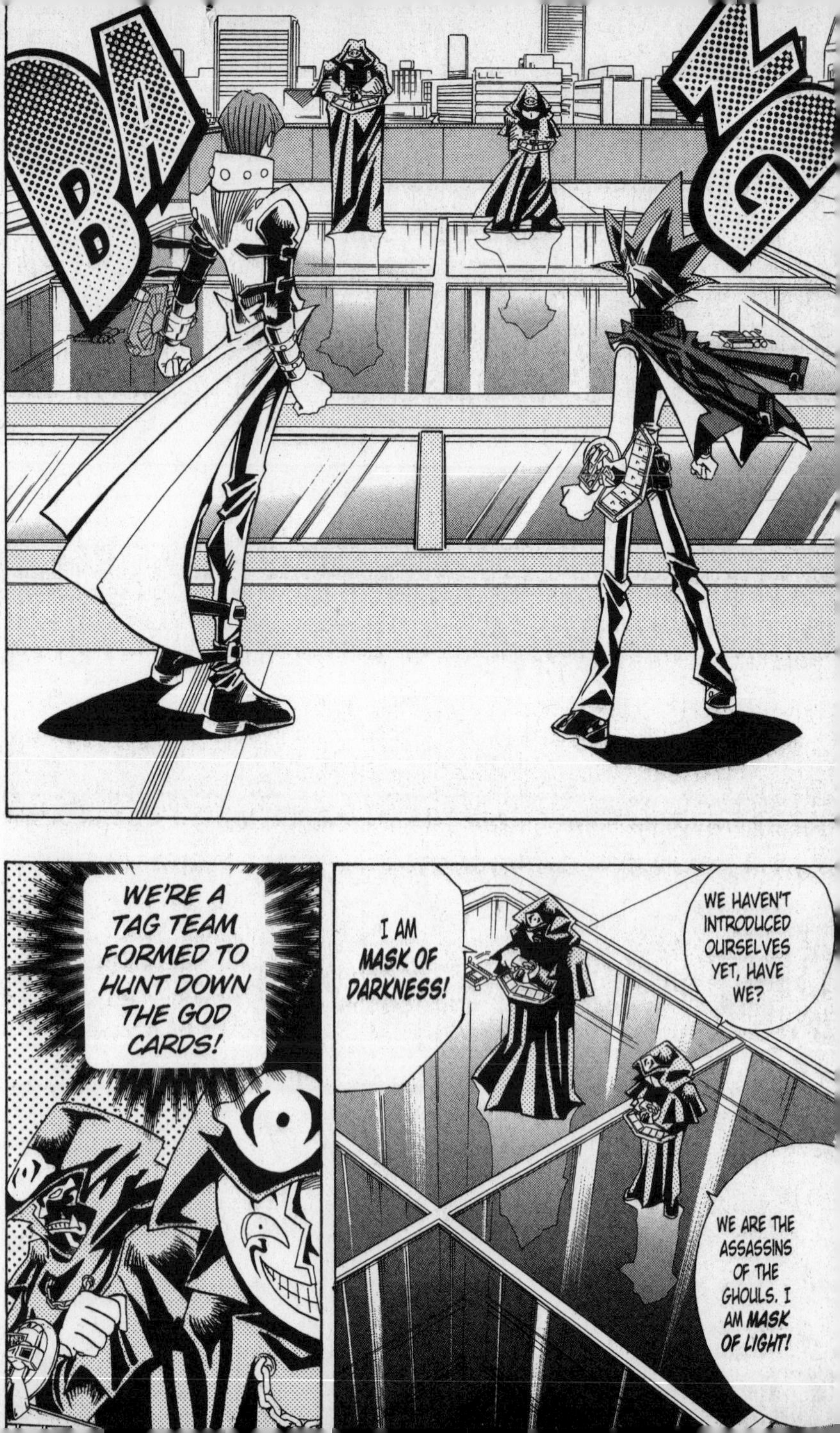
WE HAVEN'T INTRODUCED OURSELVES YET, HAVE WE?
WE ARE THE ASSASSINS OF THE GHOULS. I AM MASK OF LIGHT!
I AM MASK OF DARKNESS!
WE'RE A TAG TEAM FORMED TO HUNT DOWN THE GOD CARDS!

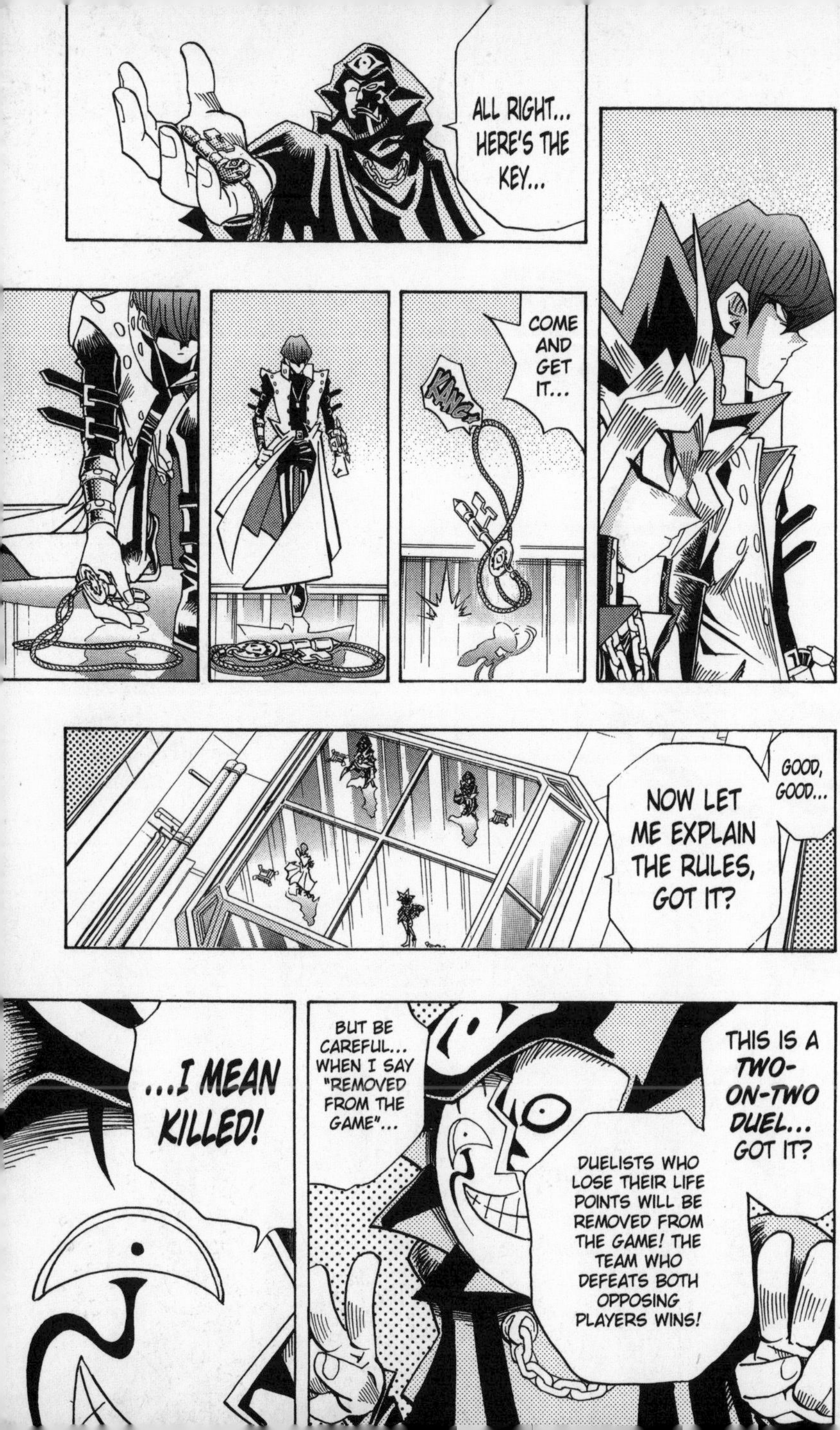
ALL RIGHT... HERE'S THE KEY...
COME AND GET IT...
KANG
GOOD, GOOD...
NOW LET ME EXPLAIN THE RULES, GOT IT?
THIS IS A TWO-ON-TWO DUEL... GOT IT?
DUELISTS WHO LOSE THEIR LIFE POINTS WILL BE REMOVED FROM THE GAME! THE TEAM WHO DEFEATS BOTH OPPOSING PLAYERS WINS!
BUT BE CAREFUL... WHEN I SAY "REMOVED FROM THE GAME"...
...I MEAN KILLED!

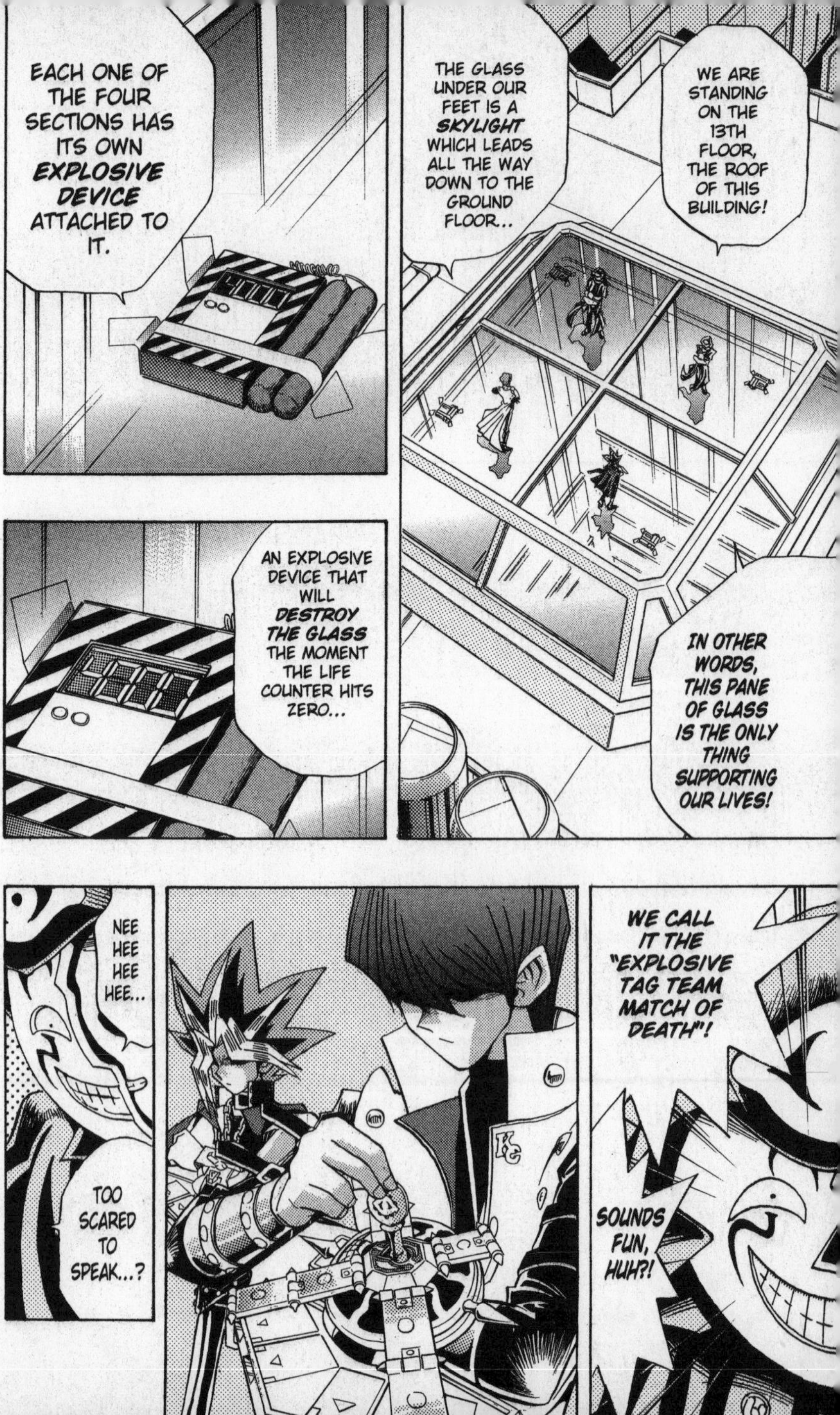
WE ARE STANDING ON THE 13TH FLOOR, THE ROOF OF THIS BUILDING!
THE GLASS UNDER OUR FEET IS A ***SKYLIGHT*** WHICH LEADS ALL THE WAY DOWN TO THE GROUND FLOOR...
IN OTHER WORDS, THIS PANE OF GLASS IS THE ONLY THING SUPPORTING OUR LIVES!
EACH ONE OF THE FOUR SECTIONS HAS ITS OWN ***EXPLOSIVE DEVICE*** ATTACHED TO IT.
AN EXPLOSIVE DEVICE THAT WILL ***DESTROY THE GLASS*** THE MOMENT THE LIFE COUNTER HITS ZERO...
WE CALL IT THE "EXPLOSIVE TAG TEAM MATCH OF DEATH"!
SOUNDS FUN, HUH?!
NEE HEE HEE HEE...
TOO SCARED TO SPEAK...?

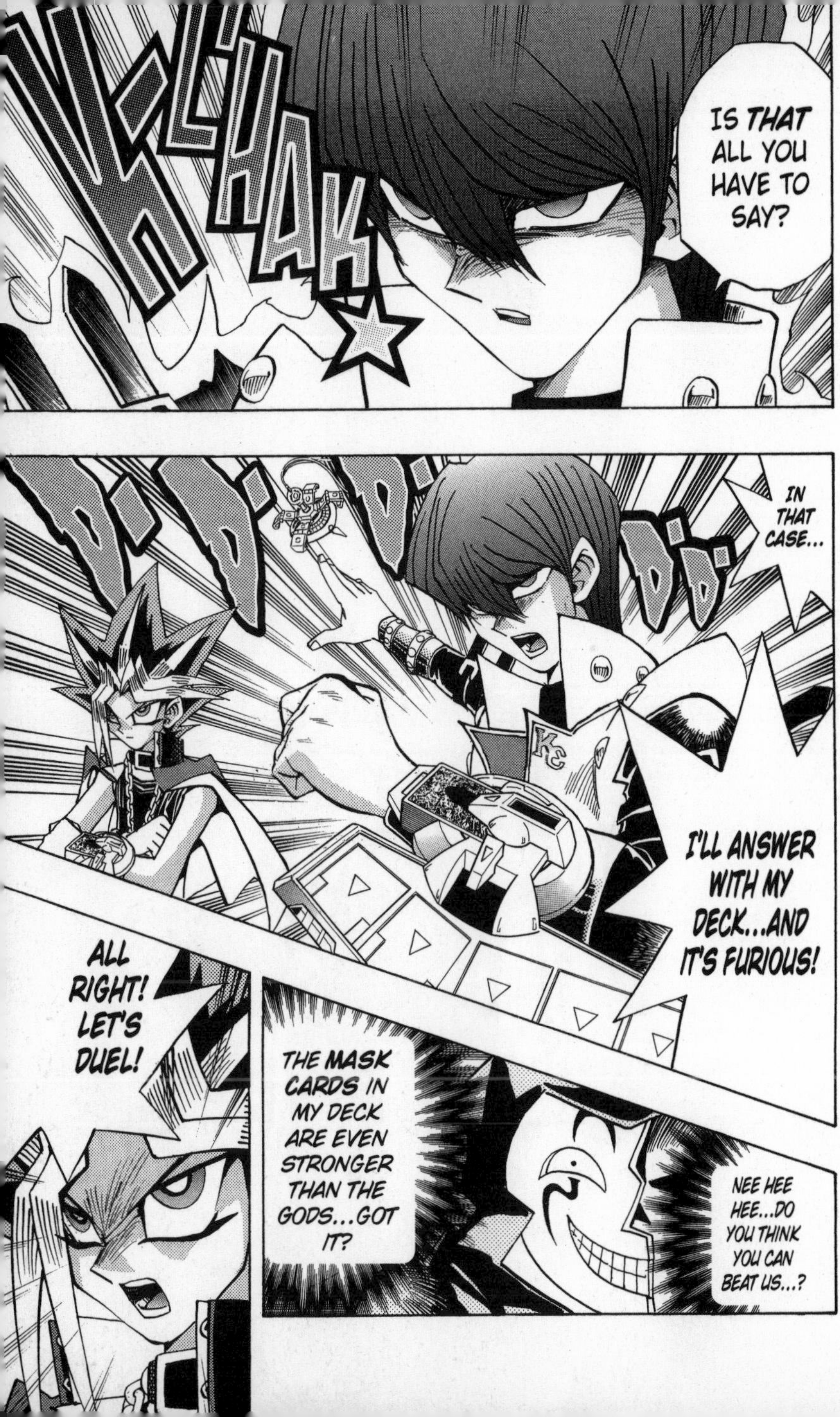
IS THAT ALL YOU HAVE TO SAY?
IN THAT CASE...
I'LL ANSWER WITH MY DECK...AND IT'S FURIOUS!
NEE HEE HEE...DO YOU THINK YOU CAN BEAT US...?
THE MASK CARDS IN MY DECK ARE EVEN STRONGER THAN THE GODS...GOT IT?
ALL RIGHT! LET'S DUEL!

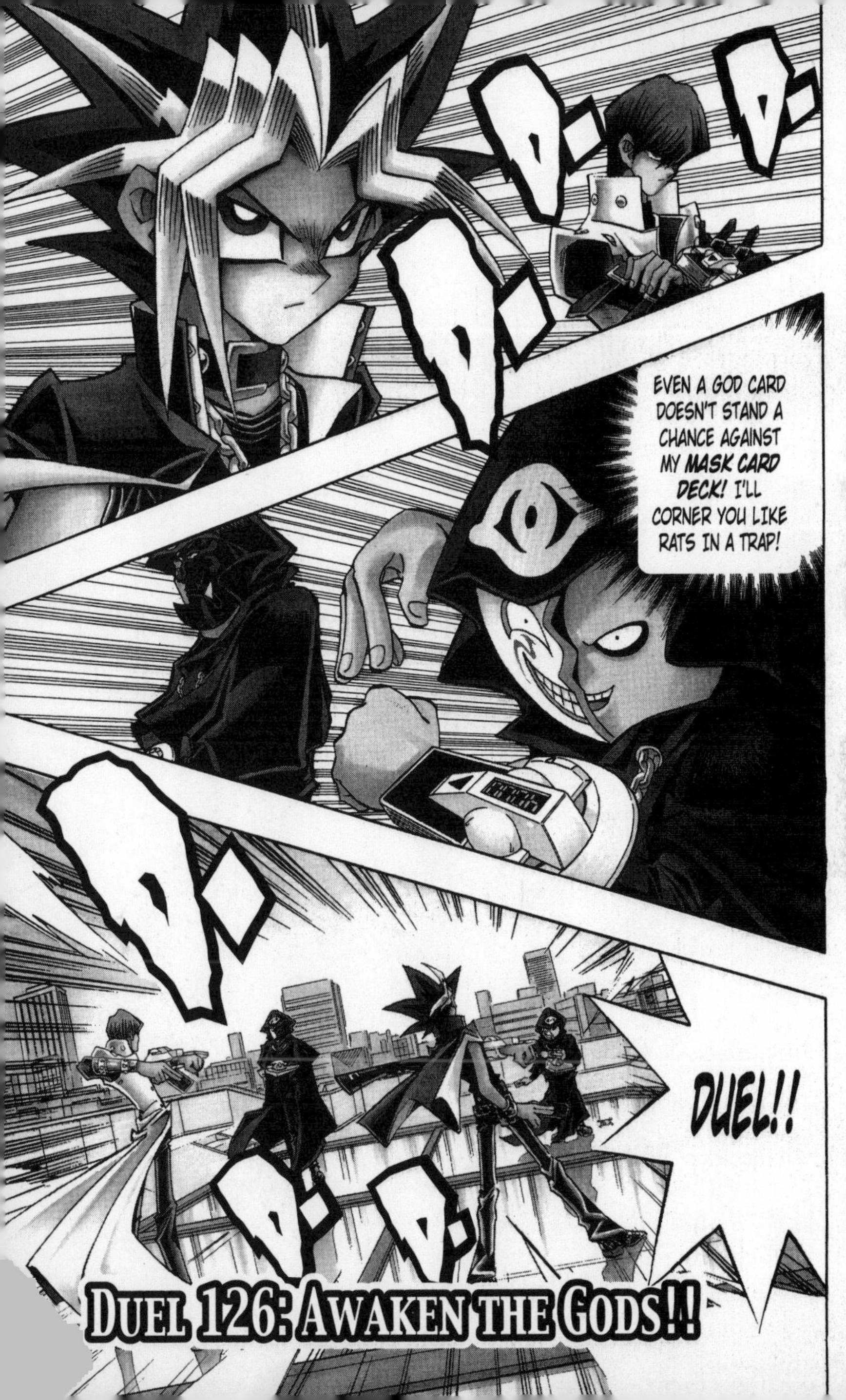
D D D D
EVEN A GOD CARD DOESN'T STAND A CHANCE AGAINST MY MASK CARD DECK! I'LL CORNER YOU LIKE RATS IN A TRAP!
D D
DUEL!!
D D

Duel 126: Awaken the Gods!!

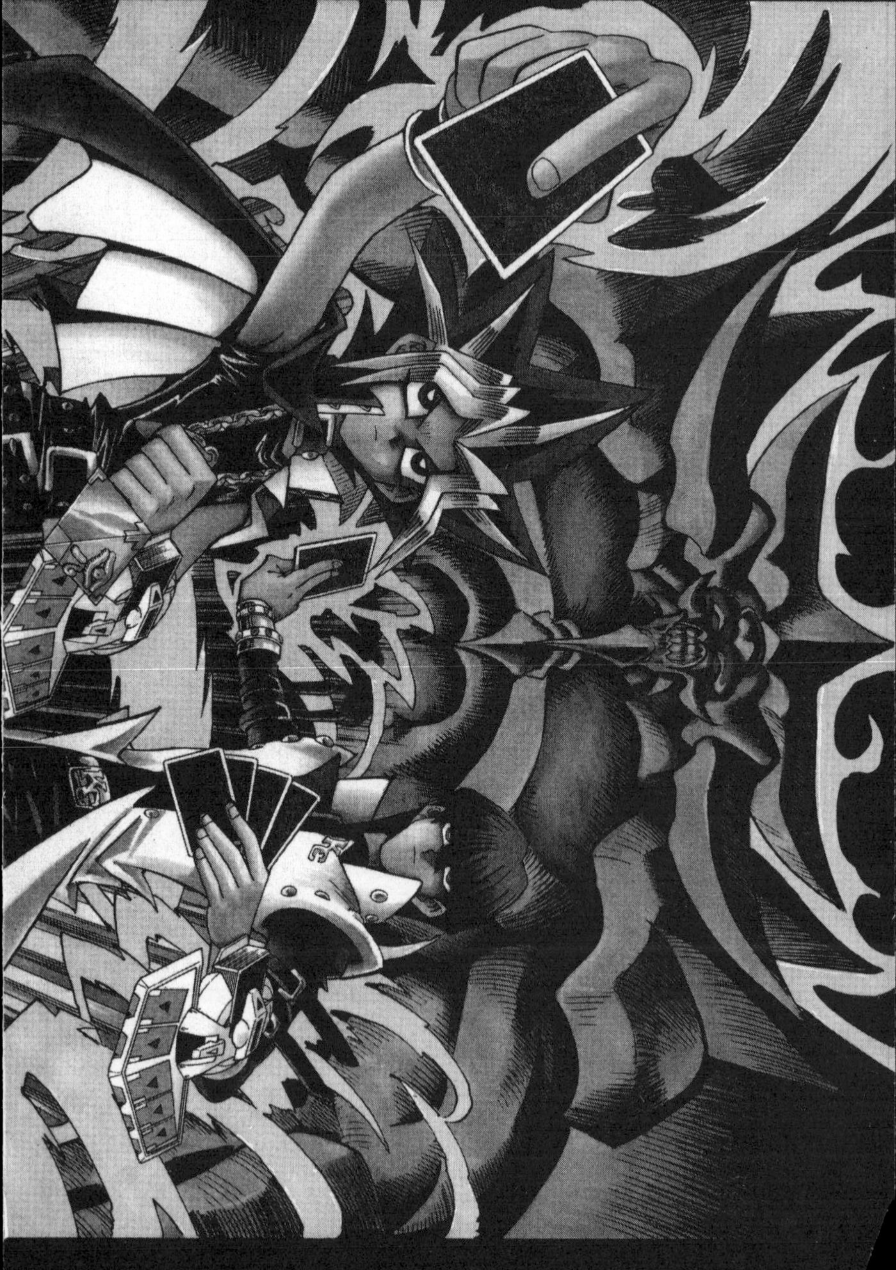

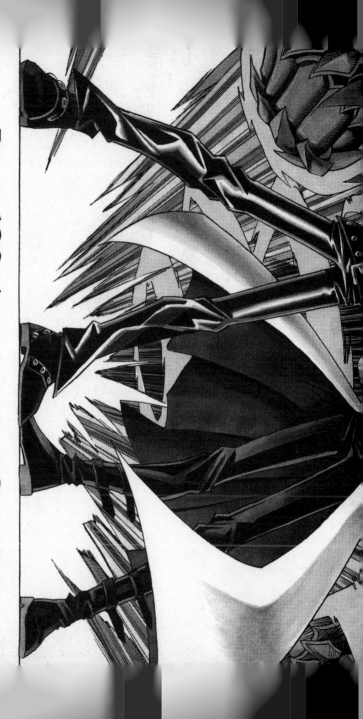

DUEL 126: AWAKEN THE GODS!!

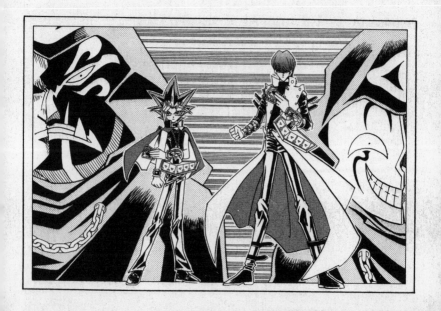

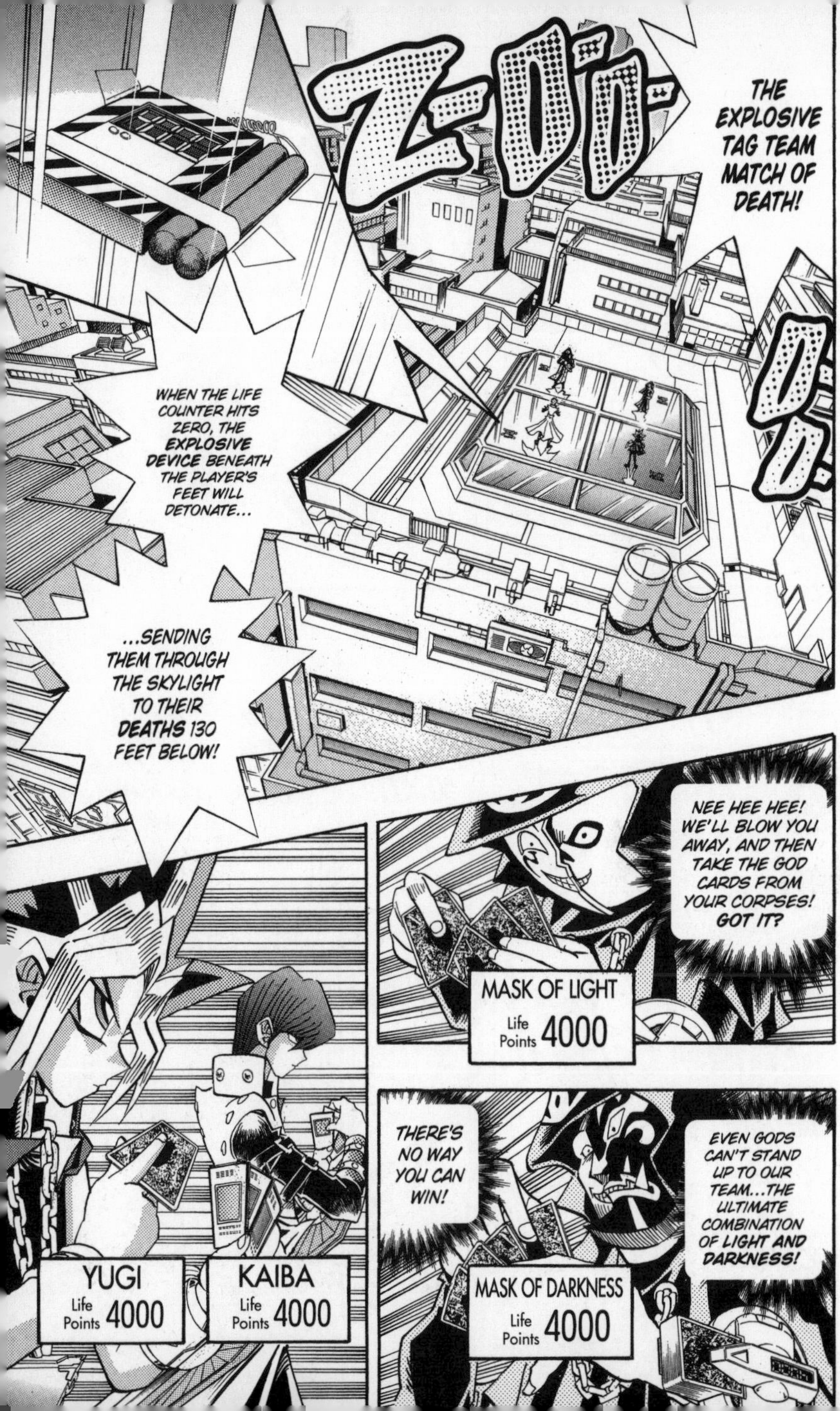
THE EXPLOSIVE TAG TEAM MATCH OF DEATH!
WHEN THE LIFE COUNTER HITS ZERO, THE **EXPLOSIVE DEVICE** BENEATH THE PLAYER'S FEET WILL DETONATE...
...SENDING THEM THROUGH THE SKYLIGHT TO THEIR **DEATHS** 130 FEET BELOW!
NEE HEE HEE! WE'LL BLOW YOU AWAY, AND THEN TAKE THE GOD CARDS FROM YOUR CORPSES! **GOT IT?**
MASK OF LIGHT Life Points 4000
EVEN GODS CAN'T STAND UP TO OUR TEAM...THE ULTIMATE COMBINATION OF **LIGHT AND DARKNESS!**
THERE'S NO WAY YOU CAN WIN!
MASK OF DARKNESS Life Points 4000
KAIBA Life Points 4000
YUGI Life Points 4000

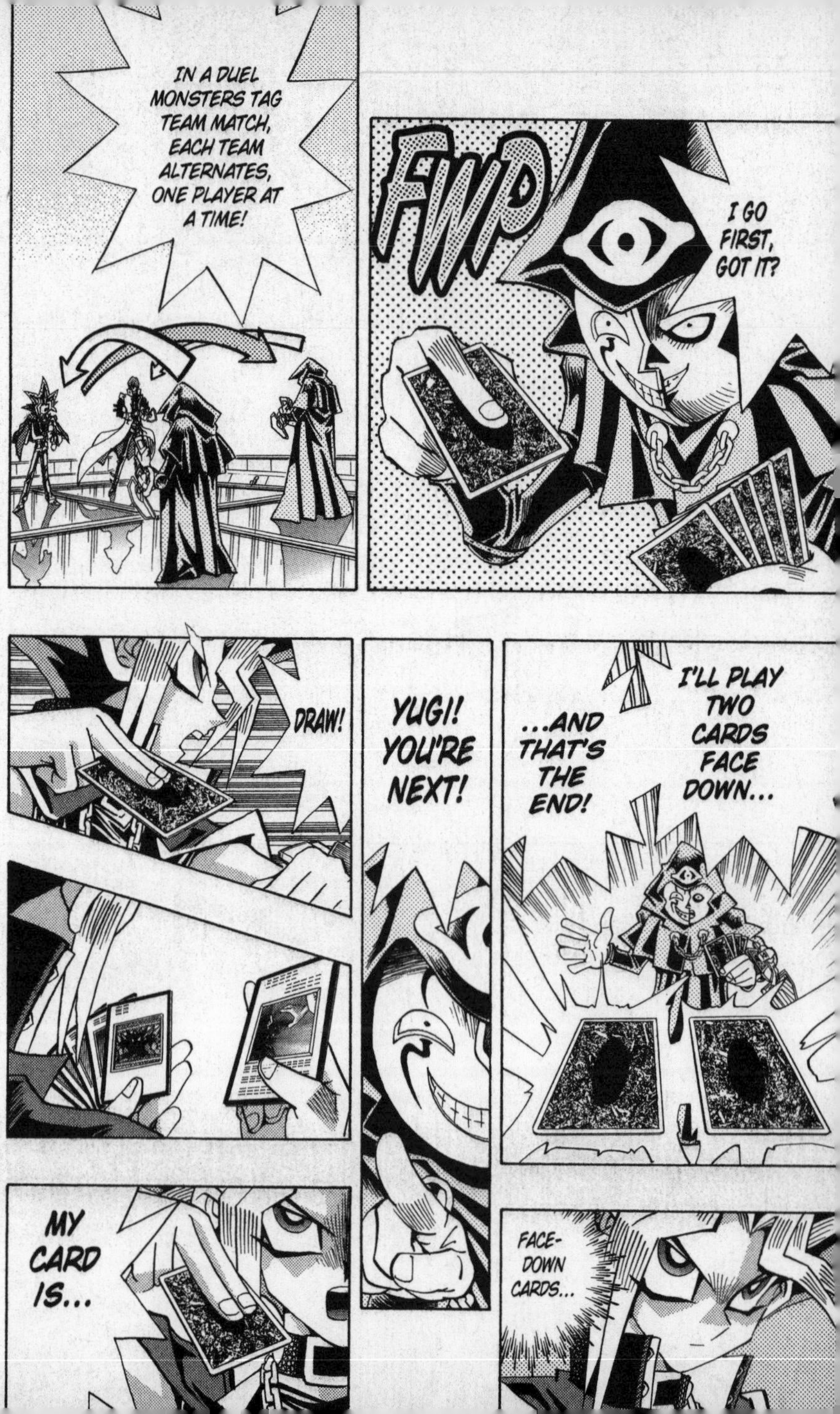
FWP
I GO FIRST, GOT IT?
IN A DUEL MONSTERS TAG TEAM MATCH, EACH TEAM ALTERNATES, ONE PLAYER AT A TIME!
I'LL PLAY TWO CARDS FACE DOWN...
...AND THAT'S THE END!
FACE-DOWN CARDS...
YUGI! YOU'RE NEXT!
DRAW!
MY CARD IS...

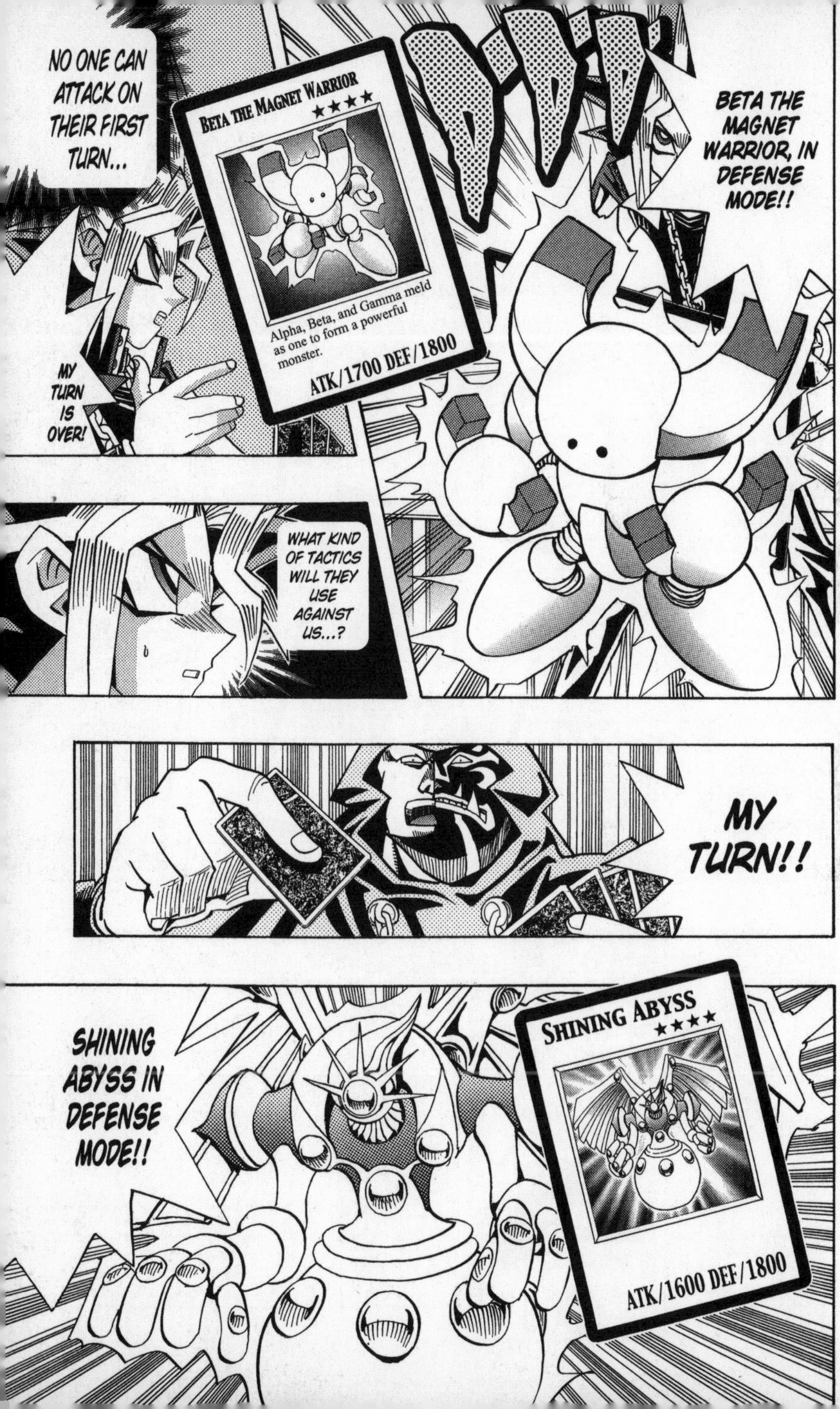
BETA THE MAGNET WARRIOR, IN DEFENSE MODE!!
Beta the Magnet Warrior
Alpha, Beta, and Gamma meld as one to form a powerful monster.
ATK/1700 DEF/1800
NO ONE CAN ATTACK ON THEIR FIRST TURN...
MY TURN IS OVER!
WHAT KIND OF TACTICS WILL THEY USE AGAINST US...?
MY TURN!!
SHINING ABYSS IN DEFENSE MODE!!
Shining Abyss
ATK/1600 DEF/1800

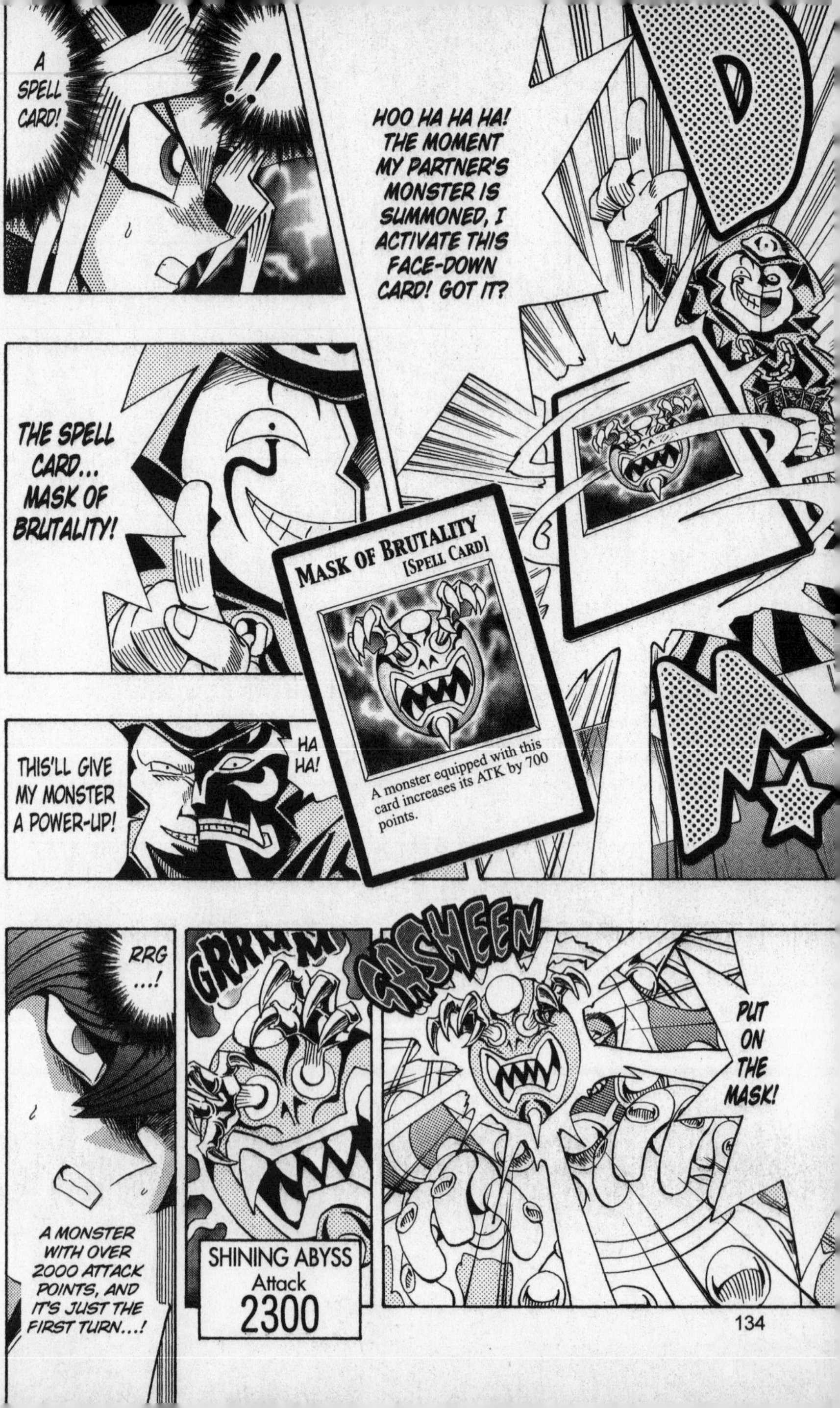
HOO HA HA HA! THE MOMENT MY PARTNER'S MONSTER IS SUMMONED, I ACTIVATE THIS FACE-DOWN CARD! GOT IT?
MASK OF BRUTALITY
[SPELL CARD]
A monster equipped with this card increases its ATK by 700 points.
!!
A SPELL CARD!
THE SPELL CARD... MASK OF BRUTALITY!
HA HA!
THIS'LL GIVE MY MONSTER A POWER-UP!
GASHEEN
PUT ON THE MASK!
GRRMM
SHINING ABYSS
Attack
2300
RRG...!
A MONSTER WITH OVER 2000 ATTACK POINTS, AND IT'S JUST THE FIRST TURN...!

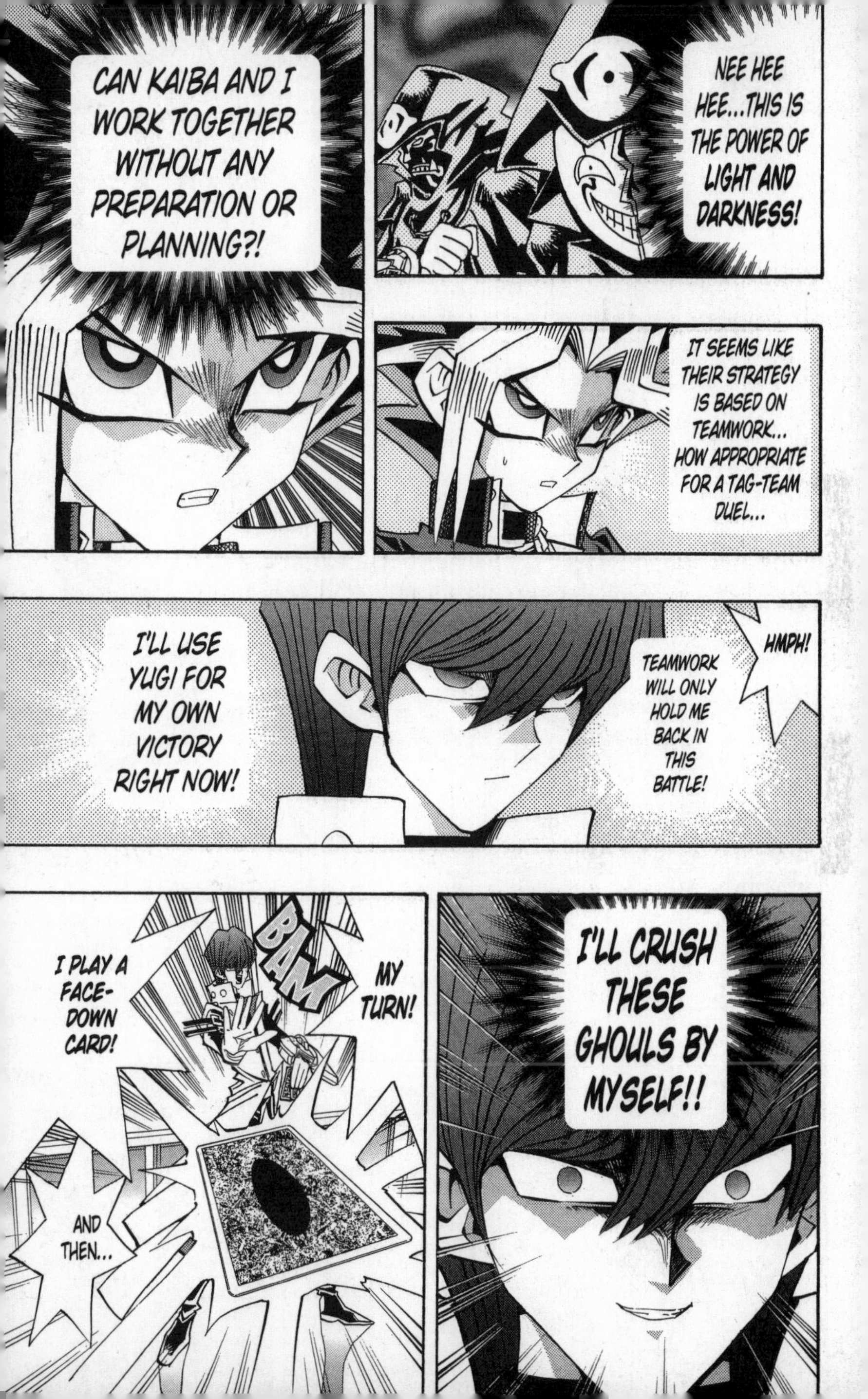
NEE HEE HEE...THIS IS THE POWER OF LIGHT AND DARKNESS!
IT SEEMS LIKE THEIR STRATEGY IS BASED ON TEAMWORK... HOW APPROPRIATE FOR A TAG-TEAM DUEL...
CAN KAIBA AND I WORK TOGETHER WITHOUT ANY PREPARATION OR PLANNING?!
HMPH!
TEAMWORK WILL ONLY HOLD ME BACK IN THIS BATTLE!
I'LL USE YUGI FOR MY OWN VICTORY RIGHT NOW!
I'LL CRUSH THESE GHOULS BY MYSELF!!
BAM
MY TURN!
I PLAY A FACE-DOWN CARD!
AND THEN...

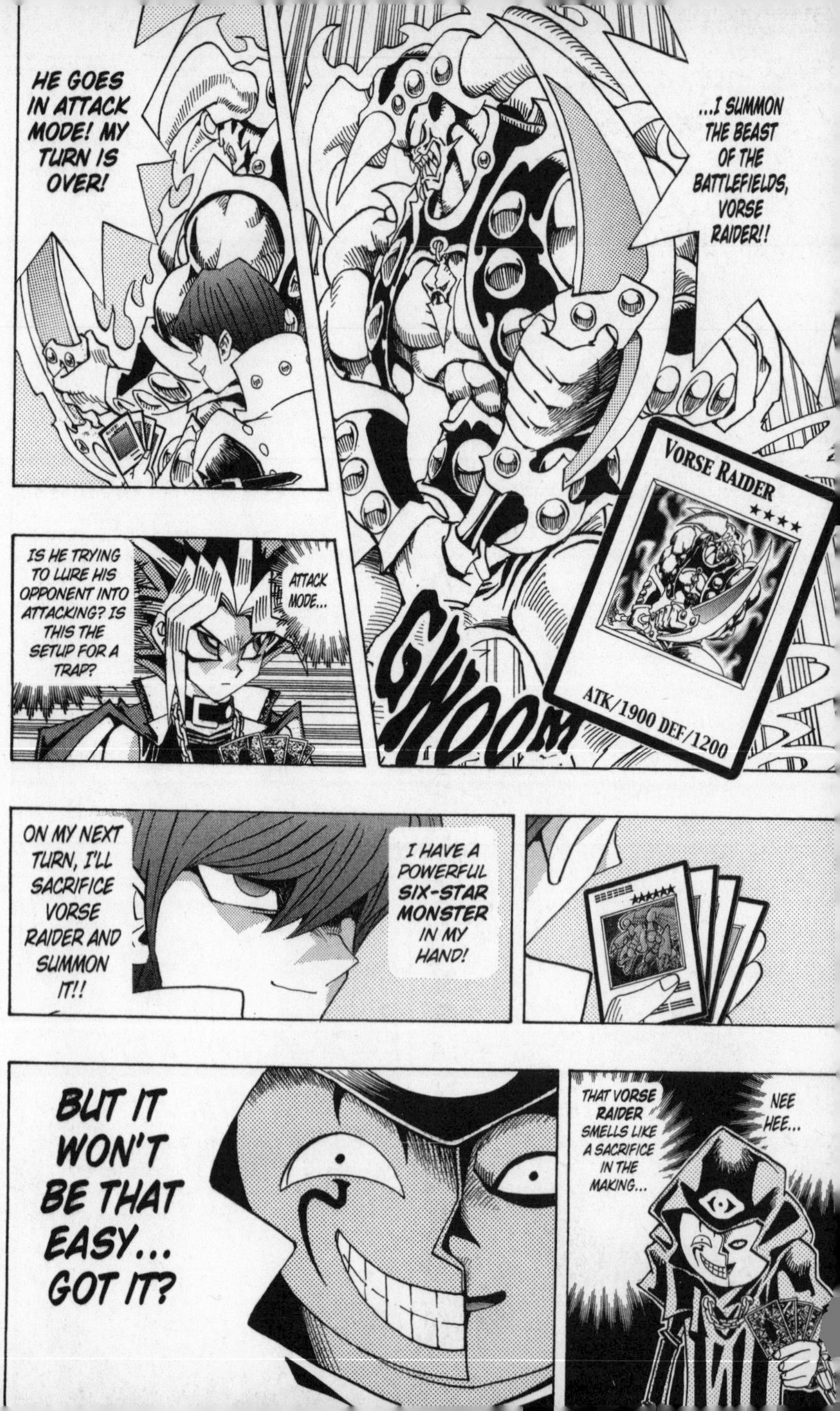
...I SUMMON THE BEAST OF THE BATTLEFIELDS, VORSE RAIDER!!
VORSE RAIDER
ATK/1900 DEF/1200
GWOOM
HE GOES IN ATTACK MODE! MY TURN IS OVER!
ATTACK MODE...
IS HE TRYING TO LURE HIS OPPONENT INTO ATTACKING? IS THIS THE SETUP FOR A TRAP?
I HAVE A POWERFUL SIX-STAR MONSTER IN MY HAND!
ON MY NEXT TURN, I'LL SACRIFICE VORSE RAIDER AND SUMMON IT!!
NEE HEE...
THAT VORSE RAIDER SMELLS LIKE A SACRIFICE IN THE MAKING...
BUT IT WON'T BE THAT EASY... GOT IT?

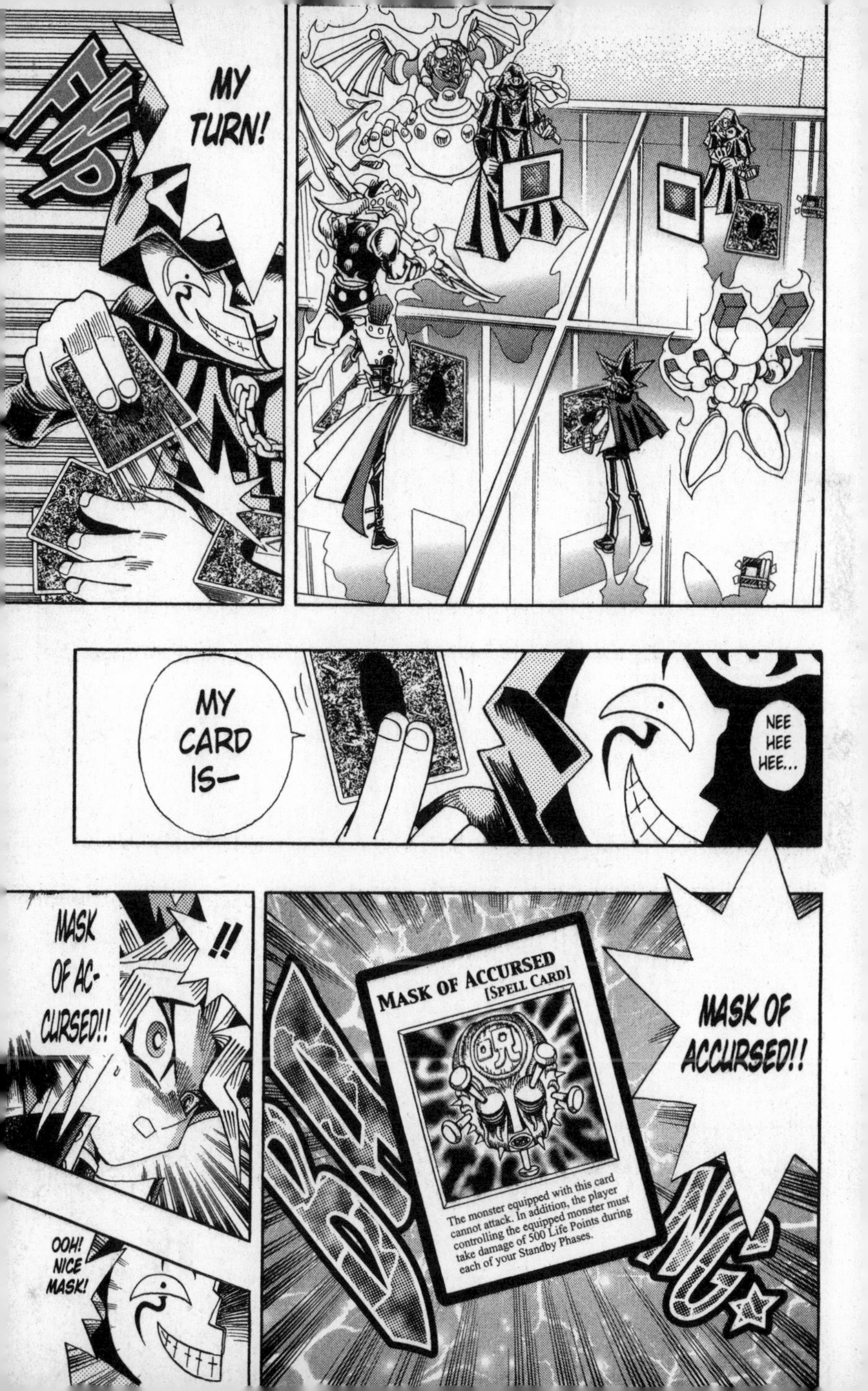
FWP
MY TURN!
NEE HEE HEE...
MY CARD IS—
MASK OF ACCURSED!!
MASK OF ACCURSED
[SPELL CARD]
The monster equipped with this card cannot attack. In addition, the player controlling the equipped monster must take damage of 500 Life Points during each of your Standby Phases.
!!
MASK OF AC-CURSED!!
OOH! NICE MASK!

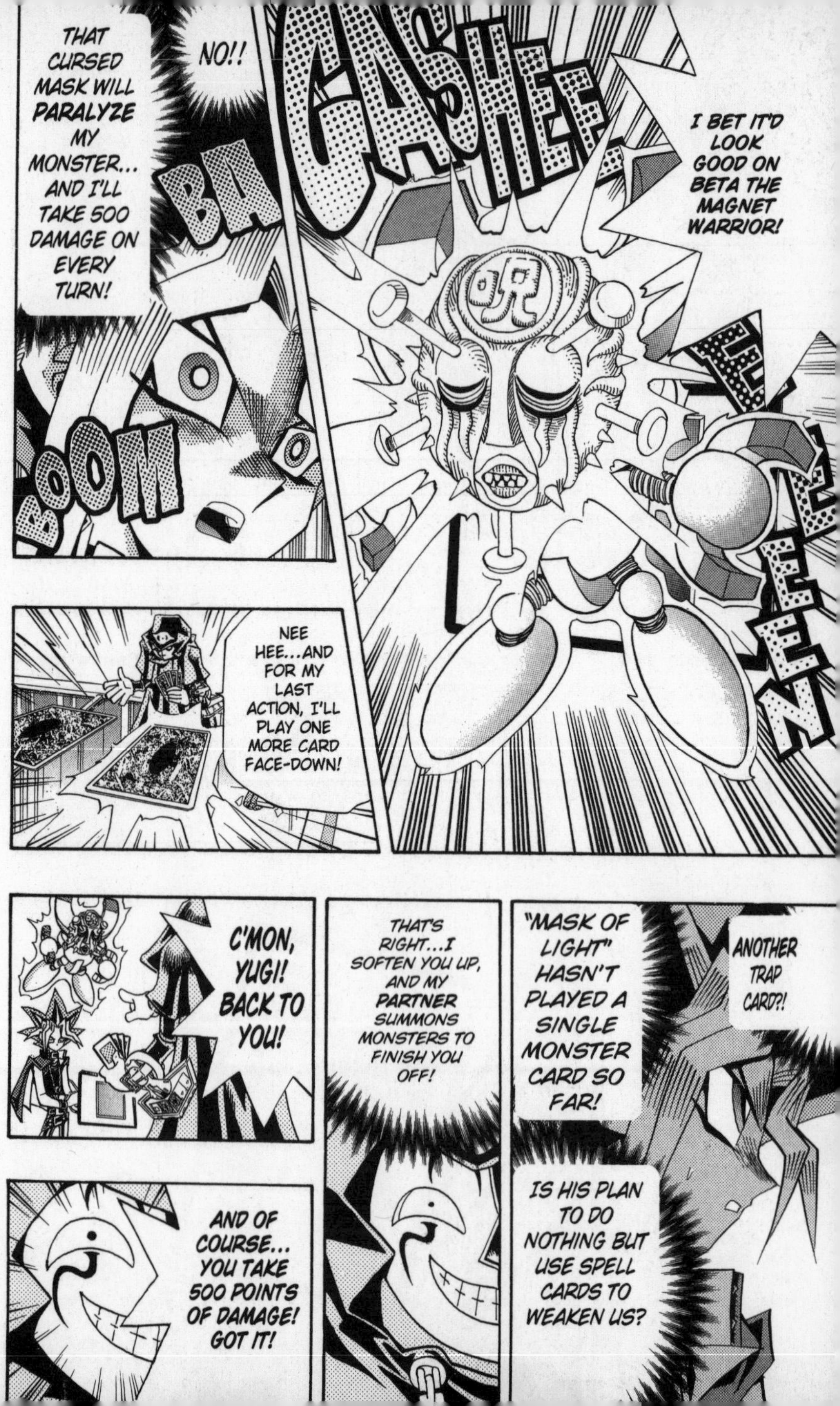
I BET IT'D LOOK GOOD ON BETA THE MAGNET WARRIOR!
NO!!
THAT CURSED MASK WILL PARALYZE MY MONSTER... AND I'LL TAKE 500 DAMAGE ON EVERY TURN!
BA
BOOM
NEE HEE...AND FOR MY LAST ACTION, I'LL PLAY ONE MORE CARD FACE-DOWN!
ANOTHER TRAP CARD?!
"MASK OF LIGHT" HASN'T PLAYED A SINGLE MONSTER CARD SO FAR!
THAT'S RIGHT...I SOFTEN YOU UP, AND MY PARTNER SUMMONS MONSTERS TO FINISH YOU OFF!
C'MON, YUGI! BACK TO YOU!
IS HIS PLAN TO DO NOTHING BUT USE SPELL CARDS TO WEAKEN US?
AND OF COURSE... YOU TAKE 500 POINTS OF DAMAGE! GOT IT!

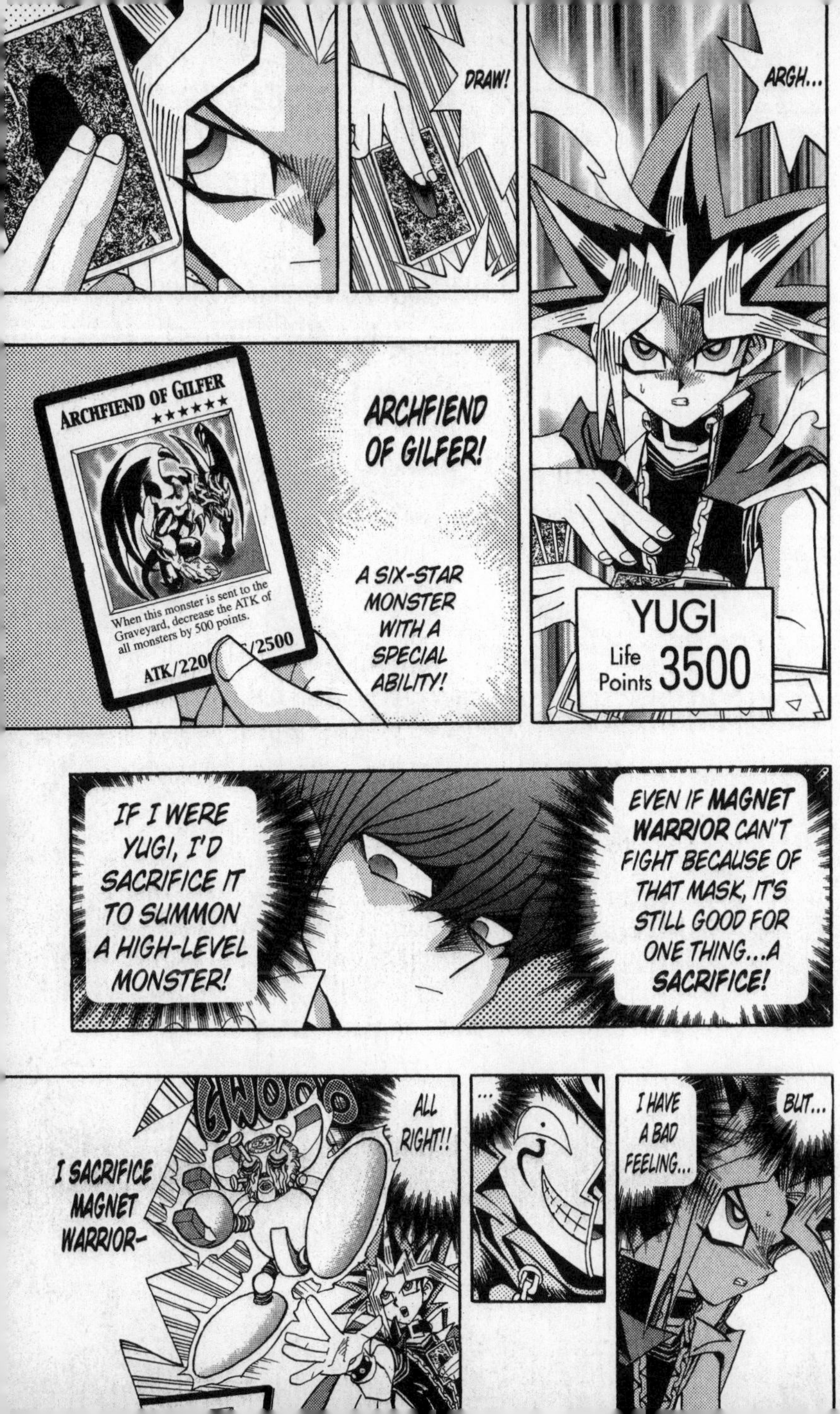
ARGH...
YUGI
Life Points 3500
DRAW!
ARCHFIEND OF GILFER
When this monster is sent to the Graveyard, decrease the ATK of all monsters by 500 points.
ATK/220
/2500
ARCHFIEND OF GILFER!
A SIX-STAR MONSTER WITH A SPECIAL ABILITY!
EVEN IF MAGNET WARRIOR CAN'T FIGHT BECAUSE OF THAT MASK, IT'S STILL GOOD FOR ONE THING...A SACRIFICE!
IF I WERE YUGI, I'D SACRIFICE IT TO SUMMON A HIGH-LEVEL MONSTER!
BUT...
I HAVE A BAD FEELING...
...
ALL RIGHT!!
I SACRIFICE MAGNET WARRIOR-

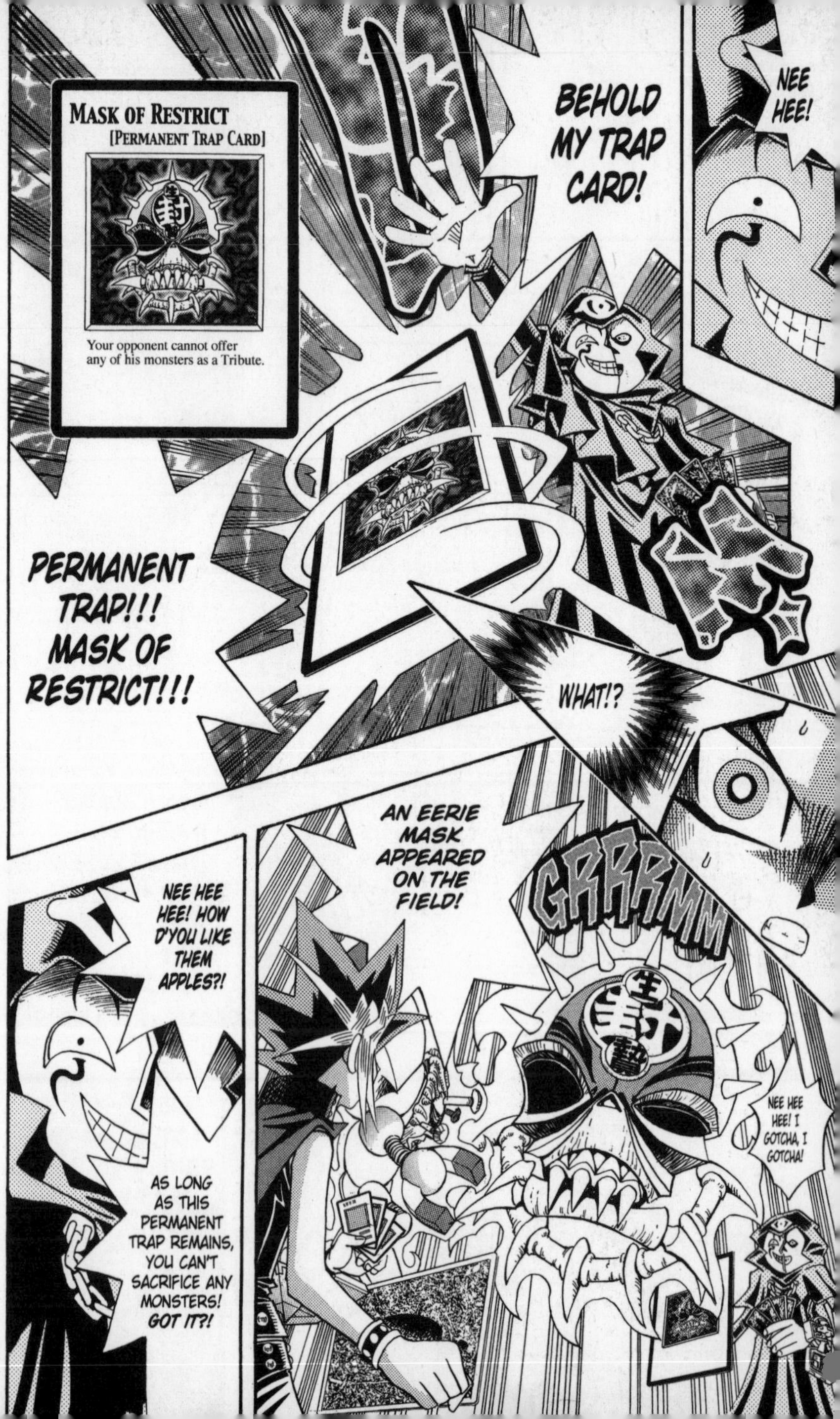
NEE HEE!
BEHOLD MY TRAP CARD!
MASK OF RESTRICT
[PERMANENT TRAP CARD]
Your opponent cannot offer any of his monsters as a Tribute.
PERMANENT TRAP!!! MASK OF RESTRICT!!!
WHAT!?
AN EERIE MASK APPEARED ON THE FIELD!
GRRRMM
NEE HEE HEE! I GOTCHA, I GOTCHA!
NEE HEE HEE! HOW D'YOU LIKE THEM APPLES?!
AS LONG AS THIS PERMANENT TRAP REMAINS, YOU CAN'T SACRIFICE ANY MONSTERS! GOT IT?!

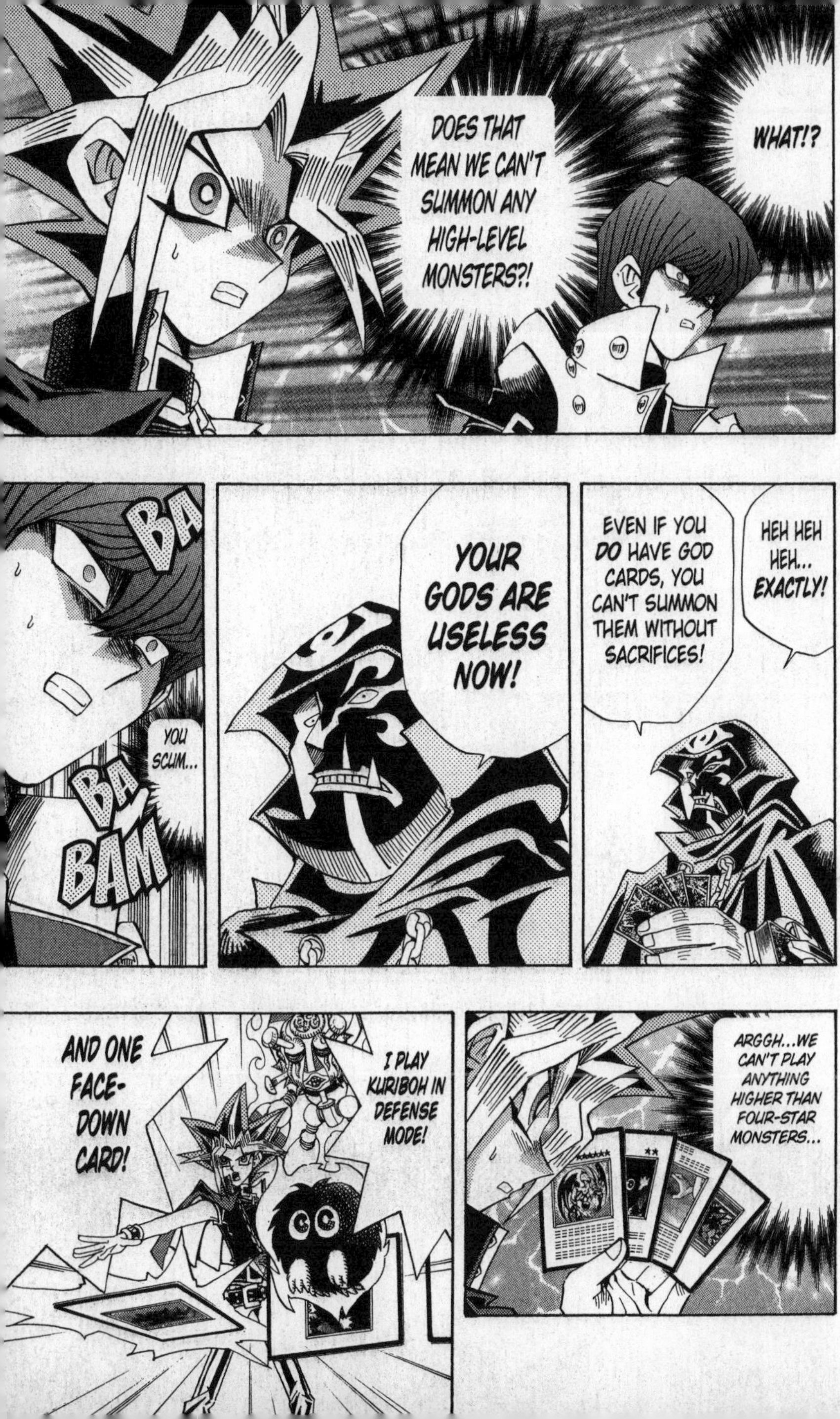
WHAT!?
DOES THAT MEAN WE CAN'T SUMMON ANY HIGH-LEVEL MONSTERS?!
HEH HEH HEH... EXACTLY!
EVEN IF YOU DO HAVE GOD CARDS, YOU CAN'T SUMMON THEM WITHOUT SACRIFICES!
YOUR GODS ARE USELESS NOW!
BA
YOU SCUM...
BA BAM
ARGGH...WE CAN'T PLAY ANYTHING HIGHER THAN FOUR-STAR MONSTERS...
I PLAY KURIBOH IN DEFENSE MODE!
AND ONE FACE-DOWN CARD!

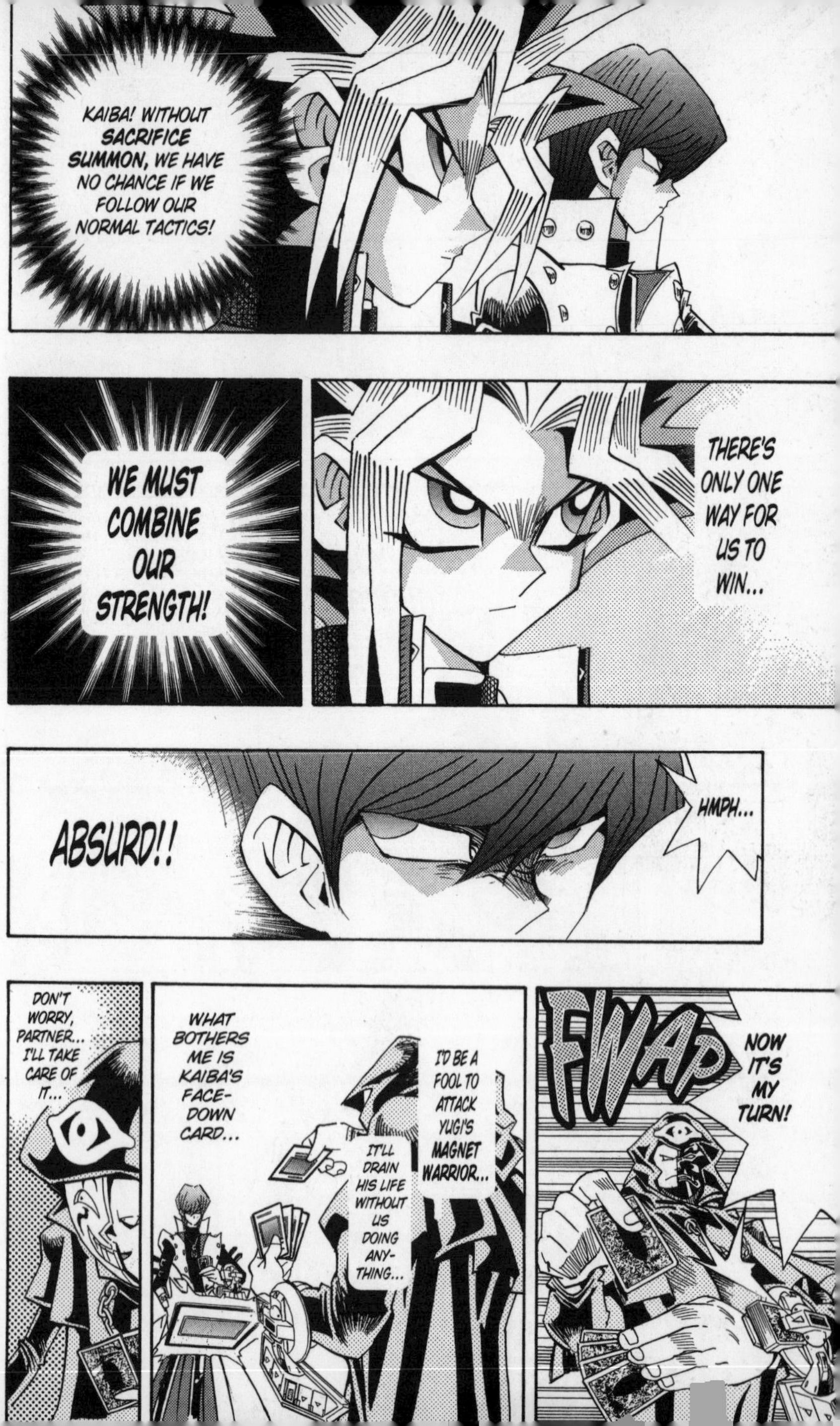
KAIBA! WITHOUT SACRIFICE SUMMON, WE HAVE NO CHANCE IF WE FOLLOW OUR NORMAL TACTICS!
THERE'S ONLY ONE WAY FOR US TO WIN...
WE MUST COMBINE OUR STRENGTH!
HMPH...
ABSURD!!
FWAP
NOW IT'S MY TURN!
I'D BE A FOOL TO ATTACK YUGI'S MAGNET WARRIOR...
WHAT BOTHERS ME IS KAIBA'S FACE-DOWN CARD...
IT'LL DRAIN HIS LIFE WITHOUT US DOING ANYTHING...
DON'T WORRY, PARTNER... I'LL TAKE CARE OF IT...

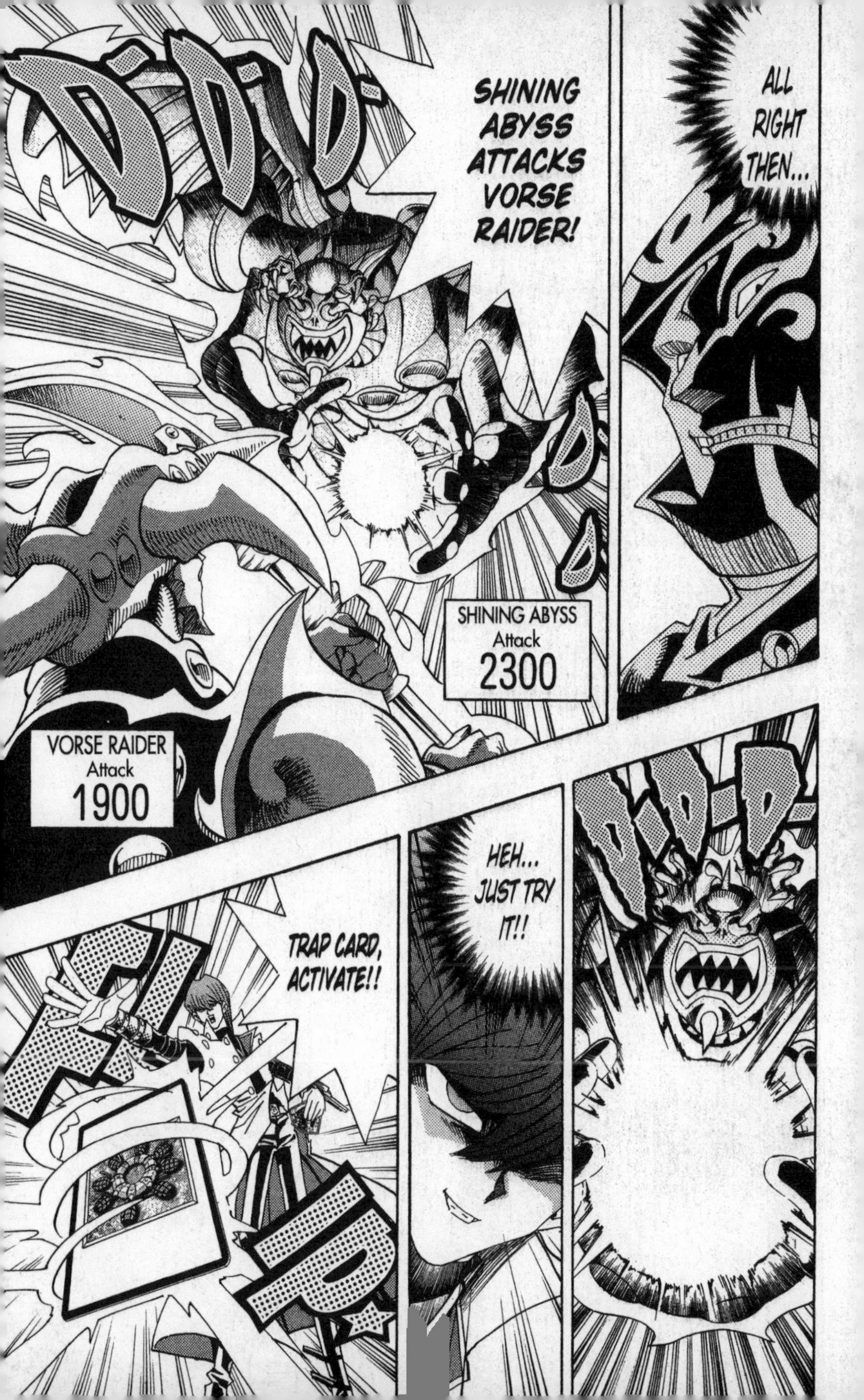
ALL RIGHT THEN...
D-D-D-
SHINING ABYSS ATTACKS VORSE RAIDER!
SHINING ABYSS Attack 2300
VORSE RAIDER Attack 1900
D-D-D-
HEH... JUST TRY IT!!
TRAP CARD, ACTIVATE!!

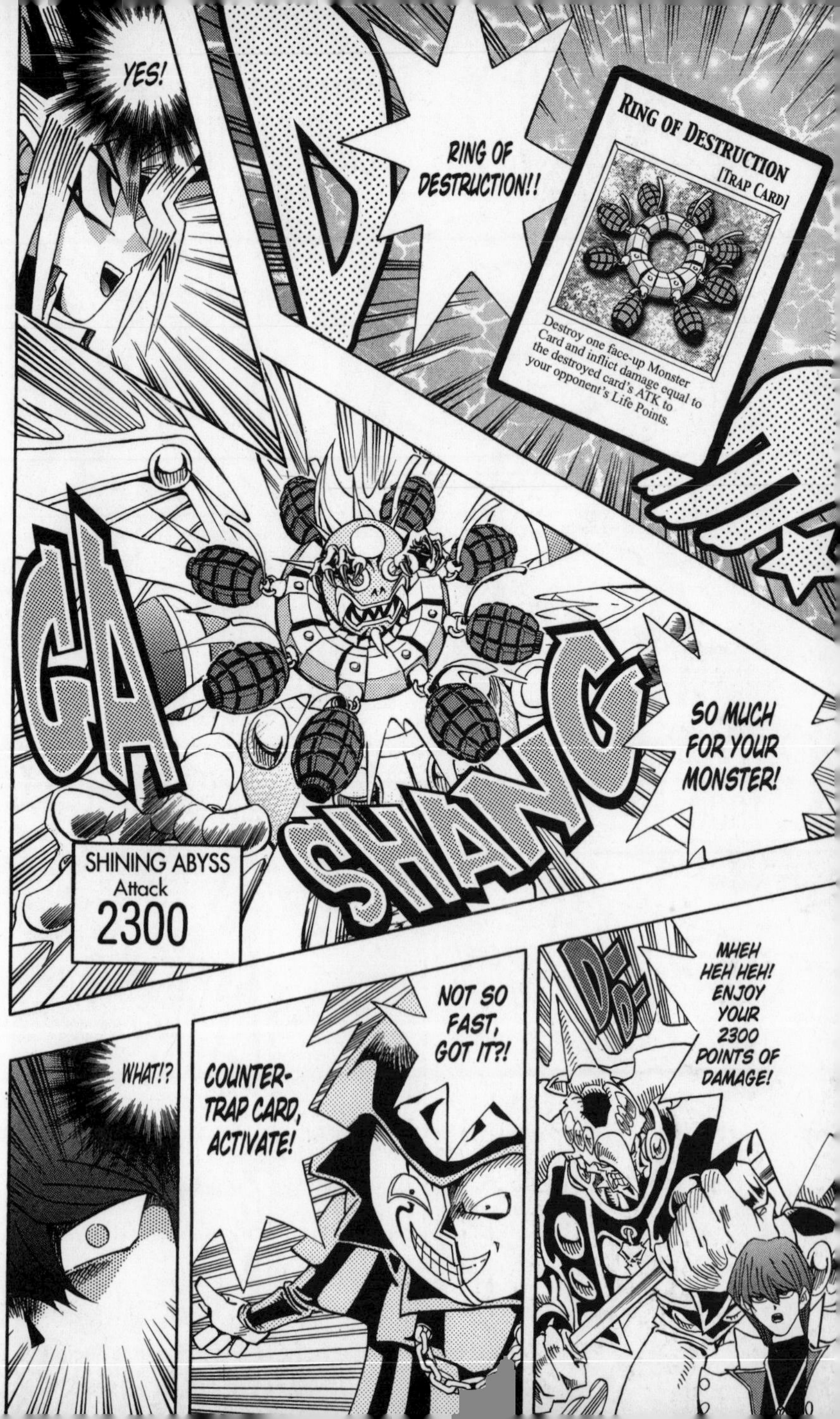
YES!
RING OF DESTRUCTION!!
Ring of Destruction
[Trap Card]
Destroy one face-up Monster Card and inflict damage equal to the destroyed card's ATK to your opponent's Life Points.
SO MUCH FOR YOUR MONSTER!
CA
SHANG
SHINING ABYSS
Attack
2300
MHEH HEH HEH! ENJOY YOUR 2300 POINTS OF DAMAGE!
NOT SO FAST, GOT IT?!
COUNTER-TRAP CARD, ACTIVATE!
WHAT!?

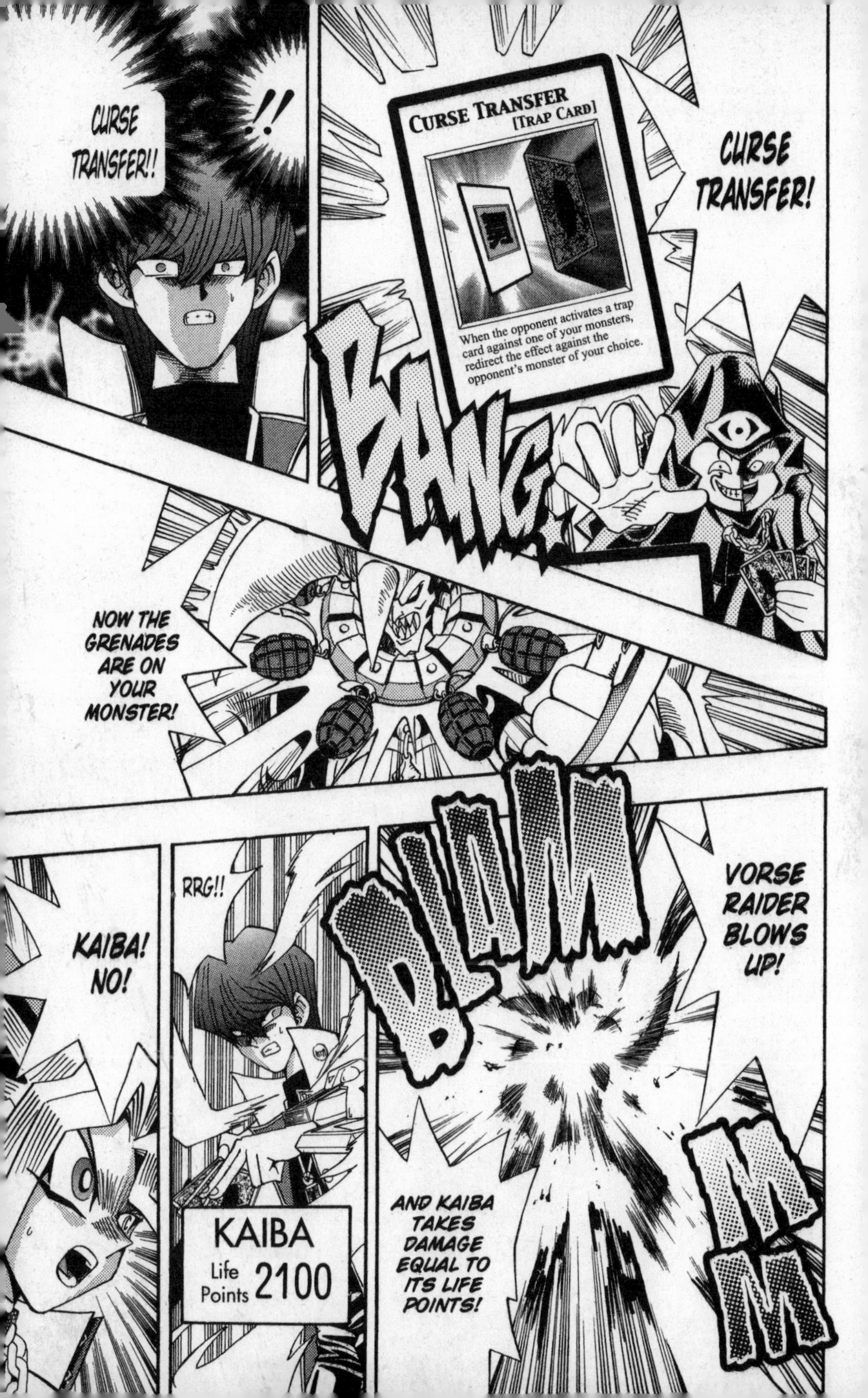
CURSE TRANSFER
[TRAP CARD]
When the opponent activates a trap card against one of your monsters, redirect the effect against the opponent's monster of your choice.
CURSE TRANSFER!
BANG
!!
CURSE TRANSFER!!
NOW THE GRENADES ARE ON YOUR MONSTER!
VORSE RAIDER BLOWS UP!
BLAM
MM
AND KAIBA TAKES DAMAGE EQUAL TO ITS LIFE POINTS!
RRG!!
KAIBA
Life Points 2100
KAIBA! NO!

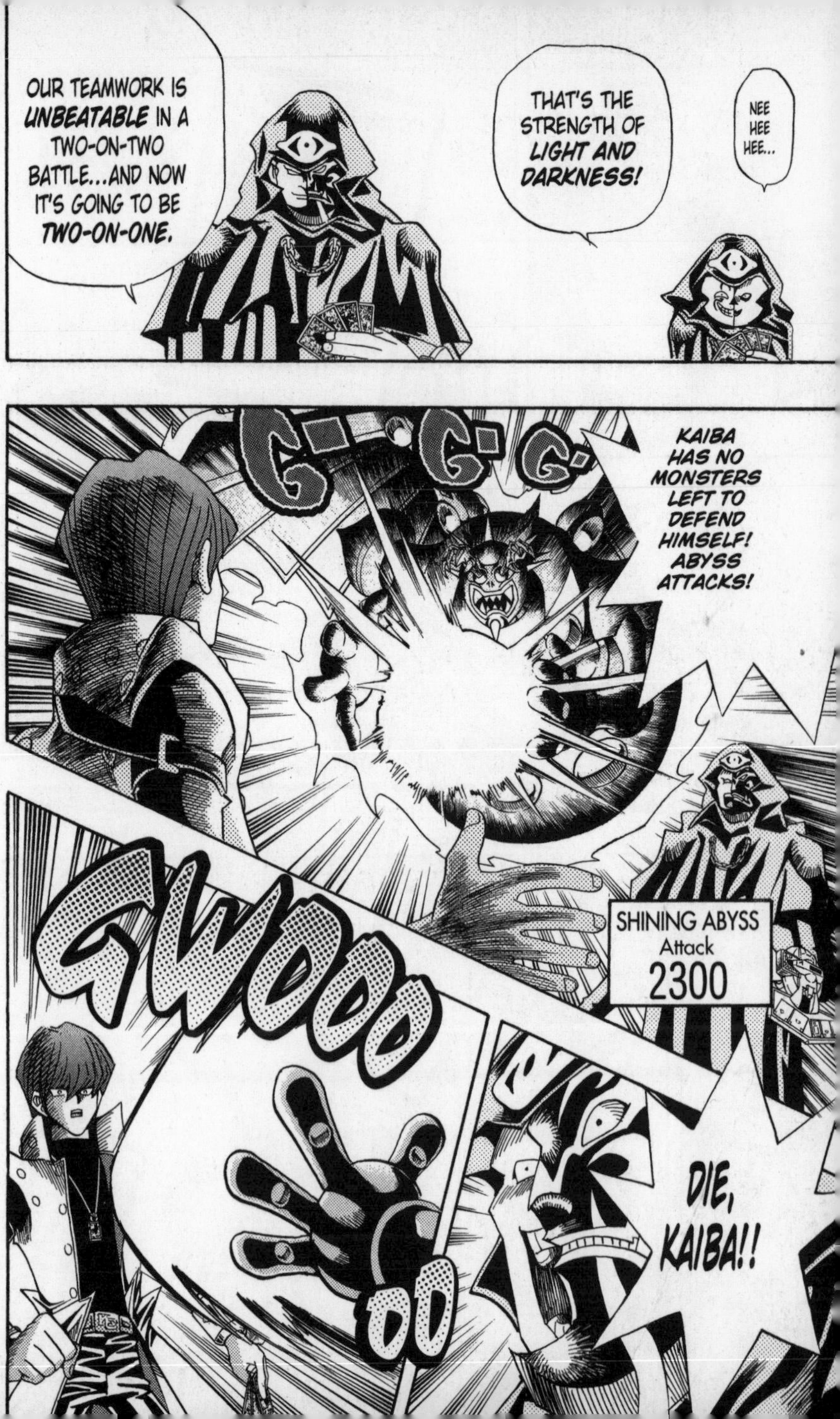
NEE HEE HEE...
THAT'S THE STRENGTH OF LIGHT AND DARKNESS!
OUR TEAMWORK IS UNBEATABLE IN A TWO-ON-TWO BATTLE...AND NOW IT'S GOING TO BE TWO-ON-ONE.
KAIBA HAS NO MONSTERS LEFT TO DEFEND HIMSELF! ABYSS ATTACKS!
G G G
SHINING ABYSS Attack 2300
GWOOO
DIE, KAIBA!!

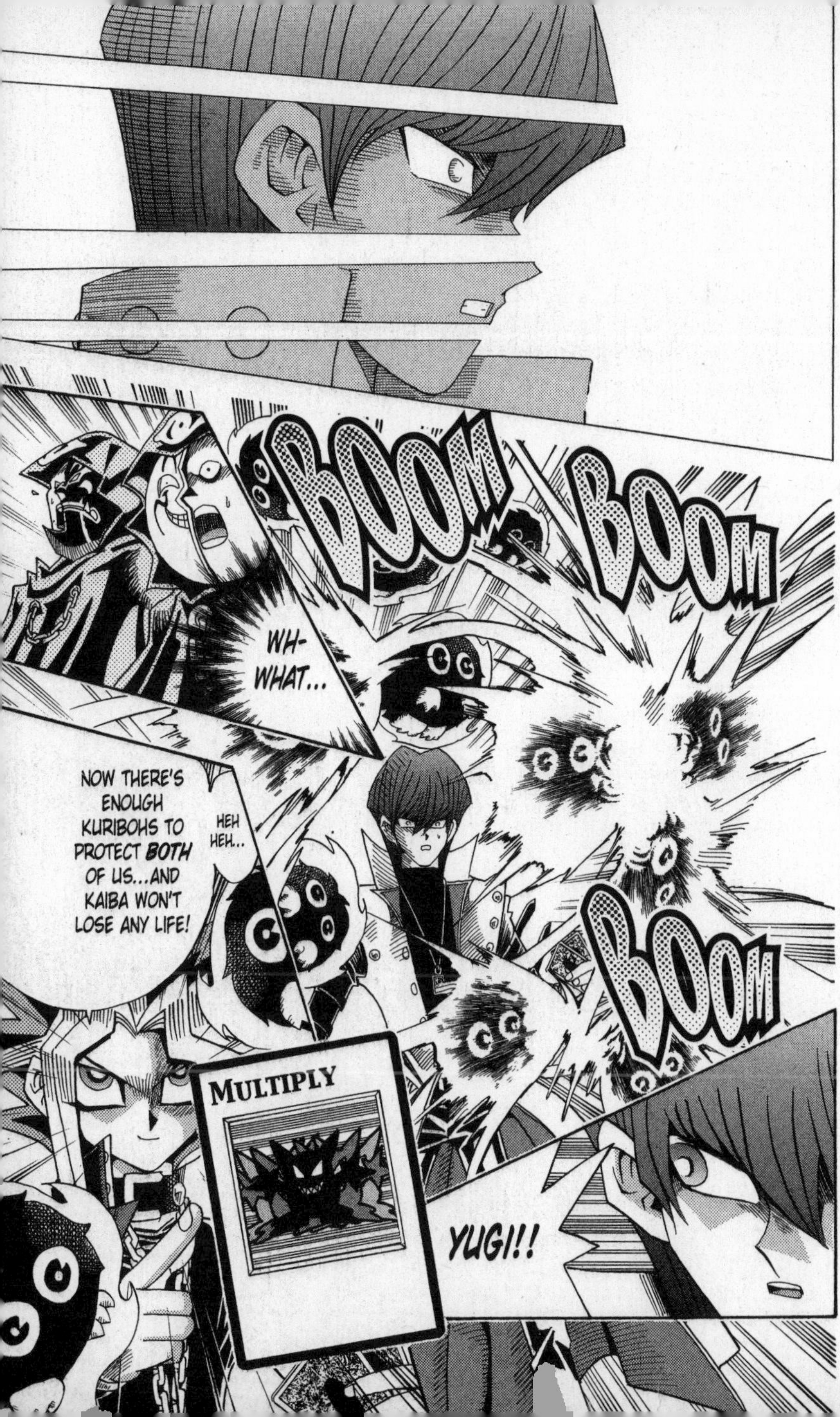
BOOM
BOOM
WH-WHAT...
BOOM
HEH HEH...
NOW THERE'S ENOUGH KURIBOHS TO PROTECT BOTH OF US...AND KAIBA WON'T LOSE ANY LIFE!
MULTIPLY
YUGI!!

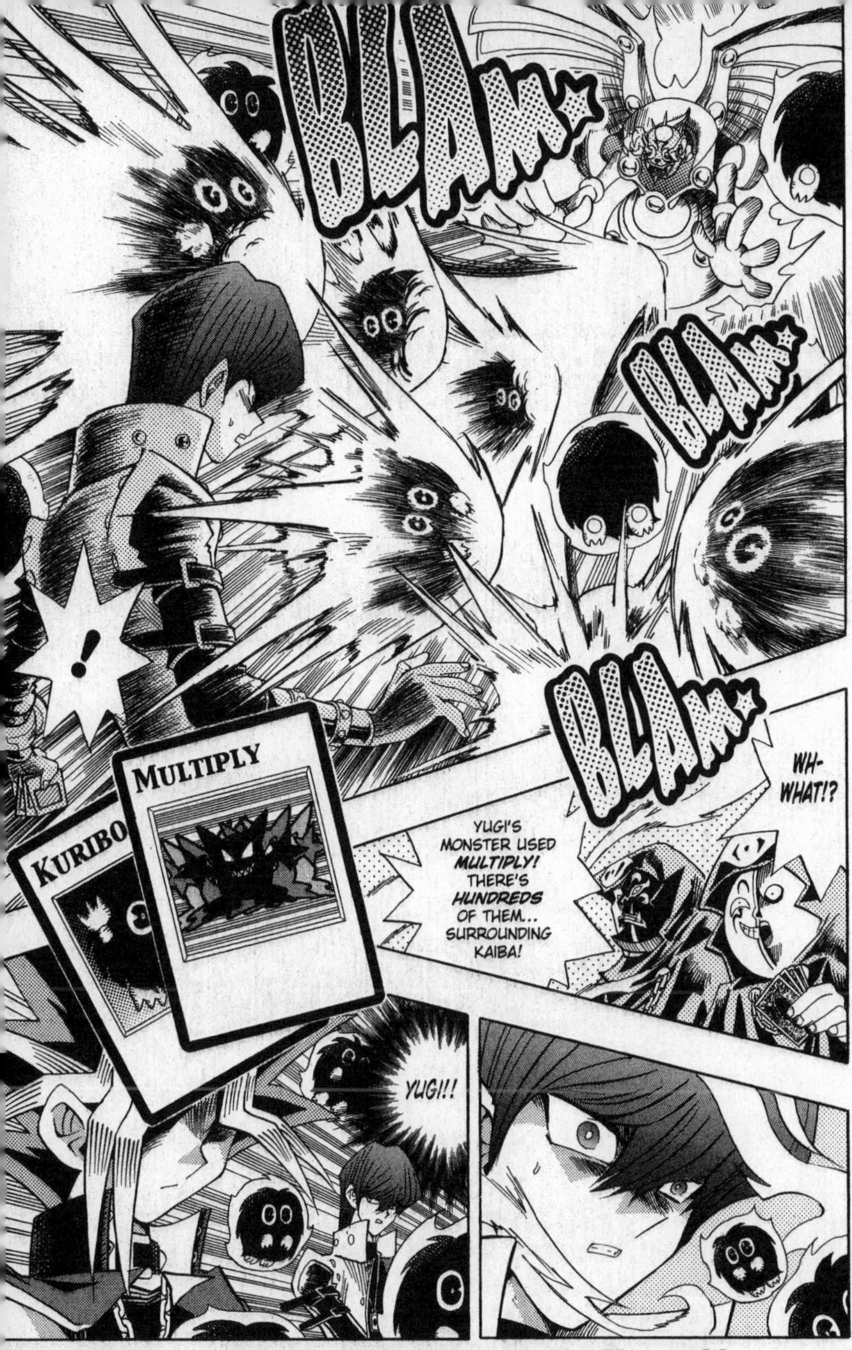
BLAM
BLAM
BLAM
!
MULTIPLY
KURIBO
WH-WHAT!?
YUGI'S MONSTER USED *MULTIPLY!* THERE'S *HUNDREDS* OF THEM... SURROUNDING KAIBA!
YUGI!!

Duel 127: Monsters Unite!!

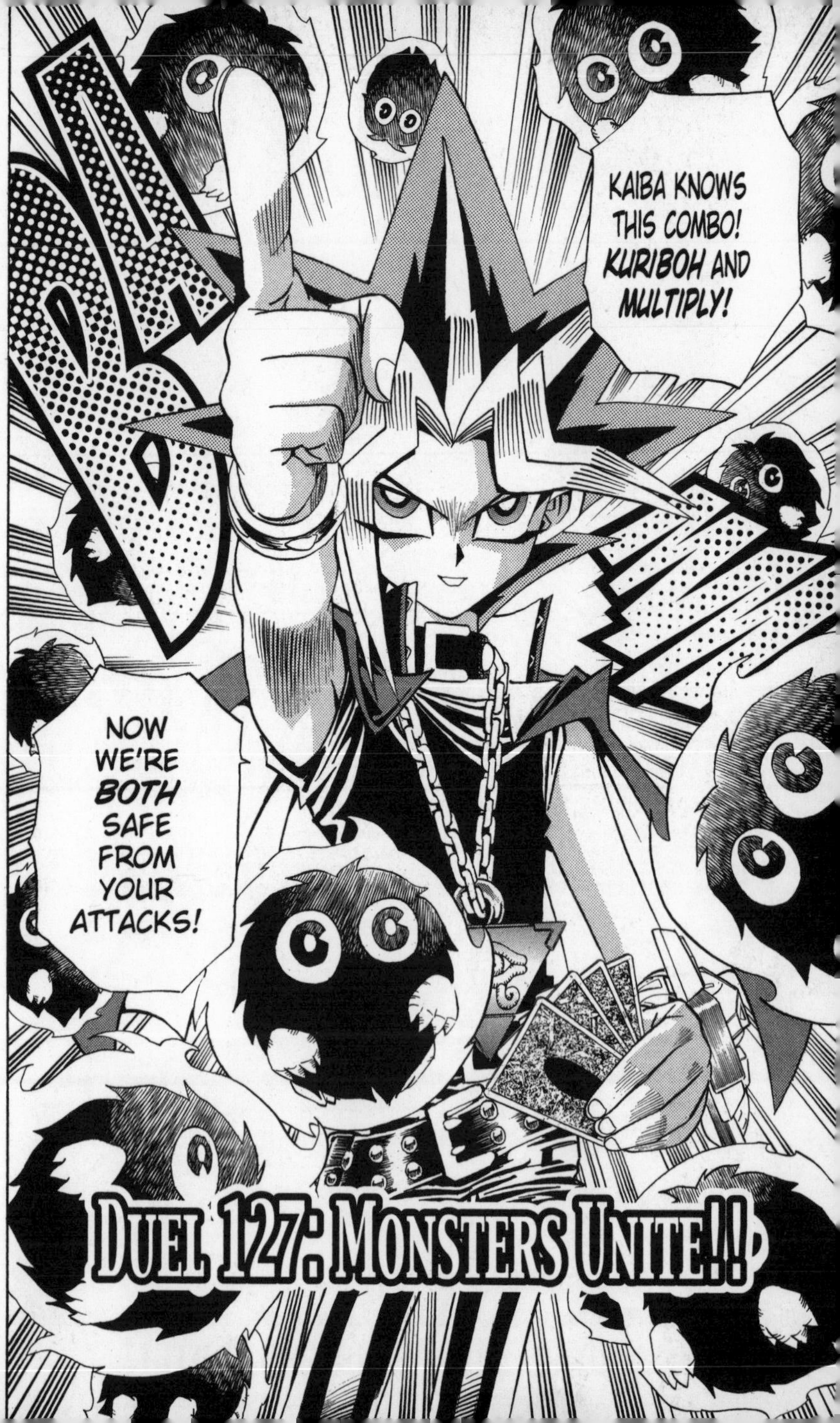
KAIBA KNOWS THIS COMBO! KURIBOH AND MULTIPLY!
NOW WE'RE BOTH SAFE FROM YOUR ATTACKS!
DUEL 127: MONSTERS UNITE!!

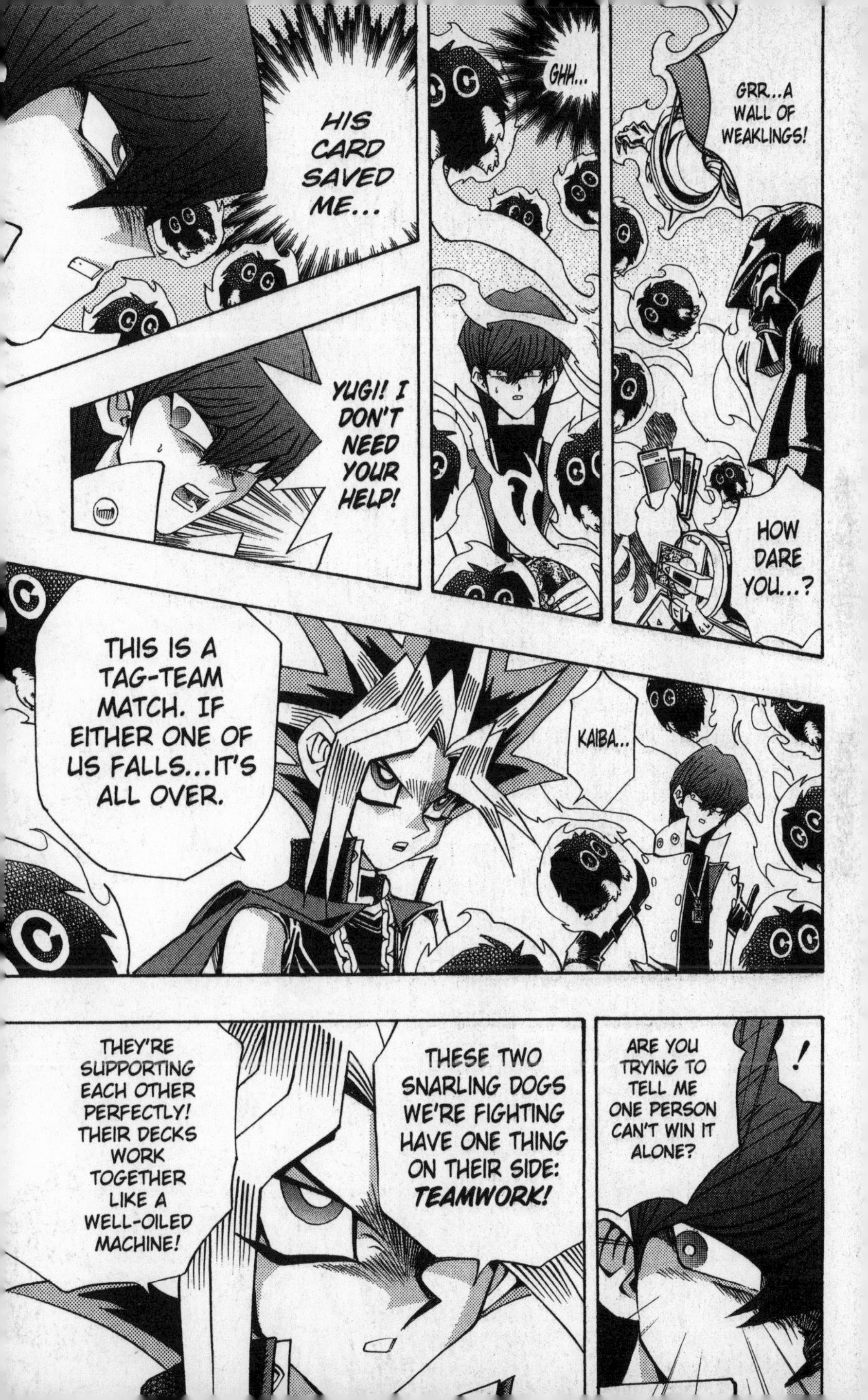
GRR...A WALL OF WEAKLINGS!
HOW DARE YOU...?
GHH...
HIS CARD SAVED ME...
YUGI! I DON'T NEED YOUR HELP!
KAIBA...
THIS IS A TAG-TEAM MATCH. IF EITHER ONE OF US FALLS...IT'S ALL OVER.
!
ARE YOU TRYING TO TELL ME ONE PERSON CAN'T WIN IT ALONE?
THESE TWO SNARLING DOGS WE'RE FIGHTING HAVE ONE THING ON THEIR SIDE: TEAMWORK!
THEY'RE SUPPORTING EACH OTHER PERFECTLY! THEIR DECKS WORK TOGETHER LIKE A WELL-OILED MACHINE!

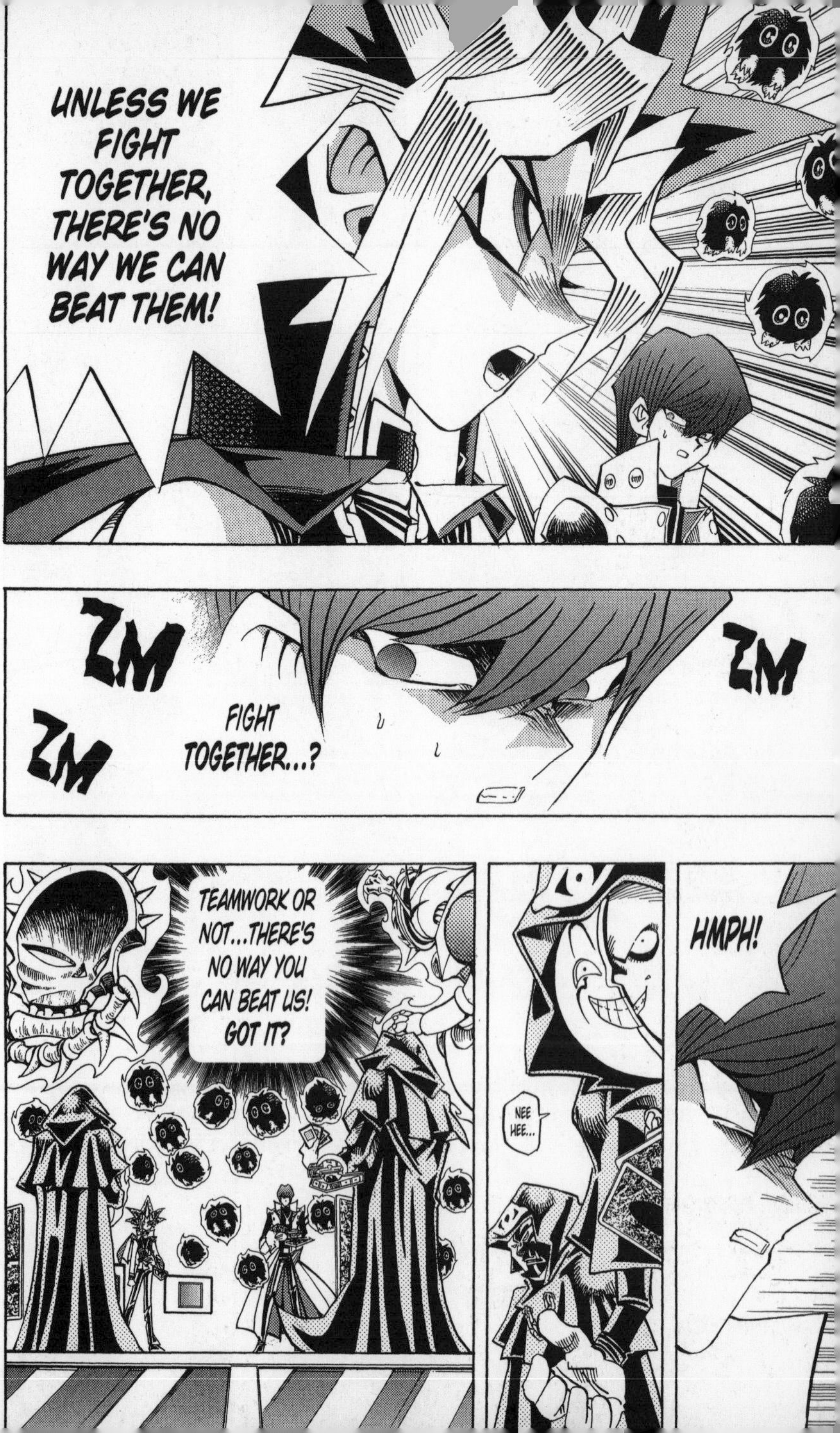
UNLESS WE FIGHT TOGETHER, THERE'S NO WAY WE CAN BEAT THEM!
ZM
ZM
FIGHT TOGETHER...?
ZM
HMPH!
NEE HEE...
TEAMWORK OR NOT...THERE'S NO WAY YOU CAN BEAT US! GOT IT?

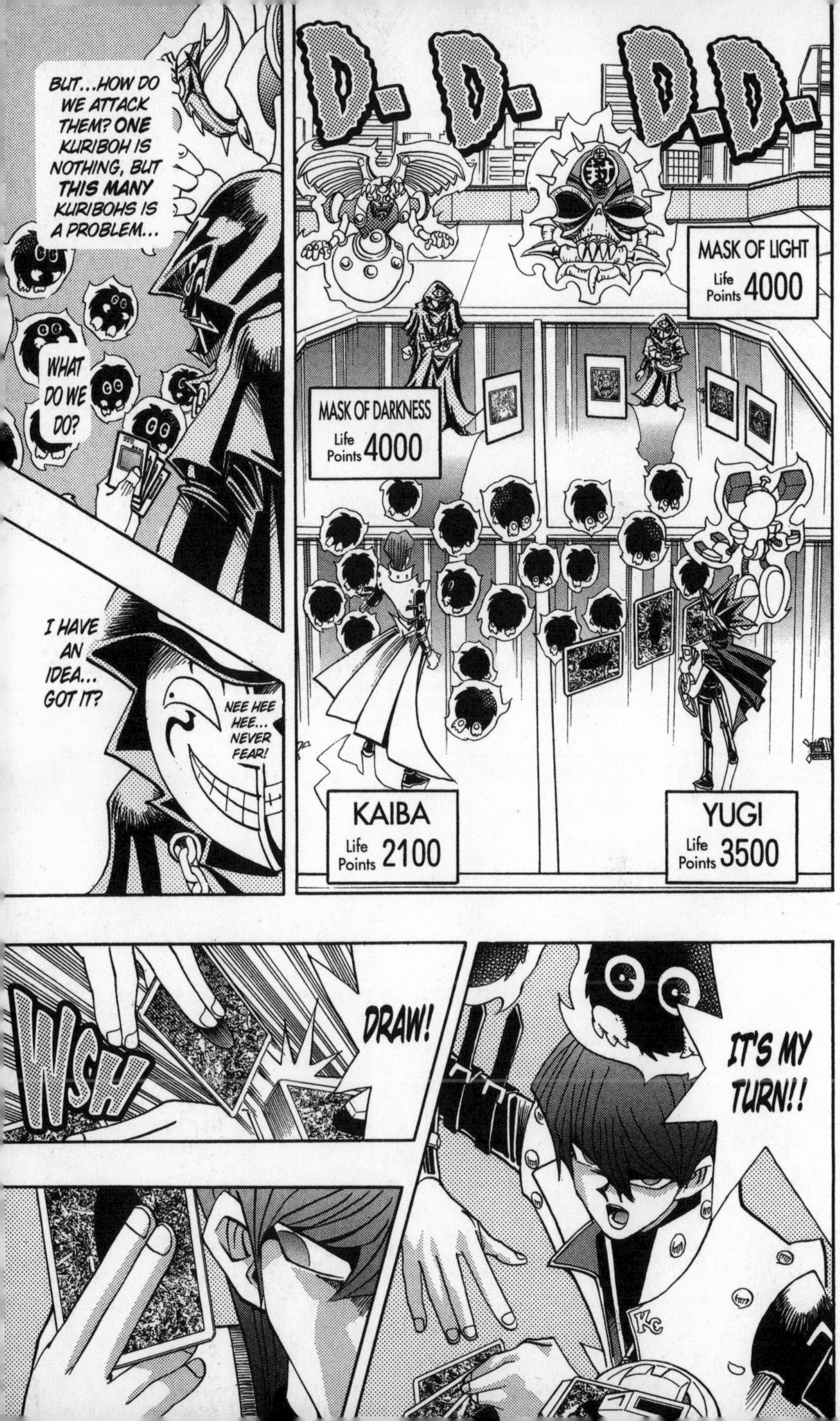
D. D. D.D.
MASK OF LIGHT Life Points 4000
MASK OF DARKNESS Life Points 4000
YUGI Life Points 3500
KAIBA Life Points 2100
BUT...HOW DO WE ATTACK THEM? ONE KURIBOH IS NOTHING, BUT THIS MANY KURIBOHS IS A PROBLEM...
WHAT DO WE DO?
NEE HEE HEE... NEVER FEAR!
I HAVE AN IDEA... GOT IT?
IT'S MY TURN!!
DRAW!
WSH

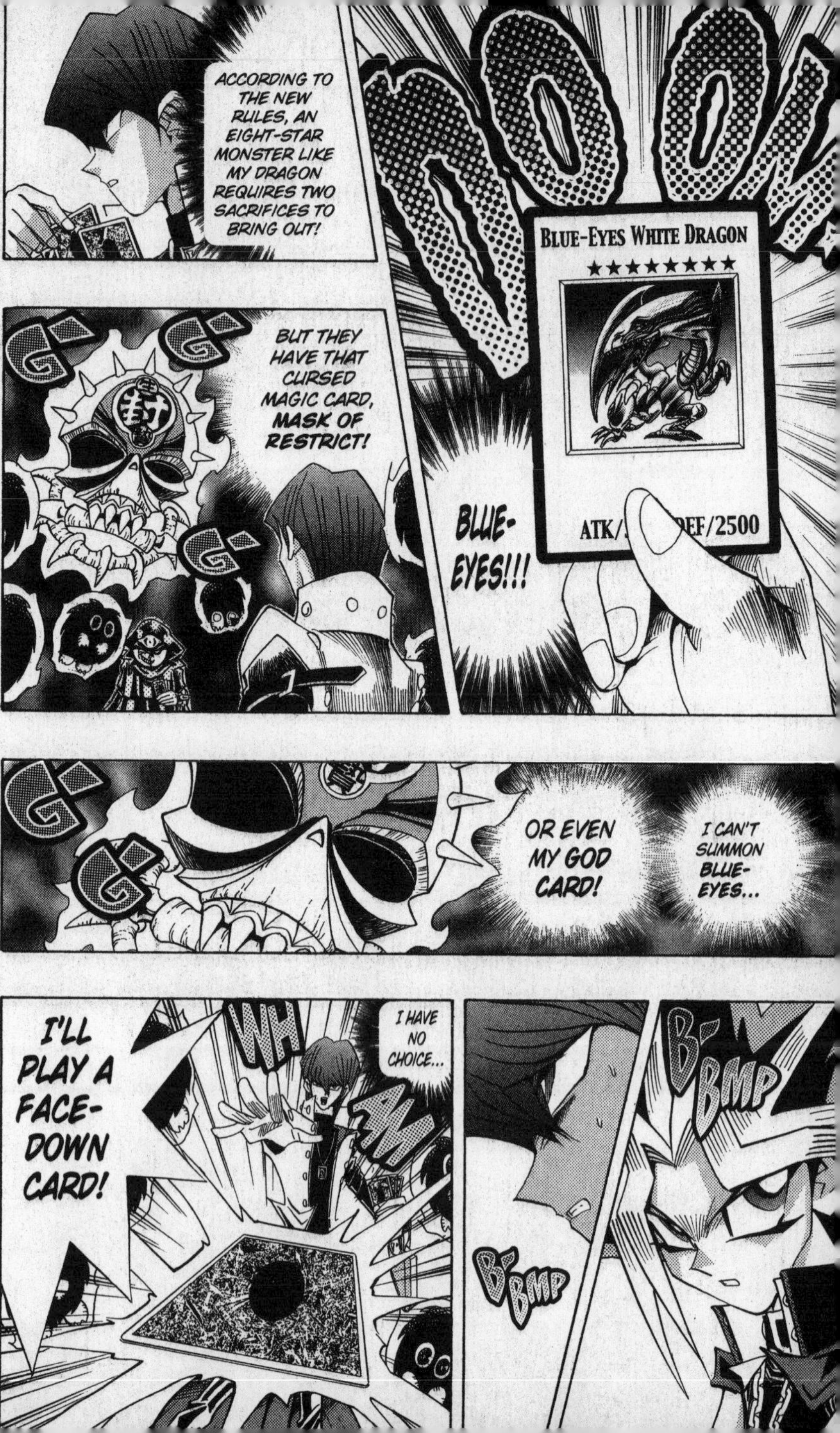
BLUE-EYES WHITE DRAGON
DEF/2500
BLUE-EYES!!!
ACCORDING TO THE NEW RULES, AN EIGHT-STAR MONSTER LIKE MY DRAGON REQUIRES TWO SACRIFICES TO BRING OUT!
G' G'
BUT THEY HAVE THAT CURSED MAGIC CARD, **MASK OF RESTRICT!**
G'
I CAN'T SUMMON BLUE-EYES...
OR EVEN MY GOD CARD!
G' G'
B-BMP
B-BMP
I HAVE NO CHOICE...
WHAM
I'LL PLAY A FACE-DOWN CARD!

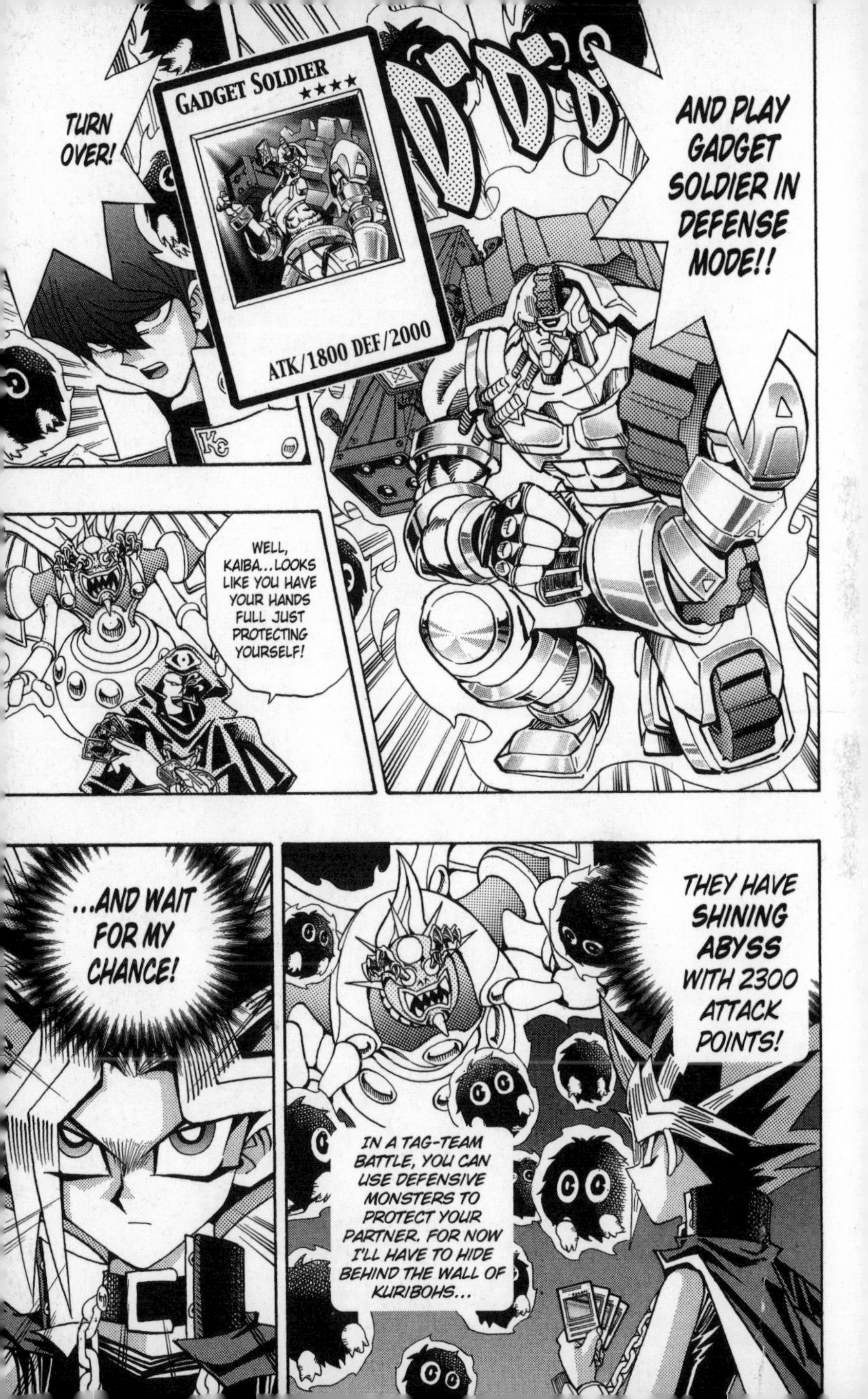
AND PLAY GADGET SOLDIER IN DEFENSE MODE!!
DDD
TURN OVER!
GADGET SOLDIER ★★★★
ATK/1800 DEF/2000
WELL, KAIBA...LOOKS LIKE YOU HAVE YOUR HANDS FULL JUST PROTECTING YOURSELF!
THEY HAVE SHINING ABYSS WITH 2300 ATTACK POINTS!
IN A TAG-TEAM BATTLE, YOU CAN USE DEFENSIVE MONSTERS TO PROTECT YOUR PARTNER. FOR NOW I'LL HAVE TO HIDE BEHIND THE WALL OF KURIBOHS...
...AND WAIT FOR MY CHANCE!

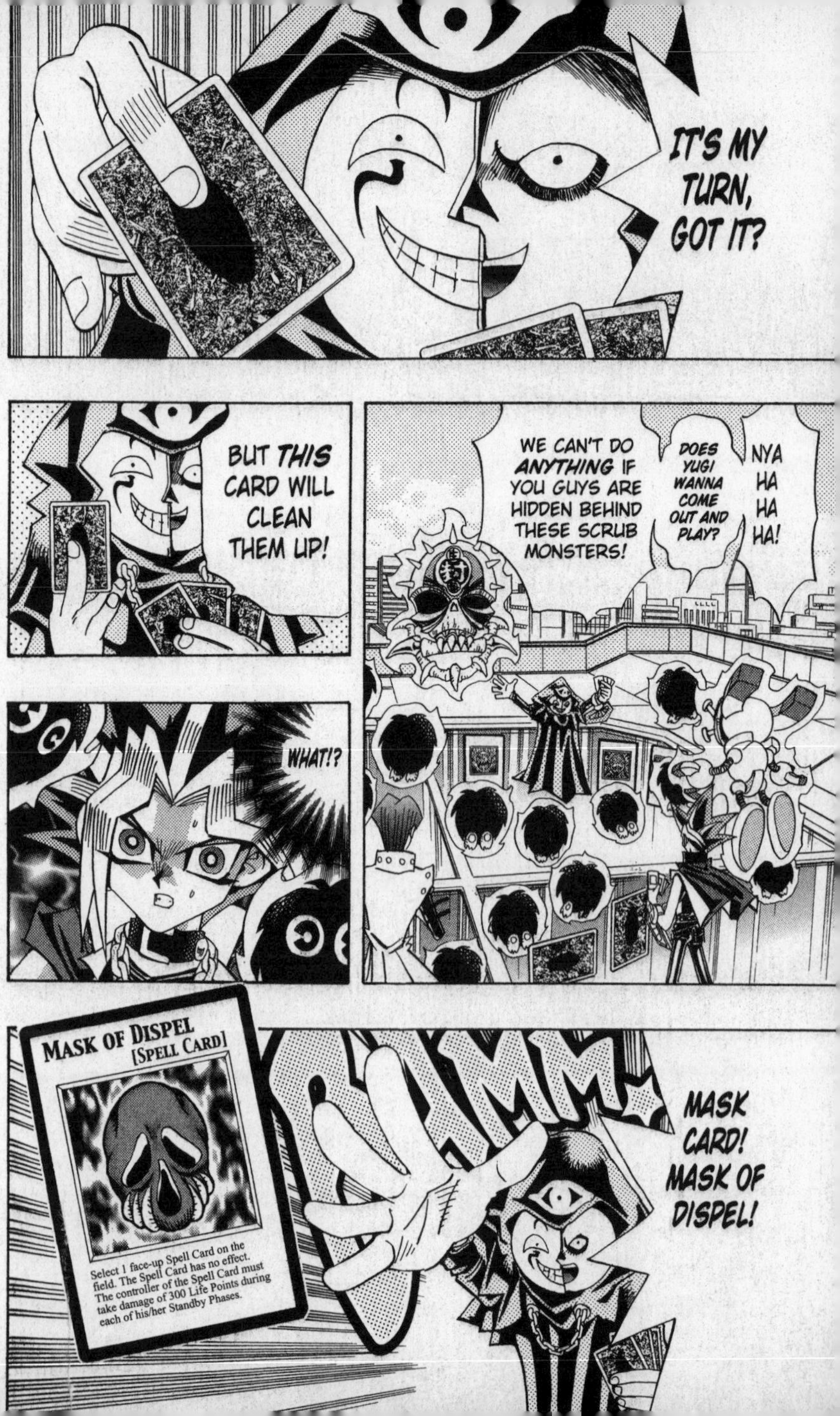

IT'S MY TURN, GOT IT?
NYA HA HA HA!
DOES YUGI WANNA COME OUT AND PLAY?
WE CAN'T DO ANYTHING IF YOU GUYS ARE HIDDEN BEHIND THESE SCRUB MONSTERS!
BUT THIS CARD WILL CLEAN THEM UP!
WHAT!?
MASK CARD! MASK OF DISPEL!
MASK OF DISPEL
[SPELL CARD]
Select 1 face-up Spell Card on the field. The Spell Card has no effect. The controller of the Spell Card must take damage of 300 Life Points during each of his/her Standby Phases.

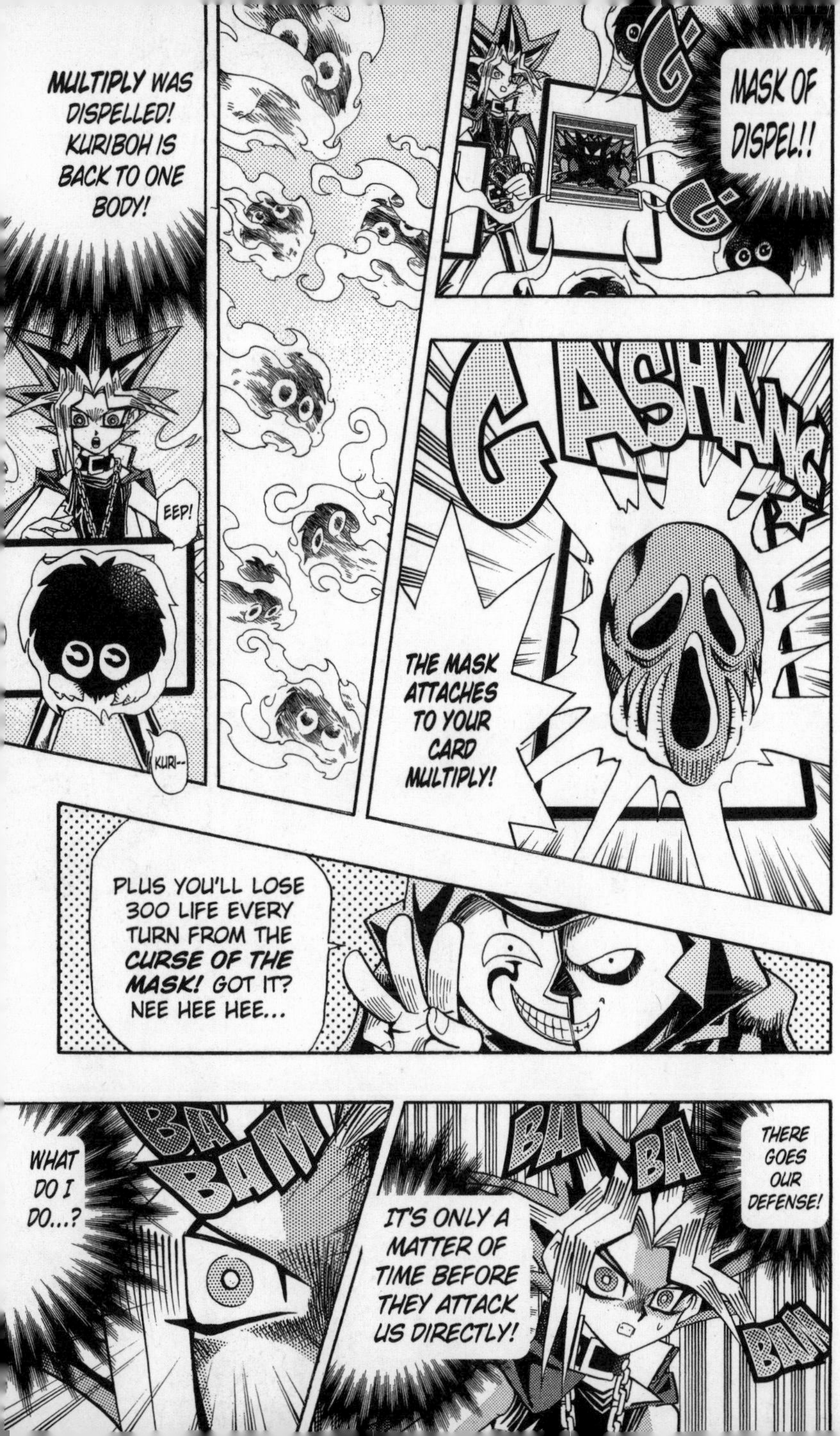
G G
MASK OF DISPEL!!
GASHANG
THE MASK ATTACHES TO YOUR CARD MULTIPLY!
MULTIPLY WAS DISPELLED! KURIBOH IS BACK TO ONE BODY!
EEP!
KURI--
PLUS YOU'LL LOSE 300 LIFE EVERY TURN FROM THE ***CURSE OF THE MASK!*** GOT IT? NEE HEE HEE...
BA BA
THERE GOES OUR DEFENSE!
IT'S ONLY A MATTER OF TIME BEFORE THEY ATTACK US DIRECTLY!
BAM
BA BAM
WHAT DO I DO...?

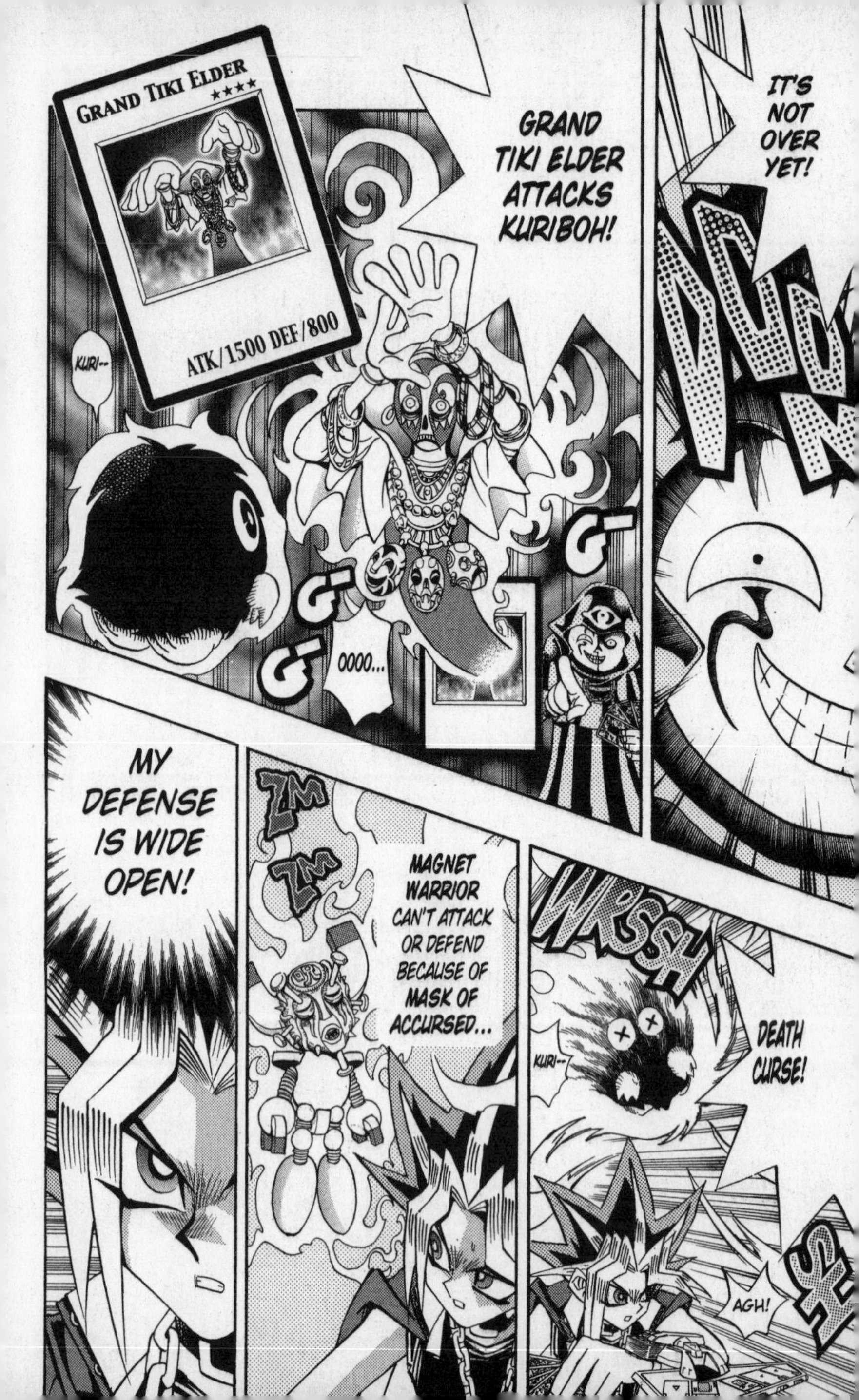
IT'S NOT OVER YET!
GRAND TIKI ELDER
ATK/1500 DEF/800
GRAND TIKI ELDER ATTACKS KURIBOH!
KURI--
OOOO...
WRSSH
DEATH CURSE!
KURI--
AGH!
ZM
ZM
MAGNET WARRIOR CAN'T ATTACK OR DEFEND BECAUSE OF MASK OF ACCURSED...
MY DEFENSE IS WIDE OPEN!

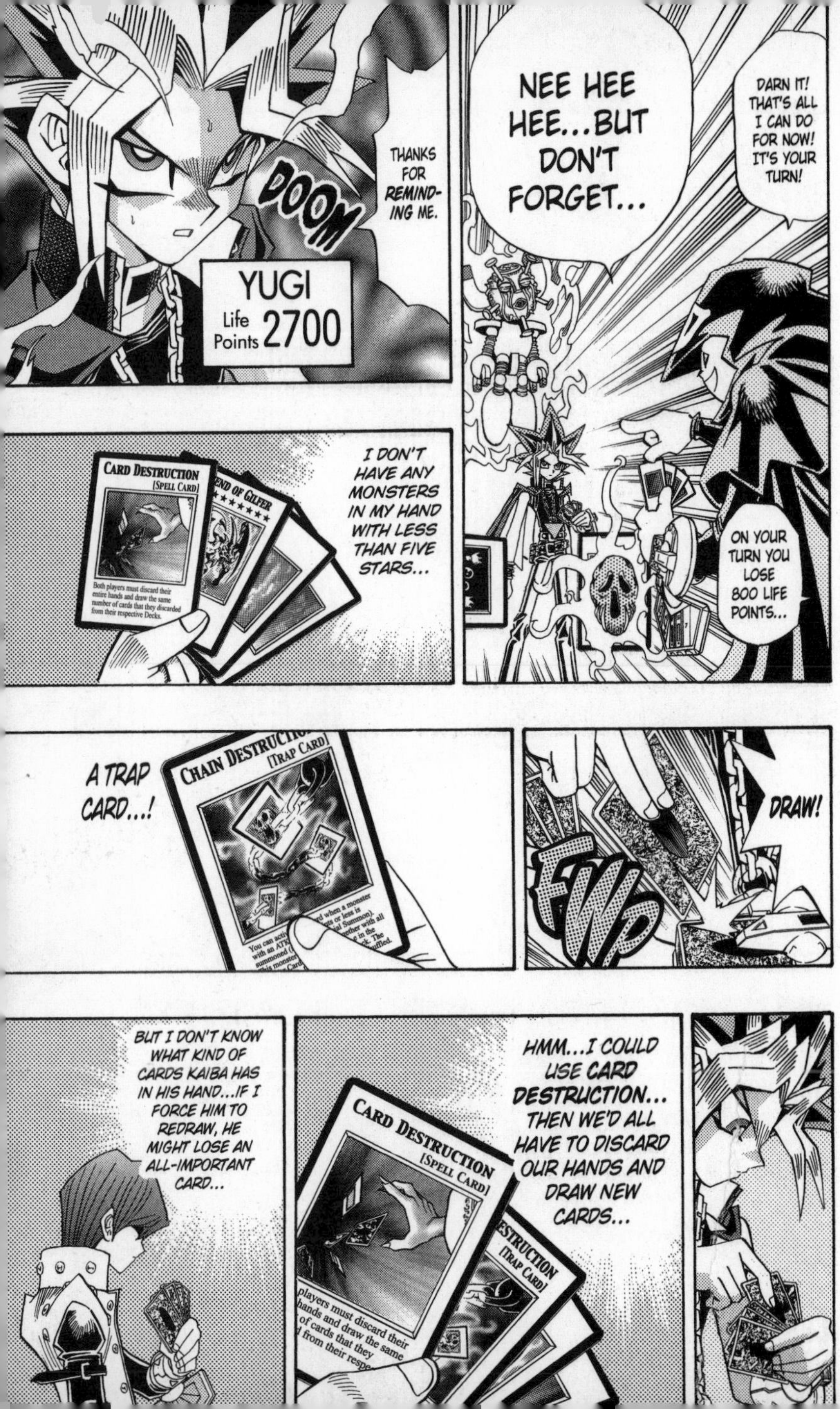
DARN IT! THAT'S ALL I CAN DO FOR NOW! IT'S YOUR TURN!
NEE HEE HEE...BUT DON'T FORGET...
ON YOUR TURN YOU LOSE 800 LIFE POINTS...
DOOM
THANKS FOR REMINDING ME.
YUGI
Life Points 2700
I DON'T HAVE ANY MONSTERS IN MY HAND WITH LESS THAN FIVE STARS...
CARD DESTRUCTION
[SPELL CARD]
Both players must discard their entire hands and draw the same number of cards that they discarded from their respective Decks.
DRAW!
FWIP
A TRAP CARD...!
CHAIN DESTRUCTION
[TRAP CARD]
HMM...I COULD USE CARD DESTRUCTION... THEN WE'D ALL HAVE TO DISCARD OUR HANDS AND DRAW NEW CARDS...
CARD DESTRUCTION
[SPELL CARD]
BUT I DON'T KNOW WHAT KIND OF CARDS KAIBA HAS IN HIS HAND...IF I FORCE HIM TO REDRAW, HE MIGHT LOSE AN ALL-IMPORTANT CARD...

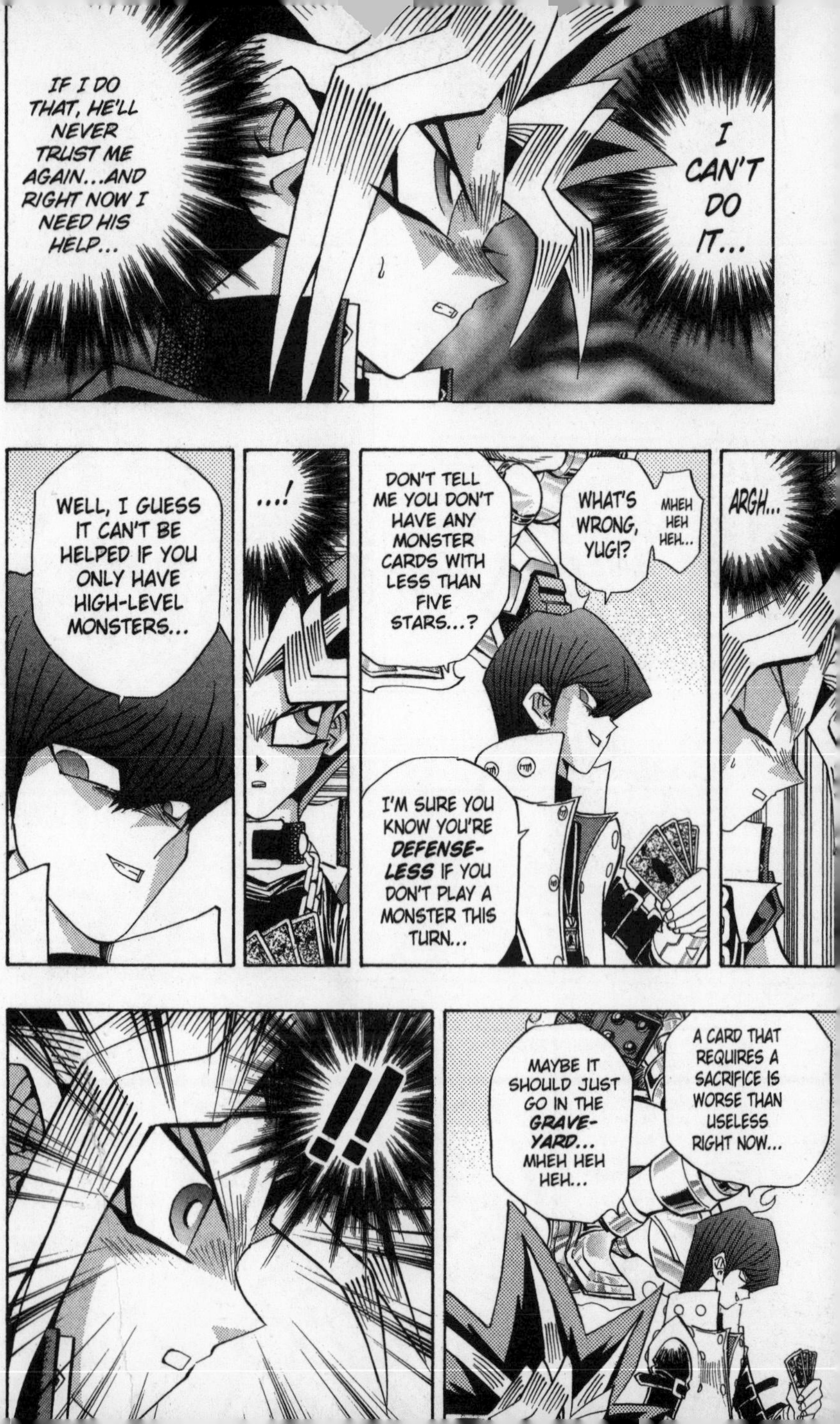
I CAN'T DO IT...
IF I DO THAT, HE'LL NEVER TRUST ME AGAIN...AND RIGHT NOW I NEED HIS HELP...
ARGH...
MHEH HEH HEH...
WHAT'S WRONG, YUGI?
DON'T TELL ME YOU DON'T HAVE ANY MONSTER CARDS WITH LESS THAN FIVE STARS...?
I'M SURE YOU KNOW YOU'RE DEFENSELESS IF YOU DON'T PLAY A MONSTER THIS TURN...
...!
WELL, I GUESS IT CAN'T BE HELPED IF YOU ONLY HAVE HIGH-LEVEL MONSTERS...
A CARD THAT REQUIRES A SACRIFICE IS WORSE THAN USELESS RIGHT NOW...
MAYBE IT SHOULD JUST GO IN THE GRAVEYARD... MHEH HEH HEH...
!!

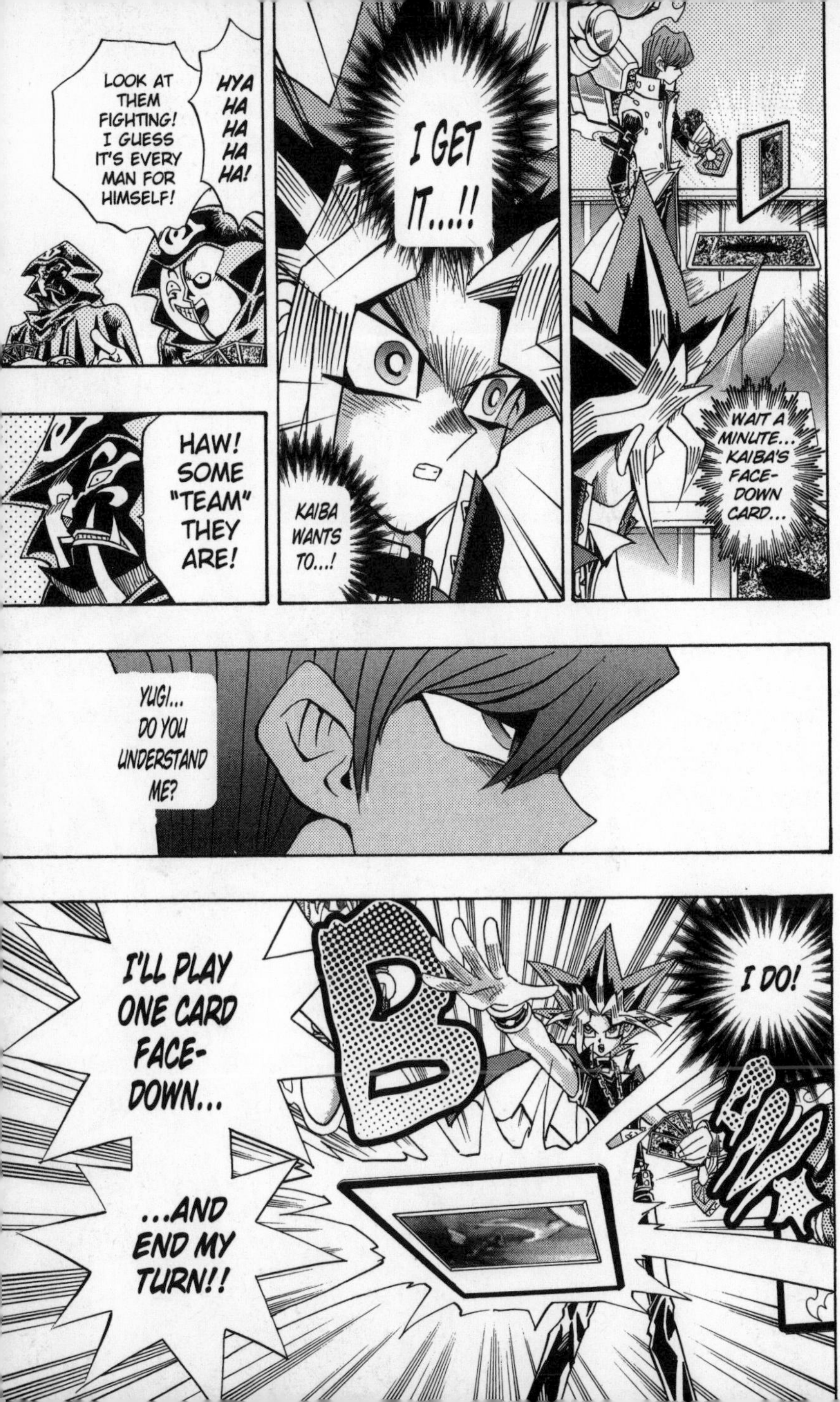
WAIT A MINUTE... KAIBA'S FACE-DOWN CARD...
I GET IT...!!
KAIBA WANTS TO...!
HYA HA HA HA HA!
LOOK AT THEM FIGHTING! I GUESS IT'S EVERY MAN FOR HIMSELF!
HAW! SOME "TEAM" THEY ARE!
YUGI... DO YOU UNDERSTAND ME?
I DO!
I'LL PLAY ONE CARD FACE-DOWN...
...AND END MY TURN!!

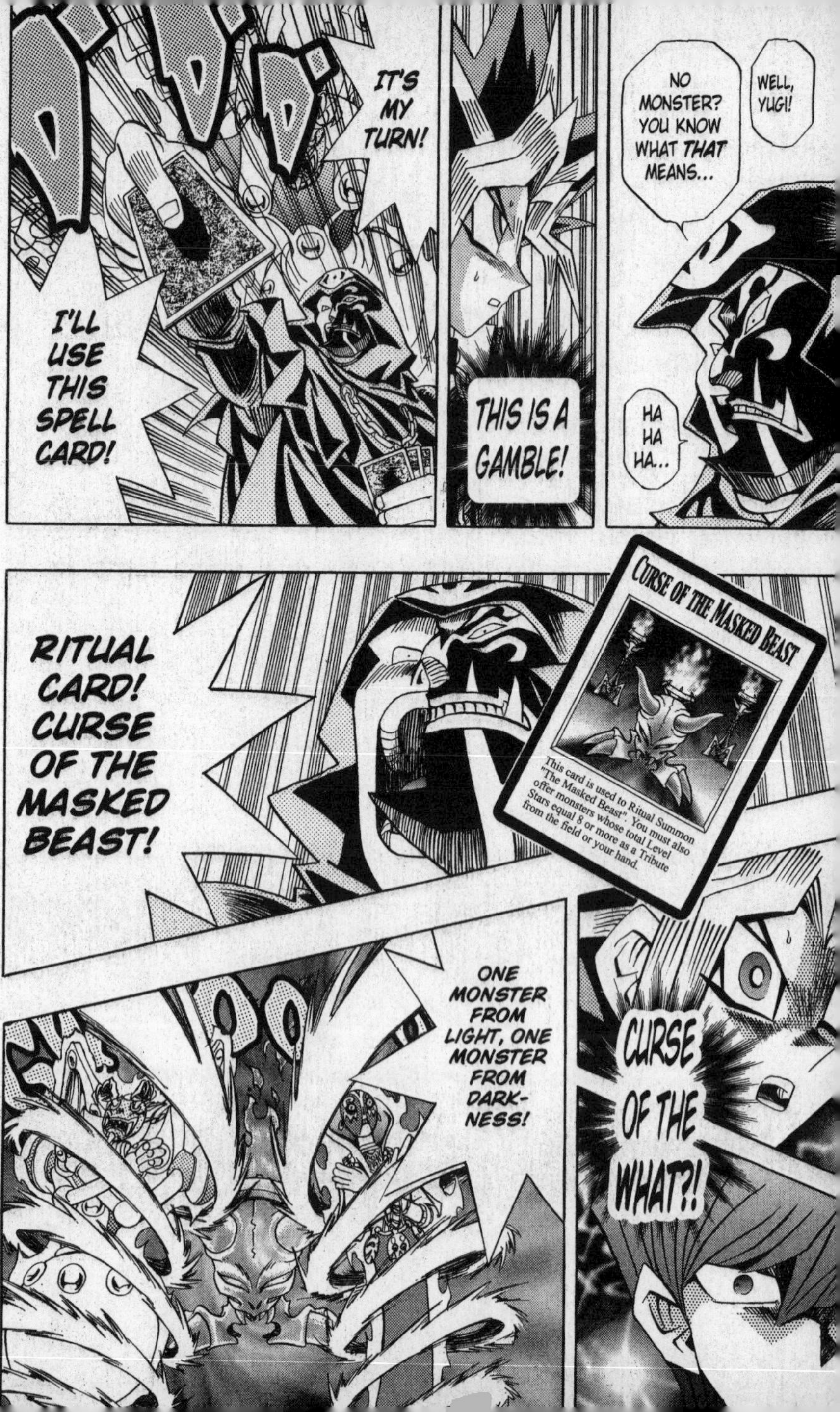
WELL, YUGI!
NO MONSTER? YOU KNOW WHAT THAT MEANS...
HA HA HA...
THIS IS A GAMBLE!
IT'S MY TURN!
I'LL USE THIS SPELL CARD!
CURSE OF THE MASKED BEAST
This card is used to Ritual Summon "The Masked Beast". You must also offer monsters whose total Level Stars equal 8 or more as a Tribute from the field or your hand.
RITUAL CARD! CURSE OF THE MASKED BEAST!
CURSE OF THE WHAT?!
ONE MONSTER FROM LIGHT, ONE MONSTER FROM DARK-NESS!

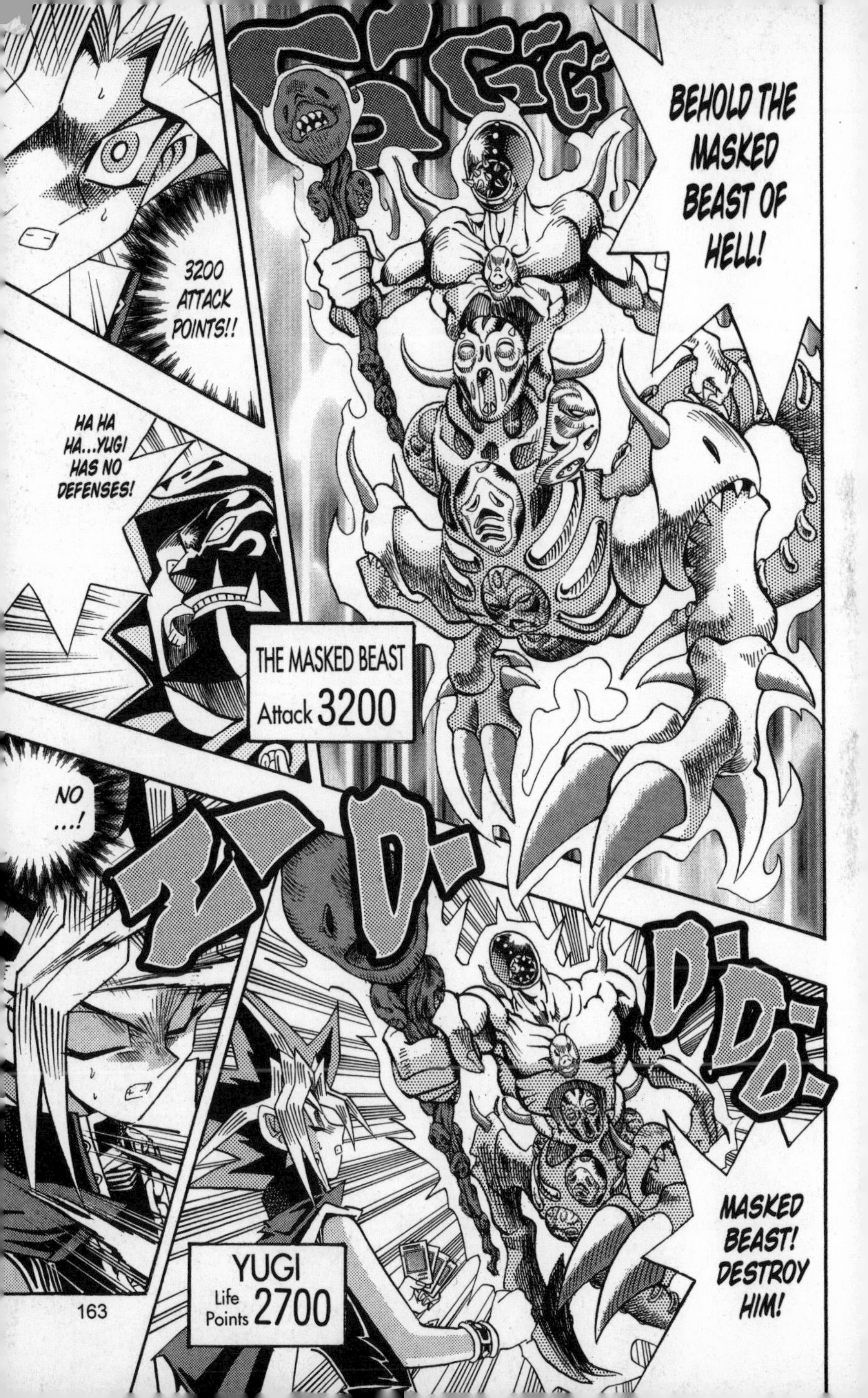

BEHOLD THE MASKED BEAST OF HELL!
3200 ATTACK POINTS!!
HA HA HA...YUGI HAS NO DEFENSES!
THE MASKED BEAST
Attack 3200
MASKED BEAST! DESTROY HIM!
NO ...!
YUGI
Life Points 2700

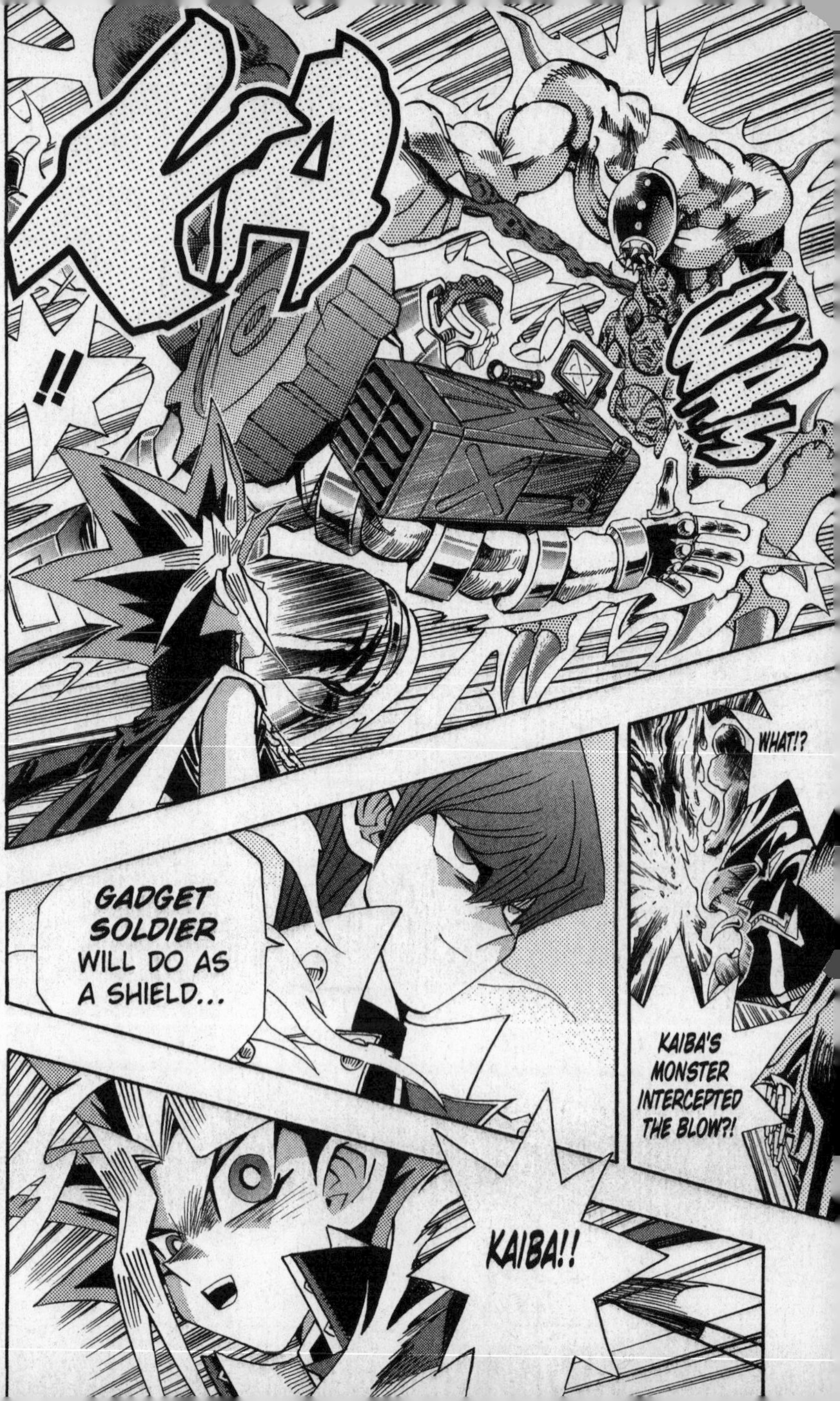
!!
WHAT!?
KAIBA'S MONSTER INTERCEPTED THE BLOW?!
GADGET SOLDIER WILL DO AS A SHIELD...
KAIBA!!

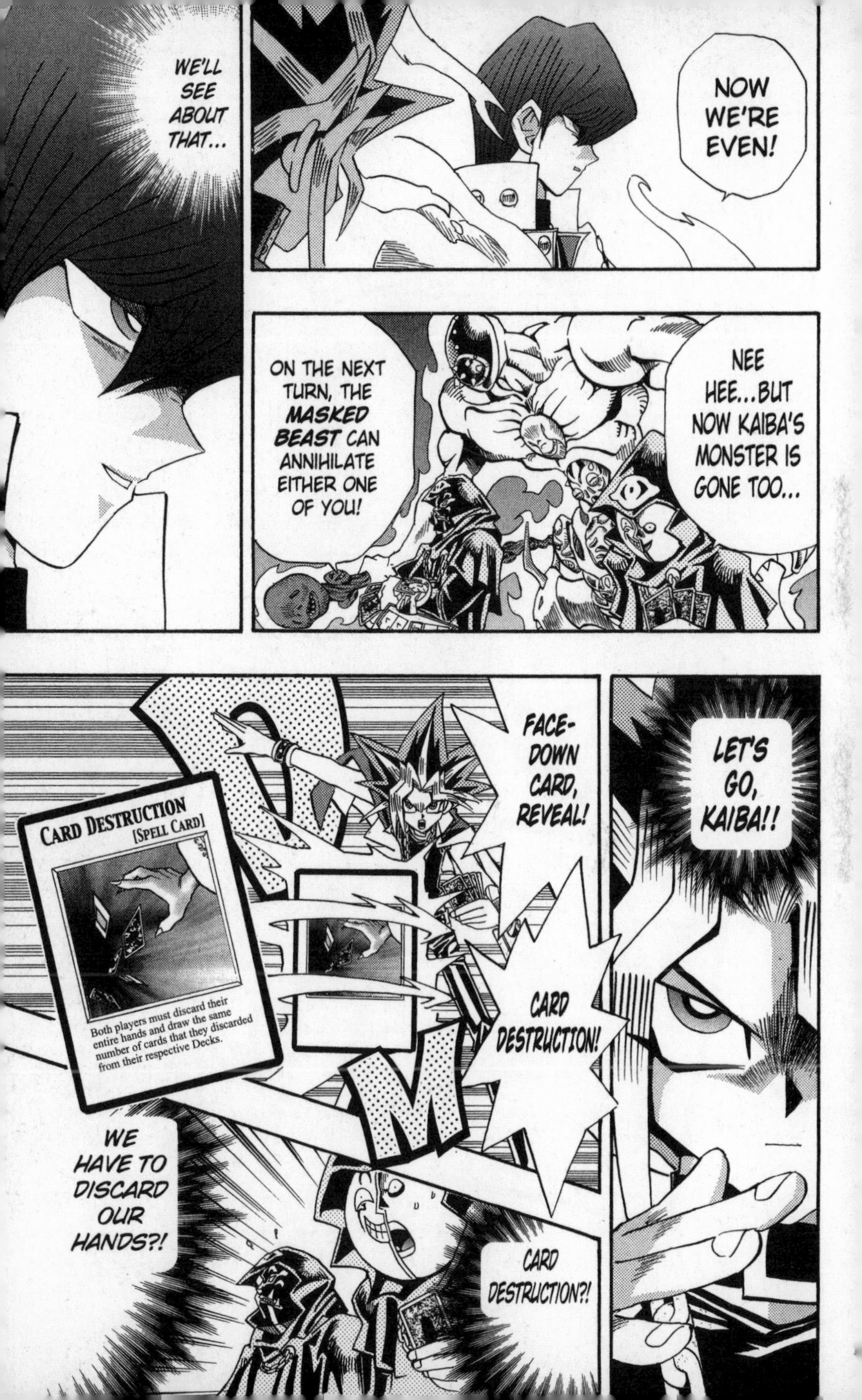
NOW WE'RE EVEN!
NEE HEE...BUT NOW KAIBA'S MONSTER IS GONE TOO...
ON THE NEXT TURN, THE MASKED BEAST CAN ANNIHILATE EITHER ONE OF YOU!
WE'LL SEE ABOUT THAT...
LET'S GO, KAIBA!!
FACE-DOWN CARD, REVEAL!
CARD DESTRUCTION!
CARD DESTRUCTION
[SPELL CARD]
Both players must discard their entire hands and draw the same number of cards that they discarded from their respective Decks.
M
WE HAVE TO DISCARD OUR HANDS?!
CARD DESTRUCTION?!

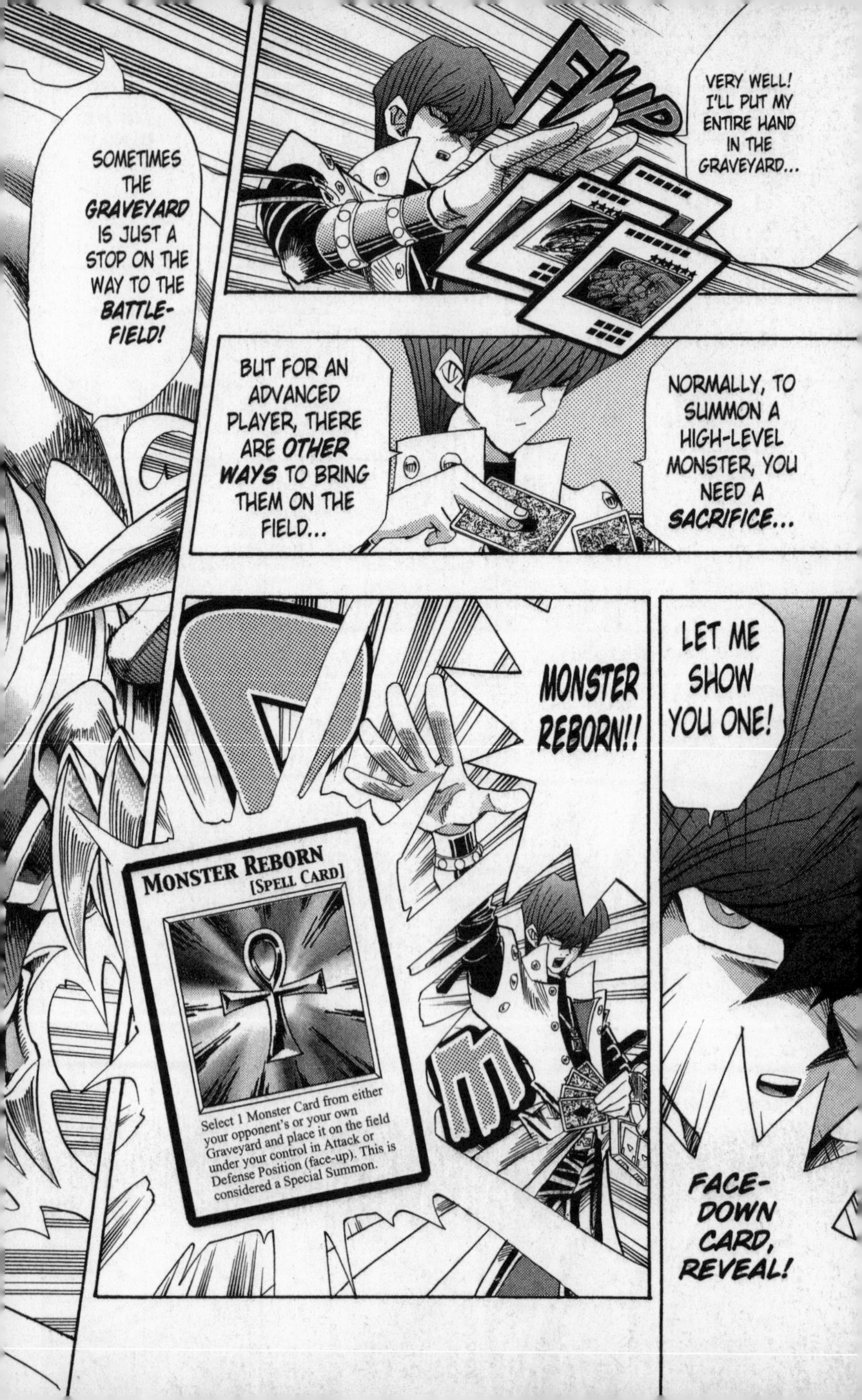
FWP
VERY WELL! I'LL PUT MY ENTIRE HAND IN THE GRAVEYARD...
NORMALLY, TO SUMMON A HIGH-LEVEL MONSTER, YOU NEED A SACRIFICE...
BUT FOR AN ADVANCED PLAYER, THERE ARE OTHER WAYS TO BRING THEM ON THE FIELD...
SOMETIMES THE GRAVEYARD IS JUST A STOP ON THE WAY TO THE BATTLE-FIELD!
LET ME SHOW YOU ONE!
FACE-DOWN CARD, REVEAL!
MONSTER REBORN!!
MONSTER REBORN
[SPELL CARD]
Select 1 Monster Card from either your opponent's or your own Graveyard and place it on the field under your control in Attack or Defense Position (face-up). This is considered a Special Summon.

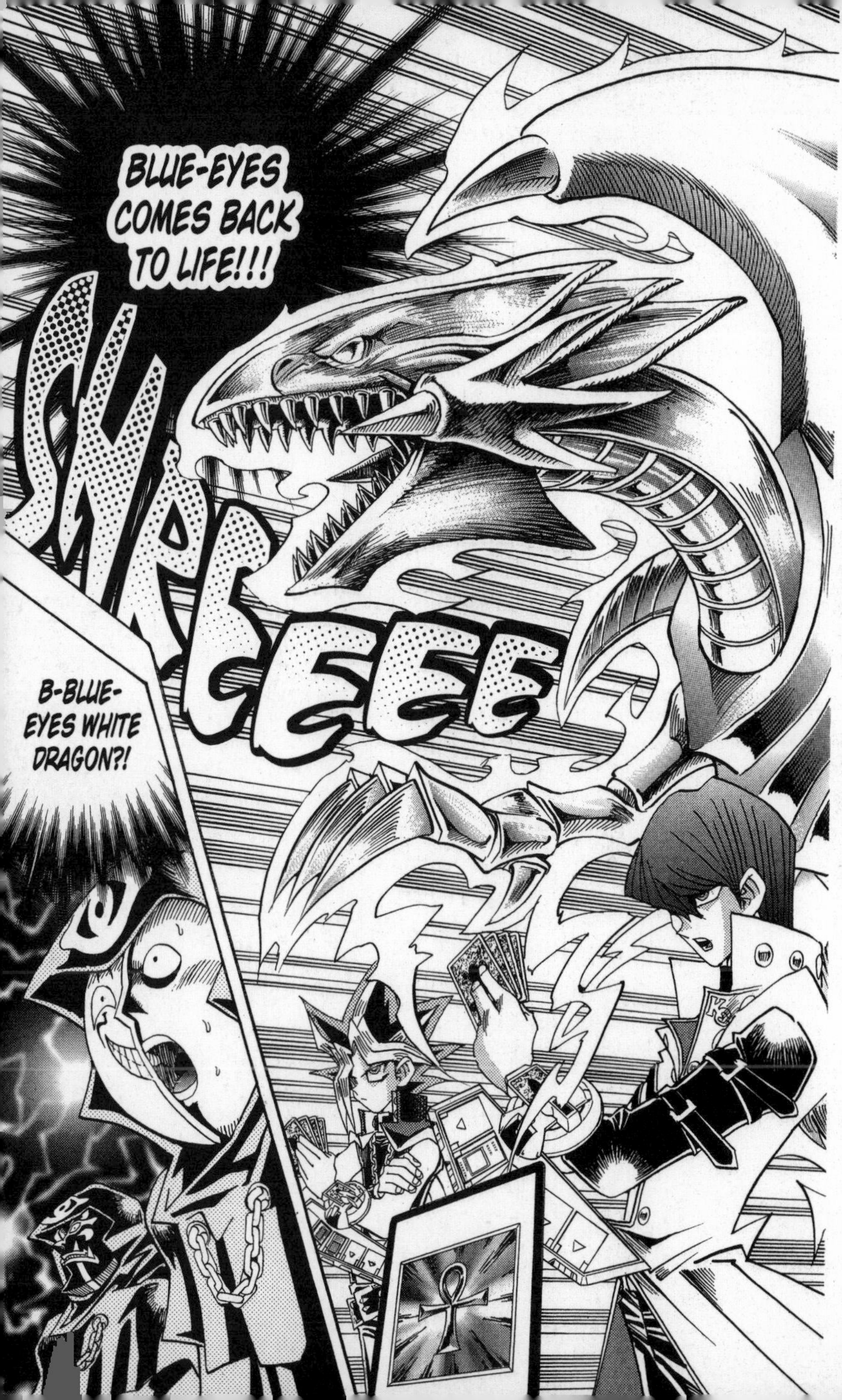
BLUE-EYES COMES BACK TO LIFE!!!
B-BLUE-EYES WHITE DRAGON?!

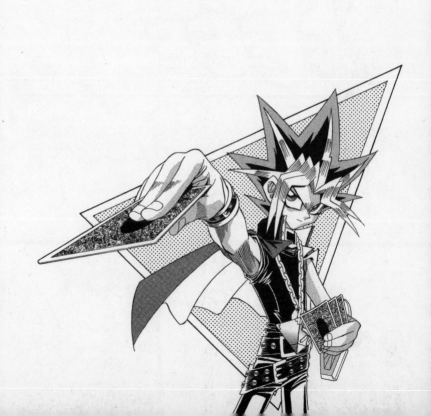

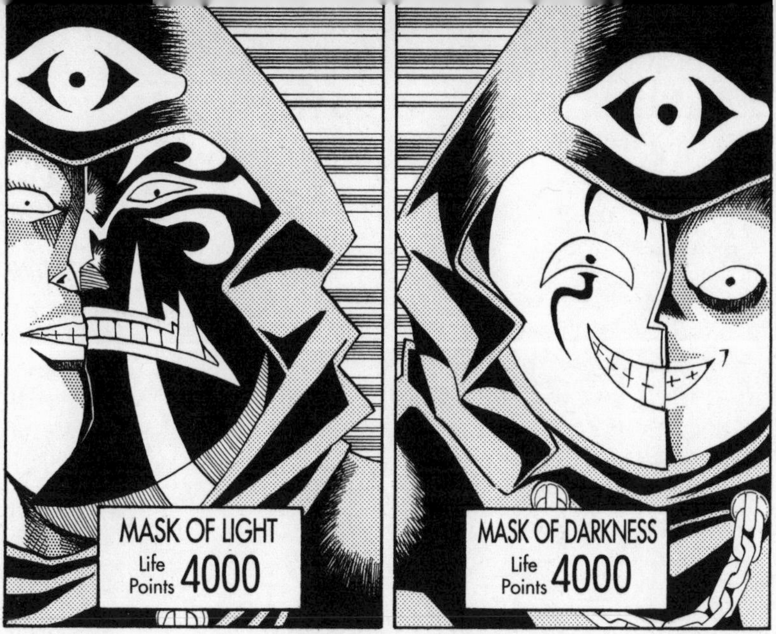
MASK OF DARKNESS
Life Points 4000
MASK OF LIGHT
Life Points 4000

DUEL 128: TEAMWORK

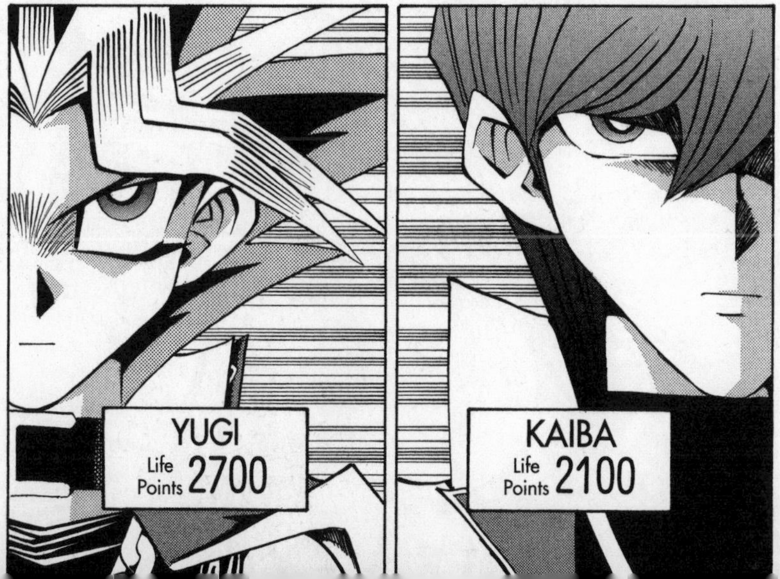
KAIBA
Life Points 2100
YUGI
Life Points 2700

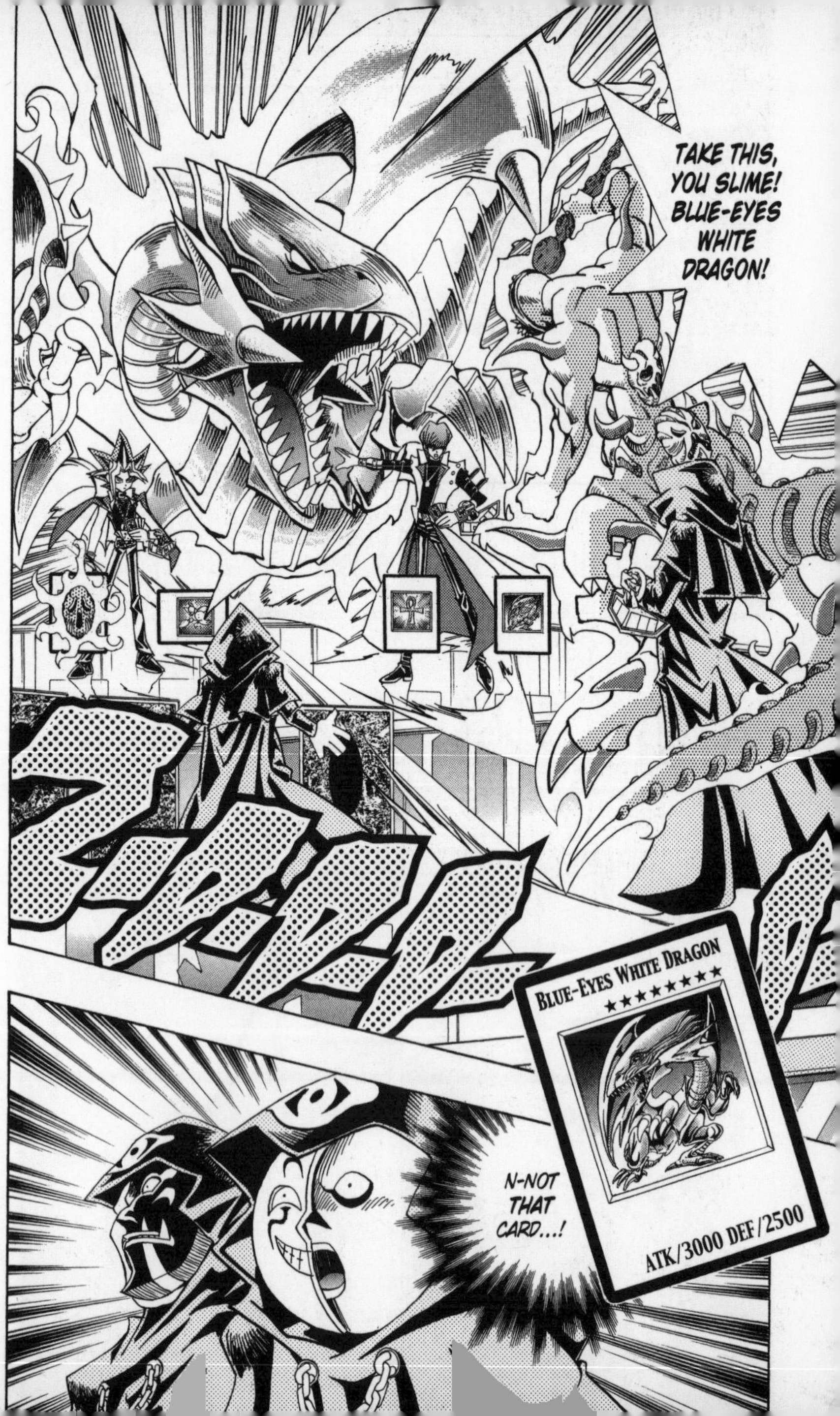
TAKE THIS, YOU SLIME! BLUE-EYES WHITE DRAGON!
BLUE-EYES WHITE DRAGON
ATK/3000 DEF/2500
N-NOT THAT CARD...!

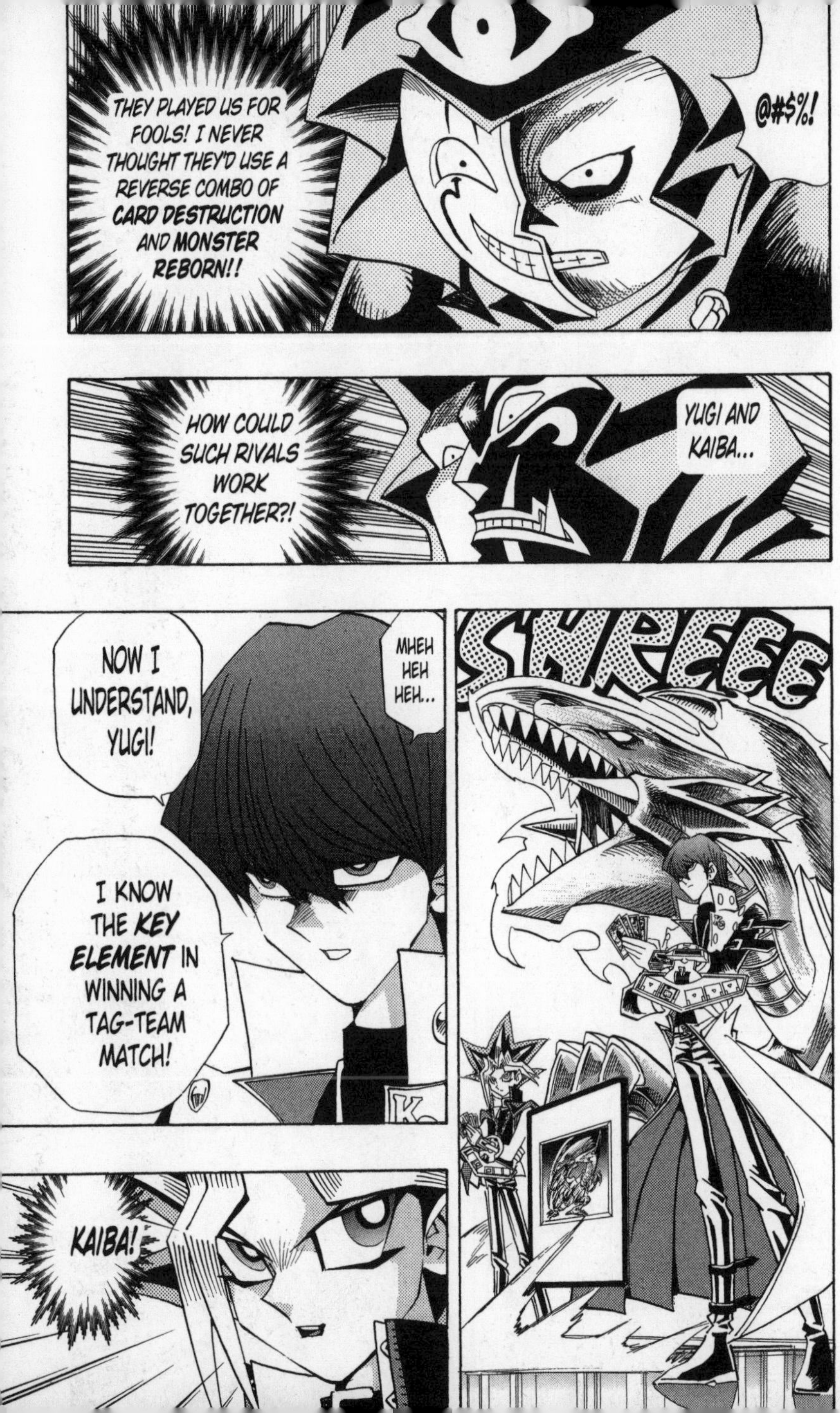
@#$%!
THEY PLAYED US FOR FOOLS! I NEVER THOUGHT THEY'D USE A REVERSE COMBO OF **CARD DESTRUCTION** AND **MONSTER REBORN**!!
YUGI AND KAIBA...
HOW COULD SUCH RIVALS WORK TOGETHER?!
SHREEE
MHEH HEH HEH...
NOW I UNDERSTAND, YUGI!
I KNOW THE ***KEY ELEMENT*** IN WINNING A TAG-TEAM MATCH!
KAIBA!

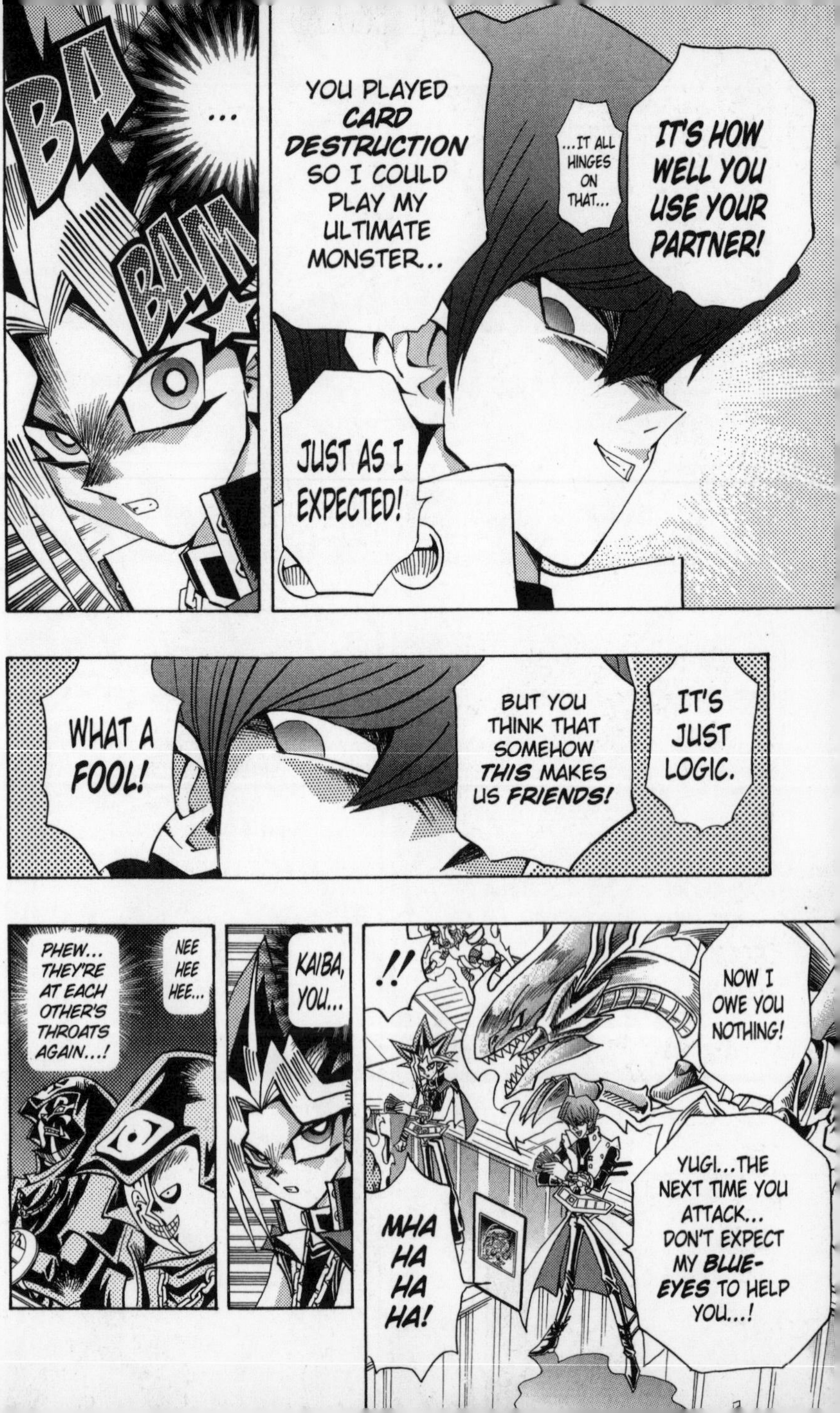
IT'S HOW WELL YOU USE YOUR PARTNER!
...IT ALL HINGES ON THAT...
YOU PLAYED CARD DESTRUCTION SO I COULD PLAY MY ULTIMATE MONSTER...
JUST AS I EXPECTED!
...
BA BAM
IT'S JUST LOGIC.
BUT YOU THINK THAT SOMEHOW THIS MAKES US FRIENDS!
WHAT A FOOL!
NOW I OWE YOU NOTHING!
YUGI...THE NEXT TIME YOU ATTACK... DON'T EXPECT MY BLUE-EYES TO HELP YOU...!
!!
MHA HA HA HA!
KAIBA, YOU...
NEE HEE HEE...
PHEW... THEY'RE AT EACH OTHER'S THROATS AGAIN...!

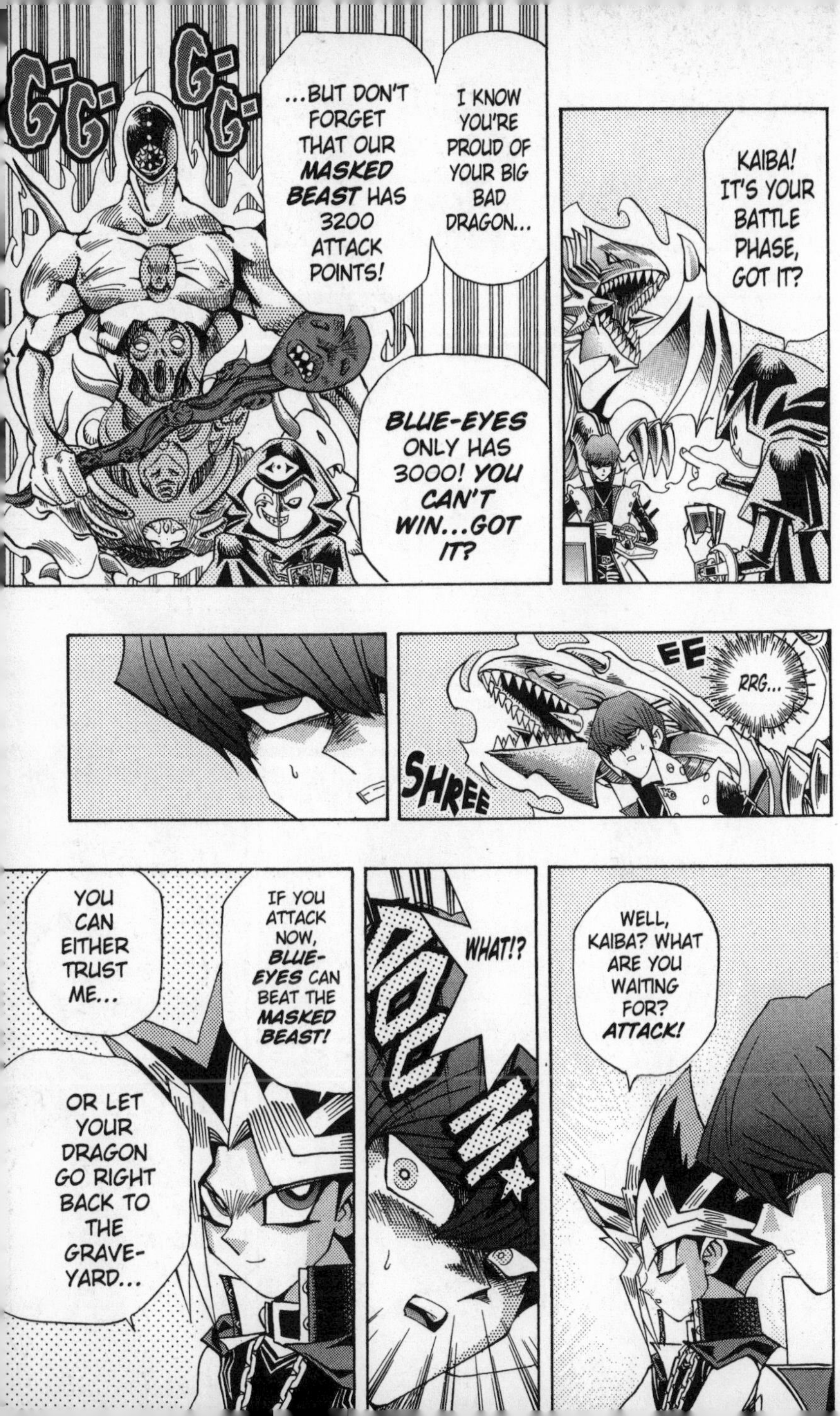
KAIBA! IT'S YOUR BATTLE PHASE, GOT IT?
G-G- G-G-
I KNOW YOU'RE PROUD OF YOUR BIG BAD DRAGON...
...BUT DON'T FORGET THAT OUR **MASKED BEAST** HAS 3200 ATTACK POINTS!
BLUE-EYES ONLY HAS 3000! **YOU CAN'T WIN...GOT IT?**
EE
RRG...
SHREE
WELL, KAIBA? WHAT ARE YOU WAITING FOR? **ATTACK!**
WHAT!?
DOOM
IF YOU ATTACK NOW, **BLUE-EYES** CAN BEAT THE **MASKED BEAST!**
YOU CAN EITHER TRUST ME...
OR LET YOUR DRAGON GO RIGHT BACK TO THE GRAVEYARD...

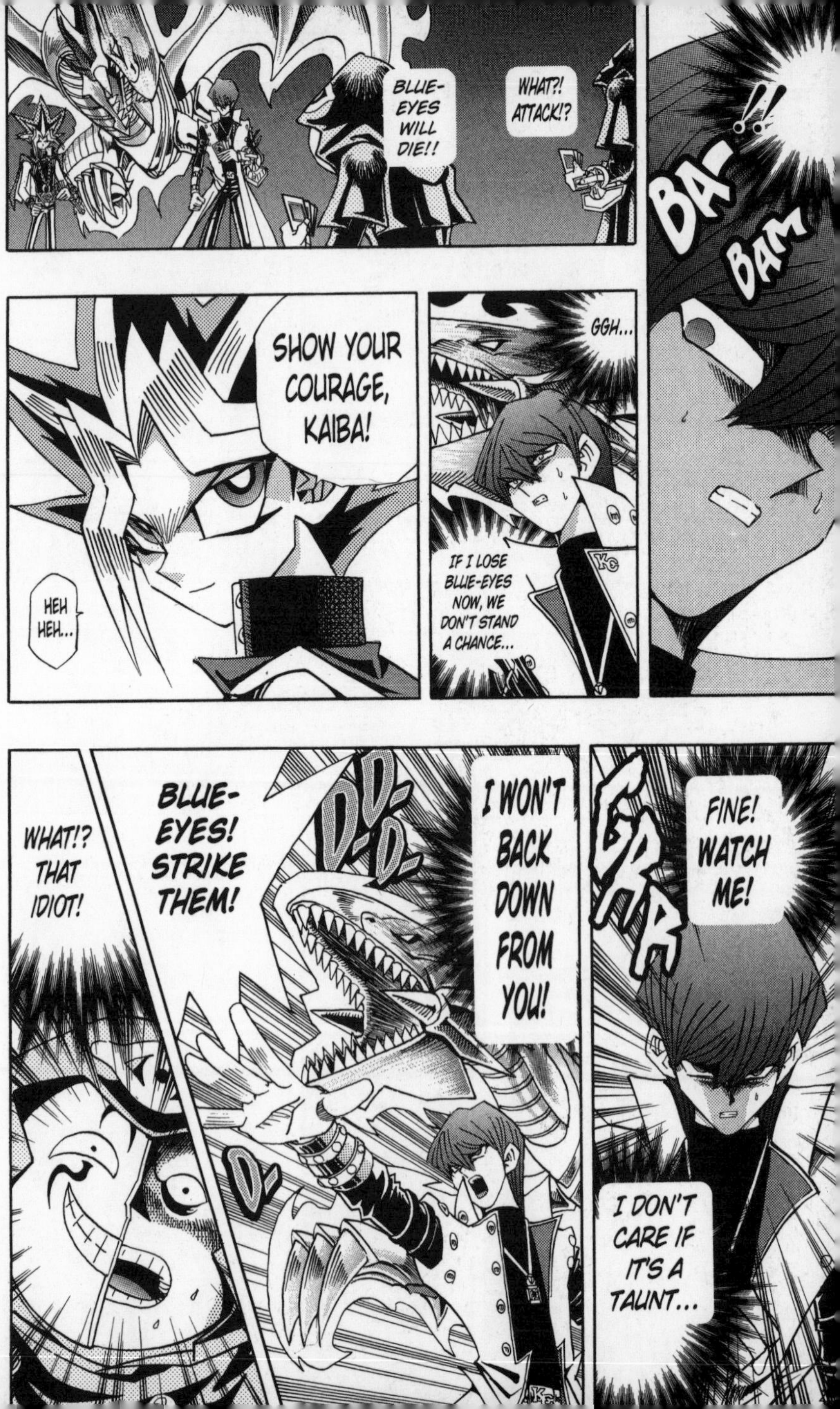
!!
BA-
BAM
WHAT?! ATTACK!?
BLUE-EYES WILL DIE!!
GGH...
IF I LOSE BLUE-EYES NOW, WE DON'T STAND A CHANCE...
SHOW YOUR COURAGE, KAIBA!
HEH HEH...
GRR
FINE! WATCH ME!
I DON'T CARE IF IT'S A TAUNT...
I WON'T BACK DOWN FROM YOU!
BLUE-EYES! STRIKE THEM!
WHAT!? THAT IDIOT!

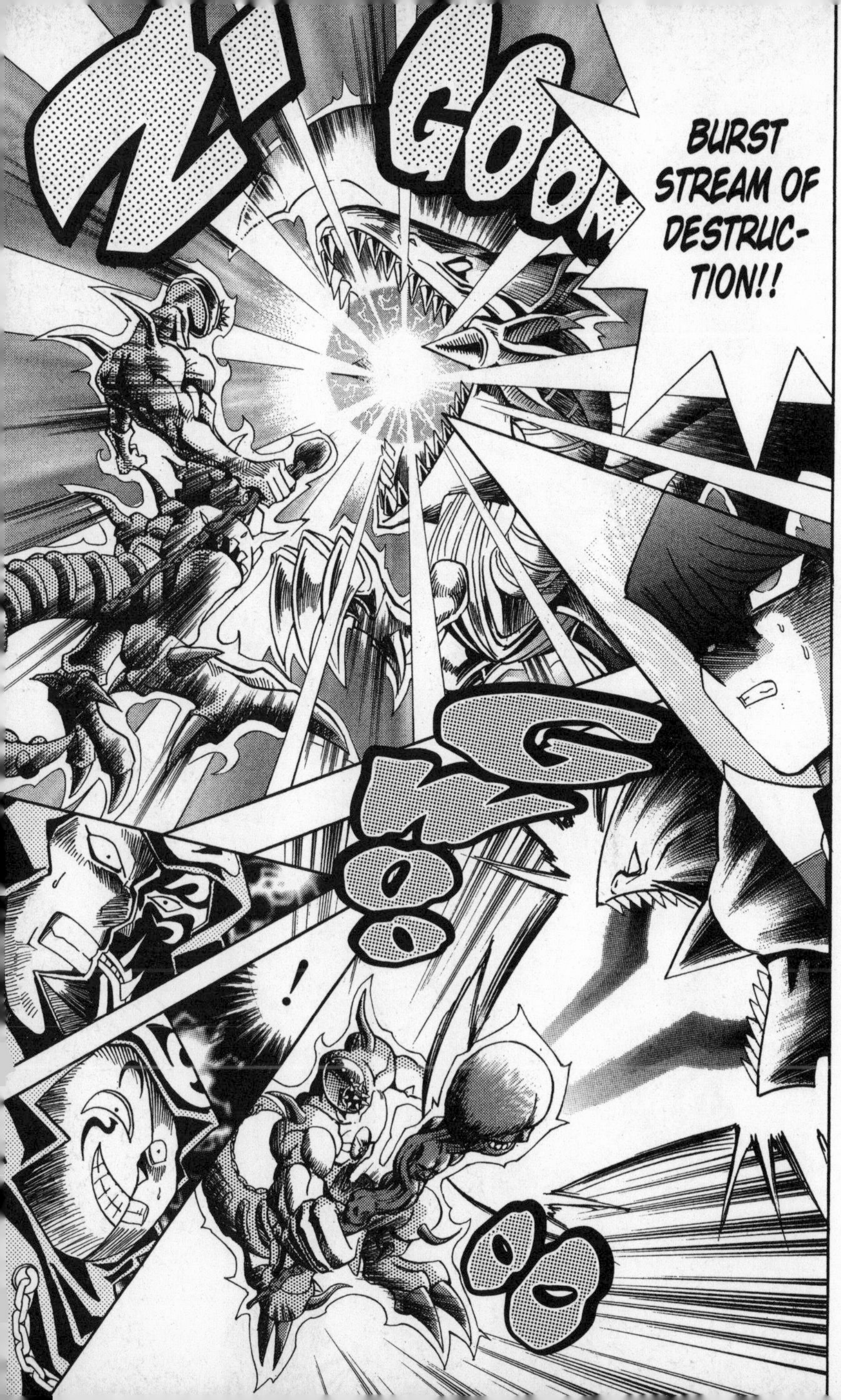
BURST STREAM OF DESTRUC-TION!!
!

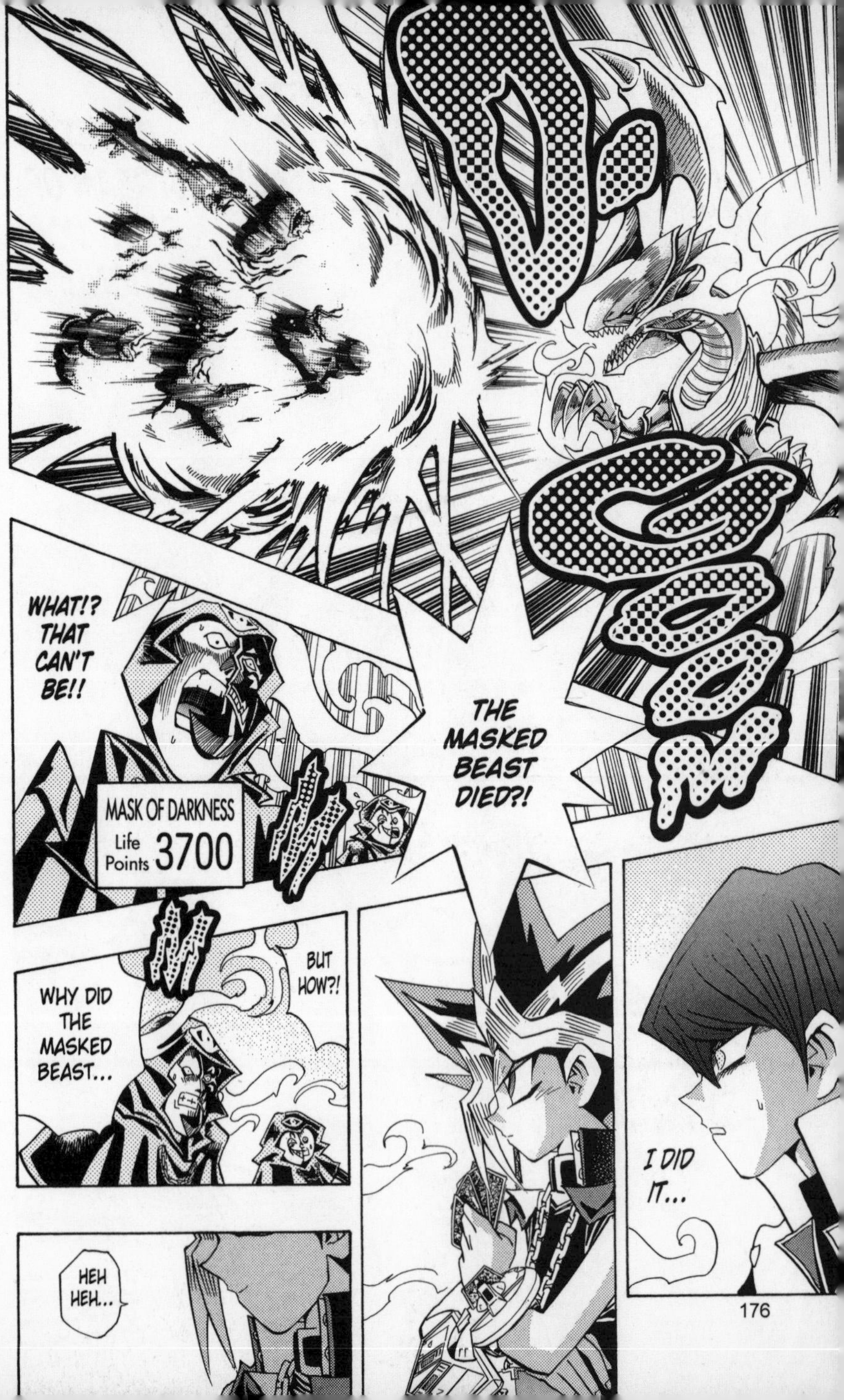
THE MASKED BEAST DIED?!
WHAT!? THAT CAN'T BE!!
MASK OF DARKNESS Life Points 3700
I DID IT...
BUT HOW?!
WHY DID THE MASKED BEAST...
HEH HEH...

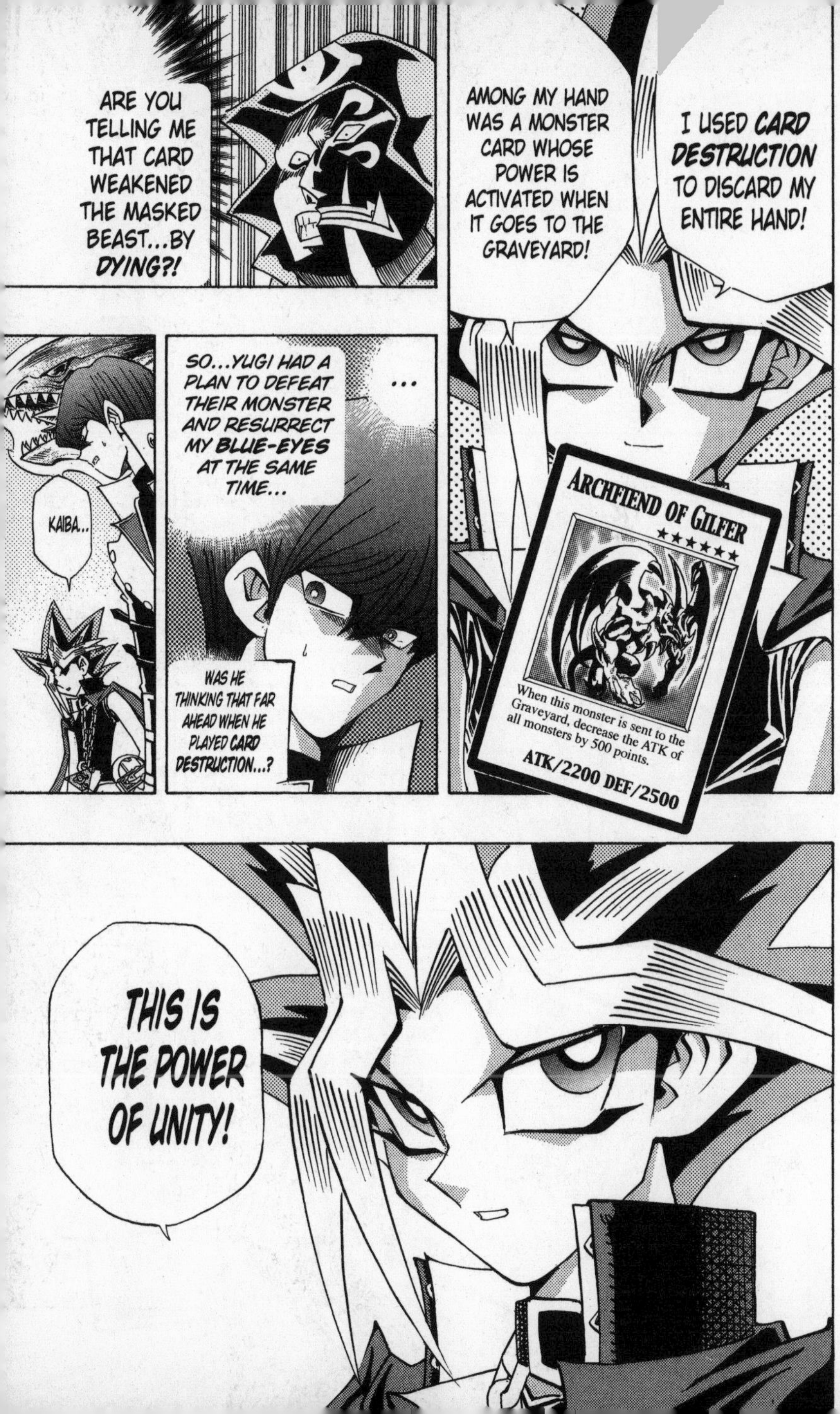
I USED CARD DESTRUCTION TO DISCARD MY ENTIRE HAND!
AMONG MY HAND WAS A MONSTER CARD WHOSE POWER IS ACTIVATED WHEN IT GOES TO THE GRAVEYARD!
ARCHFIEND OF GILFER
When this monster is sent to the Graveyard, decrease the ATK of all monsters by 500 points.
ATK/2200 DEF/2500
ARE YOU TELLING ME THAT CARD WEAKENED THE MASKED BEAST...BY DYING?!
SO...YUGI HAD A PLAN TO DEFEAT THEIR MONSTER AND RESURRECT MY BLUE-EYES AT THE SAME TIME...
...
WAS HE THINKING THAT FAR AHEAD WHEN HE PLAYED CARD DESTRUCTION...?
KAIBA...
THIS IS THE POWER OF UNITY!

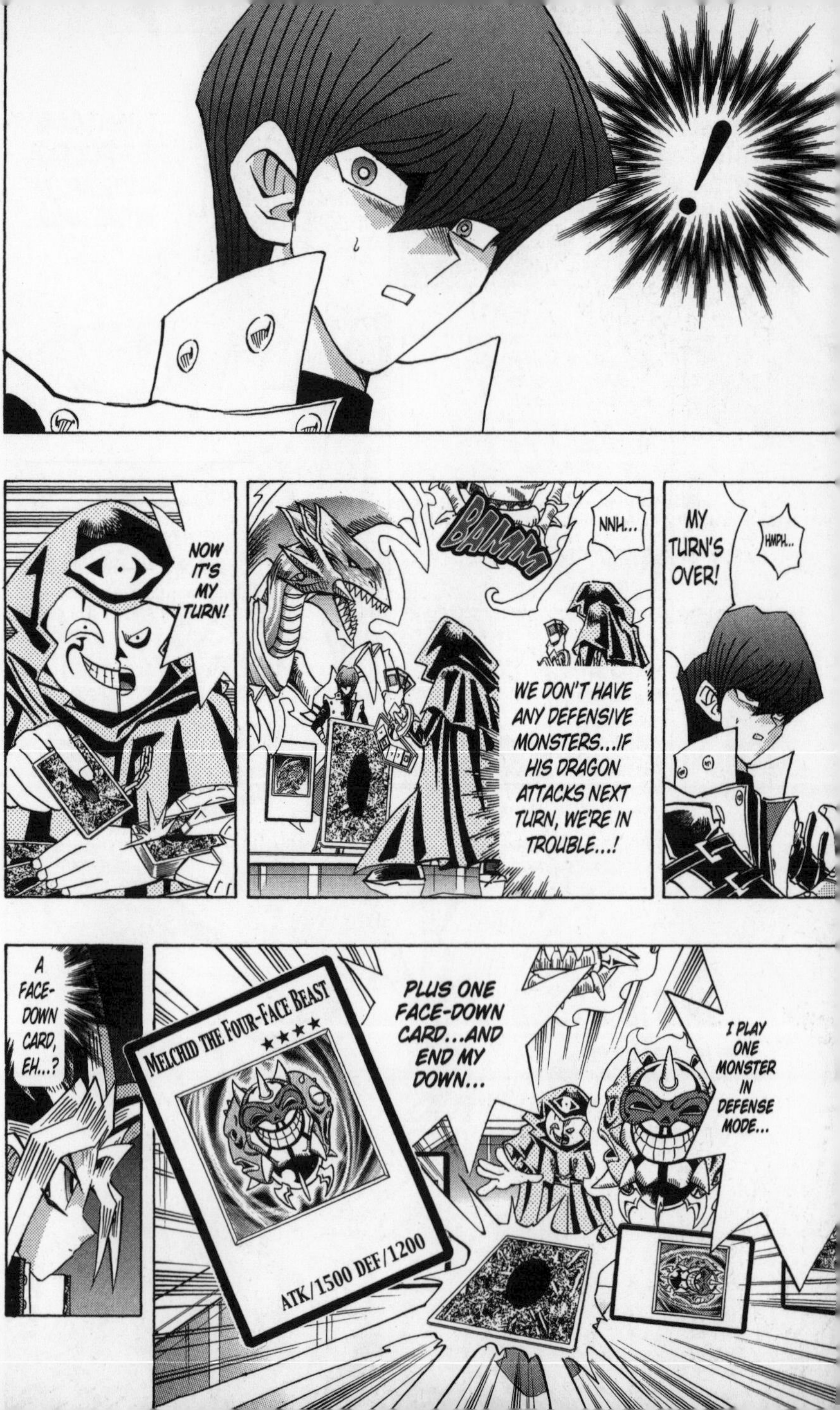
!
MY TURN'S OVER!
HMPH...
NNH...
BAMM
WE DON'T HAVE ANY DEFENSIVE MONSTERS...IF HIS DRAGON ATTACKS NEXT TURN, WE'RE IN TROUBLE...!
NOW IT'S MY TURN!
I PLAY ONE MONSTER IN DEFENSE MODE...
PLUS ONE FACE-DOWN CARD...AND END MY DOWN...
MELCHID THE FOUR-FACE BEAST
ATK/1500 DEF/1200
A FACE-DOWN CARD, EH...?

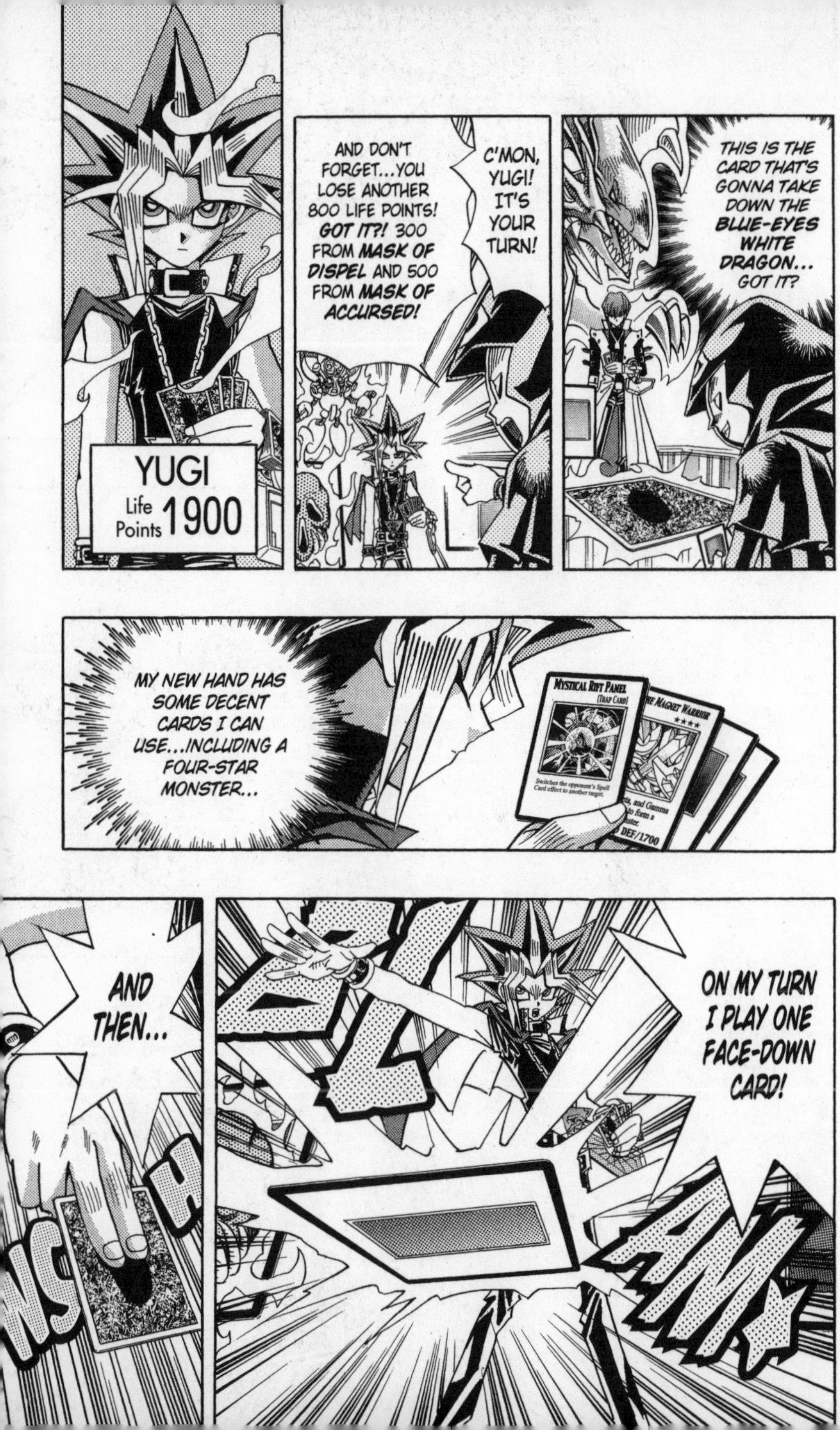
THIS IS THE CARD THAT'S GONNA TAKE DOWN THE BLUE-EYES WHITE DRAGON... GOT IT?
C'MON, YUGI! IT'S YOUR TURN!
AND DON'T FORGET...YOU LOSE ANOTHER 800 LIFE POINTS! GOT IT?! 300 FROM MASK OF DISPEL AND 500 FROM MASK OF ACCURSED!
YUGI
Life Points 1900
MY NEW HAND HAS SOME DECENT CARDS I CAN USE...INCLUDING A FOUR-STAR MONSTER...
MYSTICAL RIFT PANEL
[TRAP CARD]
Switches the opponent's Spell Card effect to another target.
DEF/1700
ON MY TURN I PLAY ONE FACE-DOWN CARD!
AND THEN...

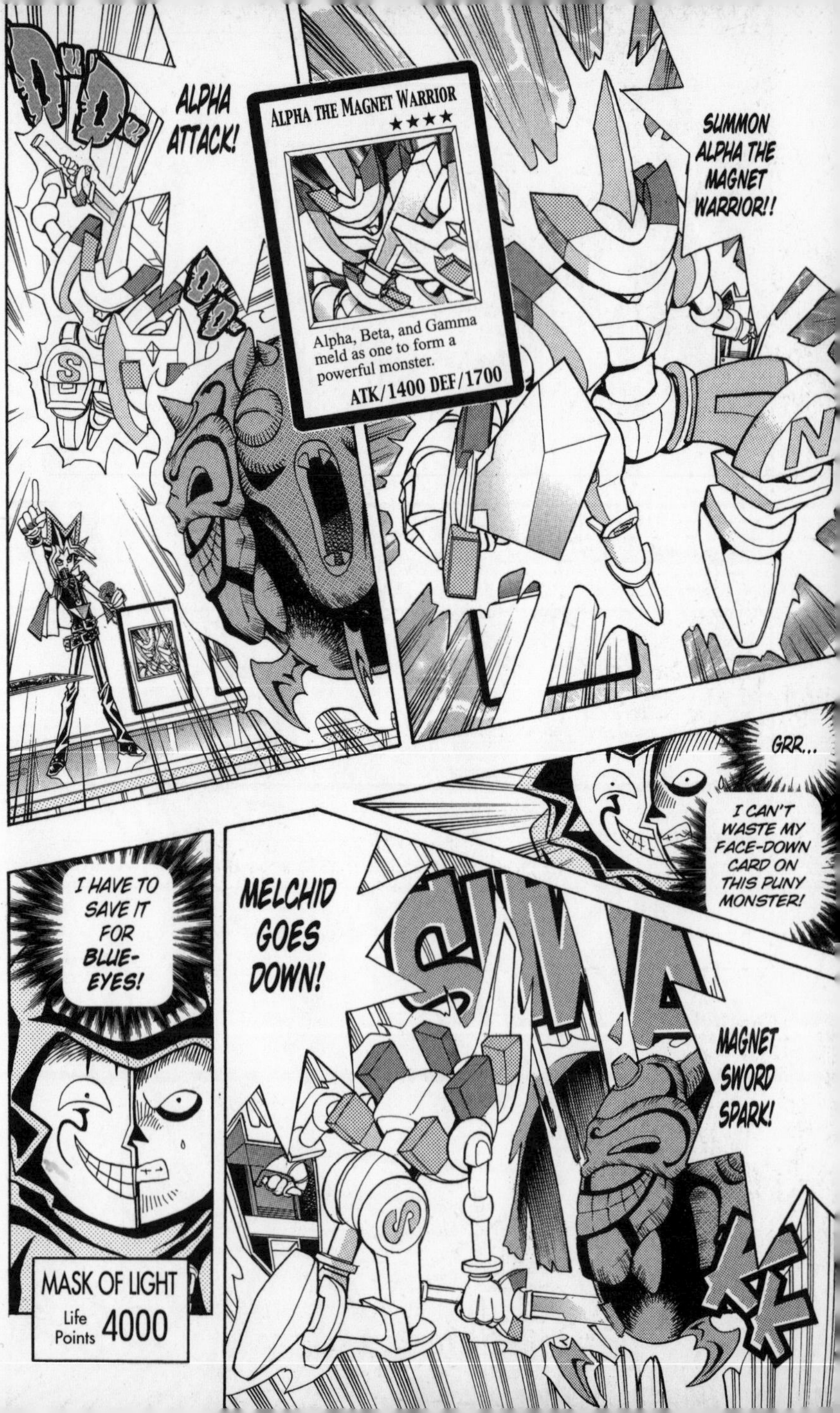
SUMMON ALPHA THE MAGNET WARRIOR!!
ALPHA THE MAGNET WARRIOR
★★★★
Alpha, Beta, and Gamma meld as one to form a powerful monster.
ATK/1400 DEF/1700
ALPHA ATTACK!
GRR...
I CAN'T WASTE MY FACE-DOWN CARD ON THIS PUNY MONSTER!
MAGNET SWORD SPARK!
MELCHID GOES DOWN!
I HAVE TO SAVE IT FOR BLUE-EYES!
MASK OF LIGHT
Life Points 4000

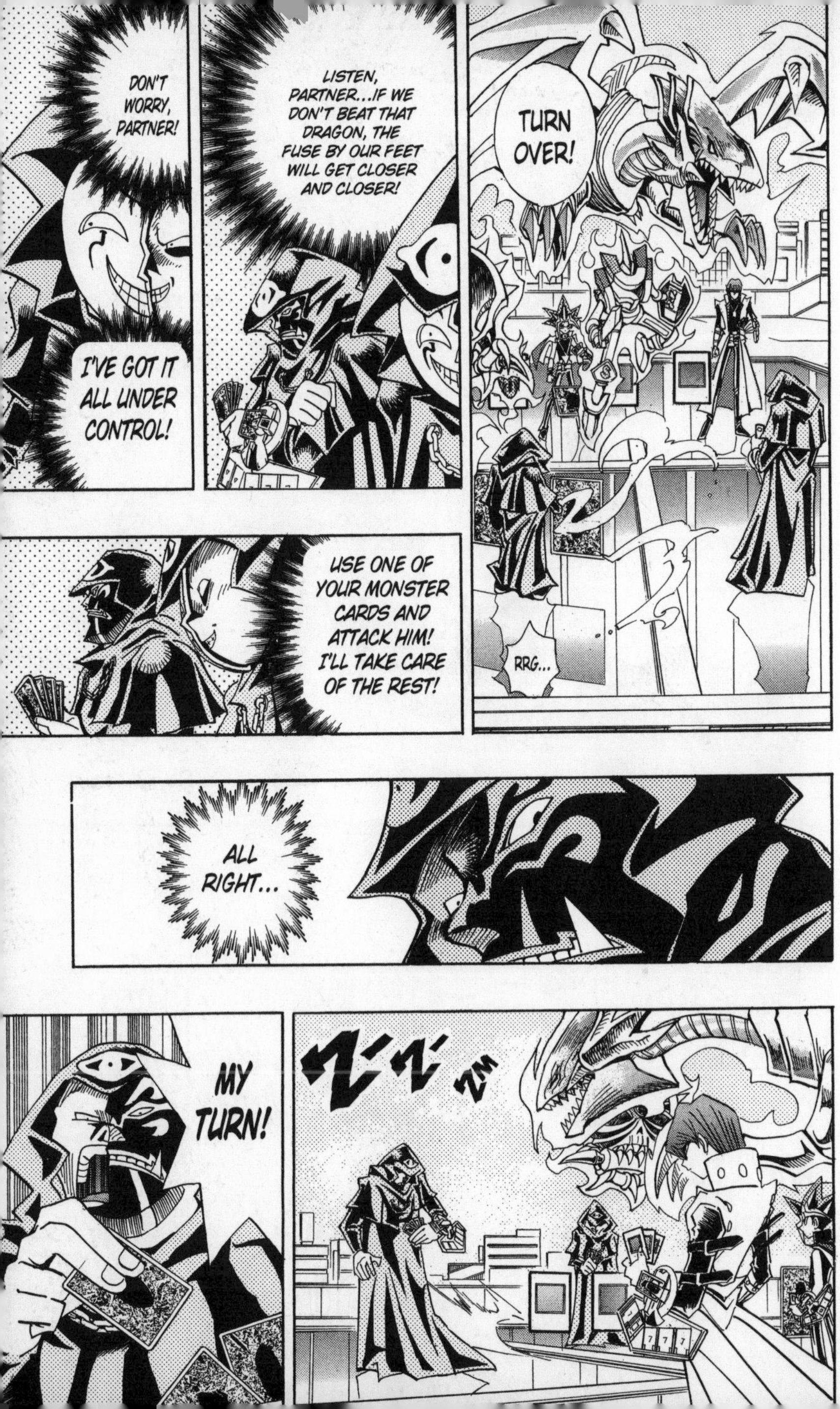
TURN OVER!
RRG...
LISTEN, PARTNER...IF WE DON'T BEAT THAT DRAGON, THE FUSE BY OUR FEET WILL GET CLOSER AND CLOSER!
DON'T WORRY, PARTNER!
I'VE GOT IT ALL UNDER CONTROL!
USE ONE OF YOUR MONSTER CARDS AND ATTACK HIM! I'LL TAKE CARE OF THE REST!
ALL RIGHT...
ZM
MY TURN!

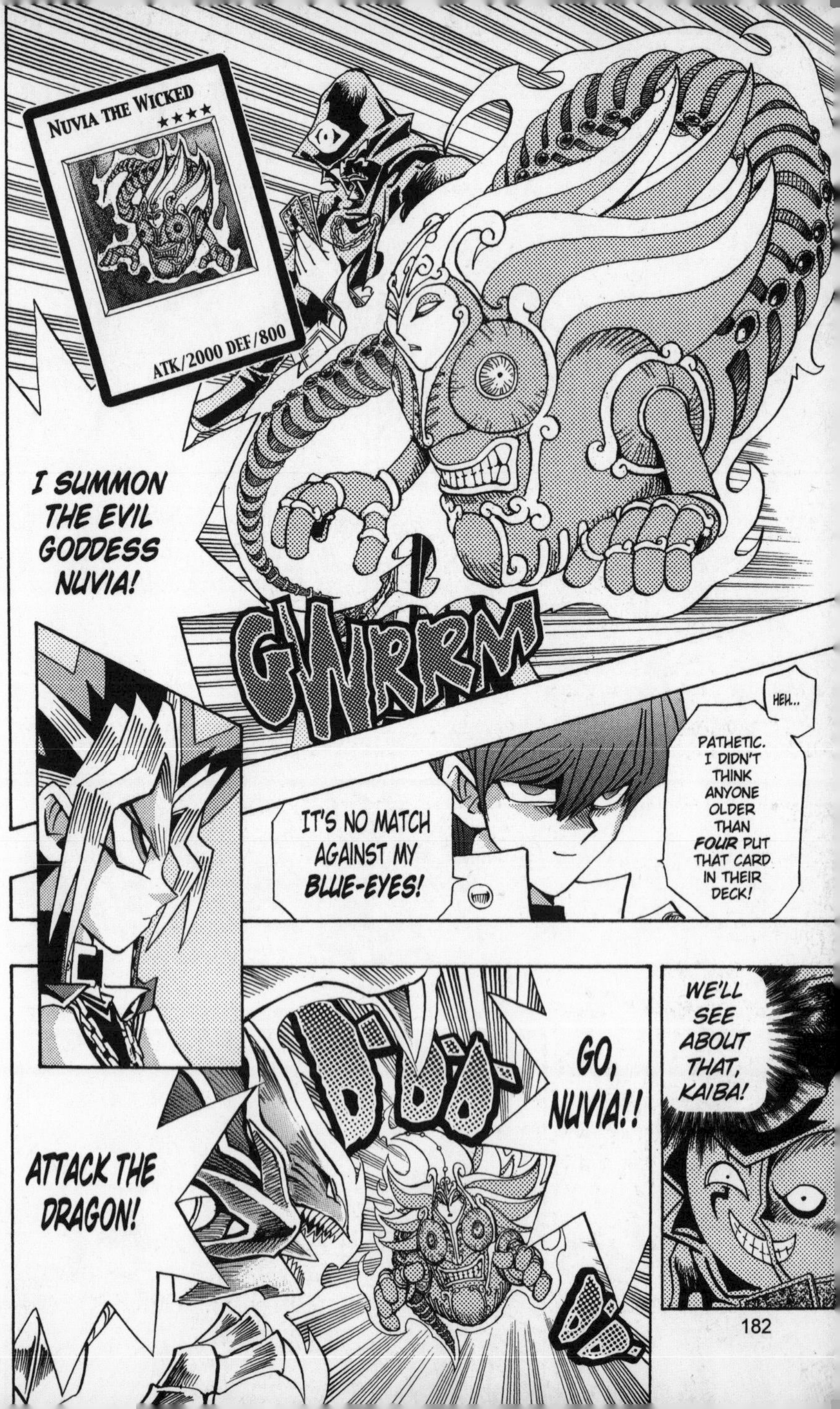
NUVIA THE WICKED
★★★★
ATK/2000 DEF/800
I SUMMON THE EVIL GODDESS NUVIA!
GWRRM
HEH...
PATHETIC. I DIDN'T THINK ANYONE OLDER THAN FOUR PUT THAT CARD IN THEIR DECK!
IT'S NO MATCH AGAINST MY BLUE-EYES!
WE'LL SEE ABOUT THAT, KAIBA!
GO, NUVIA!!
ATTACK THE DRAGON!

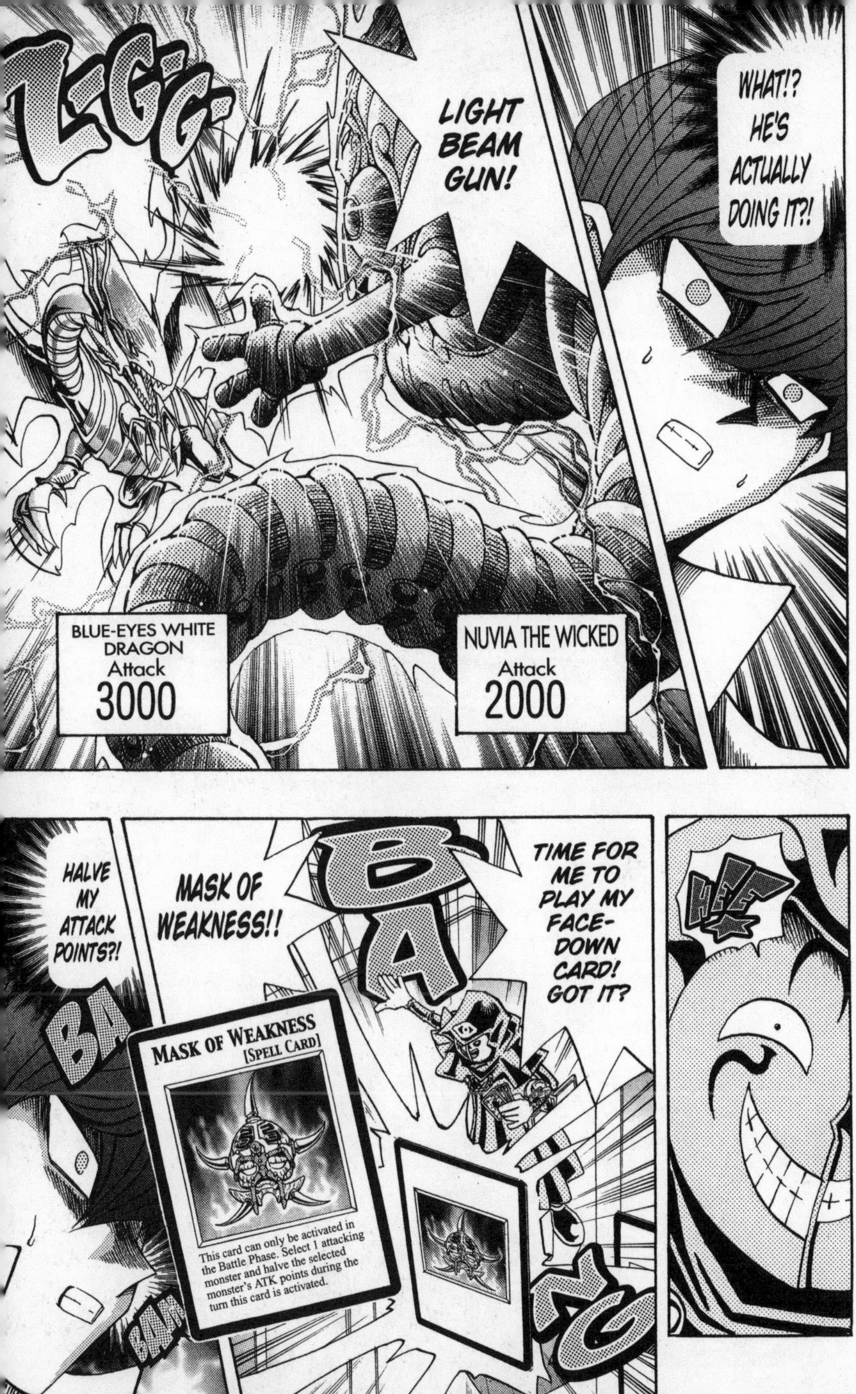
WHAT!? HE'S ACTUALLY DOING IT?!
LIGHT BEAM GUN!
Z-G-G
NUVIA THE WICKED
Attack
2000
BLUE-EYES WHITE DRAGON
Attack
3000
HEE
TIME FOR ME TO PLAY MY FACE-DOWN CARD! GOT IT?
BA
MASK OF WEAKNESS!!
MASK OF WEAKNESS
[SPELL CARD]
This card can only be activated in the Battle Phase. Select 1 attacking monster and halve the selected monster's ATK points during the turn this card is activated.
HALVE MY ATTACK POINTS?!
BA

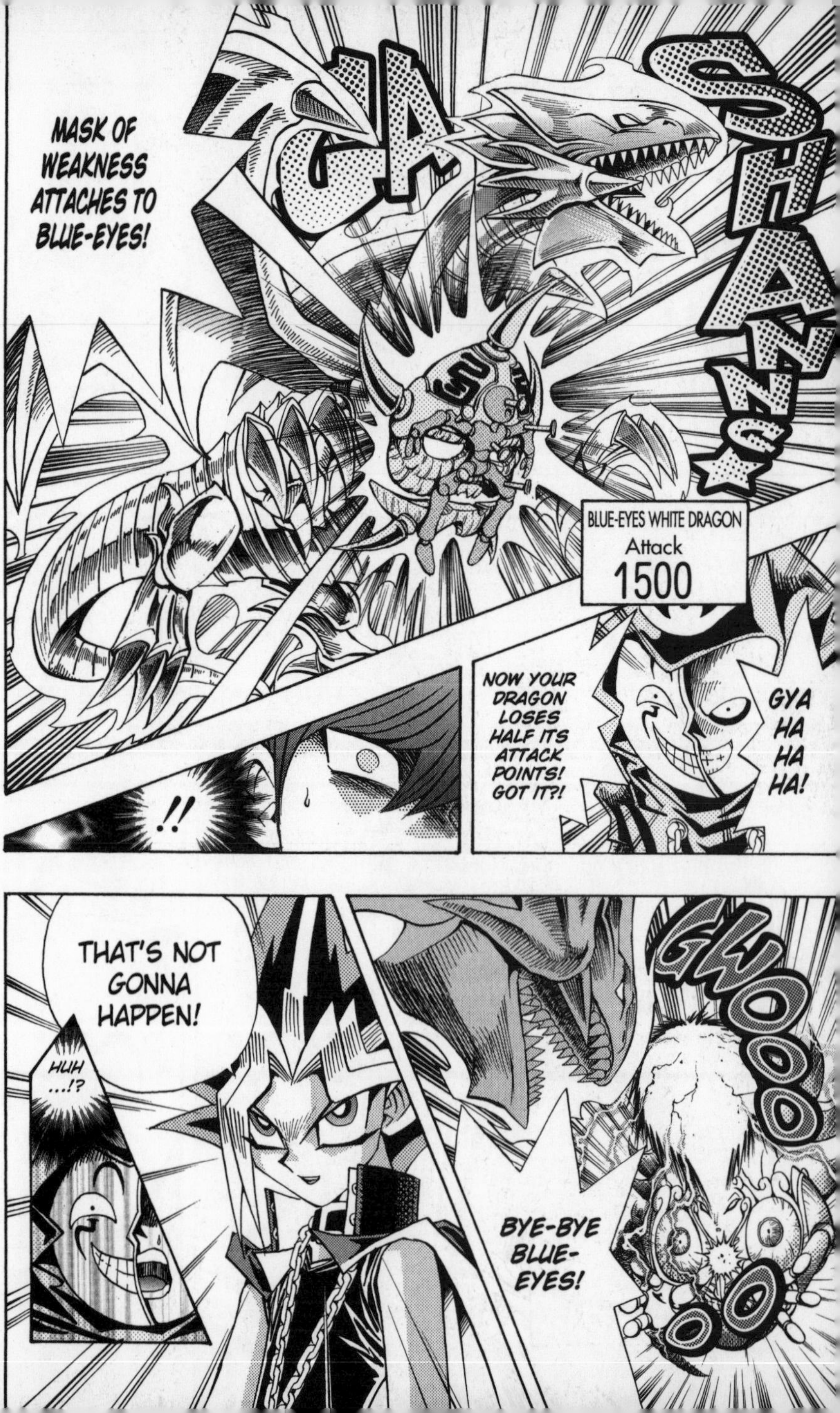
CA
SHAZANG☆
MASK OF WEAKNESS ATTACHES TO BLUE-EYES!
BLUE-EYES WHITE DRAGON
Attack
1500
GYA HA HA HA!
NOW YOUR DRAGON LOSES HALF ITS ATTACK POINTS! GOT IT?!
!!
GWOOOOO
BYE-BYE BLUE-EYES!
THAT'S NOT GONNA HAPPEN!
HUH ...!?

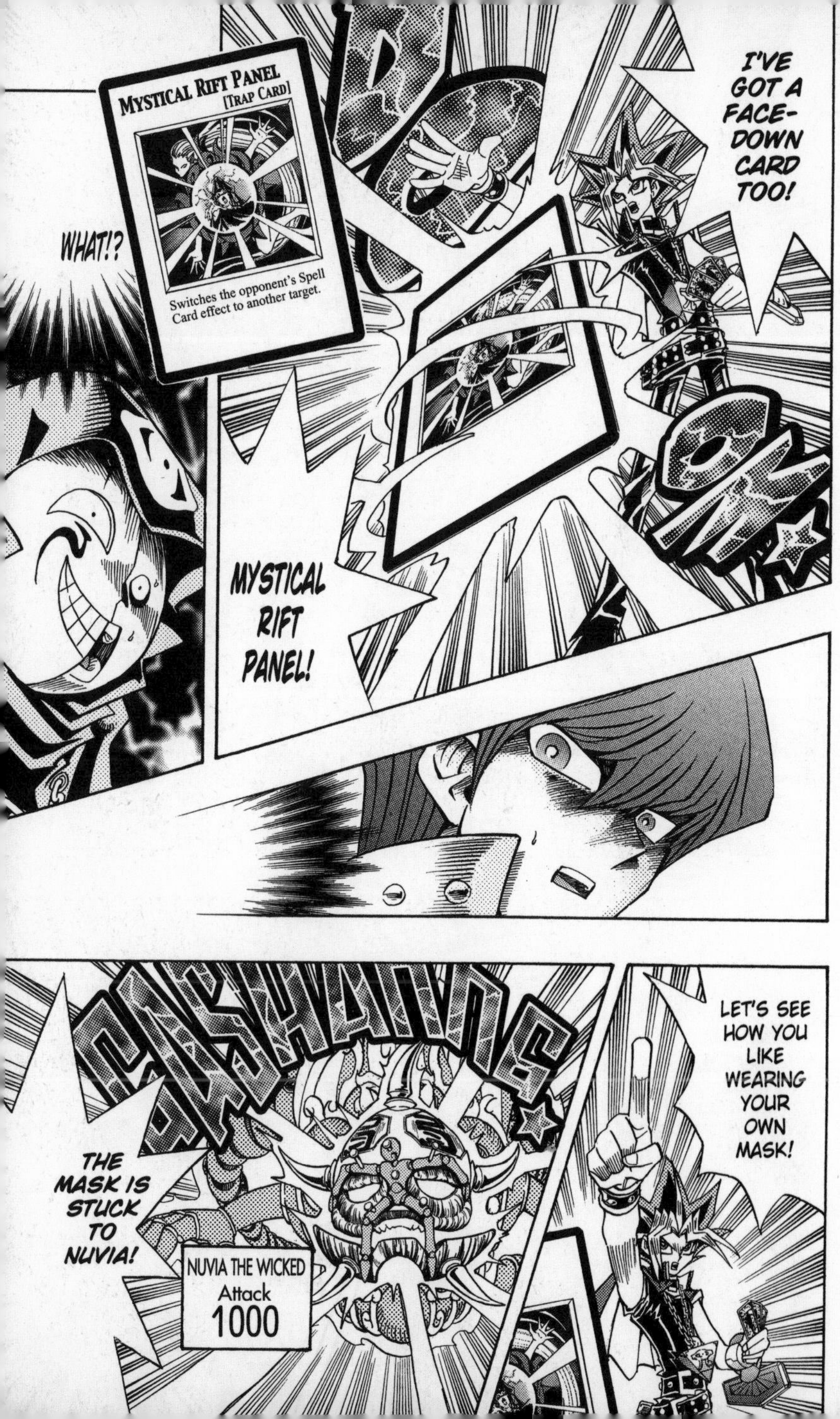
I'VE GOT A FACE-DOWN CARD TOO!
MYSTICAL RIFT PANEL!
MYSTICAL RIFT PANEL
[TRAP CARD]
Switches the opponent's Spell Card effect to another target.
WHAT!?
LET'S SEE HOW YOU LIKE WEARING YOUR OWN MASK!
THE MASK IS STUCK TO NUVIA!
NUVIA THE WICKED
Attack
1000

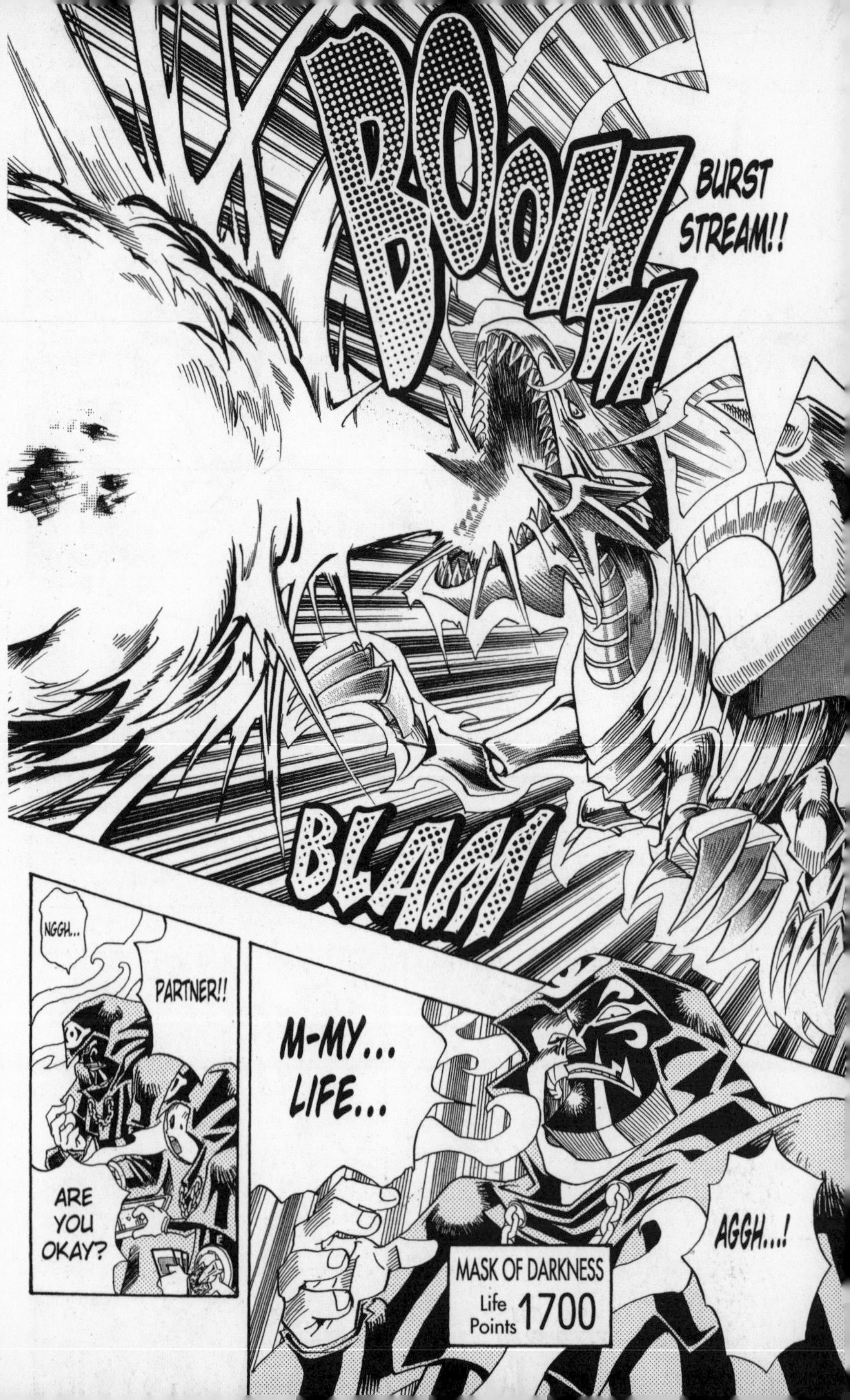
BOOM
BURST STREAM!!
BLAM
M-MY... LIFE...
AGGH...!
MASK OF DARKNESS Life Points 1700
NGGH...
PARTNER!!
ARE YOU OKAY?

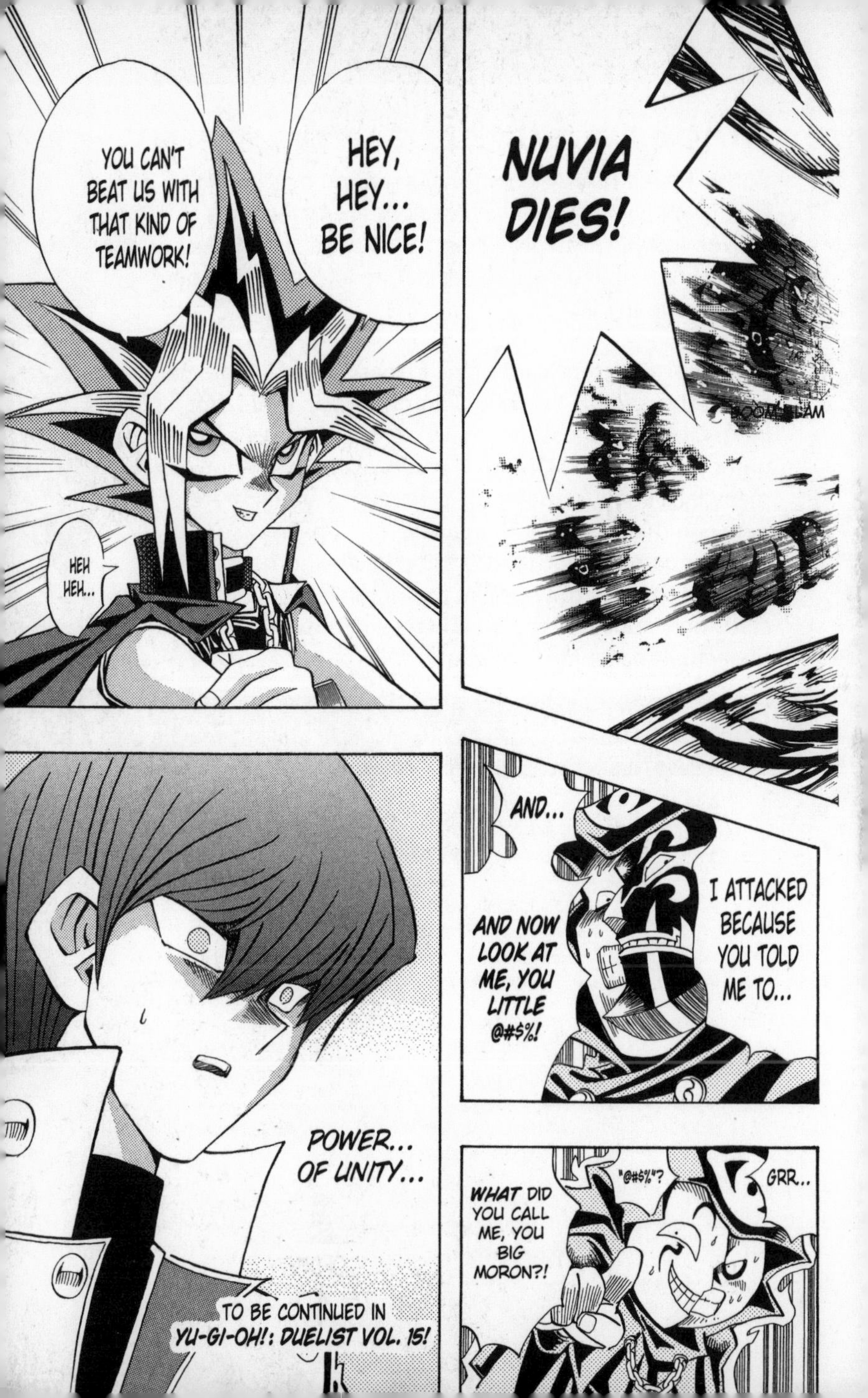
NUVIA DIES!
BOOM SLAM
HEY, HEY... BE NICE!
YOU CAN'T BEAT US WITH THAT KIND OF TEAMWORK!
HEH HEH...
I ATTACKED BECAUSE YOU TOLD ME TO...
AND...
AND NOW LOOK AT ME, YOU LITTLE @#$%!
GRR...
"@#$%"?
WHAT DID YOU CALL ME, YOU BIG MORON?!
POWER... OF UNITY...
TO BE CONTINUED IN YU-GI-OH!: DUELIST VOL. 15!

MASTER OF THE CARDS

The "Duel Monsters" card game first appeared in volume two of the original **Yu-Gi-Oh!** graphic novel series, but it's in **Yu-Gi-Oh!: Duelist** (originally printed in Japan as volumes 8-31 of **Yu-Gi-Oh!**) that it gets really important. As many fans know, some of the card names are different between the English and Japanese versions. In case you play the game, or you're interested in playing, here's a run-down of some of the cards in this graphic novel. Some cards only appear in the **Yu-Gi-Oh!** video games, not in the actual collectible card game.

FIRST APPEARANCE IN THIS VOLUME	JAPANESE CARD NAME	ENGLISH CARD NAME
p.14	*Madô Kishi Giltia* (Magic Conducting/ Guiding Knight Giltia)	Giltia the D. Knight
p.14	*Gekiryûsô* (Raging Torrent Burial)	Torrential Tribute
p.15	*Flying Fish*	Flying Fish
p.15	*Otoshiana* (Pitfall)	Chasm with Spikes
p.20	*Monster Box*	Fairy Box
p.20	*Wyvern no Senshi* (Wyvern Warrior)	Alligator Sword
p.21	*Hangyojû Fisher Beast* (Half-Fish Beast Fisher Beast)	Amphibian Beast

AMPHIBIAN BEAST

[FISH]
On land or in the sea, the speed of this monster is unmatchable.

ATK/2400 DEF/2000

SHINING ABYSS

[FAIRY]
This monster employs the powers of both Light and Darkness.

ATK/1600 DEF/1800

GRAND TIKI ELDER

[FIEND]
A masked monster that wields the most deadly of curses.

ATK/1500 DEF/ 800

FIRST APPEARANCE IN THIS VOLUME	JAPANESE CARD NAME	ENGLISH CARD NAME
p.23	*Umi* (Ocean)	Umi (NOTE: This is the first time in the manga in which "Umi" appears as a card.)
p.24	*Akuma no Saikoro* (Devil Dice)	Skull Dice
p.30	*Yûgô* (Fusion)	Polymerization
p.31	*Baby Dragon*	Baby Dragon
p.32	*Dragon ni noru Wyvern* (Dragon-riding Wyvern)	Alligator Sword Dragon
p.36	*Tornado Wall*	Tornado Wall
p.41	*Little Winguard*	Little Winguard
p.43	*Rocket Senshi* (Rocket Warrior)	Rocket Warrior
p. 44	*Yôsai Kujira* (Fortress Whale)	Fortress Whale
p.59	*Kusaritsuki Boomerang* (Chained Boomerang)	Kunai with Chain

THE MASKED BEAST

[FIEND / RITUAL]
This monster can only be Ritual Summoned with the Ritual Spell Card "Curse of the Masked Beast". You must also Tribute monsters whose total Level Stars equal 8 or more from the field or your hand.
ATK/3200 DEF/1800

MELCHID THE FOUR-FACE BEAST

[FIEND]
This monster has four different masks for four different attacks.
ATK/1500 DEF/1200

NUVIA THE WICKED

[FIEND / EFFECT]
If this monster is Normal Summoned, destroy this card. If your opponent controls any monster, decrease the ATK of this card by 100 points for each monster on your opponent's side of the field.
ATK/2000 DEF/800

FIRST APPEARANCE IN THIS VOLUME	JAPANESE CARD NAME	ENGLISH CARD NAME
p.59	*Inazuma no Ken* (Lightning Sword)	Lightning Blade
p.59	*Shikkoku no Hyôsenshi Panther Warrior* (Jet Black Panther Warrior)	Panther Warrior
p.59	*Magic Arm Shield*	Magic Arm Shield
p.60	*Sea Snake*	Sea Snake (NOTE: Not a real game card. Called "Aqua Serpent" in the video games.)
p.62	*Densetsu no Fisherman* (Legendary Fisherman)	The Legendary Fisherman
p.81	*Shisha no Seikan* (Return of the Dead)	Return of the Doomed
p.84	*Hurricane*	Giant Trunade
p.129	*Obelisk no Kyoshinhei* (Obelisk the Giant God Soldier)	God of the Obelisk (NOTE: Called "Obelisk the Tormentor" in the English anime and card game.)

MASK OF WEAKNESS
[TRAP CARD]

CURSE OF THE MASKED BEAST
[SPELL CARD]

MASK OF DISPEL
[SPELL CARD]

FIRST APPEARANCE IN THIS VOLUME	JAPANESE CARD NAME	ENGLISH CARD NAME
p.132	*Tefuda Massatsu* (Card Obliteration)	Card Destruction
p.132	*Zôshoku* (Multiply)	Multiply
p.133	*Magnet Warrior Beta*	Beta the Magnet Warrior
p.133	*Shine Abyss*	Shining Abyss
p.134	*Kyôbôka no Kamen* (Mask of Savage/Brutal Transformation)	Mask of Brutality
p.136	*Blood Vorse*	Vorse Raider
p.137	*Jukon no Kamen* (Mask of Cursed Grudge/Grudge Spell)	Mask of the Accursed (NOTE: Kanji on mask reads "curse/spell")
p.139	*Ankokumazoku Gilfer Demon* (Darkness/Black Magic/Demon Clan Gilfer Demon)	Archfiend of Gilfer
p.140	*Ikeniefûji no Kamen* (Mask of Sacrificial Offering Sealing)	Mask of Restrict (NOTE: Kanji on mask reads "sacrificial offering seal")

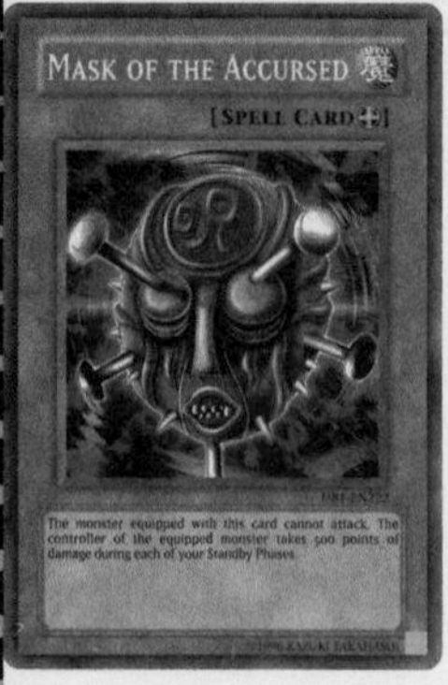
MASK OF THE ACCURSED
[SPELL CARD]
The monster equipped with this card cannot attack. The controller of the equipped monster takes 500 points of damage during each of your Standby Phases.

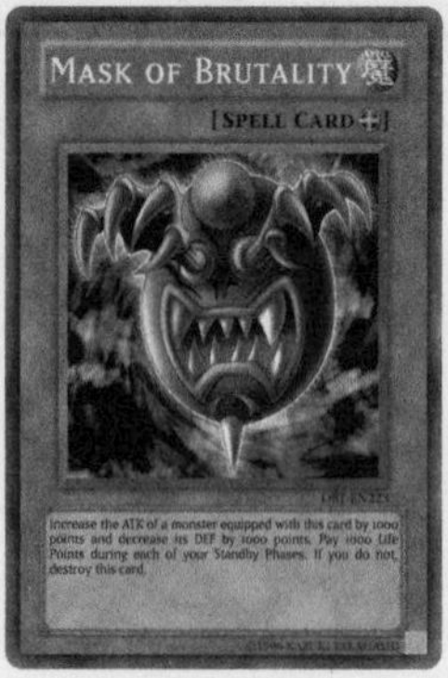
MASK OF BRUTALITY
[SPELL CARD]
Increase the ATK of a monster equipped with this card by 1000 points and decrease its DEF by 1000 points. Pay 1000 Life Points during each of your Standby Phases. If you do not, destroy this card.

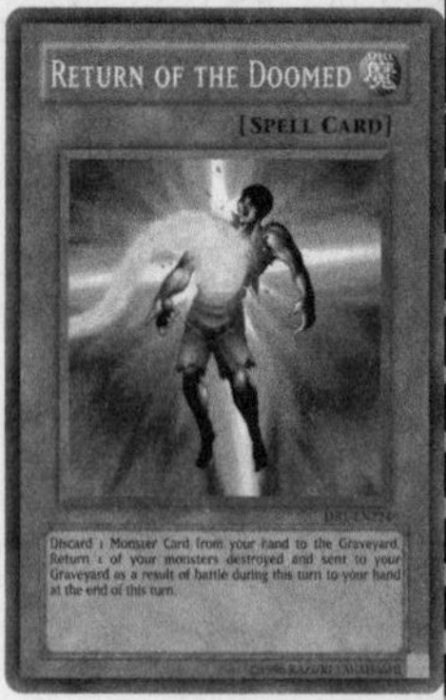
RETURN OF THE DOOMED
[SPELL CARD]
Discard 1 Monster Card from your hand to the Graveyard. Return 1 of your monsters destroyed and sent to your Graveyard as a result of battle during this turn to your hand at the end of this turn.

FIRST APPEARANCE IN THIS VOLUME	JAPANESE CARD NAME	ENGLISH CARD NAME
p.141	*Kuribo*	Kuriboh
p.143	*Hakairin* (Destruction Ring/Circle)	Ring of Destruction
p.145	*Noroi Utsushi* (Curse Transfer)	*Curse Transfer* (NOTE: Not a real game card)
p.154	*Blue-Eyes White Dragon*	Blue-Eyes White Dragon
p.155	*Gadget Soldier*	Gadget Soldier
p.156	*Maryoku Muryokuka no Kamen* (Mask of Magic-Power Nullification)	Mask of Dispel
p.158	*Kamenjujutsushi Cursed Gyura* (Mask Black Arts/Enchantment Master Cursed Gyura)	Grand Tiki Elder
p.159	*Chain Destruction* (NOTE: Japanese kanji reads "Chain Destruction")	Chain Destruction
p.162	*Kamenmajû no Gishiki* (Masked Magical/Demon Beast Ritual)	Curse of the Masked Beast